CW01082287

Does Game Theory Work?

Economic Learning and Social Evolution

General Editor

Ken Binmore, Director of the Economic Learning and Social Evolution Centre, University College London.

Does Game Theory Work?

The Bargaining Challenge

Ken Binmore

The MIT Press
Cambridge, Massachusetts
London, England

© 2007 Massachusetts Institute of Technology

All rights reserved. No part of this book may be reproduced in any form by any electronic or mechanical means (including photocopying, recording, or information storage and retrieval) without permission in writing from the publisher.

MIT Press books may be purchased at special quantity discounts for business or sales promotional use. For information, please email special_sales@mitpress.mit.edu or write to Special Sales Department, The MIT Press, 55 Hayward Street, Cambridge, MA 02142.

This book was set in Times New Roman and Syntax on 3B2 by Asco Typesetters, Hong Kong and was printed and bound in the United States of America.

Library of Congress Cataloging-in-Publication Data

Binmore, K. G., 1940–
Does game theory work? : the bargaining challenge / Ken Binmore.
    p.   cm. — (Economic learning and social evolution ; 7)
Includes bibliographical references and index.
Contents: Getting to equilibrium? — Which equilibrium? — The ultimatum game — Inequity aversion? — Outside options — Forced breakdown — Lost opportunities — Unequal bargaining power.
ISBN-13: 978-0-262-02607-9 (alk. paper)
ISBN-10: 0-262-02607-4 (alk. paper)
1. Game theory. 2. Negotiation. 3. Economics—Psychological aspects. I. Title.
HB144.B55   2007
330.01′5193—dc22   2006047238

10   9   8   7   6   5   4   3   2   1

Contents

Series Foreword

The MIT Press series on Economic Learning and Social Evolution reflects the continuing interest in the dynamics of human interaction. This issue has provided a broad community of economists, psychologists, biologists, anthropologists, mathematicians, philosophers, and others with such a strong sense of common purpose that traditional interdisciplinary boundaries have melted away. We reject the outmoded notion that what happens away from equilibrium can safely be ignored, but think it no longer adequate to speak in vague terms of bounded rationality and spontaneous order. We believe the time has come to put some beef on the table.

The books in the series so far are:

• *Evolutionary Games and Equilibrium Selection*, by Larry Samuelson (1997). Traditional economic models have only one equilibrium and therefore fail to come to grips with social norms whose function is to select an equilibrium when there are multiple alternatives. This book studies how such norms may evolve.

• *The Theory of Learning in Games*, by Drew Fudenberg and David Levine (1998). John Von Neumann introduced "fictitious play" as a way of finding equilibria in zero-sum games. In this book the idea is reinterpreted as a learning procedure and developed for use in general games.

• *Just Playing*, by Ken Binmore (1998). This book applies evolutionary game theory to moral philosophy. How and why do we make fairness judgments?

• *Social Dynamics*, edited by Steve Durlauf and Peyton Young (2001). The essays in this collection provide an overview of the field of social dynamics, in which some of the creators of the field discuss a variety of approaches, including theoretical model-building, empirical studies, statistical analyses, and philosophical reflections.

• *Evolutionary Dynamics and Extensive Form Games*, by Ross Cressman (2003). How is evolution affected by the timing structure of games? Does it generate backward induction? The answers show that orthodox thinking needs much revision in some contexts.

Authors who share the ethos represented by these books, or who wish to extend it in empirical, experimental, or other directions, are cordially invited to submit outlines of their proposed books for consideration. Within our terms of reference, we hope that a thousand flowers will bloom.

Introduction

Cleaning Test Tubes

When I started doing experimental work in the 1980s, the subject was in its infancy among economists, but one set of findings was thought to be rock solid. Game theory doesn't work in the laboratory. People don't play Nash equilibria. They don't use their maximin strategies in two-person, zero-sum games. They even cooperate in the Prisoners' Dilemma.

But the rock on which these certitudes were based has crumbled away. It is true that unmotivated subjects in unfamiliar situations don't play as game theory predicts. So if game theory had to predict interactive human behavior under all circumstances to be worthy of attention, it would indeed be a failure. But who would want to claim of any theory that it work in all environments? Just as Newton's laws of motion don't predict well at the bottom of the sea, so game theory can't reasonably be expected to work in environments in which its tacit assumptions have no chance of being true. So what is the kind of environment in which we might reasonably expect game theory to predict well?

Favorable Environments

A conservative specification of a favorable experimental environment for game theory requires that all three of the following criteria be satisfied:

- The game is simple, and presented to the subjects in a user-friendly manner.
- The subjects are paid adequately for performing well.
- Sufficient time is available for trial-and-error learning.

Critics rightly say that these criteria are too stringent to cover all the economic situations to which game theory gets applied, but who would want to defend each and every crazy application of the theory? Such enthusiasts certainly exist, but they seem to me no less misguided than the skeptics who determinedly turn a blind eye to any evidence that isn't hostile to game theory.

My three environmental criteria aren't intended to be hard-and-fast necessary and sufficient conditions for game theory to predict human behavior. Game theory sometimes works when one or more of the criteria aren't satisfied. It sometimes fails when all three criteria are satisfied. However, the successes are now so well established that the first response to finding that a game-theoretic prediction fails in a laboratory when all three criteria hold is to ask the same question that chemists ask if something unexpected happens when they mix reagents together:

Did I clean my test tubes properly?

Bargaining

My own attempts to work with clean test tubes in the laboratory largely fall into two categories: experiments on bargaining and experiments on auctions. The latter work was all conducted on behalf of governments and commercial enterprises. I don't report on it here, partly for reasons of confidentiality, but mostly because nobody seems to doubt that game theory is a useful guide to predicting human bidding behavior. All but one of the papers from my experimental repetoire that make up this volume are therefore devoted to tests of game-theoretic models of bargaining.

The case of bargaining is a particularly challenging case for game theory—perhaps the most challenging case of all. Everyone agrees that human behavior in real-life bargaining situations is governed at least partly by fairness considerations that we don't understand very well. But what happens when such fairness considerations conflict with game-theoretic predictions in the laboratory? Will people adapt their behavior so that they end up playing a novel bargaining game strategically? Or must we expect them simply to play fair?

Even when the test tubes are clean, experiments on bargaining models therefore come with the dice loaded against game theory. But I hope that the evidence to be presented will justify my boldness in defending the theory in a case where skeptics think the arguments in its favor are at their weakest.

The Behavioral Challenge

I think the claims made for game theory in the previous section would be uncontroversial if the issues weren't clouded by an emotional debate that seems to me entirely orthogonal to the issue of whether or not game theory works. This is the question of whether people are inherently selfish, or whether they care about those around them.

Although I think the question isn't central to the issue of whether game theory works, it isn't possible to get a hearing nowadays for the kind of experimental results I report here without confronting this controversy, since the behavioral economists who emphasize the importance of other-regarding or social preferences commonly believe that their findings represent a threat to traditional game theory.

No amount of denial seems capable of altering their conviction that game theorists like myself must necessarily believe that human beings have no interest whatever in playing fair when the chips are down. I sometimes try to shake their certitude by pointing out that I have probably written more on how and why fairness matters than any economist ever, but I find this gets me nowhere because the reasons why I think social preferences matter are so different from theirs (Binmore 1994, 1998, 2005).

The rest of this introduction is therefore devoted to making three points. The first is that the behavioral school could well be right in claiming that people have strong other-regarding preferences without their results presenting any challenge to game theory at all. The second is that one can believe that social preferences matter enormously in human conduct without agreeing at all with the behavioral school about how they matter. The third is that the level of scientific rigor thought adequate by some leading proponents of the behavioral school represents no improvement on that of the experts who used to claim that people nearly always cooperate in the Prisoners' Dilemma.

Are People Selfish?

Should we model the people who enter our laboratories as seeking to maximize the money in their own pockets? Or should we model them as maximizing a more complicated utility function, whose arguments take account of the welfare of others?

I think one might as well ask when you stopped beating your wife. In discussing the behavior of inexperienced laboratory subjects, the first question isn't what kind of utility function they are maximizing, but whether they can sensibly be seen as maximizing anything at all (Giger-enzer 2004).

The behavior of laboratory subjects often changes markedly over time as they learn the ropes in a new experiment. We can make the maximizing hypothesis into a tautology by introducing utility functions that correspondingly change with time, but who thinks that this would be a worthwhile activity? It is true that abandoning the maximizing hypothesis implies that we have to look beyond traditional economic theory for explanations of how inexperienced subjects learn to play games, but I see no reason why we should imagine that psychology and sociology are irrelevant when trying to make sense of boundedly rational behavior.

Only after the learning phase is over can we expect to find subjects at a Nash equilibrium, each behaving as though trying to maximize his or her own utility function given the behavior of the other subjects. But do we then not find them simply maximizing money?

The answer is that this is indeed what we usually do observe—provided that the monetary payoffs are chosen to be sufficiently large. However, we can't deduce that real people therefore don't have other-regarding preferences, because part of the reason that experimenters like myself believe that the monetary payoffs need to be relatively large is to swamp whatever other-regarding preferences may be present (Vernon Smith 1976).

The school of behavioral economists who insist that other-regarding preferences matter in real life therefore have nothing to fear from experiments that show that game theory often works—unless they want to claim that subjects care so enormously about other people that it is always impossible to control their preferences in the laboratory by paying relatively large sums of money. They therefore don't need to seek to discredit game theory by endlessly drawing attention to the fact that it mostly doesn't work for inexperienced and underpaid subjects.

Nor have game theorists anything to gain from denying that the payoffs in real-life games might sometimes be derived from other-regarding preferences. Game theory is the same whether it is used to advise Saint Francis of Assisi or Attila the Hun. We simply recognize the difference between Attila and Saint Francis by writing different payoffs in the games we model them as playing.

Prisoners' Dilemma

The Prisoners' Dilemma is the most famous of all the toy games that game theorists use to illustrate their ideas. In the payoff table of figure 1,

Figure 1
Prisoners' Dilemma

Adam's payoffs are in the bottom left of each cell and Eve's are in the top right. Adam chooses a row and Eve chooses a column. Each then receives the payoff in the cell their choices jointly determine.

The starred payoffs indicate best replies. Thus, if Eve chooses *dove*, Adam can get a payoff of 1 by choosing *dove*, and a payoff of 3 by choosing *hawk*. Since $3 > 1$, Adam's payoff of 3 is starred to show that *hawk* is his best reply to Eve's choice of *dove*. Both payoffs are starred in the cell that arises when both players choose *hawk*, which implies that the strategy pair (*hawk*, *hawk*) is a Nash equilibrium, since each player is then making a best reply to the strategy choice of the other.

The idea that it is rational to play *hawk* in the Prisoners' Dilemma has historically generated great hostility, since everyone can see that both players would get more if both played *dove*. All kinds of fallacies have therefore been invented in hopeless attempts to prove that it can be rational to play something other than the Nash equilibrium of the game (Binmore 1994). Fortunately, this activity seems to have gone out of fashion for the moment, but it remains popular to claim that laboratory experiments show that the game-theoretic analysis of the Prisoners' Dilemma has no practical relevance.

If this is your aim, then it is very easy to organize an experiment that meets your requirements. Just as alchemists can "refute" the predictions of modern chemistry by mixing their reagents in dirty test tubes, so one can "refute" game theory by confusing the subjects with complicated instructions, or by providing them with inadequate incentives, or with too little time to get to grips with the problem that has been set.

One response to such criticism is that our test tubes need to be dirty, because that's how they are in real life. Those of us who clean our metaphorical test tubes can then be accused of "fixing" our experiments to get the results we want. But who would apply the same reasoning to chemistry experiments?

Incentives

A much-quoted experiment of Robert Frank illustrates the genre I am criticizing. Despite what is commonly said, even inexperienced subjects cooperate only about half the time in the one-shot Prisoners' Dilemma (Camerer 2003, p. 46).[1] However, in Frank's (2004) modification of the usual experimental design, subjects were allowed to fraternize for half an hour before playing. It turned out that relatively few subjects were then willing to cheat on their partners by playing *hawk* after promising to play *dove*, although they could gain a dollar by doing so.

But of course not! Who is going to metaphorically stab even a new friend in the back for one measly dollar? Even Attila the Hun wouldn't bother.

Sometimes such experiments are defended with the claim that it doesn't matter whether or not you pay the subjects, as the results turn out much the same either way. Such apologists can point to experiments in which behavioral "anomalies" remain unaffected as the rewards get large. In the Ultimatum Game they can get very large indeed (Cameron 1999).

But the fact that the size of the reward is irrelevant in some environments doesn't imply that it is irrelevant in most environments. Right at the beginning of modern experimental economics, Vernon Smith (1976) observed that the amount subjects are paid can make a substantial difference in economic experiments. If this weren't true most of the time, economists presumably would have learned by now that they don't need to spend large sums of their hard-to-get research money incentifying their experimental subjects.

My own most striking experience was when I ran laboratory experiments to test a design for a major British telecom auction for which I was responsible (which eventually raised $35 billion). The pilot experiments came nowhere near the efficient outcome predicted by game theory, but when we doubled the financial incentives—so that subjects went home with about $60 on average rather than $30—the results were suddenly very close to the theoretical predictions.

Experience

Incentives therefore matter much of the time, but what I think matters most is experience. Here again, Vernon Smith (1991) was early on the scene. In a classic experiment, he found that subjects needed to be recalled to the laboratory for three separate sessions of experience with an artificial financial market before they finally learned not to create bubbles.

Despite what is commonly said to the contrary by those who don't know or care about the literature, the case of the Prisoners' Dilemma and other toy games that can be thought of as modeling the private provision of public goods is particularly clear.[2] The huge number of experimental studies available in 1995 was surveyed both by John Ledyard (1995) and by David Sally (1995), the former for Roth and Kagel's authoritative *Handbook of Experimental Economics*. Camerer's (2003, p. 46) more recent *Behavioral Game Theory* endorses their conclusions.

It is true that inexperienced subjects often cooperate (by playing *dove*), but as the subjects gain experience, they defect more and more (by playing *hawk*), until about 90 percent are defecting. One can disrupt the march toward equilibrium by intervening in various ways, but when active intervention ceases, the march resumes.

Figure 2 is from a paper by Fehr and Gächter (2000). It is included to emphasize that these conclusions are uncontested even by authors who are commonly quoted with a view to discrediting traditional game theory. The first ten periods show the standard decline in the average contribution as the subjects gain experience in a regular public goods game.[3] In the final round nearly everyone contributes nothing.

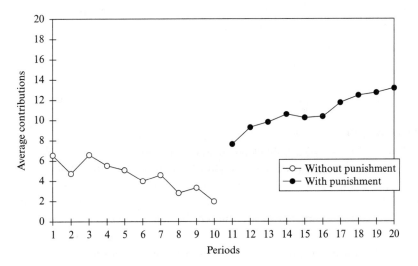

Figure 2
Public goods experiments before and after punishment (Fehr and Gächter 2000a, fig. 3B).

What Does Game Theory Predict?

But what about the behavior in the second ten periods of Fehr and Gächter's (2000) experiment?

In this part of the experiment the game is changed so that the subjects can pay a relatively small amount to reduce the payoff of free riders by a relatively large amount. They wouldn't take advantage of this opportunity to punish free riders in a subgame-perfect equilibrium of the one-shot game, but the data from the second ten periods of the experiment show that on the contrary, the threat of punishment induces the subjects to contribute more and more as they gain experience of the new game.

Behavioral economists take such data as proof that people have other-regarding preferences, but it isn't hard to think of other reasons why the equilibrium that behavioralists identify as the orthodox prediction isn't appropriate. For example, there isn't any particular reason why an adjustment process should converge on the subgame-perfect equilibrium of a one-shot game when other Nash equilibria are available—which they usually are (appendix C at the end of this volume). Nor is it obvious that we should be looking at Nash equilibria of the one-shot game when small groups of subjects play repeatedly (chapter 8).

Even if one insists on looking only at subgame-perfect equilibria of the one-shot game, it is unnecessary to postulate more than a small other-regarding component in the subjects' utility functions to create a game with a cooperative equilibrium. For example, Jakub Steiner (1972) offers a model in which the subjects feel just a little angry with free riders. He then describes an equilibrium in which only the worst free rider would get punished. The small cost of punishing then becomes tiny because it is shared among all the punishers. But the punishment is enough to support an equilibrium without free riding in the one-shot game, since a player who is the only free rider will necessarily be the most guilty (chapter 8).

No Convergence

However, the reason for spending time on the second ten periods of Fehr and Gächter's experiment isn't so much to question their claims about what game theory ought to predict about the equilibrium on which their subjects might eventually converge if the game were repeated often enough. It is to point out that although the subjects' behavior converges fairly well to the standard result in the experiment of the first ten periods, their behavior in the experiment of the second ten periods hasn't got close to converging on anything at all.

The graph of figure 2 shows the subjects' average behavior changing fairly rapidly over time. Nor is there any sign of the subjects coalescing around the average. As the authors point out, the distribution of contributions in the final round is spread out over the whole range of possibilities. It is therefore premature to ask to what extent the subjects should be seen as revealing other-regarding or selfish utilities in the second experiment. The subjects' behavior isn't consistent with maximizing any time-independent utility function at all.

This comment may seem too obvious to be worth making, but it isn't at all popular. Neoclassical economists are often as impatient as behavioral economists with the idea that people need time to adapt to a new game because they think of learning as an exclusively intellectual activity—and what is there to learn in such a simple game?

But I think the kind of learning that is going on is more akin to a sailor's learning not to walk with a rolling gait when he comes ashore after a long voyage. His mind knows perfectly well that he is on dry land, but his body hasn't figured out yet that this implies that he doesn't need to keep making ready for the next wave.

Coming Ashore

Everyone agrees that much of our interaction with other human beings is governed by *social norms*. I see such norms as analogues in social life of a sailor's rolling gait.

Just as a sailor's rolling gait is an efficient adaptation to the need to be ready for the next wave during a long voyage, so game theorists of my persuasion think it likely that cultural evolution has shaped our social norms so that their use mostly results in our coordinating on efficient equilibria in the real-life games that we play every day with those around us.

Of course, we are seldom any more aware that this is what we are doing than a sailor is conscious of walking oddly. We usually aren't even conscious that we are playing a game. For ordinary human beings, using a social norm is a piece of habituated behavior that is triggered by appropriate environmental cues.

Habits are hard to shake off—especially if you are unconscious that you have a habit in the first place. So when the *framing* of an experiment triggers the appropriate environmental cues, we often respond with the habituated response: no matter how ill-adapted it may be to the actual game being played in the laboratory. Like a sailor stepping ashore, we still roll with the waves, even though there are no longer any waves with which to roll.

I therefore think that Kahneman and Tversky's (1988) emphasis on the importance of framing in experiments is well grounded. But accepting this insight doesn't imply that we must also believe that human beings are mindless robots, irreversibly programmed with rigid social behaviors. Given time and adequate incentives, we can learn by trial and error or by imitation to adapt our behavior to novel situations. Sometimes we even think a little about what we are doing.

Presumably the rate at which different people learn depends on their personal characteristics, and the strength of their conditioning in the social norm that they must learn to abandon. Perhaps some people will never learn, no matter how long we give them or how large the incentives. The study of such inflexible folk is certainly of very great interest. But the evidence from the one-shot Prisoners' Dilemma suggests that the inflexible fraction of the student population from which subjects are usually drawn can't be more than about 10 percent of the whole.

Fairness

Although game theorists like myself have to put up with being said to be unremmitingly hostile to the idea that fairness can influence human behavior, I have devoted a substantial chunk of my life to working out a theory of how and why fairness norms matter in human societies (Binmore 1994, 1998). I even have some lingering hope that the absence of any algebra in my recent *Natural Justice* will result in the theory getting some serious attention from moral philosophers (Binmore 2005).

The basic thesis of the theory is that our sense of fairness evolved because the coordination games of which everyday social life largely consists commonly have large numbers of equilibria. A society therefore needs equilibrium selection devices if its members are to succeed in coordinating on one particular equilibrium in each game. Fairness is our name for a class of equilibrium selection devices that result in some social surplus being divided.

The conclusions to which I am led accord rather well with a psychological literature referred to as "modern equity theory" that is largely ignored by economists.[4] This literature offers experimental support for Aristotle's ancient contention, in his *Nichomachean Ethics*, that what is fair is what is proportional.

I don't plan to press the virtues of my theory of fairness in this book, since I haven't done any experimental work of my own on the subject. But two aspects of this theory are immediately relevant here. The first is the significance of the theory of repeated games. The second is the importance of evolutionary theory.

Repeated Games

The folk theorem of repeated game theory says that any contract that rational players might sign on how to play a one-shot game is sustainable as an *equilibrium* outcome when the game is played repeatedly by patient players with no secrets from each other. Cooperative agreements that can only be sustained in one-shot situations with the assistance of an external enforcement agency can therefore survive as *self-policing* social norms in a repeated environment.

The mechanism that sustains self-policing cooperative agreements in repeated games is *reciprocity*. People sometimes register their understanding of how such self-policing agreements work by saying, "I'll scratch your back if you'll scratch mine." But such a promise wouldn't be effective without the implied threat that I'll stop scratching your back (or worse) if you stop scratching mine. That is to say, what keeps the cooperative arrangement on track is that everybody recognizes that they will suffer some punishment if they don't honor the implicit deal.

The need to punish deviant behavior is explicit when Adam and Eve both use the GRIM strategy in the infinitely repeated Prisoners' Dilemma. The GRIM strategy tells you to play *dove* at each repetition of the Prisoners' Dilemma until the opponent fails to reciprocate. After an opponent plays *hawk*, the GRIM strategy tells you to play *hawk* yourself ever after. Neither player can therefore profit from deviating from the GRIM strategy by being the first to play *hawk* because the deviant will be relentlessly punished by the opponent responding by always playing *hawk* thereafter.

When we all lived in small foraging communities, there was no external enforcement agency to police the way that people played coordination games, but most of the coordination games we played together were *repeated* day after day. Moreover, as in small villages today, everyone knew everyone else's business. Given the folk theorem of repeated game theory, it is therefore perhaps no great surprise that evolution—both cultural and biological—should have generated fairness norms that allow social surpluses to be divided efficiently in favorable environments without wasteful conflict (Axelrod 1984).

The conditions of the folk theorem don't apply in large modern states, but much of our interaction with other human beings nevertheless continues to be open-ended. Even when we won't be interacting with the same person again, the way we conduct ourselves with that person is often being observed by onlookers with whom we may well interact in the future. Punishment for cheating on a partner can then be administered not by the victim (as in the GRIM strategy) but by onlookers refusing to deal with someone who has just established a reputation for being untrustworthy. That is to say, the domain within which we may reasonably expect cooperation to survive as equilibrium behavior is much wider than the narrow class of games to which formal versions of the folk theorem apply directly.

For this reason I believe that the social norms to which we unconsciously appeal in bargaining and other social situations are often best thought of as being adapted to *repeated* interactions. Such cooperative norms for repeated games sometimes get triggered in one-shot laboratory situations. This would explain why inexperienced subjects commonly play *dove* in the one-shot Prisoners' Dilemma. But after getting shafted a few times when playing the one-shot Prisoners' Dilemma over and over again (against a new opponent each time) and finding themselves unable to retaliate, most people eventually shift to playing *hawk*.

Strong Reciprocity?

A recent anthropological study highlights how social norms can be triggered in the laboratory (Henrich et al. 2004, 2005). The study confirms that inexperienced citizens of different societies play a variety of canonical toy games in different ways—presumably reflecting the fact that different societies operate different social norms. As Henrich et al. (2005) say: "Experimental play often reflects patterns of interaction found in everyday life."

The anthropologist Jean Ensminger is more explicit when commenting on why the Orma contributed generously in the public goods game she carried out as part of the study:

When this game was first described to my research assistants, they immediately identified it as the *"harambee"* game, a Swahili word for the institution of village-level contributions for public goods projects such as building a school.... I suggest that the Orma were more willing to trust their fellow villagers not to free ride in the Public Goods Game because they associated it with a learned and predictable institution. While the game had no punishment for free-riding associated with it, the analogous institution with which they are familiar does. A social norm had been established over the years with strict enforcement that mandates what to do in an exactly analogous situation. It is possible that this institution "cued" a particular behavior in this game (Henrich et al. 2004, p. 376).

The enforcement here is operated by the players themselves as envisaged in the folk theorem, and not external enforcement operated by the government. (National or cross-regional attempts at *harambee* collections are predictably corrupt.)

Despite this and similar evidence from the anthropologists who contributed to the study, Henrich et al.'s (2004) introduction insists on interpreting the data as supporting the existence of significant other-regarding preferences. But if Ensminger is right, then it would be a huge mistake to try to explain the behavior of the Orma in her public goods game on the hypothesis that their behavior was adapted to the game they played in her makeshift laboratory. In particular, inventing other-regarding utility functions whose maximization would lead to generous contribution in the public goods game would be pointless. Ensminger is suggesting that the subjects' behavior is adapted to the public goods game embedded in the *repeated* game that they play every day of their lives, for which the folk theorem provides an explanation that does not require anything at all to be invented.

It is admittedly difficult to distinguish the interpretation of the data that I share with Ensminger from the claim that the subjects have the kind of other-regarding preferences postulated by the theory of "strong reciprocity." This theory holds that people have a liking for reciprocation built into their personal utility functions. I am always puzzled by the ardor with which advocates of the theory of strong reciprocity, like Bowles and Gintis (2002) and Gintis (2002), condemn the idea that people might also sometimes reciprocate favors because this is how cooperative equilibria are sustained in indefinitely repeated games. Don't they see that the folk theorem would provide a possible evolutionary explanation for the emergence of strong reciprocity? However, my guess is that they reject the support that the theory of repeated games might offer the strong reciprocity hypothesis because everyone can see that we don't need to hypothesize strong reciprocity if we can explain the available data without going beyond the so-called weak reciprocity used to prove the folk theorem.

Evolution?

Where did the fairness norms triggered in laboratory experiments come from? I believe they evolved as equilibrium selection devices for use in those real-life games in which a surplus can be created by operating one of many cooperative equilibria. Cultural evolution must surely have been as important as biological evolution in this process, since what people regard as fair seems to depend heavily on both context and culture. Indeed I think that cultural evolution is active all the time in generating new social mini-norms for novel contexts. Some bargaining experiments can even be interpreted as snapshots of cultural evolution shaping a new fairness mini-norm while we watch (chapter 2).

But evolution is a slippery concept, easily harnessed in support of almost any doctrine. Other-regarding preferences are a case in point. It isn't good enough to argue that evolution built a regard for others into our preferences because we are all better off that way. The same argument shows that evolution should be expected to generate cooperation in the one-shot Prisoners' Dilemma. Similarly it isn't good enough to argue that evolution will select the preferences that we would choose to bind ourselves to if we knew our choices were to become common knowledge (Güth and Kliemt 1998). This is just another version of the Transparent Disposition Fallacy used by some authors in defense of rational cooperation in the one-shot Prisoners' Dilemma (Binmore 1994b). Any evolutionary defense for other-regarding preferences needs to be accompanied with a plausible story that explains *how* other-regarding mutants could have invaded our gene pool, and managed to survive once established—as, for example, in Samuelson (2004) or Weibull and Salomonsson (2005).

A Gift-Exchange Experiment

Nor can we afford to be naïve about evolutionary interpretations of laboratory experiments. An anecdote of Konrad Lorenz will serve to illustrate one particular mistake that I think it important to avoid.

Lorenz placed a totally inexperienced jackdaw on a marble-topped table, whereupon the baby bird went through all the motions of taking a bath. I think one may reasonably deduce that bath-taking behavior is genetically programmed in jackdaws, and that a trigger for this behavior is the presence of a flat, reflective surface (like water). What one isn't entitled to deduce is the absurd conclusion that bath-taking behavior somehow promotes the survival of jackdaws placed on marble-topped tables. If the jackdaw were human, we would say that its behavior was irrational, or ill-adapted to the context.

An example of the kind of interpretive mistake I am warning against is provided by a much-quoted experiment of Fehr et al. (1997) and Fehr and Gächter (2000). It can be thought of as modeling a competitive labor market in which the workers have the opportunity to reward employers who pay above the competitive rate by putting in more effort—even though the employer has no comeback if the worker just pockets the extra money and shirks.

The finding is that workers do indeed reward generous employers with more effort—that they metaphorically "exchange gifts." The authors speculate that their data supports the theory of strong reciprocity, which says that people have preferences that incorporate a positive liking for reciprocity.

But before leaping to such a conclusion, shouldn't we consider a less dramatic scenario? Although the subjects are called buyers and sellers in the experiment rather than employers and workers, its framing nevertheless cues the subjects for the *repeated* environment typical of a labor market. It therefore triggers a fairness norm that selects one of the cooperative equilibria of such a repeated game. Reciprocity therefore matters to the behavior of the subjects because reciprocity is the mechanism that sustains cooperative equilibria in repeated games.

If this dull story is true, then instead of subjects responding *rationally* to a set of preferences unconsidered in traditional economics, they just have traditional preferences but are behaving *irrationally*, in the sense that their behavior isn't adapted to the one-shot game they are deemed to be playing in the laboratory.

Ledyard's (1995) survey of experiments on the Prisoners' Dilemma and related games is obviously relevant here. What would happen if the subjects in the Fehr et al. study were allowed to play a large number of times?

We have seen that it is uncontroversial that subjects in experiments change their behavior as they gain experience, and matters are no different in the current study. The observed movement is initially *away* from the behavior that the authors assume should be the orthodox equilibrium prediction. But who can say what would happen with more than the usual ten or so repetitions? Nevertheless, in summarizing their data, Fehr et al. (1997, p. 2) say (with my italics):

These results indicate that reciprocity *motives* may indeed be capable of driving a competitive experimental market *permanently* away from the competitive outcome.

This claim is called into immediate question by the very data that the authors offer in its support. How could they have overlooked the final round effects evident in the data given in the appendix to their paper? In

16 of the 26 final rounds reported in which the worker has the opportunity to reciprocate, he doesn't. On the contrary, his effort is as small as it is possible for it to be.[5]

My own guess is that an understanding of what is really going on in the Fehr et al. experiment requires appealing to the contagion mechanism described by Kandori (1992) for sustaining cooperative equilibria in infinitely repeated games played by small groups of anonymous agents. It is true that the game of Fehr et al. is only repeated a finite number of times, but a number of authors, including Reinhard Selten (1986), have shown that the folk theorem often still works in the laboratory when the number of repetitions is finite. The fact that cooperation tends to break down in the final rounds of these experiment adds some support to my conjecture, once it is revealed that the same holds true in the experiment of Fehr et al. (chapter 8).

Social Preferences

When experimental economics was recognized in 2002 with a Nobel Prize awarded jointly to Daniel Kahneman and Vernon Smith, a joke circulated that Smith had been awarded the prize for showing that economics works in the laboratory, and Kahneman for showing that it doesn't.

The uncontroversial truth is that there are domains within which traditional economic theory—including game theory—works badly or not at all, and other domains within which it works rather well. What is controversial is how large these domains are, and where they lie.

Nowadays the followers of Daniel Kahneman and Amos Tversky[6] call themselves behavioral economists, to distinguish themselves from experimental economists like Vernon Smith or Charles Plott, who work largely in the tradition of neoclassical economics. However, on the subject of fairness in bargaining games there is a curious reversal of attitudes. Behavioral economists seem mostly to believe that the available experimental data support the hypothesis that laboratory subjects are classical optimizers whose utility functions have a social or other-regarding component.[7]

I have already explained why I think it a mistake to get into a dispute over what kind of utility function is being maximized by inexperienced and unmotivated laboratory subjects, but I want to insist that this doesn't imply that I believe that social preferences have no role to play in explaining human economic behavior in general. On the contrary, my own theory of fairness depends very heavily on the idea that social preferences matter (Binmore 2005). The rest of this section is therefore an aside that briefly examines three different ways in which I believe that social preferences can be significant.

Blood Is Thicker Than Water

Hamilton's (1995) rule offers a biological prediction of the extent to which we should care about a relative. A gene that programs its animal host to maximize the gene's fitness would do best to take into account not only the children its current host might produce but also the children of the host's relatives. The probability that they will carry a copy of the gene is smaller but much too large to be neglected.

The point was famously made in a semi-serious joke of the biologist J. B. S. Haldane. When asked whether he would give his life for another, he replied that the sacrifice would only be worthwhile if it saved two brothers or eight cousins. Haldane's joke is only funny if you know that your degree of relationship to a full brother is one-half, and your degree of relationship to a full cousin is one-eighth. These numbers are the probabilities that a recently mutated gene in your body is also to be found in the body of the relative in question.

The only experimental study on Hamilton's rule of which I know found that best friends get pretty much the same consideration as brothers or sisters (Dunbar et al. 2004). My guess is that our bodies have to deduce their degree of relationship to others from the extent to which we find ourselves in their company. If so, then the instincts that promote altruism within the family may also be triggered within a sufficiently close-knit group of unrelated individuals, as in an army platoon under combat conditions or a teenage street gang.

This is perhaps why we find ourselves feeling curiously obligated to old school friends or office colleagues, whom we may actively dislike at the conscious level. Our bodies are telling us that this pushy individual demanding an inconvenient favor must be a cousin or an aunt—as she would probably have been when we all lived in small foraging communities. Even establishing eye contact with a beggar in the street somehow creates enough inner discomfort at neglecting a potential relative that we are sometimes moved to hand over our small change with no prospect of any recompense.

I therefore accept that most people have other-regarding preferences to some degree—that they are willing to pay a small amount for no other return than the warm glow they derive from improving the lot of another human being. Perhaps there are economists who think otherwise, but I don't know who they are. One doesn't even need to appeal to the data from Dictator Games to confirm the claim, since nobody denies that nearly everyone contributes some small fraction of their income to charity. Moreover the kinship argument offers a possible evolutionary explanation of why people might be made this way. It is also doubtless true that some small fraction of people are willing to make large contributions on a regular basis toward the welfare of others, although an explanation of this behavior is not so easy to find.

However, the fact that some small fraction of the population behave like saints and that most of the rest of us are willing to treat pretty much anyone as a distant relative won't generate a warm enough glow to convert a game like the Prisoners' Dilemma into a game with an efficient equilibrium when the other player is a stranger. One needs *large* perturbations of the preferences economists traditionally attribute to players for this to happen. Matters are different in the games we play with the friends and neighbors in our extended family, but I don't believe the evidence offered in support of the claim that most of us are programmed to treat strangers like close members of the family survives serious examination.

Revealed Preference

Why do I reject the social preferences that behavioral economists fit to their experimental data? They commonly report relatively large warm-glow effects.

The theory of revealed preference tells us that we can describe the behavior of agents who choose consistently as optimization relative to some utility function. However, economists who take the orthodox neoclassical position seriously are very careful *not* to deduce that the observed behavior was generated by the agent *actually* maximizing whatever utility function best fits the data. This would be to attribute the kind of psychological foundations to neoclassical theory that its founders invented the theory to escape.

Being able to fit a utility function only tells us that the behavior is consistent—it doesn't tell us *why* the behavior is consistent. For example, one way of explaining the behavior of that half of the population of inexperienced subjects who cooperate in the one-shot Prisoners' Dilemma is to say that they are optimizing a social utility function whose arguments include the welfare of others. Another is to attribute any consistency in their behavior to the fact that they are unconsciously operating a social norm better adapted to repeated situations.

Both explanations fit the data equally well, but the former explanation is easier to criticize. What is the point of insisting that players have other-regarding utility functions built into their brains if doing so doesn't allow predictions to be made about how they will play in future, or in other games? But we know that the behavior of subjects in the one-shot Prisoners' Dilemma changes markedly over time as they pick up experience. A social utility function fitted to the behavior of an inexperienced subject will therefore fail to predict how he or she will behave when experienced—let alone when they play other games in other contexts.

None of this is to suggest that fitting utility functions to behavioral data may not be a useful way of summarizing the data—provided that we don't fall into the trap of assuming that the same utility function will necessarily predict other data without any experimental confirmation.

When evaluating an empirical claim that people have personal preferences with a large social component that has been quantified using experimental data, I therefore always ask myself what new data from other sources this claim has genuinely succeeded in predicting. I don't know of any cases at all that can be said to have unequivocally cleared this hurdle.

The theory of inequity aversion proposed by Fehr and Schmidt (1999) is usually quoted in denial of this skeptical assessment. (See chapter 4.) Fehr and Schmidt claim to have used data from ultimatum games to calibrate the parameters in the other-regarding utility function of their theory, and then used the calibrated utility function to predict the data from experiments on other games. However, Shaked (2005) has pointed out that this claim cannot possibly be true, because the data supposedly used to calibrate the parameters only restricts their range. When Fehr and Schmidt picked particular values of the parameters from within this range, they therefore made use of information that they should have denied themselves.[8]

Empathetic Preferences

Comparing utils across different individuals has been a controversial subject for a long time. Only recently have traditional economists stopped teaching the dogma that such interpersonal comparisons are intrinsically nonsensical. But how can fairness judgments be made if we have no way of comparing the welfare of those among whom a surplus is to be shared?

John Harsanyi (1977) invented a theory of interpersonal comparison of utility that makes good sense in the context of my theory of fairness (Binmore 2005). Harsanyi postulates social or empathetic preferences that exist in parallel with the standard personal preferences with which we are all familiar. With some apparently mild assumptions, Harsanyi shows that such empathetic preferences can be summarized in terms of a rate at which Eve assesses Adam's personal utils relative to her own personal utils.

Empathetic preferences live in an entirely different world from personal preferences because their content is entirely hypothetical. For example, Eve expresses an empathetic preference when she says that she would rather be herself eating an apple than Adam wearing a fig leaf—but there is no way Eve is ever going to get the opportunity to swap bodies with Adam.

I think the reason that normal people are all capable of expressing such empathetic preferences is that we need them to assess who should get how much when using fairness norms as equilibrium selection devices. The internal process by which we make such judgments is largely a mystery to us, and so it isn't surprising that we often confuse our empathetic preferences with our more readily understood personal preferences—especially those personal preferences that capture our feelings about those close to us.

Psychologists avoid this confusion by separating the notion of empathy from that of sympathy. A confidence trickster may *empathize* with an old lady by putting himself in her position to see what tall tale is most likely to persuade her to part with her money. He may compare the distress that she will feel at the loss of her life savings with his own joy in having her money to spend. He may even need to brush a tear from his eye as he contemplates her plight. But he won't be diverted from swindling her unless he also *sympathizes* with her by including her welfare among the arguments of his personal utility function.

I think economists need to make the same distinction. I agree wholeheartedly with those behavioral economists who argue that fairness matters. I also agree that we can't make sense of fairness norms without some notion of a social preference. But we don't need to identify a social preference exclusively with a sympathetic preference. I believe that the social preferences to which we appeal when making fairness judgments are mostly empathetic preferences that implicitly describe the standard of interpersonal comparison to be applied.

Straw Men

Finally, I want to address the standard criticism that people like me have to face—that we fix our experiments to get results consistent with neoclassical economics.[9] This slander is often exacarbated by characterizations of neoclassical economics that belong in horror comics rather than serious academic studies.

For example, neoclassical economists are said to be wicked for supposedly putting around the theory that people are inherently selfish. There is even a small experimental literature in which students of economics are supposedly demonstrated to be more evil than other students (Frank, Gilovich, and Regan 1993). As a result I know of at least one case in which a university senate was asked to ban the teaching of rational choice theory on the ground that it is immoral!

I agree that politically motivated economists, both of the left and the right, often use phony arguments in support of immoral policies, but I am not politically active, and neither are most traditionally minded economists. We have no interest in defending the transparently wrong proposition that people are inherently selfish. Just like anyone else, we give money to charity and help old ladies cross the road. We don't run experiments to justify an irrational prejudice in favor of neoclassical economics. We run experiments to determine the domains within which the predictions of neoclassical economics work reasonably well.

When the predictions don't work in apparently favorable environments, we ask ourselves why. Sometimes the answer is that our test tubes need cleaning, and sometimes the answer is that the theory needs fixing. Much of the attention of young neoclassical theorists in recent years has correspondingly been devoted to trying to come up with theories of bounded rationality that explain laboratory behavior better than is possible for any optimizing theory, whether neo-classical or retro-classical. (See, for example, Rubinstein 1998.)

I do not understand why this modest research program attracts such ire from behavioral economists. Behavioral economics is now triumphant in its primary aim. Everybody agrees that we need to study microeconomic behavior empirically in both the field and the laboratory. Behavioralists therefore having nothing more to gain from dismissing those experimentalists who find that traditional economics sometimes works as dishonest apologists for a failed orthodoxy.

Karl Marx said that history repeats itself, first as tragedy and then as farce. But do we really need to repeat the history of suspicion and reproach that accompanied the controversy over cooperation in the one-shot Prisoners' Dilemma? Or the more recently defunct experimental controversy over expected utility theory?

It was the latter controversy that brought Kahneman and Tversky (1979) to prominence, along with behavioral economics. But where is this controversy now? After much sound and fury, the exhausted combatants all seem to have retired from the field, leaving behind the consensus that all behavioral theories of how humans make decisions under risk are bad, but the least bad is traditional expected utility theory (Camerer and Harless 1994; Hey and Orme 1994).

Even if you are as sure about the failings of some other orthodoxy as Kahneman and Tversky were about expected utility theory, it may therefore still be worth your while to read papers that seem to defend the orthodoxy with a view to finding out what they actually say, rather than lending a credulous ear to those who attribute absurdly unrealistic beliefs to their unfortunate authors.

1   Getting to Equilibrium?

When the experiment reported in this chapter was carried out, it was still being said that Nash equilibria are irrelevant to the behavior of laboratory subjects. Even for the simplest class of games—Von Neumann's two-person, zero-sum games—the experimental reports were discouraging. The eminent psychologist Estes (1957) was particularly scathing when reporting on his test of Von Neumann's minimax theory. He agreed that game theory might be perhaps useful for something but that "game theory will be no substitute for an empirically grounded behavioral theory when we want to predict what people will actually do in competitive situations."

The negative consensus was first disturbed by a paper of Barry O'Neill (1987), but his positive conclusions were immediately attacked in *Econometrica* by Brown and Rosenthal (1990). Among other criticisms an econometric test was used to show that the theory fails because O'Neill's subjects didn't randomize *independently* between successive trials. As far as I know, all later experimenters, including myself, have found that data from two-person, zero-sum games always fails this test.

My reaction to the paper of Brown and Rosenthal was incredulity that anyone could take such a criterion seriously as a test of the Von Neumann theory. The strategy choices of players learning to play according to the minimax theory (or any other theory) will *necessarily* be correlated across successive trials. Brown and Rosenthal had therefore invented a test that treated any evidence that some kind of learning or adjustment was taking place as evidence *against* the hypothesis that the subjects were learning to play minimax.

However, Brown and Rosenthal made other criticisms of O'Neill's work that certainly did hit the spot. For this reason I joined with colleagues at the University of Michigan in putting together a new experiment on two-person, zero-sum games. Joe Swierzbinski has been a regular collaborator on experimental papers ever since.

Before designing the experiment, it was necessary to read the earlier experimental work on two-person, zero-sum games with some care. Only then did I begin to realize how slender the basis of an academic consensus can be. For example, in the experiment on which Estes based his dismissive remarks, there were only two subjects in all, who are described as being well-practiced in the reinforcement learning experiments that Estes was using to defend the (now discredited) theory of "probability matching." Neither subject knew that they were playing a game with another person. Even if they had known they were playing a game, the minimax theory would have been irrelevant to their plight, since they weren't told in advance what the payoffs of the game were. They were therefore playing a game of incomplete information, to which Von Neumann's minimax theory doesn't apply.

My colleagues and I dawdled for nearly ten years before producing a publishable paper describing our experiment. In the interval between our running the experiment and publishing our results, the academic consensus on whether Nash equilibria are relevant to the play of laboratory games had reversed itself. Nobody, then or now, finds it surprising that experienced subjects who are adequately incentified end up playing close to the minimax predictions in a user-friendly environment. But the accuracy of our results still remains of interest.

I think that there are several reasons why my experiments sometimes generate results that are closer to theoretical predictions than those of others. One reason is that I usually understand very well the ground rules of the theory being tested.

A second reason is the close attention I pay to keeping my test tubes clean. For example, the experiment of this chapter provides a good illustration of my extensive (and expensive) use of animated graphics to explain the experiment to subjects, and to keep them informed of what is happening in the game they are playing. Graphics also help make the experiment less boring than is commonly the case in the dismal science of economics.

A third reason is the quality of the *feedback* the subjects receive when they begin to play against each other—the better the feedback, the quicker and surer any convergence on a Nash equilibrium is likely to be.

Feedback

In real life we usually receive a great deal of feedback from all kinds of sources when learning how to behave in a new economic environment.

For example, rookie stockbrokers learn the ropes from their more experienced colleagues. Young economists peruse the history of Nobel laureates in the hope of finding the secret of success. Novelists tediously recycle the plots of the latest best seller. Shoppers tell each other where the best bargains are to be found. And so on.

One can completely control the quality of the feedback that subjects receive in the laboratory, but I know of very few experiments in which the feedback supplied isn't unrealistically sparse. In the experiment reported in this chapter, the feedback is comparatively rich. Subjects can compare a rolling average of their own payoff in recent games with the rolling average of the median subject in the same situation as themselves. Those who are playing badly then have an opportunity to recognize that they could do better if they played differently.

Sometimes critics say that such attempts to mimic real-life adaptive processes amount to fixing the results of an experiment. Amos Tversky often enjoyed teasing me by saying that you can "teach" laboratory subjects any behavior at all. I used to try to tease him back by telling him that you could refute any theory whatever by failing to clean your test tubes, but he always seemed to get more of a rise out of me than I was able to get out of him.

I doubt that Tversky really thought that providing subjects with the opportunity to learn in the laboratory is equivalent to conditioning them to behave in some predetermined fashion, but it isn't uncommon for his modern followers to take this line. Sometimes they claim that the results of any learning in the laboratory would be devoid of interest even in an experiment whose design wasn't supposedly biased by the prejudices of the experimenter!

As with Tversky, I am never sure how seriously such claims are intended to be taken, but after reading the paper that follows, readers can make their own judgment on whether my colleagues and I were guilty of the crime of teaching our subjects to play according to the minimax theory.

Does Minimax Work? An Experimental Study

Ken Binmore, Joe Swierzbinski, and Chris Proulx

1.1 Zero-Sum Games

Von Neumann's (1928) minimax theory of two-person, zero-sum games remains the branch of game theory with the most solid theoretical foundations. One would have thought that it would therefore have been tested to exhaustion in economics laboratories, but the small number of existing studies are mostly negative. This paper reports a laboratory experiment using modern techniques that leads to a positive conclusion.

In a zero-sum game, the players' payoffs always sum to zero whatever the outcome. In a finite, two-person, zero-sum game, Von Neumann's (1928) celebrated minimax theorem says that a player's minimax and maximin values are equal. It follows that $m_1 + m_2 = 0$, where m_i denotes player i's maximin value in the game.[1] If player I gets a payoff $x > m_1$, player II will therefore get a payoff $-x < m_2$. Since a player always has a maximin strategy that guarantees him an expected payoff no smaller than his maximin value in the game, it follows from Von Neumann's theorem that any theory of rational play for finite, two-person, zero-sum games must assign each player his maximin value.

There has been some debate about the extent to which Von Neumann was anticipated by the great mathematician Emile Borel. This debate is significant here only to the extent that the record shows that Borel

We are grateful to the National Science Foundation for funding the experiments reported in the this paper under Grant NSF-SES-882521. We also gratefully acknowledge funding from the University of Michigan to set up the Michigan Economics Laboratory, where the experiments were conducted in 1993.

1. Let $\Pi_i(p,q)$ be the expected payoff to player i in a finite, two-person game when player I uses mixed strategy p and player II uses mixed strategy q. Then player I's maximin and minimax values in the game are $m_1 = \max_p \min_q \Pi_1(p,q)$ and $M_1 = \min_q \max_p \Pi_1(p,q)$. It is always true that $m_1 \leq M_1$. Von Neumann's minimax theorem asserts that $m_1 = M_1$ when the game is zero-sum. Since $M_1 = -m_2$, it follows that $m_1 + m_2 = 0$.

formulated the minimax theorem but decided that it was probably false. It therefore seems pointless to run experiments designed to test the hypothesis that laboratory subjects are capable of duplicating Von Neumann's reasoning. Insofar as Von Neumann's minimax theory succeeds in predicting the behavior of laboratory subjects playing zero-sum games, it is not because it is common knowledge among the subjects that they are all cleverer than Borel. It is because Von Neumann's minimax theory predicts the play of Nash equilibria, and—as Nash pointed out in his thesis—Nash equilibria not only admit an eductive defense à la Von Neumann, they also admit an evolutive defense.

An evolutive defense of an equilibrium concept accepts that the players may be boundedly rational or just plain stupid. If they find their way to an equilibrium, it is therefore by some process of trial-and-error adjustment. Recent experimental work suggests that none of the dynamic adjustment processes that have been proposed fit the data well enough to justify our claiming to understand in detail how boundedly rational agents learn to play games. Nevertheless, the study of naïve idealized adjustment processes is thought to provide insight into the types of games for which a suitable equilibrium concept will provide a first approximation to how subjects end up playing after a long enough session in the laboratory.

For example, Binmore et al. (1995) and Roth and Erev (1995) show that simple adaptive models either do not converge to the subgame-perfect equilibrium in the Ultimatum Game, or else converge far too slowly for it to be possible to come close to replicating the necessary number of trials in the laboratory. By contrast, Brown (1951) and Robinson (1951) showed long since that the adaptive process called fictitious play converges reasonably quickly in two-person, zero-sum games. For example, the Nash equilibrium in the game Matching Pennies requires each player to play Heads or Tails with probability 1/2. Figure 1.1a shows a typical trajectory along which players adjusting their behavior according to the fictitious play algorithm approach this Nash equilibrium.[2] The adjustment process that receives the most attention after fictitious play is Darwinian replicator dynamics. The Nash equilibrium for Matching Pennies is a local attractor but not an asymptotic attractor for these dynamics. However, figure 1.1b shows a typical trajectory when the replicator dynamics are perturbed by introducing a small fraction of agents

---

2. The particular version of fictitious play required to generate this well-known diagram together with some adaptive stories that lead to it are described in Binmore (1987).

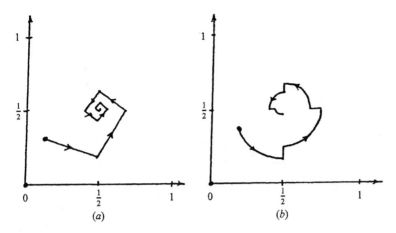

Figure 1.1
Approaching equilibrium in Matching Pennies

who know the current population mix and then optimize. Two-person, zero-sum games therefore provide an arena in which it is reasonable to hope that subjects will learn to play the equilibrium of the game within the time spans available in the laboratory.

1.2 Interpreting Mixed Strategies

If the evolutive interpretation of equilibria were valid, one would think that it would have first been confirmed for two-person, zero-sum games, but the few experimental studies that exist are not generally supportive of the minimax hypothesis. An exception is provided by a paper of O'Neill (1987).

Figure 1.2a reproduces the diagram with which O'Neill compares his results with the earlier experiments of Frenkel (1973), Estes (1957), Suppes and Atkinson (1960), and Malcolm and Lieberman (1965). It compares the observed and predicted frequencies with which the selected strategies were played in these experiments. However, O'Neill's paper was discredited by Brown and Rosenthal (1990), and we accept that his data points in figure 1.2a are unsafe. Among other concerns his decision to study repeated play between the same subjects blurs some of the issues he was seeking to clarify. Later experimental studies by Rapoport and Boebel (1992), Mookherjee and Sopher (1994, 1997), and McCabe et al. (1994) report positive conclusions only in the case of Matching Pennies. The recent field study by Walker and Wooders (1998) also rejects the

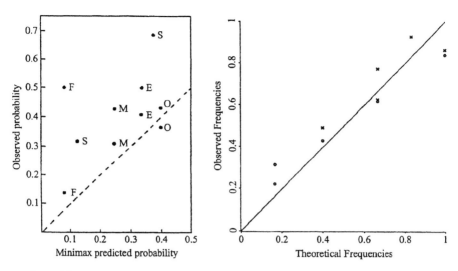

Figure 1.2
Observation versus prediction in some experimental games

minimax hypothesis for experimental data, although it finds support for minimax play by professional tennis players.

For comparison, figure 1.2b plots the average frequencies with which selected row and column strategies from each of the games in our experiments were played against the theoretical frequencies predicted by the minimax hypothesis. The symbol o in figure 1.2b denotes a row strategy and the symbol × denotes a column strategy.

Our paper differs from this literature in offering experimental support for the minimax hypothesis. We attribute our different findings partly to our using a more refined experimental technique, and partly to an insistence by previous authors on an overly literal interpretation of how one might reasonably expect a mixed equilibrium to manifest itself in the laboratory.[3]

We agree that the case of greatest interest arises when the maximin strategies are mixed, but we think it a mistake to demand that the players actively randomize before the minimax theory can be said to be relevant to their play. Real people are notoriously bad natural randomizers (although Rapaport and Budescu 1992 find that they randomize much better when playing a zero-sum game than in other situations studied in

---

3. A working paper available from the authors discusses the reasons for our differing findings in more detail.

the psychological literature). Even professional statisticians find it hard to eyeball a random sequence. When playing a repeated game against a real opponent whom one wants to keep guessing, it is therefore not necessary to behave in a manner that comes anywhere close to passing any scientific tests for randomness.

This point becomes sharper when attention is confined to the *one-shot* games that we study. In such games the players do not have to worry about offering their opponent clues as to their future play. When a mixed strategy is optimal, the players are necessarily *indifferent* among the pure strategies to which the mixed strategy assigns a positive probability. An individual player therefore has no reason to play such pure strategies with any particular probability. Although old-style game theory books proceed as though rationality demands that each player actively randomize when his maximin strategy in a two-person, zero-sum game is mixed, the theory actually offers no support for this claim. Modern eductive accounts of Nash equilibria in mixed strategies therefore stress their interpretation as equilibria in *beliefs* rather than *actions* (Binmore 1991, p. 286).

One way of realizing an equilibrium in beliefs arises when the players are drawn at random from a population whose characteristics are commonly known. It then does not matter how each individual player chooses his strategy in a two-player, zero-sum game G, provided that the frequencies with which strategies are played in the population as a whole correspond to their maximin probabilities. In extreme cases we may observe what biologists call a polymorphic equilibrium of the grand game played by the population as a whole. In such an equilibrium each member of the population may plan to use a *pure* strategy if chosen to play G, but the frequencies with which they choose different pure strategies coincide with the probabilities assigned to them by a mixed equilibrium of G. A player facing an opponent drawn at random from the population will then be in the same situation as someone whose opponent is known to randomize according to his maximin strategy. It is then optimal for him to secure his maximin value by playing any of the pure strategies assigned positive probability by his own maximin strategy.

Our experiment is designed to allow polymorphic equilibria to evolve in the laboratory. Some theoretical evolutive models in which this outcome should be expected have been studied by Hopkins (1996). Crawford's (1989) earlier evolutive study confirms that we should not expect to see each individual player ending up by actively randomizing according to his maximin probabilities, but neither are human subjects likely to

stick to just one of their pure strategies in the manner that biologists attribute to animals. Human subjects must be expected to be constantly
adjusting their strategy choice in an attempt to exploit variations in the
frequencies with which strategies are employed in the population as a
whole. Since the payoff to making such adjustments declines to zero as
the population frequencies approach their minimax values, it would be
unreasonable to expect convergence to go all the way. The best that one
can expect is that the system will find its way into a neighborhood of the
minimax outcome, wherein it will wander as the subjects find it increasingly difficult to decide between strategies among which they would be indifferent in equilibrium.

These considerations led us to predict that the frequencies with which
pure strategies are played by populations of sufficiently well-motivated
subjects will be close to the maximin probabilities, provided that adequate time for trial-and-error adjustment is available. Their payoffs will
then necessarily be close to the players' maximin values for the game.
Figure 1.2b indicates that the experiment largely confirmed our expectations. The surprise was to find that convergence to a neighborhood of the
equilibrium was so quick.

An eductive explanation of why subjects get close to their maximin
payoffs, which demands that players randomize independently each time
that they play, is not supported by our results. As with O'Neill's and later
experiments, our data fail an independence test proposed by Brown and
Rosenthal (1990). As is evident from figure 1.6, our subjects' choices are
dependent on the past history of play. A contrary finding would refute the
evolutive hypothesis that people find their way to equilibrium by some
kind of trial-and-error adjustment process.

1.3 The Experimental Design

Figure 1.3 shows player I's payoff matrices for the seven two-person,
zero-sum games played by our subjects. As indicated in the figure, there
were two "practice" and five "real" games. The asterisks in figure 1.3
indicate the row and column strategies whose frequencies of play are
plotted in figures 1.5 and 1.6 and reported in tables 1A.3, 1A.4, and
1A.5. Figure 1.3 also shows the payoff matrices for the three companion
games that we use to facilitate the analysis of the data and are discussed
in section 1.4.

In the computer implementation a subject was always shown his or her
own payoff matrix with positive values represented by the appropriate

Practice Games

Game 1

	1	2	3
1	3	−3	−2
2	2	0	−1
3	1	2	0

Game 2

	1	2
1	1	−1
2	−1	0

Real Games

Game 1

	1*	2
1*	−2	3
2	−1	−2

Game 2

	1	2*	3
1	−3	−2	−3
2*	1	−1	0
3	3	−3	−3

Game 3

	1*	2	3
1*	−2	3	−3
2	−1	−3	0
3	3	−1	1

Game 4

	1	2	3*
1	0	2	−1
2	2	0	−1
3*	−1	−1	0

Game 5

	1*	2	3	4
1*	1	−1	−1	−1
2	−1	−1	1	1
3	−1	1	−1	1
4	−1	1	1	−1

2 × 2 Companion Games for Real Games 3, 4, and 5

Game 3

	1*	2
1*	−2	3
2	0	−1

Game 4

	1–2	3*
1–2	1	−1
3*	−1	0

Game 5

	1*	2–4
1*	1	−1
2–4	−1	1/3

Figure 1.3
Payoff matrices for the row player in our experiments

number of green disks and negative values by a corresponding number of red disks. Alongside their payoff matrix, subjects were shown a "roulette wheel" that was half red and half green at the beginning of each new game. After each play of the game, the red or green region was updated to take account of the amount the player won or lost in that play. After completing all the plays of a particular game, the subjects observed a small yellow "ball" move around the circumference of the roulette wheel. Its stopping location was random. If it stopped in green, the subject won $6.00 in the games played for real (and 60 cents in the practice games). If it stopped in red, the subject won nothing. Subjects were told to think in terms of losing or winning "lottery tickets." However risk-averse a rational agent might be, his or her goal in these circumstances should be to maximize the expected number of lottery tickets.

It should be noted that all the games of figure 1.3, with the exception of O'Neill's game (real game 5), have maximin frequencies that are multiples of $1/6$. This choice reflects the fact that all games were played in sessions involving twelve subjects split into six row players and six column players, who were repeatedly matched in pairs to play a game in an unpredictable manner. This design allows mixed strategies to be "purified." For example, if a mixed strategy requires the first row to be played with probability $1/6$ and the second row with probability $5/6$, then the same effect can be achieved by having one row player choose the first row for certain while the other five row players choose the second row for certain. With the exception of O'Neill's game (real game 5), it follows that polymorphic equilibria exist in which each subject uses a pure strategy. For example, in real game 1 it would be an equilibrium if just one row player used the first row strategy and just one column player used the second column strategy.

The subjects in the experiment were undergraduate students at the University of Michigan, recruited directly from classes chosen to make any familiarity with game theory or related topics unlikely. Recruits from the same class were assigned to different sessions. Despite the administrative inconvenience, we do not use the same list of volunteers for different experiments for fear of cross-experimental contamination. Since the games are all zero-sum, it was possible to tell prospective subjects that the average amount to be expected from participation would exceed $15. Counting the $3 attendance payment and the small prizes for the practice games, the actual average was approximately $18.60. Subjects spent approximately 45 minutes in the laboratory.

Each experiment session required 12 subjects, who were seated at screened monitors. We ran 13 experimental sessions[4] in all, in each of which the subjects played all 7 games of figure 1.3 many times. Each real game was played 150 times, except for real game 2, which has a pure-strategy saddle point. Real game 2 was played 75 times. Practice game 1 was played 50 times. Practice game 2 was played 100 times.

Practice game 1 was played fairly slowly to allow subjects to familiarize themselves with the controls. Practice game 2 was played faster, and the real games were played so quickly that a subject who wished to change his or her strategy at every play needed to pay very close attention to what was going on. A subject's opponents were switched after every play in an unpredictable manner. A subject remained a row or a column player during the play of any particular game, but the sets of row and column players were reshuffled each time that the game changed.

A row player chose his or her strategy by pressing the *up* and *down* arrow keys. This led to different rows being highlighted on the screen. Every so often, a column would be highlighted, indicating the choice made by the opponent in the game just played. The roulette wheel showing the subject's accumulated number of lottery tickets would then be updated. Column players chose strategies by pressing the *left* and *right* arrow keys but were not otherwise distinguished from row players.

Starting with the second practice game, subjects were also shown two graphs updated in real time. A green graph showed the subject's payoff averaged over the last six plays. A white graph showed the same statistic for the median of the other players in the same situation as the subject. That is, a row player saw the median payoff of the other row players and a column player the median payoff of the other column players. Row players were, of course, only matched against column players in the game currently being played. The graphs were intended to allow him to compare his performance with the other subjects in the same situation as himself. We attach considerable importance to this feature of the experiment, which has no correlate in other experimental work on two-person, zero-sum games as far as we know.

We will be very pleased to send copies of our experimental software to interested parties.

---

4. More sessions were organized, but we were unlucky with computer crashes and the behavior of one subject. Our policy is to throw away data if anything untoward occurs, whatever the cause.

1.4   Results

Recall that 13 experiments were run, each with 12 subjects. In each experiment, all subjects played 2 practice games and 5 real games. In any given game, half the subjects were row players and half were column players. The results of the experiments are summarized in figure 1.4 to 1.7. Figure 1.2, which is provided for purposes of comparison with O'Neill's (1987) data, has already been mentioned. Table 1A.1 to 1A.6 provide additional information on the results.

Figures 1.4 and 1.5 and the accompanying tables 1A.1 and 1A.2 show that, both in terms of average payoffs and the average frequencies with which various strategies were used, the behavior of our subjects is close to that predicted by the minimax hypothesis. Figure 1.6 and the accompanying table 1A.5 contains information on how our subjects responded to opportunities for increasing their payoffs. Figure 1.7 and table 1A.6 indicate how the subjects responded to the information presented in our graphical display. Perhaps the most striking results of our experiments concern tables 1A.3 and 1A.4, which show that the maximin frequencies are good predictions of the play-by-play behaviour of individual groups of subjects.

Figure 1.4a to 1.4e shows histograms of moving averages of the payoffs obtained by row players in real games 1 to 5 respectively. For example, figure 1.4a describes the first real game. For each subject who was a row player and for each play of the game, we calculate the moving average of that subject's payoff in the current and preceding 23 plays. Starting with play 24, the top line indicates, at each play, the maximum of the 78 moving averages calculated this way. The connected dots indicate the medians of the moving averages at each play, and the bottom line indicates the minimum of the moving averages. The intermediate lines indicate the top and bottom quartiles respectively. The horizontal lines in figure 1.4a to 1.4e indicate the maximin payoffs for a row player. For each real game the median moving average is always very close to this line. The vertical distance between the top and bottom quartile lines indicates the range of moving averages obtained by the middle half of the subjects at each play.[5] For comparison, the vertical axis in each graph runs from the minimum to the maximum payoff attainable by a row player and so indicates the full range of values that these moving averages can take on. For each

---

5. By construction, the 21st to 58th largest values are guaranteed to fall between the bottom and top quartiles. This turns out to be one less than half of the values.

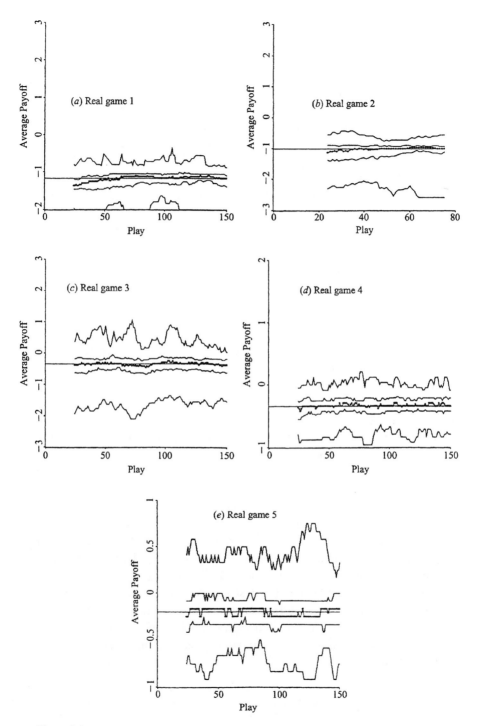

Figure 1.4
Summary statistics for the moving averages of payoffs

game the middle half of the moving averages remains clustered very narrowly around the minimax payoff.

Table 1A.1 provides further information concerning the average payoffs received by the row players in each real game.

Table 1A.2 reports the average frequency with which row and column players used each strategy. As in figure 1.3, row strategies are labeled numerically, starting from the top of the payoff matrix for each game, and column strategies are numbered from left to right. The first part of table 1A.2 involves averages over all the experiments. It reports the theoretical maximin frequency predicted for each strategy by the minimax hypothesis together with the actual frequency with which each strategy was played, both averaged over all the plays of the game and also over only the last third of plays. The second part of table 1A.2 reports the average frequency with which each strategy was used in all the plays of each separate experiment.

Figure 1.5a to 1.5e displays some of the information in table 1A.2 in graphical form. For the row and column strategies of each real game marked with asterisks in figure 1.3 and table 1A.2, the average frequencies with which these strategies were used in each of the 13 experiments are plotted. The row frequencies are shown on the horizontal axes in figure 1.5 and the column frequencies on the vertical axes. For comparison, horizontal and vertical lines in each graph also indicate the maximin row and column frequencies for each strategy. The average frequencies plotted in figure 1.5 are clearly close to the theoretical maximin predictions. On the other hand, it is also evident that there are small but systematic deviations from the maximin frequencies.[6]

The dashed boxes in figure 1.5a to 1.5e indicate the best unit box predictor for each game. As discussed in more detail below, more than 60 percent of all the frequencies observed in different plays fall within this box for each real game.

Tables 1A.3 and 1A.4 and the dashed boxes in figure 1.5 and figure 1.6 provide information on the frequencies with which individual groups of subjects used selected strategies in individual plays of the games. In figure 1.5 the strategies considered are those marked with an asterisk in figure 1.3 and table 1A.2.

---

6. For example, the standard Hotelling T^2 tests reject the hypothesis that the clouds of points in figure 1.5 are drawn from bivariate normal distributions with means at the maximin frequencies.

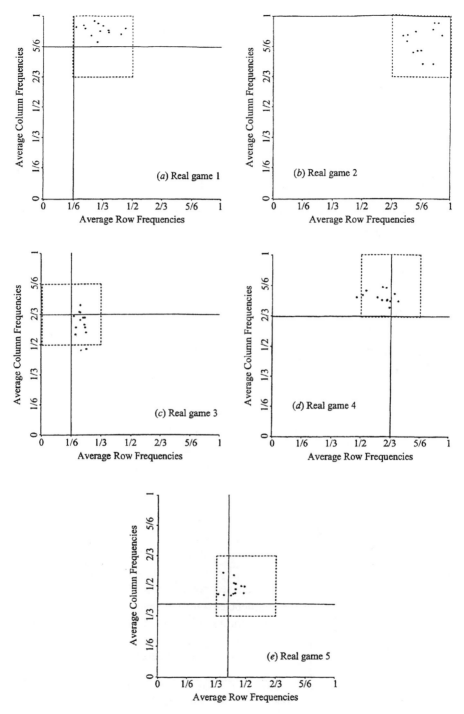

Figure 1.5
Average frequencies of play in each of the 13 experiments

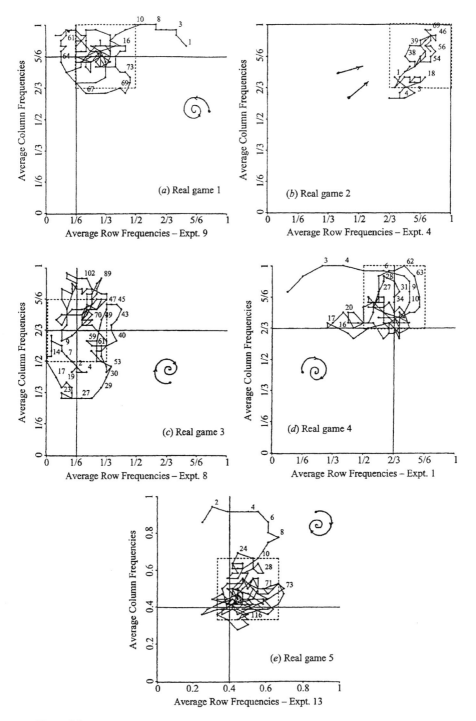

Figure 1.6
Trajectories of frequency of play for selected experiments

For each real game the group of subjects was divided into six row players and six column players. Hence only frequencies that were a multiple of 1/6 were observed in a single play of a game. For each observable combination of row and column frequencies, the entries in table 1A.4 indicate the fraction of the total number of plays in all the experiments in which that particular combination was observed. For comparison, the numbers in parentheses indicate the probabilities that the designated combinations of row and column frequencies will be observed if all players behave purely randomly, choosing their strategies randomly and independently with an equal probability of choice assigned to each strategy.

The information contained in table 1A.4 is summarized in various ways in table 1A.3. In addition the first row of entries in table 1A.3 shows the fraction of all plays where there was a net change in the number of row and/or column players playing the designated strategies from that play to the next. For each real game, the frequency of net changes was very high. Little tendency to purify mixed strategies was therefore observed.

The next set of entries in table 1A.3 describes the performance of the maximin point predictor. We use the term "point predictor" to refer to a prediction that a single combination of the row and column frequencies indicated in table 1A.4 will be observed in a play of the game. For each game the maximin point predictors select the combinations of row and column frequencies that are to be played according to the minimax hypothesis.[7] Depending on the game, the designated strategies were played at exactly the frequencies predicted by the minimax hypothesis in from 7 to 20 percent of the total plays.

The set of entries labeled "best point predictor" in table 1A.3 indicate the single frequency combination that was observed most often in each real game. These "most likely" frequency combinations are always close to the maximin frequencies, differing at most by the choice of one subject. For games 2 and 3 the maximin frequencies are the combinations observed most often. Also note that the fraction of plays occurring at the most likely frequency combinations are no more than 2 percent greater than the fractions of plays at the maximin frequencies, except for game 1 where the difference exceeds 10 percent.

As another point of comparison, the numbers listed in parentheses under the fractions of plays for the maximin and best point predictors in

7. The exact maximin frequencies for game 5 are not a multiple of 1/6 and so cannot be observed in the play of a single game. For game 5, the maximin point predictor is the observable frequency combination that has the highest probability of occurrence when subjects choose their strategies randomly and independently using the exact maximin probabilities.

table 1A.3 give the predictions of two probabilistic theories. As in table 1A.4, the first of the two numbers is the probability that each frequency combination will occur if all subjects behave purely randomly. The second number in parentheses is the probability that the designated frequency combination will occur if all subjects choose their strategies randomly and independently using the maximin probabilities. It is interesting to note that although the observed fractions of plays occurring at exactly the maximin frequencies seem small, the fractions predicted by this strong form of the minimax hypothesis are also small (except, of course, for game 2, where minimax behavior does not involve mixed strategies). Indeed, for games 3 and 4 the observed and predicted fractions of plays at exactly the maximin frequencies are not statistically different.[8]

Given the large fraction of plays where there was a net change in the frequencies with which strategies were used from one play to the next, it is unsurprising that we do not observe a large proportion of plays occurring at any one frequency combination. Since point predictors fail to recognize the noisy nature of the subjects' choices, the rest of table 1A.3 considers unit box predictors. We use the term "unit box" to refer to a square centered at one of the observable frequency combinations shown in table 1A.4. The square has a height of $1/3$ to allow for a net change (up or down) of one in the number of column players using their designated strategy at the central frequency combination. Similarly the square has a width of $1/3$ to allow for a net change of one in the number of row players using their designated strategy at the central combination. For purposes of comparison, we thought it best to keep all unit boxes the same size, although this requires displacing the centers of boxes when these involve the use of a pure strategy.

We use the term "unit-box predictor" to refer to a prediction that one of the nine adjacent combinations of observable row and column frequencies contained in some unit box will be observed in a play of the game. To make a unit box prediction is to claim that the number of row players and the number of column players using their designated strategies will each differ by at most one from the numbers of players indicated by the frequency combination at the center of the unit box under consideration.

---

8. If strategies are chosen randomly using the maximin probabilities, the observed fraction of plays is a binomial random variable with a standard deviation of $\sqrt{p(1-p)/N}$, where p is the predicted probability of observing the maximin frequency combination, and $N = 1,950$ is the total number of plays for game 3 and game 4. The observed fractions of plays for games 3 and 4 are within one standard deviation of the predicted fractions.

Where possible, the maximin unit-box predictor uses the unit box centered at the exact maximin frequencies to predict the outcomes of individual games. For game 2, the center of the maximin unit box predictor is offset from the boundary $(1, 1)$ to $(5/6, 5/6)$ so that the box contains the same number of possible frequency combinations as other games. The exact maximin frequencies for game 5 are not a multiple of $1/6$, and so a square the same size as a unit box but centered at the exact maximin frequencies will not contain the same number of observable frequency combinations as the boxes for other games. The maximin unit box for game 5 is therefore centered at one of the observable frequency combinations closest to the exact maximin frequencies. The unit box chosen has the highest probability of occurrence when all subjects randomly and independently choose their strategies using the maximin probabilities.

One of the important results of our experiments is the large number of plays in which the observed row and column frequencies fall within the maximin unit boxes. Depending on the game, the fraction of plays falling within the maximin unit box ranges from 49 to 88 percent.

As with point predictors, one can ask which of the unit boxes for each game contains the frequency combinations most often observed in the play of that game. We call this box the best unit box. The best unit box for each game is drawn in table 1A.4 and is also shown as a dashed box in figures 1.5 and 1.6. Information on the best unit box predictors is summarized in table 1A.3. It is worth emphasising that although the dashed boxes in figures 1.5 and 1.6 appear large, any smaller squares centered at the same points contain only one of the frequency combinations that can be observed in a single play of the game.

The best unit-box predictor for each game is a good prediction of the outcome of the individual plays in that game. Depending on the game, from 61 to 88 percent of the total number of plays occur at one of the frequency combinations contained in the best unit box. The best unit-box predictor is always close to the maximin prediction. For every game the exact maximin frequency combination is one of those contained in the best unit box. For games 2 and 3, the maximin and best unit boxes are identical. As can also be observed in table 1A.3, the fractions of plays contained in the best unit boxes are typically not much larger than the fractions contained in the maximin unit boxes.

The numbers in parentheses in table 1A.3 under the listing of the fraction of plays for the maximin and best unit-box predictors give the same information as for the point predictors. The first number is the probability that one of the frequency combinations contained in the designated box will occur when subjects choose their strategies purely randomly. The second number is the probability that one of these frequency combinations will occur when subjects choose their strategies using the maximin probabilities. In game 5 the probability of observing a frequency combination contained in the maximin unit box is large, both when subjects behave purely randomly and when they choose strategies using the maximin probabilities. Except in this case, the fraction of total plays contained in the maximin unit box is far higher than if subjects chose their strategies randomly with equal probabilities.[9] Clearly, some sort of systematic behavior keeps the subjects' choices close to the maximin frequencies.

The last part of table 1A.3 uses unit-box predictors to compare the predictive power of alternative theories with that of the minimax hypothesis. The alternative hypotheses compared with the minimax hypothesis are as follows:

1. *Random play* Brown and Rosenthal (1990) propose comparing O'Neill's (1987) results with the hypothesis that each player chooses each of his strategies with equal probability.

2. *Optimizing against random play* Kadane and Larkey (1982) argue that equilibrium considerations should be irrelevant to a strict Bayesian who simply maximizes his expected payoff relative to his subjective beliefs about the play of the opponent. We consider a player who believes that his opponent will use each of his strategies with equal probability.

3. *Minimax regret* Savage (1951) offers the minimax-regret criterion as a decision-making principle for large world contexts to which he believes that Bayesian decision theory does not apply. We adapt the theory to the case of mixed strategies in the natural way.

4. *Probability matching* As documented in a survey by Vulkan (1996), the hypothesis that animals and people do not optimize but match probabilities has a wide following in the psychological literature. It is not entirely clear how the hypothesis should be adapted to a game-theoretic context, but we take it to be the theory that a player uses his best reply to an opponent's strategy with the same probability that the opponent uses that strategy.

For the selected row and column strategies from each game, table 1A.3 first reports the probability for these strategies predicted by each of the

9. When subjects behave purely randomly, the standard deviation of the fraction of total plays falling within the maximin unit box is given by the same formula as in note 9, except that p is now the probability of observing a single play within the unit box.

four alternate theories listed above. We then consider the unit boxes corresponding to each of these predictions. Except where the predictions of the alternative theories coincide with the maximin predictions, the fractions of games whose frequency combinations fall within the unit boxes of the alternative theories are much less than the fractions falling within the corresponding maximin unit boxes.

For the pairs of row and column strategies that we have been considering and each real game, figure 1.6 shows a trajectory of moving averages of the frequencies with which these strategies were played in particular experiments. Each dot indicates the average frequency with which the strategies were used in six plays of the game. The numbers by some of the dots indicate the first plays in the corresponding averages. As in figure 1.5, the horizontal and vertical lines in each graph indicate the predicted maximin row and column frequencies, and the dashed boxes indicate the best unit boxes for each game. It is interesting how quickly the moving averages enter the best unit boxes. It is also worth recalling that except for game 2, which has a saddle point, the payoff from using each strategy is almost the same when opponents play their strategies with probabilities close to the maximin frequencies. It is therefore not surprising that the trajectories wander rather unpredictably once they get close to the maximin frequencies.

For a 2×2 game, a point in the "frequency space" depicted in figures 1.5 and 1.6 completely determines which pure strategy is a best reply for each player when he or she believes that the opponent will play according to the indicated frequency. Hence we associate a companion 2×2 game to each of games 3, 4, and 5.[10] The payoff matrices for the row player in these companion games are listed in figure 1.3.

If certain assumptions are maintained, then play in one of the 2×2 companion games should mirror play in the original game. For example, the 2×2 game associated with game 5 is obtained by assuming that the interchangeability of the second, third, and fourth pure strategies is reflected in their being played with equal probabilities. To play the first pure strategy in the companion game corresponds simply to playing the first pure strategy in the original game. To play the second pure strategy in the companion game, labeled 2–4, corresponds to playing each of the other pure strategies in the original game with probability $1/3$. In a similar way a companion 2×2 game is obtained for game 4 by exploiting the

10. Since it is fully dominance solvable, it is not interesting to compare real game 2 with a 2×2 companion game.

interchangeability of the first and second strategies in that game. The companion 2×2 game for real game 3 is obtained by deleting row strategy 2, which is strictly dominated, and then column strategy 3.[11]

The counterclockwise spiral inset in figure 1.6a indicates the direction in which that trajectory should "wind" if subjects tend to switch to whichever strategy is their best reply. Similarly the spirals inset in figure 1.6c to 1.6e indicate the directions in which the corresponding trajectories should move if subjects tend to switch to their best replies in the companion 2×2 games for each figure. Although the evolution of the trajectories is obviously noisy, each trajectory appears to wind in the predicted direction. The data reported in table 1A.5 support this conclusion.

Table 1A.5 considers plays of the games where there were nonzero net changes in the frequencies with which row or column players used their designated strategies from those plays to the next. The designated strategies are those whose frequencies are graphed in figures 1.5 and 1.6.

Consider, for example, the row strategy for game 1. This strategy is a strict best reply for row players if and only if the column players in game 1 use their designated strategy with a frequency less than the maximin column frequency. (Both row strategies are best replies when column players play their strategies with exactly the maximin frequencies.) Hence, if subjects tend to switch to their best replies, we should observe more positive than negative changes in the numbers of row players playing their designated strategy after plays where column players use their own designated strategy with less than the maximin frequency, and more negative than positive changes in the reverse situation. Similar predictions apply for the column players in game 1 and row and column players in the 2×2 companion games for games 3, 4, and 5.

The first part of table 1A.5 reports data pooled over all the experiments. The data show an increased use of those strategies which were strict best replies to the opponents' previous play either for the game itself (for game 1) or the companion 2×2 games (for games 3, 4, and 5). Whenever a strict best reply exists, the fraction of plays for which there was a shift toward that best reply is always greater than the fraction with a shift in the opposite direction. The second part of table 1A.5 reports the data separately for each experiment. In a large majority of the individual experiments, we also observe that the fraction of plays

11. Assuming that the row player does not use his strictly dominated strategy, it is not optimal for the column player in game 3 to use strategy 3 unless the probability that the row player uses strategy 1 is greater than $1/2$. As can be seen in table 1A.2, this probability is much higher than either the predicted maximin frequency or the observed frequency with which strategy 1 was played in the various experiments.

with a shift toward a strict best reply is greater than the fraction with a shift in the opposite direction.

As discussed in section 1.3, during each game subjects were provided with a real-time display that showed a moving average of their own payoffs as well as information about the average payoff of other players like themselves. One way that subjects might respond to such information is to switch strategies when the display indicates that the performance of their current choice is poor.

Figure 1.7 is a histogram that shows the frequencies with which individual row players in game 5 switched from the strategy that they used in the previous play of the game as a function of the moving averages of their own payoffs in the previous six plays. The height of each bar in figure 1.7 gives the frequency with which subjects switched strategies when

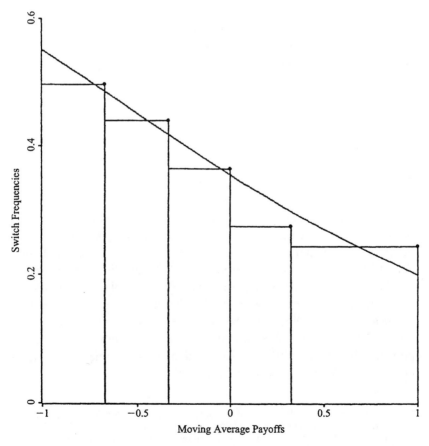

Figure 1.7
Switching frequency versus payoff for row players in game 5

their average payoffs were within the indicated interval. The data are pooled over all the plays of game 5 by the 78 subjects who were row players in that game.

It is clear from the figure that subjects tended to switch strategies more frequently when their average payoffs were low. Although the relationships are not always as smooth as that displayed in figure 1.7, similar negative relationships between the frequency of switching and the subjects' own average payoffs can be observed in the histogram for the column players in game 5 and the histograms for the row and column players in each of the other games. Table 1A.6 provides further evidence on this point.

The curve superimposed on the histogram of figure 1.7 represents the predicted probability of switching obtained from a logit model. For the row and column players in each real game, table 1A.6 reports the estimated coefficients of logit models that relate the probability of switching strategies to the two statistics contained in the subjects' graphical display. In every case there is a highly significant negative relationship between the probability of switching and the moving average of the subjects' own payoffs. The relation between the probability of switching and the median moving average of the other players' payoffs is less clear. In some cases, this relation was negative, in others positive, and in still other cases, no significant relationship existed.[12]

1.5 Conclusion

Two-person, zero-sum games are the heartland of game theory. It is therefore frustrating that the empirical evidence should have carried so little weight in determining the prevailing orthodoxy, which treats Von Neumann's minimax theory as sacred. However, the hypothesis that real people are better natural gamesmen than Emile Borel is not well supported by this or any other experiment. But the question that matters is whether real people are willing and able to *learn* to play like gamesmen using trial-and-error methods. This and other experiments on simple noncooperative games whose equilibria are easily accessible using simple adjustment processes would seem to establish that the answer is a firm *yes*, provided that the incentives are adequate and ample time and information is available to allow learning to take place.

---

12. In considering the results presented in figure 1.7 and table 1A.6, one should keep in mind that subjects had other sources of information about their own payoffs in addition to the graphical display. Subjects received an indication each time they won or lost, and they could also observe changes in their cumulative winnings, which were displayed on a roulette wheel as described in section 1.3.

Appendix Tables

Table 1A.1

Average payoffs obtained by row players for each of the games of our experiments. The first part of the table reports payoffs averaged over all the experiments. For comparison, the second column of the first part reports the minimax payoff for row players in each game. The third and fourth columns report the payoff obtained by the row players averaged over all the plays and the last third of the plays respectively. The columns in the second part of the table report the average payoff obtained in all the plays of each experiment.

Game	Minimax	All	Last 3rd
1	-1.1667	-1.2399	-1.2023
2	-1	-1.1297	-1.0923
3	-0.3333	-0.3870	-0.4013
4	-0.3333	-0.3413	-0.3282
5	-0.2	-0.1976	-0.1882

Average payoff in each experiment

Game	Experiment												
	1	2	3	4	5	6	7	8	9	10	11	12	13
1	-1.2700	-1.2933	-1.1611	-1.1422	-1.2667	-1.1733	-1.3233	-1.2622	-1.2189	-1.2622	-1.2956	-1.1467	-1.3033
2	-1.0733	-1.1222	-1.0711	-1.1622	-1.3000	-1.2511	-1.2422	-0.9044	-0.9733	-1.0756	-1.1400	-1.0933	-1.2778
3	-0.3133	-0.3576	-0.2489	-0.3767	-0.5356	-0.3822	-0.3633	-0.3600	-0.3700	-0.4433	-0.3311	-0.6244	-0.3256
4	-0.3500	-0.4067	-0.3144	-0.3389	-0.3600	-0.3167	-0.3656	-0.3500	-0.3533	-0.2689	-0.3444	-0.3500	-0.3178
5	-0.2267	-0.1889	-0.2067	-0.2222	-0.1978	-0.1867	-0.2289	-0.2311	-0.1689	-0.2044	-0.1933	-0.1689	-0.1444

Table 1A.2
Average frequencies with which row and column players used each strategy in the games of our experiments. The first part of the table involves averages over all the experiments. It reports the theoretical maximin frequency predicted for each strategy by the minimax hypothesis along with the actual frequency that each strategy was played over all the plays of the game and also over only the last third of plays. The second part of the table reports the average frequency with which each strategy was played in all the plays of each separate experiment. Strategies for row players are numbered from top to bottom of the payoff matrices shown in figure 1.3. Column strategies are numbered from left to right. Strategies marked with an asterisk are those whose frequencies are plotted in figures 1.5 and 1.6 and reported in tables 1A.3, 1A.4, and 1A.5.

	Row frequencies			Column frequencies		
Strategy	Maximin	All	Last 3rd	Maximin	All	Last 3rd
Game 1						
1*	0.1667	0.3143	0.2508	0.8333	0.9256	0.9146
2	0.8333	0.6857	0.7492	0.1667	0.0744	0.0854
Game 2						
1	0	0.0562	0.0441	0	0.0171	0.0113
2*	1	0.8386	0.8877	1	0.8622	0.9179
3	0	0.1051	0.0682	0	0.1207	0.0708
Game 3						
1*	0.1667	0.2222	0.2051	0.6667	0.6201	0.6469
2	0	0.0679	0.0562	0.3333	0.2876	0.2785
3	0.8333	0.7098	0.7387	0	0.0923	0.0746
Game 4						
1	0.1667	0.2132	0.2072	0.1667	0.0608	0.0813
2	0.1667	0.1717	0.1328	0.1667	0.1691	0.1705
3*	0.6667	0.6150	0.6600	0.6667	0.7702	0.7482
Game 5						
1*	0.4	0.4295	0.4392	0.4	0.4885	0.4479
2	0.2	0.1762	0.1874	0.2	0.2579	0.2664
3	0.2	0.2281	0.2236	0.2	0.1093	0.1118
4	0.2	0.1662	0.1497	0.2	0.1443	0.1738

Average frequencies in each experiment

	Experiment												
Strategy	1	2	3	4	5	6	7	8	9	10	11	12	13
Game 1—Row frequencies													
1*	0.3367	0.4333	0.2678	0.1822	0.3078	0.2233	0.4611	0.3189	0.3022	0.2878	0.3644	0.2322	0.3678
2	0.6633	0.5667	0.7322	0.8178	0.6922	0.7767	0.5389	0.6811	0.6978	0.7122	0.6356	0.7678	0.6322
Game 1—Column frequencies													
1*	0.9467	0.9000	0.8933	0.9400	0.9611	0.9500	0.9311	0.9167	0.8567	0.9722	0.9222	0.9322	0.9111
2	0.0533	0.1000	0.1067	0.0600	0.0389	0.0500	0.0689	0.0833	0.1433	0.0278	0.0778	0.0678	0.0889
Game 2—Row frequencies													
1	0.0378	0.0711	0.0467	0.0822	0.0733	0.1133	0.0711	0.0044	0.0200	0.0244	0.0244	0.0489	0.1133
2*	0.8400	0.7867	0.9000	0.8111	0.7289	0.7556	0.8022	0.9000	0.9533	0.9333	0.8311	0.9089	0.7511
3	0.1222	0.1422	0.0533	0.1067	0.1978	0.1311	0.1267	0.0956	0.0267	0.0422	0.1444	0.0422	0.1356
Game 2—Column frequencies													
1	0.0200	0.0556	0.0067	0.0067	0.0333	0.0133	0.0133	0.0244	0.0156	0.0044	0.0133	0.0044	0.0111
2*	0.7378	0.8000	0.9267	0.8089	0.8911	0.8956	0.9156	0.7378	0.8956	0.9644	0.8111	0.9644	0.8600
3	0.2422	0.1444	0.0667	0.1844	0.0756	0.0911	0.0711	0.2378	0.0889	0.0311	0.1756	0.0311	0.1289
Game 3—Row frequencies													
1*	0.2178	0.1911	0.2500	0.2167	0.2178	0.2333	0.2433	0.2100	0.1933	0.2522	0.2400	0.2411	0.1822
2	0.0611	0.0511	0.0489	0.0389	0.1222	0.0444	0.0322	0.0644	0.0400	0.0822	0.0300	0.2244	0.0433
3	0.7211	0.7578	0.7011	0.7444	0.6600	0.7222	0.7244	0.7256	0.7667	0.6656	0.7300	0.5344	0.7744
Game 3—Column frequencies													
1*	0.6367	0.5556	0.5667	0.6767	0.7156	0.6500	0.5944	0.6789	0.5944	0.4756	0.6100	0.6489	0.6578
2	0.2722	0.3089	0.3222	0.2478	0.2033	0.2567	0.3111	0.2456	0.3444	0.3600	0.2733	0.3200	0.2733
3	0.0911	0.1356	0.1111	0.0756	0.0811	0.0933	0.0944	0.0756	0.0611	0.1644	0.1167	0.0311	0.0689

Table 1A.2
(continued)

Average frequencies in each experiment

Experiment

Strategy	1	2	3	4	5	6	7	8	9	10	11	12	13
Game 4—Row frequencies													
1	0.2144	0.2389	0.1844	0.1600	0.1811	0.1589	0.2667	0.2000	0.2433	0.2256	0.2100	0.2033	0.2856
2	0.1922	0.2844	0.1589	0.1333	0.1778	0.1556	0.2022	0.1822	0.0956	0.1300	0.1678	0.1511	0.2011
3*	0.5933	0.4767	0.6567	0.7067	0.6411	0.6856	0.5311	0.6178	0.6611	0.6444	0.6222	0.6456	0.5133
Game 4—Column frequencies													
1	0.0344	0.0756	0.0900	0.0900	0.0567	0.0833	0.0378	0.0333	0.0411	0.1056	0.0244	0.0722	0.0456
2	0.1978	0.1567	0.1989	0.1644	0.1244	0.1300	0.1567	0.2144	0.2133	0.1433	0.1511	0.1722	0.1744
3*	0.7678	0.7678	0.7111	0.7456	0.8189	0.7867	0.8056	0.7522	0.7456	0.7511	0.8244	0.7556	0.7800
Game 5—Row frequencies													
1*	0.4322	0.4878	0.3711	0.4400	0.3456	0.3767	0.4433	0.4322	0.4289	0.4156	0.4433	0.4922	0.4744
2	0.1456	0.1222	0.1811	0.1822	0.2544	0.1811	0.1789	0.1600	0.1467	0.2078	0.1889	0.1822	0.1589
3	0.2778	0.2189	0.2989	0.1778	0.2367	0.2367	0.2022	0.1956	0.2867	0.2444	0.2167	0.1800	0.1933
4	0.1444	0.1711	0.1489	0.2000	0.1633	0.2056	0.1756	0.2122	0.1378	0.1322	0.1511	0.1456	0.1733
Game 5—Column frequencies													
1*	0.5144	0.4600	0.5711	0.4600	0.4533	0.4489	0.5100	0.5578	0.4556	0.4456	0.4800	0.4956	0.4978
2	0.3533	0.3333	0.2189	0.2789	0.2289	0.2744	0.2300	0.2256	0.2067	0.2678	0.2522	0.1767	0.3067
3	0.0378	0.1156	0.0700	0.1333	0.1222	0.1456	0.0578	0.1278	0.1833	0.1278	0.1267	0.0911	0.0822
4	0.0944	0.0911	0.1400	0.1278	0.1956	0.1311	0.2022	0.0889	0.1544	0.1589	0.1411	0.2367	0.1133

Table 1A.3
Summary information about the frequencies with which populations of subjects used their designated strategies in individual plays of the games. The row and column strategies considered for each game are those marked with an asterisk in figure 1.3 and table 1A.2. See the text for a definition and discussion of the summary statistics reported in this table. An entry of 0.0000 indicates a value less than 0.00005.

	Game 1	Game 2	Game 3	Game 4	Game 5
Frequencies of net changes	0.7274	0.6778	0.8436	0.8363	0.8947
Maximin point predictor					
Coordinates of point	(1/6, 5/6)	(1, 1)	(1/6, 4/6)	(4/6, 4/6)	(2/6, 2/6)[a]
Fraction of total plays at designated point	0.0959	0.2082	0.1272	0.1067	0.0744
	(0.0088, 0.1615)	(0.0000, 1.0)	(0.0217, 0.1323)	(0.0068, 0.1084)	(0.0880, 0.0967)
Best point predictor					
Coordinates of point	(1/6, 1)	(1, 1)	(1/6, 4/6)	(4/6, 5/6)	(2/6, 3/6)
Fraction of total plays at designated point	0.1995	0.2082	0.1272	0.1097	0.0964
	(0.0015, 0.1346)	(0.0000, 1.0)	(0.0217, 0.1323)	(0.0014, 0.0867)	(0.0391, 0.0860)
Unit-box predictors					
Maximin unit-box predictor					
Coordinates of center	(1/6, 5/6)	(5/6, 5/6)[b]	(1/6, 4/6)	(4/6, 4/6)	(2/6, 2/6)[c]
Fraction of total plays within designated box	0.7041	0.88	0.7174	0.6108	0.4995
	(0.1182, 0.8793)	(0.0100, 1.0)	(0.2165, 0.7615)	(0.1013, 0.6595)	(0.6153, 0.5993)
Best unit-box predictor					
Coordinates of center	(2/6, 5/6)	(5/6, 5/6)	(1/6, 4/6)	(4/6, 5/6)	(3/6, 3/6)
Fraction of total plays within designated box	0.7544	0.88	0.7174	0.6867	0.6123
	(0.2202, 0.6155)	(0.0100, 1.0)	(0.2165, 0.7615)	(0.0319, 0.5525)	(0.2129, 0.5267)
Unit-box predictors for alternate theories					
Minimax regret					
Theoretical prediction	(5/6, 5/6)	(3/5, 3/6)	(3/6, 6/7)	(0, 4/6)	(2/5, 2/5)[d]
Coordinates of center	(5/6, 5/6)	(4/6, 3/6)[e]	(3/6, 5/6)[e]	(1/6, 4/6)[f]	(2/6, 2/6)[e]
Fraction of total plays within designated box	0.1133	0.1538	0.2369	0.1215	0.4995

Table 1A.3
(continued)

Random strategy choice					
Theoretical prediction	(3/6, 3/6)	(2/6, 2/6)	(2/6, 2/6)	(2/6, 2/6)	(1/4, 1/4)
Coordinates of center	(3/6, 3/6)	(2/6, 2/6)	(2/6, 2/6)	(2/6, 2/6)	(1/6, 1/6)[e]
Fraction of total plays within designated box	0.0374	0.0133	0.3200	0.0441	0.1723
Best reply to random strategy choice					
Theoretical prediction	(1, 1)	(1, 1)[g]	(0, 1)	(0, 1)	(0, 1)
Coordinates of center	(5/6, 5/6)[f]	(5/6, 5/6)[f]	(1/6, 5/6)[f]	(1/6, 5/6)[f]	(1/6, 5/6)[f]
Fraction of total plays within designated box	0.1133	0.8800	0.5256	0.1446	0.1569
Probability matching					
Theoretical prediction	(3/6, 3/6)	(1, 1)[d]	(3/6, 0)	(3/6, 3/6)	(2/5, 2/5)[g]
Coordinates of center	(3/6, 3/6)	(5/6, 5/6)[f]	(3/6, 1/6)[f]	(3/6, 3/6)	(2/6, 2/6)[e]
Fraction of total plays within designated box	0.0374	0.8800	0.0615	0.2985	0.4995

a. As recorded in table 1A.2, the exact maximin prediction for game 5 is (2/5, 2/5), which is not a frequency that can be observed in a single play by a single population of players. The indicated point predictor is the frequency combination with the highest probability of occurrence in a single play when all subjects randomly and independently choose strategies using the maximin probabilities.

b. The exact maximin prediction for game 2 is (1, 1). A square box centered at this point would contain only four rather than nine frequency combinations that could occur in a single play, since frequencies must lie between 0 and 1. In order to maintain comparability with the unit-box predictors for other games and other theories, the center of the unit box is therefore "offset" to (5/6, 5/6).

c. Since the exact maximin prediction for game 5 is not a frequency combination that can be observed in a single play of the game, a square box which is the same size as a unit box but centered at this prediction would not contain the same number of observable frequency combinations as a unit box, which is centered at an observable combination. In order to maintain comparability with other unit-box predictors, we choose as the maximin unit-box predictor that box which is (1) centered at an observable frequency combination and (2) has the highest probability of occurrence when all subjects randomly and independently choose strategies using the maximin probabilities.

d. This predicted frequency combination is also the one predicted by the minimax hypothesis.

e. For the reasons discussed in note c, the unit box is not centered at the exact prediction for this game and theory. Rather it is the unit box which is (1) centered at an observable frequency combination and (2) has the highest probability of occurrence when all subjects randomly and independently choose whether or not to play their designated strategy using the probabilities predicted by the relevant theory.

f. For the same reasons as were discussed in note b, the center of the unit box in this case is "offset" from the "boundary" value predicted by the theory.

g. The theory in this case predicts a range of possible frequency combinations including the frequencies predicted by the minimax hypothesis, as shown in the table.

Table 1A.4

For selected row and column strategies from each game, showing frequencies with which individual groups of subjects used these strategies in individual plays of the game. The strategies considered are those marked with an asterisk in figure 1.3 and table 1A.2. Since there were six row and six column players in each group, only frequencies which are a multiple of one sixth can be observed in a single play. The possible frequencies for row players are indicated at the top of the table for each game and the frequencies for column players are shown in the first column of the table. For each combination of row and column frequencies, the entries in the table indicate the fraction of the total number of plays in all the experiments where that particular combination was observed. For each game, the numbers in parentheses indicate the probabilities that each combination of row and column frequencies will occur when all players choose strategies randomly with an equal probability of choice assigned to each strategy. For games 1 through 4, the maximin row and column frequencies are indicated with an asterisk. The boxes in the table surround the nine entries in the table that correspond to the frequency combinations contained in the best unit box for each game. See the text for a further discussion of unit-box predictors. An entry of 0.0000 indicates a value less than 0.00005.

Game 1—Fraction of total plays at each combination of frequencies

	0	1/6*	2/6	3/6	4/6	5/6	1
1	0.0846 (0.0002)	0.1995 (0.0015)	0.1590 (0.0037)	0.1077 (0.0049)	0.0533 (0.0037)	0.0144 (0.0015)	0.0036 (0.0002)
5/6*	0.0364 (0.0015)	0.0959 (0.0088)	0.0959 (0.0220)	0.0554 (0.0293)	0.0251 (0.0220)	0.0062 (0.0088)	0.0015 (0.0015)
4/6	0.0051 (0.0037)	0.0123 (0.0220)	0.0154 (0.0549)	0.0133 (0.0732)	0.0056 (0.0549)	0.0031 (0.0220)	0.0005 (0.0037)
3/6	0.0005 (0.0049)	0.0005 (0.0293)	0.0015 (0.0732)	0.0005 (0.0977)	0.0005 (0.0732)	0.0010 (0.0293)	0.0010 (0.0049)
2/6	0.0000 (0.0037)	0.0000 (0.0220)	0.0000 (0.0549)	0.0005 (0.0732)	0.0000 (0.0549)	0.0000 (0.0220)	0.0000 (0.0037)
1/6	0.0000 (0.0015)	0.0000 (0.0088)	0.0000 (0.0220)	0.0000 (0.0293)	0.0000 (0.0220)	0.0000 (0.0088)	0.0000 (0.0015)
0	0.0000 (0.0002)	0.0000 (0.0015)	0.0000 (0.0037)	0.0000 (0.0049)	0.0000 (0.0037)	0.0000 (0.0015)	0.0000 (0.0002)

Game 2—Fraction of total plays at each combination of frequencies

	0	1/6	2/6	3/6	4/6	5/6	1*
1*	0.0000 (0.0001)	0.0000 (0.0004)	0.0021 (0.0005)	0.0174 (0.0003)	0.0544 (0.0001)	0.1723 (0.0000)	0.2082 (0.0000)
5/6	0.0000 (0.0014)	0.0010 (0.0043)	0.0051 (0.0054)	0.0236 (0.0036)	0.0646 (0.0014)	0.1251 (0.0003)	0.1128 (0.0000)
4/6	0.0000 (0.0072)	0.0000 (0.0217)	0.0031 (0.0271)	0.0113 (0.0181)	0.0359 (0.0068)	0.0626 (0.0014)	0.0441 (0.0001)
3/6	0.0000 (0.0193)	0.0000 (0.0578)	0.0031 (0.0723)	0.0082 (0.0482)	0.0123 (0.0181)	0.0174 (0.0036)	0.0062 (0.0003)
2/6	0.0000 (0.0289)	0.0000 (0.0867)	0.0000 (0.1084)	0.0010 (0.0723)	0.0031 (0.0271)	0.0021 (0.0054)	0.0010 (0.0005)
1/6	0.0000 (0.0231)	0.0000 (0.0694)	0.0000 (0.0867)	0.0010 (0.0578)	0.0010 (0.0217)	0.0000 (0.0043)	0.0000 (0.0004)
0	0.0000 (0.0077)	0.0000 (0.0231)	0.0000 (0.0289)	0.0000 (0.0193)	0.0000 (0.0072)	0.0000 (0.0014)	0.0000 (0.0001)

Game 3—Fraction of total plays at each combination of frequencies

	0	1/6*	2/6	3/6	4/6	5/6	1
1	0.0169	0.0164	0.0154	0.0026	0.0015	0.0000	0.0000
	(0.0001)	(0.0004)	(0.0005)	(0.0003)	(0.0001)	(0.0000)	(0.0000)
5/6	0.0421	0.0769	0.0636	0.0190	0.0041	0.0000	0.0000
	(0.0014)	(0.0043)	(0.0054)	(0.0036)	(0.0014)	(0.0003)	(0.0000)
4/6*	0.0713	0.1272	0.0959	0.0292	0.0056	0.0005	0.0000
	(0.0072)	(0.0217)	(0.0271)	(0.0181)	(0.0068)	(0.0014)	(0.0001)
3/6	0.0513	0.1118	0.0774	0.0256	0.0056	0.0000	0.0000
	(0.0193)	(0.0578)	(0.0723)	(0.0482)	(0.0181)	(0.0036)	(0.0003)
2/6	0.0215	0.0390	0.0318	0.0123	0.0021	0.0000	0.0000
	(0.0289)	(0.0867)	(0.1084)	(0.0723)	(0.0271)	(0.0054)	(0.0005)
1/6	0.0046	0.0092	0.0087	0.0041	0.0010	0.0000	0.0000
	(0.0231)	(0.0694)	(0.0867)	(0.0578)	(0.0217)	(0.0043)	(0.0004)
0	0.0015	0.0026	0.0010	0.0005	0.0000	0.0000	0.0000
	(0.0077)	(0.0231)	(0.0289)	(0.0193)	(0.0072)	(0.0014)	(0.0001)

Game 4—Fraction of total plays at each combination of frequencies

	0	1/6	2/6	3/6	4/6*	5/6	1
1	0.0046	0.0103	0.0231	0.0503	0.0600	0.0410	0.0149
	(0.0001)	(0.0004)	(0.0005)	(0.0003)	(0.0001)	(0.0000)	(0.0000)
5/6	0.0026	0.0154	0.0472	0.0913	0.1097	0.0718	0.0164
	(0.0014)	(0.0043)	(0.0054)	(0.0036)	(0.0014)	(0.0003)	(0.0000)
4/6*	0.0036	0.0056	0.0323	0.0831	0.1067	0.0728	0.0185
	(0.0072)	(0.0217)	(0.0271)	(0.0181)	(0.0068)	(0.0014)	(0.0001)
3/6	0.0010	0.0031	0.0108	0.0236	0.0292	0.0226	0.0082
	(0.0193)	(0.0578)	(0.0723)	(0.0482)	(0.0181)	(0.0036)	(0.0003)
2/6	0.0005	0.0005	0.0000	0.0056	0.0072	0.0046	0.0005
	(0.0289)	(0.0867)	(0.1084)	(0.0723)	(0.0271)	(0.0054)	(0.0005)
1/6	0.0005	0.0000	0.0005	0.0000	0.0000	0.0000	0.0000
	(0.0231)	(0.0694)	(0.0867)	(0.0578)	(0.0217)	(0.0043)	(0.0004)
0	0.0005	0.0000	0.0000	0.0000	0.0000	0.0000	0.0000
	(0.0077)	(0.0231)	(0.0289)	(0.0193)	(0.0072)	(0.0014)	(0.0001)

Game 5—Fraction of total plays at each combination of frequencies

	0	1/6	2/6	3/6	4/6	5/6	1
1	0.0015	0.0031	0.0046	0.0056	0.0015	0.0015	0.0000
	(0.0000)	(0.0001)	(0.0001)	(0.0000)	(0.0000)	(0.0000)	(0.0000)
5/6	0.0062	0.0159	0.0221	0.0251	0.0092	0.0026	0.0005
	(0.0008)	(0.0016)	(0.0013)	(0.0006)	(0.0001)	(0.0000)	(0.0000)
4/6	0.0072	0.0262	0.0703	0.0621	0.0379	0.0072	0.0000
	(0.0059)	(0.0117)	(0.0098)	(0.0043)	(0.0011)	(0.0001)	(0.0000)
3/6	0.0128	0.0421	0.0964	0.0949	0.0508	0.0215	0.0026
	(0.0235)	(0.0469)	(0.0391)	(0.0174)	(0.0043)	(0.0006)	(0.0000)
2/6	0.0067	0.0359	0.0744	0.0821	0.0436	0.0123	0.0005
	(0.0528)	(0.1056)	(0.0880)	(0.0391)	(0.0098)	(0.0013)	(0.0001)
1/6	0.0036	0.0128	0.0308	0.0303	0.0149	0.0062	0.0000
	(0.0634)	(0.1267)	(0.1056)	(0.0469)	(0.0117)	(0.0016)	(0.0001)
0	0.0005	0.0021	0.0056	0.0056	0.0010	0.0000	0.0000
	(0.0317)	(0.0634)	(0.0528)	(0.0235)	(0.0059)	(0.0008)	(0.0000)

Table 1A.5
Plays of the games where there were net changes in the frequencies with which selected row or column strategies were used from that play to the next. The strategies considered are those marked with an asterisk in figure 1.3 and table 1A.2. For these plays, the table describes how the fraction of changes that were positive depends on the opponents' play. The heading "lt. mm." indicates a frequency "less than the maximin frequency" and similarly for the other headings. See the text for further discussion. The first part of the table reports data pooled over all the experiments. The first number in each entry is the number of plays in that category with a nonzero net change. The second number is the fraction of those net changes that were positive. The numbers in parentheses are the 95 percent confidence interval for the probability that a net change is positive under the assumption that this probability is constant across plays in a given category. The second part of the table reports the data separately for each experiment. The number in parentheses in each entry is the total number of plays in the indicated category and experiment where there was a nonzero net change from that play to the next. The other number is the fraction of these net changes that were positive. As discussed further in the text, the categories of plays where the designated strategies are strict best replies are marked with a † in the second part of the table. The corresponding fractions of positive net changes are marked with a † in the first part of the table.

Fractions of nonzero net changes that were positive, pooled over all the experiments

	Row players: Frequency of opponents' play			Column players: Frequency of opponents' play		
	lt. mm.	eq. mm.	gt. mm.	lt. mm.	eq. mm.	gt. mm.
Game 1	76, 0.6316 (0.5193, 0.7312)	381, 0.5774 (0.5273, 0.6260)	673, 0.4309 (0.3940, 0.4686)	96, 0.4583 (0.3622, 0.5577)	206, 0.4757 (0.4086, 0.5437)	401, 0.5511 (0.5022, 0.5991)
Game 3	486, 0.5391 (0.4946, 0.5829)	390, 0.5205 (0.4710, 0.5697)	298, 0.3993 (0.3453, 0.4559)	268, 0.4291 (0.3713, 0.4890)	467, 0.4882 (0.4432, 0.5335)	477, 0.5577 (0.5128, 0.6016)
Game 4	166, 0.2831 (0.2201, 0.3560)	396, 0.4116 (0.3642, 0.4607)	646, 0.6130 (0.5749, 0.6498)	456, 0.6162 (0.5708, 0.6597)	363, 0.4408 (0.3906, 0.4922)	297, 0.4242 (0.3694, 0.4811)
Game 5[a]	150, 0.3733 (0.3000, 0.4530)	772, 0.4650 (0.4301, 0.5003)	380, 0.6421 (0.5927, 0.6887)	216, 0.6481 (0.5824, 0.7087)	793, 0.5132 (0.4785, 0.5479)	272, 0.3125 (0.2604, 0.3699)

Table 1A.5
(continued)

Fractions of nonzero net changes that were positive—Each experiment

Frequency of opponents' play	Experiment												
	1	2	3	4	5	6	7	8	9	10	11	12	13
Game 1—Row players													
lt. mm.:	0.5 (2)	0.5 (4)	0.5455 (11)	0.6 (5)	1.0 (1)	0.0 (1)	0.6667 (3)	0.6364 (11)	0.75 (20)	1.0 (1)	0.7143 (7)	— (0)	0.5 (10)
eq. mm.	0.72 (25)	0.5614 (57)	0.5294 (34)	0.6786 (28)	0.65 (20)	0.5625 (16)	0.5455 (44)	0.6087 (23)	0.5106 (47)	0.7 (10)	0.4516 (31)	0.6364 (22)	0.5833 (24)
gt. mm.	0.4118 (68)	0.4043 (47)	0.3714 (35)	0.4063 (64)	0.4068 (59)	0.45 (60)	0.4844 (64)	0.4364 (55)	0.3243 (37)	0.4524 (42)	0.5098 (51)	0.4 (30)	0.4754 (61)
Game 1—Column players													
lt. mm.:	0.4 (5)	— (0)	0.375 (8)	0.45 (20)	0.5 (10)	0.5 (22)	0.0 (1)	0.5 (10)	0.5455 (11)	0.3333 (3)	0.5 (2)	0.0 (1)	0.3333 (3)
eq. mm.	0.4737 (19)	0.4286 (7)	0.5 (34)	0.5833 (12)	0.4545 (11)	0.5263 (19)	0.5 (6)	0.4 (10)	0.3478 (23)	0.5 (14)	0.4118 (17)	0.5 (20)	0.5714 (14)
gt. mm.	0.5476 (42)	0.5278 (36)	0.5714 (35)	0.6 (10)	0.5294 (34)	0.5 (20)	0.5313 (64)	0.5652 (23)	0.6111 (36)	0.6 (15)	0.5682 (44)	0.625 (8)	0.5 (34)
Game 3—Row players													
lt. mm.:	0.6129 (31)	0.475 (40)	0.4915 (59)	0.6957 (23)	0.6667 (21)	0.4516 (31)	0.5417 (48)	0.5417 (24)	0.5435 (46)	0.5625 (64)	0.5111 (45)	0.5 (28)	0.5385 (26)
eq. mm.	0.4667 (30)	0.6071 (28)	0.6071 (28)	0.5143 (35)	0.5429 (35)	0.5 (42)	0.4091 (22)	0.5294 (17)	0.3889 (18)	0.45 (20)	0.5429 (35)	0.5455 (44)	0.5556 (36)
gt. mm.	0.3333 (27)	0.4167 (12)	0.4167 (12)	0.375 (24)	0.3846 (52)	0.4483 (29)	0.3333 (18)	0.5152 (33)	0.4286 (14)	0.0 (6)	0.3636 (22)	0.3704 (27)	0.5 (22)

Game 3—Column players

lt. mm.	0.5652 (23)	0.4643 (28)	0.3529 (17)	0.4516 (31)	0.4828 (29)	0.2941 (17)	0.5 (20)	0.375 (16)	0.45 (20)	0.3529 (17)	0.5455 (11)	0.3333 (18)	0.3333 (21)
eq. mm.	0.4483 (29)	0.3953 (43)	0.5455 (22)	0.5349 (43)	0.4872 (39)	0.4688 (32)	0.4878 (41)	0.5588 (34)	0.4571 (35)	0.5789 (38)	0.4242 (33)	0.4545 (33)	0.5111 (45)
gt. mm.	0.5641 (39)	0.5946 (37)	0.6190 (42)	0.4848 (33)	0.4359 (39)	0.6364 (33)	0.5217 (46)	0.5357 (28)	0.6522 (23)	0.5 (48)	0.5333 (45)	0.6667 (42)	0.5455 (22)

Game 4—Row players

lt. mm.	0.1818 (11)	0.5 (10)	0.2609 (23)	0.4444 (9)	0.5 (6)	0.4 (10)	0.0 (5)	0.35 (20)	0.2 (15)	0.1875 (16)	0.2857 (7)	0.2353 (17)	0.2353 (17)
eq. mm.	0.3333 (24)	0.3721 (43)	0.4194 (31)	0.4222 (45)	0.3913 (23)	0.4828 (29)	0.3103 (29)	0.5161 (31)	0.4054 (37)	0.4615 (26)	0.3333 (24)	0.4688 (32)	0.4091 (22)
gt. mm.	0.6889 (45)	0.5833 (48)	0.8 (30)	0.6923 (26)	0.5152 (66)	0.5246 (61)	0.6316 (57)	0.6 (50)	0.7045 (44)	0.5636 (55)	0.5806 (62)	0.6818 (44)	0.6034 (58)

Game 4—Column players

lt. mm.	0.5926 (27)	0.5362 (69)	0.5455 (33)	0.8125 (16)	0.6 (30)	0.9167 (12)	0.5345 (58)	0.6970 (33)	0.6538 (26)	0.6667 (36)	0.7083 (24)	0.6563 (32)	0.5833 (60)
eq. mm.	0.3469 (49)	0.2 (10)	0.5667 (30)	0.28 (25)	0.4706 (34)	0.45 (20)	0.56 (25)	0.3913 (23)	0.5517 (29)	0.4667 (30)	0.6296 (27)	0.4194 (31)	0.3 (30)
gt. mm.	0.75 (12)	0.5714 (7)	0.3889 (36)	0.5556 (36)	0.4074 (27)	0.375 (16)	0.3333 (9)	0.36 (25)	0.3889 (36)	0.3704 (27)	0.3333 (24)	0.4516 (31)	0.3636 (11)

Table 1A.5
(continued)

Frequency of opponents' play	Experiment												
	1	2	3	4	5	6	7	8	9	10	11	12	13
Game 5—Row players[a]													
lt. mm.	0.4444	0.3636	0.5	0.1667	0.4211	0.4375	0.3333	0.3333	0.25	0.3889	0.4444	0.4444	0.375
	(9)	(11)	(6)	(12)	(19)	(16)	(15)	(6)	(12)	(18)	(9)	(9)	(8)
eq. mm.	0.3770	0.4655	0.4	0.4894	0.5	0.4559	0.5526	0.5263	0.4237	0.5	0.3651	0.5	0.5
	(61)	(58)	(45)	(47)	(64)	(68)	(38)	(57)	(59)	(70)	(63)	(62)	(80)
gt. mm.	0.6923	0.6875	0.5556	0.7222	0.52	0.6552	0.5938	0.5435	0.7667	0.8571	0.8077	0.6061	0.5758
	(26)	(16)	(45)	(18)	(25)	(29)	(32)	(46)	(30)	(21)	(26)	(33)	(33)
Game 5—Column players[a]													
lt. mm.	0.7143	0.5455	0.7083	0.9091	0.5625	0.5	0.5	0.6923	0.6	0.8095	0.7857	0.5	0.6
	(21)	(11)	(24)	(11)	(32)	(24)	(14)	(13)	(10)	(21)	(14)	(6)	(15)
eq. mm.	0.4603	0.5373	0.4444	0.5455	0.5079	0.5143	0.4607	0.4902	0.54	0.5294	0.5	0.5806	0.6122
	(63)	(67)	(63)	(55)	(63)	(70)	(89)	(51)	(50)	(51)	(60)	(62)	(49)
gt. mm.	0.3529	0.3333	0.2727	0.15	0.5	0.2667	0.4091	0.25	0.3529	0.1923	0.36	0.3214	0.3103
	(17)	(36)	(11)	(20)	(14)	(15)	(22)	(12)	(17)	(26)	(25)	(28)	(29)

a. The exact maximin frequencies for game 5 are not a multiple of 1/6 and so would never be observed in a single play of the game. For game 5, the observed frequency with which opponents used their designated strategy was classified as "equal to the maximin frequency" if that frequency was either 2/6 or 3/6. The exact maximin frequency for both row and column players is 0.4.

Table 1A.6
For the row and column players of each real game, the estimated coefficients of logit models on the probability that an individual subject switches from the strategy he or she used in the previous play of the game to the two variables whose moving averages were displayed graphically for each subject during the game. The variable own-plot refers to the moving average of the subject's own payoffs in the preceding six plays. The variable other-plot refers to the median of the average payoffs of the other players of the same type in the previous six plays. The models were estimated via maximum likelihood, and the asymptotic standard errors of the coefficients are reported in parentheses. To estimate each model, the data were pooled over all the plays of the indicated game by the 78 subjects who were the indicated type of player in that game. See the text for further discussion.

	Row players		Column players	
Game	Own-plot	Other-plot	Own-plot	Other-plot
1	−0.7458	−0.4529	−1.2003	−0.1261
	(0.0592)	(0.0911)	(0.0662)	(0.1557)
2	−2.0522	−0.6299	−1.5492	1.0573
	(0.0729)	(0.1400)	(0.0960)	(0.1703)
3	−0.6433	−0.1825	−0.5001	0.1061
	(0.0362)	(0.0699)	(0.0369)	(0.0683)
4	−1.3190	−0.0798	−1.3172	−0.2924
	(0.0658)	(0.1067)	(0.0700)	(0.1271)
5	−0.7894	0.1278	−0.7878	−0.0272
	(0.0456)	(0.0737)	(0.0479)	(0.0772)

References

Binmore, K. 1987. Modeling rational players II. *Economics and Philosophy* 4: 179–214.

Binmore, K. 1991. *Fun and Games*. Lexington, MA: D.C. Heath.

Binmore, K., J. Gale, and L. Samuelson. 1995. Learning to be imperfect: The ultimatum game. *Games and Economic Behavior* 8: 56–90.

Binmore, K., and L. Samuelson. 1997. Muddling through: Noisy equilibrium selection. *Journal of Economic Theory* 74: 235–65.

Brown, G. 1951. Iterative solution of games by fictitious play. In T. Koopmans, ed., *Activity Analysis of Production and Allocation*. New York: Wiley.

Brown, J., and R. Rosenthal. 1990. Testing the minimax hypothesis: A re-examination of O'Neill's game experiment. *Econometrica* 58: 1065–81.

Crawford, V. 1989. Learning and mixed strategy equilibria in evolutionary games. *Journal of Theoretical Biology* 140: 537–50.

Estes, W. 1957. Of models and men. *American Psychologist* 12: 609–17.

Frenkel, O. 1973. A study of 78 non-iterated 2 × 2 games. University of Toronto, unpublished draft.

Hopkins, E. 1996. Learning, evolution and price dispersion. PhD thesis. European University Institute.

Kadane, J., and P. Larkey. 1982. Subjective probability and the theory of games. *Management Science* 28: 113–20.

Malcolm, D., and B. Lieberman. 1965. The behavior of responsive individuals playing a two-person zero-sum game requiring the use of mixed strategies. *Psychonomic Science* 2: 373–74.

McCabe, K., A. Mukherji, and D. Runkle. 1994. An experimental study of learning and limited information in games. University of Minnesota discussion paper.

Mookherjee, D., and B. Sopher. 1994. Learning behavior in an experimental matching pennies game. *Games and Economic Behavior* 8: 62–91.

Mookherjee, D., and B. Sopher. 1997. Learning and decision costs in experimental constant sum games. *Games and Economic Behavior* 19: 97–132.

O'Neill, B. 1987. Nonmetric test of the minimax theory of two-person zero-sum games. *Proceedings of the National Academy of Sciences* 84: 2106–2109.

Rapaport, A., and D. Bludescu. 1992. Generation of random series in two-person strictly competitive games. *Journal of Experimental Psychology* 121: 352–63.

Rapaport, A., and R. Boebel. 1992. Mixed strategies in strictly competitive games: A further test of the minimax hypothesis. *Games and Economic Behavior* 4: 261–83.

Robinson, J. 1951. An iterative method of solving a game. *Annals of Mathematics* 54: 296–301.

Roth, A., and I. Erev. 1995. Learning in extensive-form games: Experimental data and simple dynamic models in the medium term. *Games and Economic Behavior* 8: 164–212.

Savage, L. 1951. *The Foundations of Statistics*. New York: Wiley.

Suppes, P., and R. Atkinson. 1960. *Applications of a Markov Model to Multiperson Interactions*. Stanford: Stanford University Press.

Von Neumann, J. 1928. Zur theorie der gesellschaftsspiele. *Mathematische Annalen* 100: 295–320.

Vulkan, N. 1996. A survey and assessment of the probability matching literature. University College London Discussion Paper.

Walker, M., and J. Wooders. 1998. Minimax play at Wimbledon. Draft. Department of Economics, University of Arizona.

2   Which Equilibrium?

We have just looked at an experiment that shows that subjects can learn to play Nash equilibria in games, even when the equilibria call for the use of mixed strategies. But the games of the previous chapter each have only one Nash equilibrium, and so the equilibrium selection problem doesn't arise.[1]

However, one can't study bargaining games without facing up to the equilibrium selection problem. This is part of the reason that bargaining games present such a challenging case for game theory. How will people behave when there are many Nash equilibria that they might learn to play?

Focal Points

Thomas Schelling (1960) argued that societies develop *focal points* to solve such equilibrium selection problems in the games of everyday life. For example, the Driving Game we play every morning on our way to work has three Nash equilibria: we can all drive on the left, we can all drive on the right, or we can all choose the side of the road on which to drive at random. The first equilibrium is focal in Britain and the second in the United States. When some Turks told me that the third equilibrium was focal in their country, I thought it was a joke, but I take the idea more seriously now that I have visited Turkey myself.

I think the bargaining experiment reported in this chapter is best seen as a representation in miniature of the manner in which different focal points can evolve in different societies to solve the same equilibrium selection problem. We found that all our groups of experimental subjects ended up playing close to one of the game's efficient Nash equilibria but that *different* groups ended up near *different* equilibria. As usual in my later experiments, the feedback the subjects received was much richer than in most comparable experiments.

What led some groups to one equilibrium and others to another? My guess is that the effect is partly random and partly a function of where the group started. But when the subjects were debriefed, they didn't see it like this. They were willing to say that the focal point that had evolved within their group of experimental subjects was close to the "fair" solution to the bargaining problem they were set. It can therefore take only an hour or so for cultural evolution to create a new fairness norm in a small minisociety, even when the amount of interaction within the minisociety is severely restricted.

I should hasten to qualify this last remark by observing that to say that new fairness norms can be created in the laboratory for restricted purposes isn't the same as saying that we can easily persuade people to abandon the fairness criteria that they are accustomed to use in regulating their everyday lives. If our bargaining problem had been framed less sparsely, we would doubtless have triggered whatever focal point was conventional for the social environment with which the trigger is normally associated. One might, for example, adopt a frame in which the first player is said to be an employer and the second a worker in a wage negotiation. Or one could frame the problem as that of sharing a sum of money, so that it is obvious what counts as a fifty:fifty split. I would still expect to see eventual divergence from the conventional focal point if this isn't a Nash equilibrium of the bargaining game being played, but who knows how long that might take?

Conditioning

Although I think the main lesson to be learned from the experiment reported in this chapter is that the Nash equilibrium selected in a game is likely to be partly a function of historical events or accidents that occur while or before or a group of players are finding their way to an equilibrium, this wasn't its initial aim at all. All the efficient outcomes of our bargaining game are *approximate* Nash equilibria; the extra money a player could gain by deviating is so small that it would normally be regarded as negligible. I thought that we should therefore be able to treat *all* the efficient outcomes of the bargaining game as effective Nash equilibria. The idea was then to see how easy it would be to *condition* players on whichever of four focal points that we chose beforehand.

But it turns out not to be so easy to educate subjects as Amos Tversky liked to claim. Even though the gains were negligible and the movements of the cursor necessary to achieve the gains almost imperceptible on their screens, subjects nevertheless moved away from anything that wasn't an *exact* Nash equilibrium. Our attempt to persuade some groups to make the outcome that utilitarians hold to be fair into a focal point cut particularly little ice. Nor was our attempt to focalize Rawls's theory of justice with other groups very much more successful. Only a small number of trials was necessary to see subjects begining to diverge from these widely canvased fairness norms. Although both norms called for the play of strategies that were very nearly an equilibrium, all groups eventually moved away to one or other of the exact equilibria—a result I found so unexpected that Joe Swierzbinski had to spend half an hour repeatedly showing me diagrams of the exact Nash equilibria and the final experimental outcomes before I was able to grasp that they were two different diagrams.

Nash's Demand Game

The bargaining game chosen for the experiment was John Nash's (1950) classic Demand Game. Each player makes a demand. If the two demands are compatible with what is available, both players receive their demands; otherwise, both get nothing. This toy game strips the bargaining process to an irreducible minimum, and so exposes the equilibrium selection problem that lies at its root. All efficient ways of dividing the surplus correspond to Nash equilibria; if each player demands his or her share in any efficient division of the surplus, neither player can gain from unilaterally demanding more, since the new joint demand will be infeasible.

Nash (1950) proposed solving the severe equilibrium selection problem that arises in his Demand Game by inventing what later came to be known as trembles. He introduced some doubt about whether a pair of demands close to the boundary of the feasible set would be counted as feasible. In this *smoothed* Nash Demand Game, all Nash equilibria converge on the Nash bargaining solution as the size of the tremble is allowed to become vanishingly small. We included Nash's trembles in the experiment more to counter possible criticism from theorists than because we thought they would be important behaviorally, but in this we were mistaken.

For those who are interested, here is a simple version of Nash's argument. In the smoothed Nash Demand Game the players' reaction curves

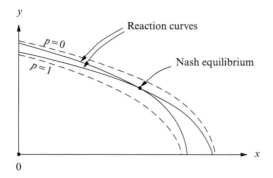

Figure 2.1
Reaction curves in Nash's smoothed Demand Game

look like those of figure 2.1. Under mild conditions, the curves cross only once, which implies that there is only one Nash equilibrium (Binmore 1987).

If $p(x, y)$ is the probability that the pair of demands (x, y) is counted as feasible, then one player wants to maximize $xp(x, y)$ and the other $yp(x, y)$. They will simultaneously achieve their aims—and hence be at the only Nash equilibrium of the game—if they choose x and y so that the product $xyp(x, y)$ is maximized.

As we allow the uncertain world represented by the probability function p to collapse onto certainty, the pair of demands (x, y) that maximizes $xyp(x, y)$ converges on the pair of demands that maximizes xy in the certain world. But one of many defining criteria for the Nash bargaining solution is that it maximizes the Nash product xy. It follows that the unique Nash equilibrium in the smoothed Demand Game approximates the Nash bargaining solution when the level of uncertainty is sufficiently small.

One can't capture the mathematical elegance of this argument in a computerized version of the smoothed Nash Demand Game, since the players don't have a continuous range of demands available. The reaction curves of figure 2.1 then become finite sets of points, which can't easily be made to intersect in a single point as in Nash's model. In our case they overlay each other for some of their length. Each of the many points they have in common is an exact Nash equilibrium that lies close to one of the efficient outcomes of the unsmoothed bargaining game. However, it turned out to be fortunate that most efficient outcomes of the unsmoothed game aren't close to such an exact Nash equilibrium.

Focal Points and Bargaining

Ken Binmore, Joe Swierzbinski, Steven Hsu, and Chris Proulx

Early mankind soon reached the grand generalization that everything has its price, everything can be paid for. Here we have the oldest and most naïve moral canon of justice, of all "fair play," "good will," and "objectivity." Justice at this level is good will operating among men of roughly equal power, their readiness to come to terms with one another, to strike a compromise.... (Friedrich Nietzsche, *The Generalogy of Morals*)

2.1 Introduction

If I wait in the coffee shop for my wife while she searches for me in the car park, we are experiencing a coordination failure. Schelling's (1960) well-known essay on coordination stresses the importance of focal points in such a context. The side of the road on which people drive is the standard example. Before any legislation appeared, it became focal to drive on the left in England, but to drive on the right in France.

Although the idea of a focal point is of great practical importance, the manner in which focal points become established and survive after their establishment remains a mystery. No consensus even exists about how this mystery should be investigated. Some authors emphasize rationality considerations to the exclusion of all else. However, it seems doubtful that the equilibrium selection problem of game theory is likely to be solvable by a technique that ignores what may be common knowledge among the players about the social norms of their culture. At the other extreme are authors who argue that social norms are so important that

We are grateful to the National Science Foundation for funding the experiments reported in this paper under Grant NSF-SES-8821521. We also gratefully acknowledge funding from the University of Michigan to set up the Michigan Economics Laboratory, where the experiments were conducted. We would also like to thank Richard Stallman and the Free Software Foundation for developing EMACS, Luke Tierney for developing LISPSTAT, and Hal Varian for showing us how to use both.

strategic issues can be neglected altogether. This view tends to be expressed most forcefully when the coordination problem is framed in a bargaining context. Fairness norms then enter the picture—and there is much evidence that such norms often do take precedence over strategic considerations in determining the behavior of subjects in certain types of laboratory experiments.

The story is further confused by the fact that those who emphasize rationality do not argue that real people are likely to find their way to what rationality supposedly recommends simply by thinking about the problem. Where pregame, cheap-talk sessions are not possible, the claim is that people will be able to find their way to the rational solution by trial-and-error if given long enough to gain experience of the game's strategic realities and the behavior of other members of the game-playing population. Nor are the views of those who emphasize social norms free from complication. They argue that several distinct social norms may compete for attention in certain contexts. So how do people decide which social norm should be honored?

This paper seeks to investigate such questions experimentally, using an archetypal example of a focal point problem. The example studied is the Nash (1950) bargaining problem in which two players can achieve any point x in a given feasible set X provided that they can reach agreement. If they cannot agree, the result is a fixed disagreement point ξ in the set X. Although the paper can be seen as a contribution to the expanding literature on experimental bargaining games, its potential applications to bargaining theory were a secondary consideration in our choosing the Nash bargaining problem for study. The primary reasons are twofold:

1. The literature contains numerous rival candidates as focal points in the Nash bargaining problem. We consider the Nash (1950) bargaining solution, the Kalai-Smorodinsky (1975) bargaining solution, the utilitarian solution associated with Harsanyi (1977) and the equal increments solution[2] associated with Rawls (1972).

2. Unlike the situations studied in the related work of Cooper et al. (1991) and Van Huyck et al. (1991a, b), the Nash bargaining problem has a *continuous* strategy space. In a discrete problem, it may be hard to destabilize an established focal point. A population, for example, cannot gradually drift from driving on the left to driving on the right.

---

2. The Pareto efficient point $x \in X$ with $x_1 - \xi_1 = x_2 - \xi_2$.

In order to study the Nash bargaining problem, it is necessary to say what the players need to do to reach an agreement. The most primitive mechanism is represented by the Nash (1950) demand game, and so we use this. In our experiment a population of subjects plays the same Nash demand game repeatedly, half the time as player I and half the time as player II, switching partners unpredictably after each play. At each play a subject currently in the role of player I makes a demand x_1 and a subject in the role of player II makes a demand x_2. Each subject makes his demand in ignorance of the current demand of the other subject. (However, in our experiment much information about *past* plays of the population as a whole was made available using a graphic display to be described later.) If the point $x = (x_1, x_2)$ of a partnered pair of subjects proves to be feasible, each receives his or her demand. Otherwise, each receives the disagreement payoff. In our case this was always zero (i.e., $\xi = 0$).

Since conventional wisdom holds that the outcome in such a game depends on the players' attitudes toward risk, it is important to control for risk aversion. The standard technique is to pay subjects off in lottery tickets. In our case the subjects had the opportunity to win $10 with a probability equal to the number of lottery tickets they had accumulated divided by 100. Rational agents would then be induced to behave as though they were risk neutral. To further impress the subjects with the importance of risk, lotteries were also introduced into each play of the game by fuzzing the boundary of the feasible set X. That is to say, the boundary of X was expanded into a narrow strip. The feasibility of pairs of demands falling in this strip was uncertain. If, for example, the pair of demands fell on an 80 percent contour running through the strip, it would be found feasible by the computer with probability 0.8.

We had a secondary motive in fuzzing the boundary, which needs to be mentioned at an early stage because the fuzzing was instrumental in generating results that took us by surprise. This was a desire to be faithful to Nash's (1950) original conception. He transferred his attention from the original Nash Demand Game to a version with a fuzzed or smoothed boundary because, without the smoothing, any individually rational, Pareto efficient x in X is a Nash equilibrium for the Nash demand game. With the smoothing, all Nash equilibria approximate the Nash bargaining solution. (See papers 4 and 8 of Binmore and Dasgupta 1987.)

To see why such smoothing might help in responding to a comment on the possible results of the experiment, consider what conclusions might be drawn if the subjects were to coordinate on the utilitarian solution. Harsanyi (1977) might argue that such subjects were motivated by moral considerations. A welfare economist might argue that the explanation is that the utilitarian solution is Pareto efficient for the population as a whole over the course of the experiment. However, a game theorist of the variety that believes that thinking alone is adequate to get subjects immediately to the "right" Nash equilibrium would not be willing to admit that such normative considerations were necessarily relevant if the boundary of X were not fuzzed. He could simply point to the fact that the utilitarian solution is a Nash equilibrium like every other individually rational, Pareto efficient outcome of X.

Although we prepared defenses in advance against certain potential criticisms by paying subjects off in lottery tickets (rather than directly in money) and by fuzzing the boundary of the feasible set, we did not seriously anticipate that these refinements would have any impact on our results. Our guess was that subjects are effectively risk neutral already with respect to the small sums of money we are able to pay. Moreover, after the fuzzing of the boundary of the feasible set, all the focal points we considered were within 0.1 of an ε-equilibrium with $\varepsilon = 0.1$. It did not occur to us at the outset that subjects would be interested in discriminating at the 0.1 level, since 0.1 of a lottery ticket was worth only about a dime. However, our guess about the level at which subjects would choose to discriminate turned out to be badly wrong, and the results are perhaps more interesting than would have been the case if we had guessed right. To see why, it is necessary to continue outlining the design of the experiment.

After a hands-on interactive session at their computer to learn the mechanics of the program, the subjects first played ten "practice" games "against the computer." Both when playing the computer and when playing real opponents, subjects sometimes occupied the role of player I and sometimes the role of player II. Throughout the experiment, the subjects were shown the last demands made by all of their potential partners, both when the potential partner was player I and when he or she was player II. In the "practice games" this information display was used in a (successful) attempt to condition the subjects to begin the games against real opponents at one of the four "focal points" that we chose to study. For example, in the treatment designed to study the equal increments solution as a possible focal point, the simulated potential partners that the subjects faced during the ten "practice games" were designed to converge slowly from a fixed initial configuration toward the equal increments solution.

After being conditioned to begin by making demands at or near the equal increments solution, the question was then whether the subjects would continue to use this focal point once play against real opponents began.

We would not have been surprised to find that all the focal points we studied were stable. We thought the utilitarian solution might be particularly attractive. However, this proved to be the hardest to condition for in our main experiment. But the chief conclusion to which we were led by the data swept aside our initial expectations. We found a very strong tendency of the median subject to *optimize relentlessly*. Indeed, the extent of the optimization is almost absurd, since the subjects seem to have been sensitive to payoff differences right down to 0.01 of a lottery ticket (about a penny). It is important to understand that the subjects were provided with graphic aids that made this possible for them to do reasonably efficiently if they so chose. In particular, they were provided with a display that allowed them to zero-in on the demand that would maximize their expected number of lottery tickets in the current game if their potential partners were to behave as they did the last time that they occupied their current role. Nevertheless, we were taken aback to find it necessary to compute the *exact* Nash equilibria of the *discrete* game that the digital character of computer technology made it necessary to present to the subjects in place of the continuous version that we had in mind as our basic model.

In our experiment this required looking at a 100×50 payoff matrix in which each player's pure strategies consist of all possible locations for the cursor that he or she used in specifying what demand to make. The cursor moved in steps of 0.1 of a lottery ticket. Each lottery ticket increases the probability of winning \$10 by 0.01. Thus 0.1 of a lottery ticket corresponds to about one dime.

Figure 2.2 is intended to illustrate the main conclusions (case 1) reported in this paper. The region shown represents the feasible set X in each repetition of the Nash demand game. (The boundary shown is the 100 percent probability contour.) Coordinates are given as numbers of lottery tickets. The equal increments solution, the Kalai-Smorodinsky solution, the Nash bargaining solution and the utilitarian solution are indicated by the letters E, K, N, and U respectively. The box contains all Nash equilibria of the *discrete* game. (Any Nash equilibrium of the continuous version approximates N.)

The arrows in figure 2.2 do not indicate trajectories. Each of the 16 sets of arrows corresponds to a different group of 12 subjects and

Chapter 2

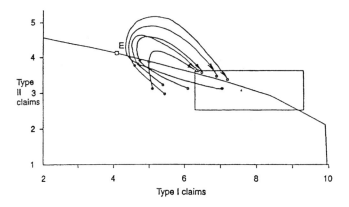

Figure 1(a) : Case 1E

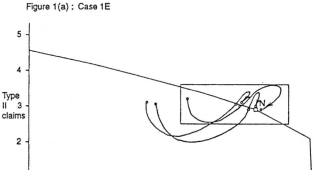

Figure 1(c) : Case 1N

Figure 2.2
Summary of results in case 1

summarizes their experience by linking three points. Each point is a pair of *median*[3] demands. The x-coordinate is the median demand of players I. The y-coordinate is the median demand of players II. The three stages of the experiment at which these numbers are reported in the figure are:

1. At the very beginning—the first and second practice games before any experience had been gained.[4]

3. The median of a set of numbers with an even number of elements is the mean of the two middle numbers.

4. The computer updated its display every *second* play.

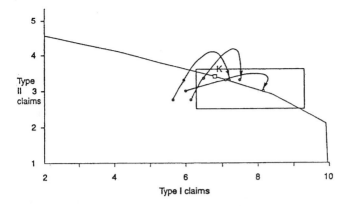

Figure 1(b) : Case 1K

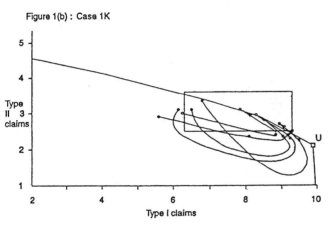

Figure 1(d) : Case 1U

Figure 2.2
(continued)

2. Immediately after the practice games—the 11th and 12th plays that followed the 10 conditioning practice games.

3. At the very end—the 49th and 50th plays, after 10 practice games and 40 real games.

Three preliminary conclusions are listed below:

• Whatever social norms the subjects may bring into the laboratory are easily erasable in the circumstances of the experiment. The subjects can be conditioned to begin playing for real close to any of the four focal points E, K, N, or U.

• The focal points E and U are not stable.

• The explanation that groups of subjects converge on an exact Nash equilibrium of the discrete game that they actually played fits the data very well.

It is natural to ask whether the Kalai-Smorodinsky solution K would have been stable if it had not been included in the Nash equilibrium box. (One cannot, of course, exclude the Nash bargaining solution from the box.) One might also ask how the subjects would perform if not assisted with such a helpful graphic display. It is also interesting to know how the subjects responded to questions about "fairness" after playing the game.

The first question is not easily answered because it is difficult to adapt our experimental design to separate the Kalai-Smorodinsky solution and the Nash bargaining solution adequately. The extent to which our graphic display was essential to the results was explored in case 2. Case 1E was modified so that the subjects were deprived of expected utility information in the graphic display. (Case 2 was otherwise identical to case 1E.) Perhaps surprisingly, the subjects' behavior was not very different from that when the expected utility information was provided. Even the amount of variance in the data was only slightly higher. However, we only gathered data on this issue in the case when subjects were conditioned on the equal increments solution.

Finally, the median of the claims reported as fair by each set of subjects after the experiment turned out to be closely correlated with the median of the claims actually made at the end of the experiment in which the subjects had participated. Very similar results were reported in Binmore et al. (1991). Perhaps we are therefore learning something about the *origin* of "fairness" norms.

2.2   Theory

This section begins by describing the ideas from cooperative bargaining theory used to locate the focal points in the experiment. Roth (1979) discusses the properties and axiomatic characterization of the concepts. The remainder of the section briefly examines the problem of computing Nash equilibria in the smoothed Nash Demand Game.

2.2.1   Cooperative Solution Concepts
The unsmoothed feasible set X shown in figure 2.3 is the convex hull of the points $(0,0)$, $(10,0)$, $(0,5)$, $(4.1, 4.1)$, $(6.8, 3.4)$, $(8.4, 2.9)$, and

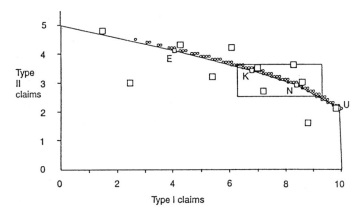

Figure 2.3
Feasible set, focal points, the exact Nash equilibrium box, ε-equilibria of the discrete game with $\varepsilon = 0.1$, and initial robot claims

(9.9, 2.1). (In the smoothed case a belt of fuzz surrounds X as described in section 2.2.2 and section 2.3.) The shape of X was determined by the need to separate the focal points E, K, N, and U from each other. These four focal points are denoted by small boxes and labeled by letter in figures 2.2, 2.3, and 2.5. The disagreement point ξ is always $(0, 0)$.

Equal Increments Solution E This is a special case of a *proportional bargaining solution* as studied by Raiffa (1953), Isbell (1960), Kalai (1977), Myerson (1977), Roth (1979), Peters (1986), and others. Like the utilitarian solution to be considered shortly, the equal increments solution requires that there be some basis for interpersonal comparison of utilities. This was provided in our experiments by the fact that the subjects alternated roles and were paid off in equally valuable lottery tickets both as player I and as player II. This same feature would also seem to justify restricting attention to cooperative bargaining solutions whose characterizations include a symmetry axiom. A proportional bargaining solution places the bargaining outcome at the Pareto efficient point of X that lies on a line of fixed positive slope through the disagreement point ξ. The slope of this line equals the rate at which player I's utils are to be compared with player II's. With a symmetry axiom this rate is 1, and so the relevant line through ξ has slope 1. The equal increments solution therefore awards each player the same increment on his or her disagreement payoff. For the bargaining set described above, the equal increments solution is $E = (4.1, 4.1)$. It is worthwhile noting that E is the point of X that will be selected by Rawls's (1972) maximin criterion.

Kalai-Smorodinsky Solution *K* Kalai and Smorodinsky (1975) offer this solution as an alternative to the Nash bargaining solution. Neither of these solutions depends on interpersonal comparisons of utility. The Kalai-Smorodinsky solution is found in our case by first locating the (infeasible) "utopian point" $(10, 5)$ at which each player gets his or her maximum possible demand. A straight line is then drawn joining the disagreement point ξ and the utopian point. The Kalai-Smorodinsky solution $K = (6.8, 3.4)$ is the Pareto efficient point of X on this line.

Nash Bargaining Solution *N* Nash (1950) characterized $N = (8.4, 2.9)$ as the value of x in X satisfying $x \geq \xi$ at which the Nash product $(x_1 - \xi_1)(x_2 - \xi_2)$ is maximized.

Utilitarian Solution *U* The utilitarian solution $U = (9.9, 2.1)$ is the value of x in X at which $x_1 + x_2$ is maximized. Harsanyi (1977) discusses its merits.

2.2.2 Nash Equilibria in the Smoothed Game
The details of how the Nash demand game was smoothed for the experiment are now described. The continuous case is described first and then the discrete approximation.

The Continuous Version The smoothed version of the Nash Demand Game was obtained by making some of the demand pairs $x = (x_1, x_2)$ outside X available with a specified probability $p(x)$. If the polar coordinates of x are (r, θ), and (R, θ) is on the Pareto boundary of X, then

$$p(x) = 1 - \left\{ \frac{1 - (r/R)}{\gamma} \right\}^2, \qquad R \leq r \leq (1 + \gamma)R.$$

If $r < R$, then $p(x) = 1$. If $r > (1 + \gamma)R$, then $p(x) = 0$. Notice that $\partial p / \partial r = 0$ when $r = R$, so probabilities change smoothly across the outermost 100 percent probability contour. Notice also that the region in which it is uncertain whether a particular demand pair x is available shrinks to nothing as $\gamma \to 0$. In the experimental implementation, we took $\gamma = 0.1$.

Binmore (1987, p. 65) studies the reaction curves of the two players in smoothed Demand Games, and confirms Nash's claim that all nontrivial[5]

---

5. Excluding those equilibria when both players make demands that are too large to be feasible whatever the other player may demand.

Nash equilibria converge on the Nash bargaining solution (under mild conditions) in the limiting case as $\gamma \to 0$. (The case of a piecewise linear boundary is not substantially different from the case where X has a smooth boundary, which can be treated very easily as in Binmore 1987, p. 159.)

With our choice of the function p, the reaction curves cross at just one point when $\gamma > 0$. It follows that there is always a unique Nash equilibrium in the continuous case when $\gamma > 0$. However, since the reaction curves are trapped in the region where $0 < p < 1$, they get very close together when γ becomes small. In fact, given any $\varepsilon > 0$, we can make any individually rational, Pareto efficient x in X an ε-equilibrium by taking γ sufficiently small.

The Discrete Version We restricted players to making demands in multiples of 0.1 of a lottery ticket in the belief that we were thereby approximating the continuous version sufficiently closely for practical purposes. Figure 2.4 shows the reaction curves for the resulting discrete game.

Notice that the reaction curves in figure 2.4 are very close together where things matter. Thus many points along the boundary are ε-equilibria for small values of ε. Note also that the reaction curves actually overlap over some of their range. Thus there are multiple exact Nash equilibria.

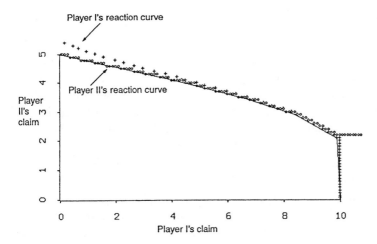

Figure 2.4
Reaction curves for the discrete game

The small circles along the boundary in figure 2.3 indicate all the nontrivial ε-equilibria with $\varepsilon = 0.1$. There are 83 such equilibria, some of which are also ε-equilibria for smaller values of ε. These ε-equilibria indicate a long and narrow region of relative stability where the gains from a unilateral deviation are small. There are 12 nontrivial exact Nash equilibria of the Discrete Game: $(6.3, 3.6)$, $(6.7, 3.5)$, $(7.0, 3.4)$, $(7.3, 3.3)$, $(7.6, 3.2)$, $(8.0, 3.1)$, $(8.3, 3.0)$, $(8.5, 2.9)$, $(8.7, 2.8)$, $(8.9, 2.7)$, $(9.1, 2.6)$, and $(9.3, 2.5)$. These equilibria are contained in the large rectangular box shown in figure 2.3 (and also in figures 2.2, 2.5, and 2A.1). This is the smallest box that contains all 12 equilibria.

Near the boundary of the feasible set, small changes in position can have large effects. For example, the point $(4.7, 4.0)$ is an ε-equilibrium for $\varepsilon = 0.05$. However, at the nearby point $(4.7, 3.8)$, a type I player can increase his expected payoff by more than 0.7 lottery tickets by deviating from the choice 4.7 when his counterpart chooses 3.8.

2.3 Practice

The experiment was conducted at the Michigan Economics Laboratory using undergraduates of the University of Michigan. The subjects were recruited directly from classes rather than from a list of participants in previous experiments. Each subject was given a specific time to appear at the laboratory[6] and promised \$2 for turning up on time, together with:

... the opportunity to win substantially more depending on how well you bargain and the circumstances in which you are placed. On average, subjects go away with between \$10 and \$30, but you might end up with more or less.

Each experimental session used 12 subjects who sat at networked microcomputers that were screened from each other. After reading the written instructions (given as appendix A1), the subjects participated in an interactive demonstration with the computer that was designed to familiarize them with how lottery tickets are converted into money and how demands are made and converted into lottery tickets.

Recall that after each 10 games a subject who has accumulated N lottery tickets in these games wins \$10 with probability N percent. This was operationalized by showing a "roulette wheel" split into a green winning region and a red losing region. A small yellow "ball" ran round the circumference of the wheel making appropriate noises, finally stopping in ei-

6. We did not want friends together in the same session.

ther the green or the red region. Where it stopped was fixed in advance only in the two demonstrations of its operation. Otherwise, everything advertized as random was indeed random.

The feasible set X was shown as a blue region relative to white Cartesian coordinate axes against a black background. The fuzzy boundary was indicated as a halo shading gradually into black. An artist with a trained eye would perhaps have been able to deduce the probability that a demand pair in the halo would be accepted from the shade of blue at that point. Recall that the subjects occupied the role of player I about half the time.[7] They were therefore given experience of both roles.

Player I made demands by moving a cursor along the x-axis. The cursor was accompanied by a vertical line. After practicing moving the cursor, a subject was shown the payoffs that he or she might receive for various demands that player II might make:

1. A horizontal line first appeared that intersected player I's vertical line well inside the blue feasible region. The point of intersection was then indicated with a flashing white circle. It was explained that each player gets his or her demand for certain.

2. Next a horizontal line appeared so that the point of intersection lay well inside the black region. The point of intersection was indicated with a flashing red circle. It was explained that each player gets nothing for certain.

3. Finally a horizontal line appeared so that the point of intersection lay in the fuzzy boundary region on the 80% probability contour. The point of intersection was indicated with a flashing white circle and the 80 percent probability contour was shown in white. It was explained that both players would get their demands 80 percent of the time and both players would get nothing 20 percent of the time.

4. Subjects received similar information after each practice and real game. After subjects registered their demands, a line was added to each subject's display indicating the demand of the opponent with whom he or she had been matched. If the intersection of the two demands was well inside the feasible set, the message "These claims are always acceptable. You both get your claims." was displayed. If the intersection was well outside the feasible set, the message "These claims are never acceptable. You both get nothing." was shown.

7. They did not strictly alternate roles since then they would not get the chance to play all other subjects. But they never occupied the same role three times in succession.

If the intersection fell near the boundary, for example, on the 65 percent contour, then the computer displayed the message "These claims
are acceptable 65 percent of the time. The computer accepts/rejects this
pair of claims." The word "accepts" was shown in white alternating
with the word "rejects" in red, the former remaining on the screen 65 percent of the time. Clicking sounds accompanied the changes in the words
displayed. Eventually the alternation stopped and the subjects were informed whether or not they had received their demands on that particular
occasion.

After practicing in player I's role, each subject went through a similar experience in the role of player II. Note that we were anxious not to suggest
any focal points at this stage, and so it was always left to the subject to
choose where to place his or her demand cursor during the demonstration. Moreover, when the computer simulated an opponent, its placing
of the opponent's cursor was made a function of the placing of the subject's cursor.

   The next step in the demonstration was to teach the subjects to understand the information about their potential opponents that would be supplied. They were shown a screen with small yellow squares superimposed
on the blue feasible region. It was explained that each yellow square represents one of the other subjects, each of whom is equally likely to be
your next opponent. The x-coordinate of the center of a square represents
the demand that the subject represented by that square last made when
occupying the role of player I. The y-coordinate represents the demand
that he or she last made when occupying the role of player II. The
computer moved player I's cursor back and forward to show how a yellow square becomes red as the demand represented by the current placing
of player I's cursor becomes incompatible with the demand last made by
the subject represented by that square when occupying the role of player
II. When there is only a probability p of the demand pair being incompatible, only a fraction p of a yellow square becomes red. As player I's
cursor is moved, the impression is therefore of a collection of small square
vessels being slowly filled with blood.

   Subjects in case 2 were offered *only* this information about the other
subjects. Subjects in the main experiment (case 1) were offered more information. After the screens that explained the yellow squares, they were
shown the same screens again with the addition of an "expected utility indicator" on the x-axis. This took the form of a second cursor that showed
the expected number of lottery tickets that player I would receive if he or
she made the demand indicated by the current placing of his or her de-

mand cursor, and the other subjects made the demands indicated by the current placing of the yellow squares. The part of the x-axis between the origin and the second cursor was highlighted in yellow and the part of the x-axis between the second cursor and the demand cursor was highlighted in red. Trials with the equipment indicate that differences in expected utility as small as 0.025 lottery tickets could be detected with this indicator.

As the demand cursor moved, the second cursor acting as an "expected utility indicator" moved also. When it reached its maximum point, it left behind a third stationary cursor (like a max-min thermometer). It was therefore relatively easy for a subject so minded to locate the demand that maximized his or her expected utility on the *myopic* assumption that other subjects would play as they did last time.

After seeing the screens that described how information is presented to player I, the subjects were invited to move player I's demand cursor back and forward to see how the display changes as the cursor moves. They were then shown the whole thing over again from player II's viewpoint.

Those who have no experience of presenting information to subjects through interactive computer programs may feel that the subjects must have been overwhelmed by such a complicated demonstration. However, subjects seemed to have very little difficulty in absorbing the information offered. They almost never used the facility for calling the assistant to answer questions, and seldom reported any confusion about what was expected of them in the questionnaire that they completed after the experiment. Perhaps this is not so surprising, since everybody has experience of video games requiring the need to absorb far more information much more quickly.

After the demonstration, each subject played ten "practice games" against "robot opponents." These practice games were not simply to familiarize the subjects with the way the games were played. The practice games were a deliberate attempt to condition the subjects to use one of the focal points on which the experiment concentrated. In each case the subjects were told that in the practice games the yellow squares each represented a robot opponent that they might be playing. The initial distribution of robot squares is shown by the larger, unlabeled squares in figure 2.3.

Case 1 was separated into four treatments. In case 1E, the robots were programmed to converge slowly on the equal increments solution, E. In case 1K, the robots converged on K, in case 1N on N, and in case 1U on U. Case 2 was the same as case 1E but without the "expected utility

indicator." Throughout the experiment, subjects' screens were updated
with information about their potential opponents' every *second* game. Note
also that convergence was deliberately not total. The robots converged
only to the extent that they arrived in the *neighborhood* of the selected
focal point at the time of the last update during the practice games.

At the end of the ten practice games, subjects were shown the roulette
wheel and discovered whether they would win or lose a prize for the practice session. They were forewarned that the prize for the practice games
would be only $1 instead of the $10 prize that was at stake in each of the
four sets of ten games that were subsequently to be played for real.

In each game, subjects were matched at random with the constraints
that no subject ever played the same opponent twice in succession or
occupied the same player role three times in succession. The interaction
between paired subjects was anonymous. Except for their opponent's current demand, subjects were not given any information about the identify
of their partner.

After each game, subjects were shown a roulette wheel that exhibited
how many lottery tickets they had accumulated since it was last "spun."
At the end of each set of ten games the roulette wheel was spun for a
prize of $10. Our strong impression is that such "intermittent reinforce-
ment" does indeed quicken the interest of subjects (as psychologists report). However, perhaps more important, it also provides some mildly
entertaining interludes in an experimental session, which although only
half an hour or so long, can easily become very dull if not broken up
into bite-size pieces.

After playing 50 games (10 for practice and 40 for real), the subjects
were told how much money they had won, and asked to complete a brief
computerized questionnaire before leaving. Finally, they were called to be
paid off one by one with the aim of minimizing interaction among subjects as they left the vicinity of the laboratory.

2.4   Results

Recall that case 1 was split into four treatments in which an attempt was
made to condition subjects to use one of the four focal points E, K, N, or
U (by programming their robot opponents to converge on one of these
focal points during the practice games). Only treatment E was used in
case 2, which differed from case 1E only in that no "expected utility indicator" was provided.

In each case 10 practice games were followed by 40 real games with pauses to spin a roulette wheel every tenth game. The experiment concluded with a brief computerized questionnaire.

2.4.1 Case 1

Figure 2.2 summarizes the overall picture. The figure shows the median demand pairs before the subjects had any experience, immediately after they had been conditioned by the practice games, and at the end of the experiment. All that need be added to the discussion of figure 2.2 given in the Introduction is that the data better fits the hypothesis that the subjects were conditioned to play a *best response* to the robot opponents they faced rather than to play the focal point itself. This point is discussed further in section 2.5 and is, of course, consistent with our overall explanation of the data: namely that the story is one of relentless optimization by the median player. Table 2A.1 gives the data from which figure 2.2 was constructed, together with the corresponding data for case 2.

Figure 2A.1a through 2A.1e show some typical trajectories for median demand pairs over the entire 50 games. For the practice games the trajectories show the median claims of both the subjects and their robot opponents. In practice games 1, 4, 6, 7, and 9 the subjects made claims as player I while the computer made claims as player II. The roles were reversed in the other practice games. When interpreting the trajectories, it is helpful to keep in mind that the x-coordinate of the point labeled "10" represents robot rather than human claims. Table 2A.1, on the other hand, reports the median human claims in games 9 and 10. That is, table 2A.1 reports the median human claims as player I from game 9 and the median human claims as player II from game 10.

Unlike figures 2.2 and 2.5, each point in figure 2A.1 represents the median demands by type I and type II players in a single game rather than a pair of games. The numbers in figure 2A.1 indicate the games that correspond to various points. It was not possible to label the same set of games on each trajectory and keep the figures legible.

From the positions of points 9 and 10 on the trajectories for case 1U, one can see that the human claims in the last practice games are close to the utilitarian focal point but the trajectories quickly move away from the focal point in the first few real games. This pattern, which indicates the difficulty we encountered in conditioning subjects to use the utilitarian focal point U, was also observed in the other three trajectories for case 1U. (One could also turn to table 2A.1 and, for each treatment, and compare the median claims made by player I in games 9 and 10 with the median type I claims made in games 11 and 12.)

The extent of the variation in individual claims can also be assessed using tables 2A.1 and 2A.3. The variation indicates that subjects did not always use the "expected utility indicator" with any precision, if at all. Such variation in behavior should not be dismissed as mere "noise." Computer simulations of myopic adjustment that we conducted before experimenting with real subjects exhibited much slower movement along the boundary away from a "focal point" than was observed in the experiment. We believe that the slow convergence of the simulated claims was due to the absence of variation in the simulation.

Other points that can be checked by examining table 2A.1 are the extent to which the subjects within each population group finally converged on the same claim and the number of games required for the median claims in each experiment to converge. In each experiment there is little or no difference between the median of the claims in the last two games and the median of the claims in the last ten games. That is to say, the median claims had already converged by the 41st game.

2.4.2   Case 2
This was an attempt to see how important the "expected utility indicator" is for the conclusions of case 1. It was replication of case 1E without the expected utility indicator. Figure 2.5 is the equivalent of figure 2.2 for case 2. The relevant data appears in table 2A.1. Figure 2A.1f shows a typical trajectory.

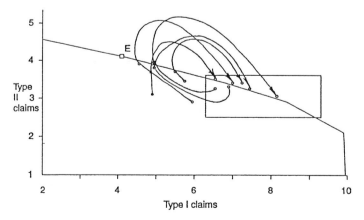

Figure 2.5
Summary of results in case 2

The results are broadly similar to those reported in case 1E. This came as yet another surprise. How did the subjects manage to behave as though they were optimizing when deprived of the means to do so with the accuracy that their behavior seems to indicate?

2.4.3 Questionnaire

In a previous paper (Binmore et al. 1991), a strong tendency was noted for people asked after the experiment for their views on what is "fair" to give answers that correlate with their experience of what actually happened in the bargaining game they had just played. We now briefly explore this issue. The relevant data is contained in table 2A.1.[8]

For each experiment figure 2.6 plots against the median of the last claims made as player I the median claim said to be "fair" for player I in reply to the question:

What do you feel would be a fair amount for each player to get?

Move each player's cursor to the fair amount.

Notice the marked tendency to report as fair what actually happened.

The line shown in figure 2.6 is the least squares regression line obtained by regressing the median fair claims on the median last claims. It satisfies the equation $y = -0.3970 + 0.9999x$. The standard errors of the intercept and slope are 1.0748 and 0.1401 respectively and $R^2 = 0.7282$.

It is perhaps interesting that the points in figure 2.6 whose residuals have the greatest absolute value are from experiments 17 and 18, both from case 2. If only data from case 1 are used, the results are essentially the same except that the R^2 increases to 0.8977. The results are also unaffected if the median last and median fair claims for player II are used instead of the claims for player I. In all cases we obtain a highly significant relationship between the median fair claims and the median last claims and a regression line with an intercept close to 0 and a slope close to 1.

If, for all 252 subjects, we regress the claim that each individual designated as fair for player I (y) against the last claim made by that individual as player I (x), then we obtain the equation $y = 2.2261 + 0.6382x$ with standard errors 0.7699 and 0.1007 and $R^2 = 0.1385$. There is still a

---

8. Because a subject could be player I or player II for two games in a row, the median claims in games 49 and 50 are almost but not quite identical to the median last claims. In experiment 17, the median of the last claims made as player I was 7.60 and in experiment 21 was 6.70. In all other cases the difference between the median claims in games 49 and 50 and the median last claims did not exceed 0.1 lottery tickets. Figure 2.6 was constructed using the median last claims rather than the median claims in games 49 and 50.

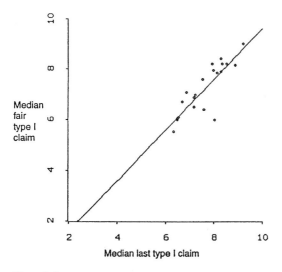

Figure 2.6
Comparison of the medians of the last actual claims made by player I in each experiment
with the medians of the claims said to be "fair" for player I

significant relationship, but the unexplained variation in the individual
claims is much higher than for the median claims.

A later question asked:

Is this the sort of situation in which people ought to "play fair," or is it
socially acceptable to use whatever bargaining power one has?

Of the 252 subjects who participated in the entire experiment, 89 subjects,
approximately 35 percent, said that one ought to "play fair." The rest
said that it was acceptable to use one's bargaining power.

2.5   Statistics

This section reports numerical summaries of the data that complement
the graphical summaries in figures 2.2 to 2.6 and figure 2A.1.

Recall that the subjects' information about the play of their potential
opponents was updated every second game. In order to compare the
effects of the different treatments in case 1 and to study the stability of
the focal points, we consider the subjects' claims in the last practice
games, 9 and 10, the first real games, 11 and 12, and the last real games,
49 and 50. For each treatment table 2.1 reports information about the
median claims in these pairs of games.

Table 2.1
For selected pairs of games, this table reports Euclidean and standardized measures of distance from the populations of median claims in each treatment to the appropriate focal points and to the median myopic best replies to the robot claims in games 9 and 10. The table also reports the means of the maximum gains obtained by unilateral deviations from each pair in the designated sets of median claims. Table 2.1 uses the median claims reported in table 2A.1 and the maximum gains from a unilateral deviation reported in table 2A.3 as input.

Games	Focal point		Myopic best reply		Mean maximum gain from a deviation
	Euclidean distance	p-Value for Hotelling's T^2	Euclidean distance	p-Value for Hotelling's T^2	
Case 1E					
9 & 10	0.690	0.0057	0.210	0.2412	0.514
11 & 12	0.708	0.0007	0.234	0.0065	0.609
49 & 50	2.637	lt. .0001	2.127	0.0002	0.011
Case 1K					
9 & 10	0.261	0.1157	0.134	0.1316	0.584
11 & 12	0.295	0.2675	0.589	0.2559	0.655
49 & 50	0.841	0.3460	0.554	0.5756	0.048
Case 1N					
9 & 10	0.237	0.1267	0.097	0.2712	0.254
11 & 12	0.409	0.0378	0.201	0.0322	0.214
49 & 50	0.130	0.2765	0.117	0.4508	0.018
Case 1U					
9 & 10	0.160	0.0576	0.117	0.1786	0.160
11 & 12	0.977	0.0095	0.860	0.0480	0.564
49 & 50	1.548	0.0015	1.413	0.0041	0.025
Case 2E					
9 & 10	0.620	0.0544	0.156	0.1451	0.379
11 & 12	0.905	0.0315	0.399	0.1335	0.295
49 & 50	3.274	0.0028	2.765	0.0053	0.036

The data used to construct table 2.1, as well as figures 2.2, 2.5, and 2.6, is contained in tables 2A.1 and 2A.3 of appendix A2 and summarized in table 2A.2. For each experiment table 2A.1 reports the median and the standard deviation of the populations of type I and type II claims in selected pairs of games. Table 2A.1 also reports the median and standard deviation for the populations of claims in the last 10 games, 41 through 50, and for the populations of claims that were designated as "fair" for each type of player in the questionnaire at the end of the experiment.

We can regard each of the pairs of type I and type II median claims reported in table 2A.1 as a single data point. The replications of each treatment then provide a population of data points for each pair of games. Table 2A.2 reports summary statistics for each of these populations. The statistics in table 2.1 were also constructed by treating the pairs of median claims in table 2A.1 as two-dimensional data points.

The second column of table 2.1 reports the Euclidean distance between the center of gravity of each population of median claims and the relevant focal point. (The coordinates of the centers of gravity are reported in columns 2 and 4 of Table 2A.2.[9]) These distances confirm the impression left by figures 2.2 and 2.5 that for each case and treatment the distance between the population of medians in the last practice or first real games and the treatment's focal point is always small compared, for example, to the distance between adjacent focal points.

For case 1U the jump in the distance to the utilitarian focal point from the last practice to the first real games is an indication of the difficulty we had in conditioning subjects to begin play at the utilitarian point. Note also that the distance from the populations to their respective focal points increases substantially from the first to the last real games for cases 1E and 1U and for case 2. The distance increases somewhat for case 1K and actually decreases for case 1N. The change in the distance from the populations of medians to their focal points over the course of the real games is one index of the relative stability of the four focal points.

Is the distance between the center of gravity of each population and the relevant focal point small or large relative to the variation within the population? If the data were one-dimensional, the t-statistic could be used to measure the distance from the sample mean to the focal point in units of the estimated standard deviation of the sample mean. Column 3 of table 2.1 measures distances using Hotelling's T^2 statistic, which is a multidimensional generalization of the t-statistic.[10]

Just as the t-statistic can be used to construct confidence intervals around the sample mean, the two-dimensional T^2 statistic can be used to construct confidence ellipses around a sample's center of gravity. Rather than directly reporting the value of T^2, column 3 of table 2.1 reports the p-value of the confidence ellipse that surrounds the center of gravity of each population of median claims and passes through the appropriate focal point.

Smaller p-values correspond to ellipses that are *further* from the center of gravity. Under the assumption that the population of median claims

9. The x and y coordinates of the center of gravity of a cloud of two-dimensional points are the means of the x and y coordinates of the points in the cloud.

10. See Rao (1973) (or any good text on multivariate statistics) for a definition and discussion of the properties of Hotelling's T^2 statistic.

represents a sample drawn from a bivariate normal distribution, a p-value less than 0.05 implies that one can reject the hypothesis that the center of gravity of the true distribution is equal to the focal point with a level of confidence greater than 95 percent. However, caution should be used in interpreting the standardized distances in this way, especially in light of the small numner of observations (3 or 5) in each sample.

If the median subject in the practice games of each experiment optimized myopically against his or her robot opponents, then the median claim in the last practice games would not necessarily be close to the focal point. Instead, this claim would be close to the myopic best reply to the population of robot opponents in games 9 and 10.

The population of robot opponents varied slightly from subject to subject within the same treatment. However, by games 9 and 10, the myopic best replies to the possible populations of robots within each treatment were virtually identical.[11] Let E_{br} denote the ordered pair of medians of the myopic best replies by type I and type II players respectively to the robot populations in games 9 and 10 of case 1E (and case 2). $E_{br} = (4.6, 4.0)$. For case 1K, $K_{br} = (7.1, 3.4)$. For case 1N, $N_{br} = (8.2, 3.0)$. For case 1U, $U_{br} = (9.8, 2.2)$.

Columns 4 and 5 of table 2.1 report the same statistics as columns 2 and 3 except that the distances measured are those between the centers of gravity of each population and the relevant median myopic best replies rather than the relevant focal points.

For case 2 and each treatment of case 1, the Euclidean distance from the center of gravity of the median claims in games 9 and 10 to the median myopic best reply is less than the distance to the corresponding focal point. In each case the p-value measuring the standardized distance to the focal point is smaller (so the standardized distance is greater) than the p-value measuring the distance to the myopic best reply. If Hotelling's T^2 statistic were used as the basis of a hypothesis test, we would be unable to reject the hypothesis that the center of gravity of the true distribution of each sample of median claims in games 9 and 10 is the relevant

11. In the real games, subjects were shown the previous claims of each of their 11 possible opponents. However, in the practice games only 10 (out of a possible 11) robot squares were displayed at a time, and which squares were displayed varied randomly from subject to subject. By games 9 and 10, the 11 possible populations of robot opponents in each treatment were all very similar, so this source of variation had almost no effect on the myopic best replies. For each treatment, the difference between the largest and the smallest myopic best reply for player I in games 9 and 10 was less than or equal to 0.2 lottery tickets. For best replies by player II, the difference was less than or equal to 0.1 lottery ticket.

myopic best reply. Statistical tests on the populations of individual subjects' claims in games 9 and 10 support a similar conclusion.[12]

In other respects the alternate distance measures in columns 3, 4, and 5 of table 2.1 reinforce the information conveyed by the distances reported in column 2. For case 1E, case 1U, and case 2 the Euclidean distance from the myopic best reply increases considerably from the first to the last pair of real games. The corresponding p-values for both the focal point and myopic best reply all decrease. The Euclidean distance to the myopic best reply in case 1K is relatively small and approximately the same in games 11 and 12 and games 49 and 50. The Euclidean distances to the best reply for case 1N are even smaller than for case 1K and the distance from the center of gravity in games 49 and 50 is less than the distance in games 11 and 12. All four p-values in games 11 and 12 and games 49 and 50 of case 1K are relatively large. The p-values for case 1N increase from the first to the last pair of real games.[13]

By comparing the median claims reported in table 2A.1 for games 49 and 50 with the coordinates of the exact Nash equilibria reported in section 2.2.2, one can confirm that the median claims in each experiment typically end up very close to one of the exact Nash equilibria of the discrete demand game. Table 2A.3 of appendix A2 further investigates the convergence of the subjects' claims to ε-equilibria of the discrete game.

For the designated games of each experiment, table 2A.3 reports the maximum expected gain that a player can achieve by deviating from the median claim for his type that was reported in table 2A.1 when the player expects his opponent to make the corresponding median claim that was reported for her type in table 2A.1. The reported gain is the maximum of that achievable by either type I or type II players. The last column in

---

12. A sign test was used to test the hypothesis that the median of the population of type I claims made by each subject in game 9 pooled across all replications of the same treatment was the same as the median of the myopic best replies to the populations of robot claims for that treatment. (See, for example, Gibbons and Chakraborti (1992) for a description and analysis of the sign test.) For each treatment we were unable to reject this hypothesis at the usual 5 percent level of significance. A similar test for the populations of type II claims in game 10 was unable to reject the hypothesis for each of the four populations of type II claims in case 1. For the type II claims in case 2 the sign test would reject the hypothesis at the 5 percent but not the 1 percent level of significance.

13. The correlation coefficients reported in table 2A.2 indicate that the populations of medians in games 49 and 50 are almost "one-dimensional." One might therefore wonder if, after all, a one-dimensional standardized distance might be more appropriate than one based on Hotelling's T^2 statistic. It turns out that p-values based on the t-statistic for the populations of median type I claims exhibit qualitative behavior which is similar to that of the p-values reported in table 2.1.

table 2.1 reports the mean of the maximum expected gains in table 2A.3 for each series of experiments.

In every experiment, including those where there was no expected utility indicator, table 2A.3 shows that by the last real games the median subjects had found their way to ε-equilibria for remarkably small values of ε.

As indicated in tables 2.1 and 2A.3, at least one type of player could typically receive an expected gain of about 0.5 lottery tickets (or 1 nickel) by unilaterally deviating from the median claim in the first real games of an experiment. An expected gain of that size would have been easily observable with the expected utility indicator provided to subjects in case 1. Moreover an increase of 0.5 lottery tickets in each of 40 real games corresponds to a 20 percent greater chance of winning 10 dollars or an expected gain of 2 dollars. Such a gain, while not large, might not have been negligible in the eyes of the subjects. By the last real games of the experiment, the typical gain obtained by a unilateral deviation from the median claims had shrunk to about 0.03 lottery tickets (about $1/3$ of a penny or 12 cents over the course of 40 games).

The standard deviations reported in table 2A.1 show that not all subjects made claims close to the median especially in the early games of an experiment. The numbers reported in parentheses in table 2A.3 help assess the implications of this variability.

For each pair of games and each experiment, one can calculate the maximum expected gain that a player can achieve by deviating from a particular claim when the player's opponent chooses randomly from the 12 opposing claims actually made in these games. By calculating a maximum expected gain in this way for each of the the 24 type I and type II claims actually made in a particular pair of games, one obtains a population of 24 maximum expected gains from a deviation. The first number of each pair in parentheses in table 2A.3 is the median of such a population of maximum expected gains. The second number is the 90th percentile of these gains.

The median expected gain defined in this way differs from the expected gain discussed earlier partly because in one case each claim is matched against a population of opposing claims while in the other case a claim is matched only against the single opposing median claim. Nevertheless, the two statistics behave similarly. In almost all experiments the median expected gain decreases from the first to the last pair of real games. In addition the median expected gain in the last real games is often less than 0.1 lottery ticket (that is less than 1 dime) and always less than 0.2 lottery tickets.

The 90th-percentile expected gains also typically decrease from the first to the last pair of real games in each experiment. Part of this decrease is probably due to the tightening of the distributions of claims around their medians which is also shown by the changes in the standard deviations reported in table 2A.1. However, the magnitudes of the 90th-percentile expected gains are also noteworthy. In a number of experiments, this percentile is greater than 0.5 lottery tickets even in the last pair of real games. This supports the conclusion stated earlier that although the median subject may optimize relentlessly, this is not necessarily true of every subject in every game.

2.6   Conclusions

The results of this series of experiments provide no comfort for those who argue that strategic considerations have little relevance to how people resolve coordination problems. If people are equipped with social norms that are relevant to the problem faced by our subjects, then it seems that a small amount of conditioning is sufficient to displace them in favor of a focal point of the experimenter's choice. Thereafter the median subject seems to optimize insofar as circumstances allow. In our experiment, this means optimizing right down to fractions of a penny. However, the subjects seem to see no contradiction between such optimizing and "fair" behavior, since the median subject reports as fair pretty much what actually happened towards the end of the games that he or she played. These results are consistent with a view that regards behavior as being shaped by social norms in the minds of the subjects, but which sees the social norms themselves as being determined by evolutionary considerations of which the subjects are only dimly aware.

However, we do not think it appropriate to make any wide claims for game theory as a predictor of human behavior, in spite of what we regard as the remarkable sharpness of our results. The reason is that we are vulnerable to the criticism that we made the process of "myopic adjustment" focal by featuring it in our graphic display.[14] One reply to this criticism is to note the similarity between the results in case 1E and case 2, even though the expected utility indicator was absent in the second situation. However, the important point is much less tendentious.

14. We do not accept that such criticism can be neglected because it involves a "Catch 22." Nobody anticipates that subjects would optimize if they were not provided with information in an easily digestible form that indicates what optimal behavior is. The catch is that the necessary information cannot be provided without focusing attention on what is optimal.

We do not argue that social norms that isolate particular focal points are unimportant in determining how people behave both inside and outside the laboratory. This paper is about how social norms get established and extinguished. In particular, we believe that it is a major error to suppose that social norms are commonly so rigid that they are able to sustain behavior in the long run that is not in equilibrium. Our experiment shows that it is relatively easy to displace whatever norms our subjects brought into the laboratory by norms that are consistent with an optimizing scenario.

Appendix

Instructions

Bargaining Experiment In this experiment, you will bargain via the computing equipment in front of you with the people seated at the the other machines in the room. You will participate in a large number of very short bargaining sessions. Whether you are player I or player II in these sessions is determined randomly. Sometimes you will be player I and sometimes player II. After each session, you will be randomly paired with a new bargaining partner.

In each bargaining session, you and your counterpart for that session will have the opportunity to split a "cake" between you. The cake will be represented by a blue region on your monitor screen. You will each simultaneously make a claim. If the pair of claims made by you and your counterpart lies well within the blue region on your screen, then you each get your claims. If the pair of claims lies well outside the blue region, you both get *nothing* in that session. If the pair of claims lies close to the boundary of the blue region, then the computer will sometimes allow the claims and sometimes it will disallow them. The closer the pair of claims is to the boundary of the blue region, the less likely the computer is to find them acceptable.

You will be bargaining for lottery tickets. After every ten bargaining sessions, each player may possibly win $10. Each lottery ticket that you acquired during the preceding ten bargaining sessions gives you one chance of a win. How many lottery tickets you get during the bargaining will depend partly on chance. If you bargain so as to maximize the number of lottery tickets that you would get on average, this will make the probability of winning $10 largest. Since you will take part in forty sessions in all, you will have four separate opportunities of winning $10. If

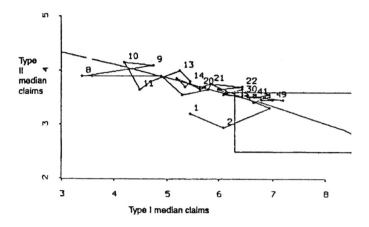

Figure A1(a) : Case 1E, Expt. 1

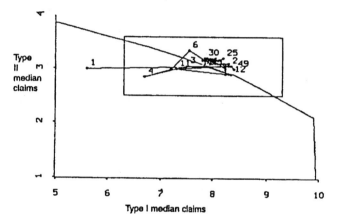

Figure A1(c) : Case 1N, Expt. 11

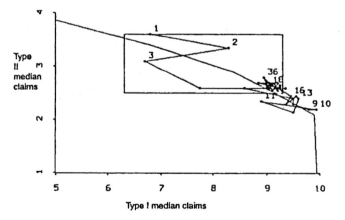

Figure A1(e) : Case 1U, Expt. 13

Figure 2A.1
Trajectories of median claims for selected experiments

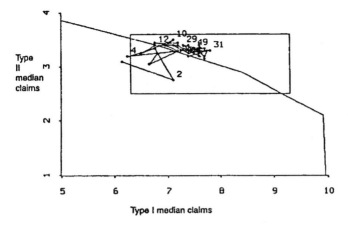

Figure A1(b) : Case 1K, Expt. 8

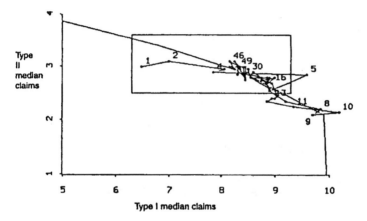

Figure A1(d) : Case 1U, Expt. 12

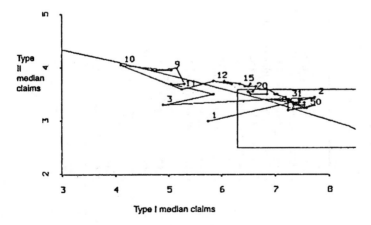

Figure A1(f) : Case 2, Expt. 17

Figure 2A.1
(continued)

Table 2A.1
For each experiment, this table reports the median of the claims made by type I and type II players in selected pairs of games, the median of the claims in the last 10 games, and the median of the claims designated as "fair" for each type of player. (The standard deviation of each set of claims is reported in parentheses.)

Experiment	Games 1 & 2		Games 9 & 10		Games 11 & 12		Games 49 & 50		Games 41–50		Fair	
	Type I	Type II	Type I	Type II	Type I	Type II	Type I	Type II	Type I	Type II	Type I	Type II
Case 1E												
1	5.45	2.95	4.75	4.15	4.60	3.75	6.90	3.45	6.90	3.50	7.10	3.40
	(1.438)	(0.294)	(1.119)	(0.421)	(0.478)	(0.387)	(0.305)	(0.176)	(0.356)	(0.143)	(0.803)	(0.191)
2	5.10	3.10	4.80	4.00	5.00	3.85	6.35	3.60	6.30	3.60	5.55	3.65
	(1.455)	(0.410)	(0.611)	(0.329)	(0.423)	(0.303)	(0.403)	(0.235)	(0.424)	(0.173)	(1.741)	(0.714)
3	7.05	3.10	4.95	4.20	4.70	3.80	7.20	3.35	7.10	3.40	6.50	3.50
	(1.422)	(0.534)	(1.251)	(1.153)	(0.523)	(0.276)	(0.510)	(0.124)	(0.490)	(0.240)	(1.639)	(0.587)
4	6.10	3.10	4.95	4.10	4.75	3.90	6.50	3.55	6.50	3.60	6.00	3.60
	(1.598)	(0.696)	(0.698)	(0.348)	(0.389)	(0.480)	(0.344)	(0.090)	(0.393)	(0.233)	(1.102)	(0.284)
5	5.40	3.20	4.50	4.00	4.70	3.80	6.40	3.60	6.40	3.50	6.05	3.50
	(1.020)	(0.601)	(1.274)	(0.274)	(0.278)	(0.329)	(0.128)	(0.130)	(0.314)	(0.127)	(0.553)	(0.157)
Case 1K												
6	5.65	2.75	6.65	3.55	5.95	3.30	7.20	3.30	7.20	3.30	6.90	3.35
	(1.666)	(0.586)	(0.585)	(0.738)	(1.214)	(0.151)	(0.261)	(0.123)	(0.204)	(0.110)	(1.591)	(0.425)
7	6.00	3.00	7.50	3.50	7.10	3.30	8.15	3.00	8.10	3.10	7.85	3.10
	(1.658)	(0.489)	(0.989)	(0.224)	(0.408)	(0.124)	(0.178)	(0.144)	(0.243)	(0.184)	(0.689)	(0.416)
8	6.15	2.75	6.95	3.50	6.50	3.35	7.50	3.30	7.60	3.30	7.60	3.15
	(1.696)	(0.538)	(2.555)	(0.215)	(1.807)	(0.322)	(0.271)	(0.135)	(0.520)	(0.165)	(0.414)	(0.221)

Case 1N												
9	5.35 (1.691)	3.10 (0.730)	8.05 (1.014)	3.10 (0.124)	7.85 (0.735)	3.05 (0.173)	8.00 (0.183)	3.10 (0.090)	8.00 (0.191)	3.10 (0.094)	7.95 (1.152)	3.00 (0.368)
10	6.50 (1.312)	3.20 (0.173)	8.45 (0.501)	3.10 (0.188)	7.95 (0.401)	3.00 (0.094)	8.55 (0.249)	2.90 (0.095)	8.50 (0.282)	2.90 (0.095)	8.20 (1.475)	3.10 (0.491)
11	5.60 (1.945)	3.05 (0.444)	8.25 (1.134)	3.05 (0.178)	8.20 (1.097)	2.90 (0.329)	8.40 (0.108)	3.00 (0.097)	8.30 (0.325)	3.10 (0.213)	8.20 (1.296)	2.95 (0.921)
Case 1U												
12	6.50 (1.379)	3.10 (0.379)	9.70 (2.964)	2.15 (0.401)	9.05 (1.853)	2.35 (0.268)	8.30 (0.295)	2.95 (0.137)	8.30 (0.306)	3.00 (0.140)	7.90 (1.634)	2.95 (0.543)
13	6.80 (1.301)	3.35 (0.368)	9.80 (0.377)	2.20 (0.424)	9.50 (0.867)	2.25 (0.234)	8.95 (0.248)	2.70 (0.074)	9.00 (0.169)	2.70 (0.099)	8.15 (2.058)	2.55 (0.701)
14	5.60 (1.280)	2.90 (0.642)	9.75 (1.775)	2.20 (0.476)	8.10 (1.466)	2.35 (0.298)	9.30 (0.293)	2.50 (0.198)	9.25 (1.206)	2.50 (0.149)	9.00 (1.740)	2.35 (0.740)
15	6.25 (2.290)	3.00 (0.346)	9.60 (3.711)	2.20 (0.617)	8.85 (1.742)	2.40 (0.417)	7.85 (0.292)	3.10 (0.190)	7.90 (0.264)	3.10 (0.192)	8.20 (1.246)	2.90 (0.460)
16	6.15 (1.438)	3.10 (0.432)	9.85 (1.522)	1.75 (0.621)	9.25 (1.468)	2.230 (0.291)	8.30 (0.312)	2.95 (0.131)	8.20 (0.695)	3.00 (0.186)	8.40 (0.921)	2.90 (0.368)
Case 2E												
17	5.75 (1.163)	3.45 (0.303)	5.05 (0.932)	4.05 (0.310)	5.50 (0.612)	3.70 (0.282)	7.45 (0.429)	3.25 (0.405)	7.50 (0.351)	3.30 (0.286)	6.40 (1.056)	3.45 (0.315)
18	4.90 (1.431)	3.10 (0.509)	4.75 (0.587)	4.15 (0.904)	4.90 (0.489)	3.90 (1.095)	8.15 (0.186)	3.05 (0.267)	8.10 (0.388)	3.10 (0.222)	6.00 (2.522)	3.35 (0.814)
19	6.90 (1.047)	3.30 (0.490)	4.80 (0.569)	4.00 (1.167)	4.95 (0.846)	3.80 (0.748)	7.25 (0.586)	3.40 (0.079)	7.20 (0.485)	3.40 (0.114)	7.00 (1.127)	3.40 (0.284)
20	6.55 (0.639)	3.25 (0.294)	4.75 (0.601)	4.20 (0.211)	4.95 (0.257)	3.95 (0.231)	6.55 (0.373)	3.50 (0.256)	6.60 (0.413)	3.50 (0.153)	6.10 (0.844)	3.60 (0.238)
21	5.95 (1.312)	2.90 (0.651)	4.25 (0.789)	4.10 (0.341)	4.55 (0.328)	3.90 (0.789)	7.00 (0.474)	3.40 (0.148)	6.75 (0.498)	3.50 (0.205)	6.70 (1.300)	3.45 (0.496)

Table 2A.2
Summary statistics describing the median type I and type II claims reported in table 2A.1 for each treatment and selected pairs of games

Games	Type I claims		Type II claims		Correlation coefficient
	Mean	Standard deviation	Mean	Standard deviation	
Case 1E, 5 experiments					
9 & 10	4.790	0.185	4.090	0.089	0.634
11 & 12	4.750	0.150	3.820	0.057	0.585
49 & 50	6.670	0.367	3.510	0.108	−0.997
Case 1K, 3 experiments					
9 & 10	7.033	0.431	3.517	0.029	−0.770
11 & 12	6.517	0.575	3.317	0.029	−0.025
49 & 50	7.617	0.486	3.200	0.173	−0.951
Case 1N, 3 experiments					
9 & 10	8.250	0.200	3.083	0.029	0.000
11 & 12	8.000	0.180	2.983	0.076	−0.999
49 & 50	8.317	0.284	3.000	0.100	−0.967
Case 1U, 5 experiments					
9 & 10	9.740	0.096	2.100	0.197	−0.627
11 & 12	8.950	0.533	2.330	0.057	−0.617
49 & 50	8.540	0.578	2.840	0.238	−0.995
Case 2E, 5 experiments					
9 & 10	4.720	0.291	4.100	0.079	−0.218
11 & 12	4.970	0.340	3.850	0.100	−0.772
49 & 50	7.280	0.591	3.320	0.175	−0.972

you are very lucky, you may therefore win $40 on top of your participation free. But please do not complain if you win nothing at all. When things are done at random, it is unavoidable that some people will be unlucky.

After the bargaining sessions are over, you will be asked to complete a computerized questionnaire. When *all* subjects have completed the questionnaire, the computer will display how much we owe you. The amount will include your $2 attendance fee, and any money you won during the experiment. Please remain in your seat until the supervisor calls your seat number and then bring your seat tag so that you can be paid.

This is not an experiment to find out what kind of person you are. When we see the results, we will neither know nor care who did what. We are only interested in what happens on average. So please don't feel that some particular sort of behavior is expected of you. However, we do ask that you do not talk to the other subjects or look at their screens. It is

Table 2A.3
Maximum expected gain that a player can achieve by deviating from the median claim for his type that was reported in table 2A.1 when the player expects his opponent to make the corresponding median claim that was reported for her type in table 2A.1. The gain is the maximum of that achievable by player I and player II. The numbers assigned to each experiment are the same as those assigned in table 2A.1. (The numbers in parentheses are the median and 90th percentile of the maximum expected gains obtained by deviating optimally from each of the type I or type II claims made in the designated pair of games. The maximum expected gain in this case is calculated assuming that a claim is matched randomly against one of the 12 opposing claims actually made in the designated games.)

Games	Experiment				
	1	2	3	4	5
Case 1E					
9 & 10	0.523	0.007	1.311	0.541	0.188
	(0.352 1.962)	(0.183 1.480)	(1.083 2.582)	(0.605 1.917)	(0.153 0.461)
11 & 12	1.021	0.247	0.734	0.308	0.734
	(0.326 0.770)	(0.103 0.532)	(0.169 0.528)	(0.119 0.436)	(0.130 0.575)
49 & 50	0.014	0.000	0.005	0.013	0.025
	(0.074 0.344)	(0.057 0.874)	(0.103 0.614)	(0.057 0.308)	(0.034 0.344)
	6	7	8		
Case 1K					
9 & 10	0.065	1.558	0.129		
	(0.254 1.425)	(0.964 2.548)	(0.533 3.090)		
11 & 12	1.274	0.124	0.567		
	(0.263 1.885)	(0.030 0.385)	(0.186 0.717)		
49 & 50	0.039	0.034	0.071		
	(0.061 0.133)	(0.052 0.126)	(0.173 0.520)		
	9	10	11		
Case 1N					
9 & 10	0.019	0.690	0.053		
	(0.057 0.611)	(0.731 2.286)	(0.277 1.874)		
11 & 12	0.166	0.221	0.256		
	(0.079 0.841)	(0.060 0.457)	(0.245 1.053)		
49 & 50	0.000	0.006	0.047		
	(0.008 0.150)	(0.029 0.392)	(0.171 0.441)		
	12	13	14	15	16
Case 1U					
9 & 10	0.155	0.018	0.041	0.161	0.428
	(0.260 2.221)	(0.212 0.460)	(0.300 1.826)	(0.116 2.458)	(0.284 2.039)
11 & 12	0.427	0.167	1.377	0.531	0.322
	(0.149 1.440)	(0.108 1.024)	(0.229 1.807)	(0.097 1.952)	(0.169 1.471)
49 & 50	0.041	0.021	0.000	0.023	0.041
	(0.062 0.183)	(0.040 0.250)	(0.125 0.985)	(0.085 0.417)	(0.010 0.409)

Table 2A.3
(continued)

Games	Experiment				
	17	18	19	20	21
Case 2E					
9 & 10	0.404	0.523	0.007	0.866	0.093
	(0.228 1.614)	(0.514 1.771)	(0.523 2.210)	(0.650 1.481)	(0.107 0.871)
11 & 12	0.307	0.159	0.484	0.017	0.508
	(0.121 0.786)	(0.245 1.175)	(0.208 1.255)	(0.033 0.550)	(0.225 1.406)
49 & 50	0.003	0.004	0.130	0.043	0.000
	(0.118 0.608)	(0.043 0.229)	(0.189 0.765)	(0.122 0.613)	(0.077 0.373)

Note: There are 24 type I or type II claims and, hence, 24 maximum expected gains associated with each pair of games and each experiment. The median is the average of the 12th and 13th largest maximum expected gains. The 90th percentile is the average of the 3rd and 4th largest expected gains.

important to the experiment that our subjects interact *only* via the computer equipment.

Now press the SPACE BAR on your keyboard. You will see a demonstration that will review the information in these instructions and give you hands-on experience of how claims are made. Remember to keep pressing the SPACE BAR to see a new screen. There is no need to hurry. You may have to wait for the other subjects to be ready anyway. If you still have questions after seeing the demonstration, there will then be an opportunity to ask the supervisor.

References

Binmore, K., and P. Dasgupta. 1987. *The Economics of Bargaining*. Oxford: Blackwell.

Binmore, K., P. Morgan, A. Shaked, and J. Sutton. 1991. Do people exploit their bargaining power: An experimental study. *Games and Economic Behavior* 3: 295–322.

Cooper, J., D. DeJong, R. Forsythe, and T. Ross. 1991. Selection criteria in coordination games: Some experimental results. *American Economic Review* 80: 218–33.

Gibbons, J., and S. Chakraborti. 1992. *Nonparametric Statistican Inference*, 3rd ed. New York: Dekker.

Harsanyi, J. 1977. Rational behavior and bargaining equilibrium in games and social situations. Cambridge: Cambridge University Press.

Isbell, I. 1960. A modification of Harsanyi's bargaining model. *Bulletin of the American Mathematical Society* 66: 70–73.

Kalai, E. 1977. Proportional solutions to bargaining situations: Interpersonal utility comparisons. *Econometrica* 45: 1623–30.

Kalai, E., and M. Smorodinsky. 1975. Other solutions to Nash's bargaining problem. *Econometrica* 45: 1623–30.

Myerson, R. 1977. Two-person bargaining and comparable utility. *Econometrica* 45: 1631–37.

Nash, J. 1950. The bargaining problem. *Econometrica* 18: 155–62.

Peters, H. 1986. Bargaining game theory. PhD thesis, Proefschritt Universitat Nijmegen.

Raiffa, H. 1953. Arbitration schemes for generalized two-person games. In H. Kuhn and A. Tucker, eds., *Contributions to the Theory of Games II*. Princeton: Princeton University Press.

Rao, C. 1973. *Linear Statistical Inference and Its Applications*, 2nd ed. New York: Wiley.

Rawls, J. 1972. *A Theory of Justice*. Oxford: Oxford University Press.

Roth, A. 1979. *Axiomatic Models of Bargaining*. Berlin: Springer-Verlag.

Schelling, T. 1960. *The Strategy of Conflict*. Cambridge: Harvard University Press.

Van Huyck, J., R. Battalio, and R. Beil. 1991. Strategic uncertainty, equilibrium selection principles and coordination failure. *American Economic Reviews* 80: 234–38.

Van Huyk, J., R. Battalio, S. Mathur, A. Ortmann, and P. Van Huyck. 1991. On the origin of convention: Evidence from symmetric bargaining games. Working Paper, Economics Department, Texas A&M University.

3   The Ultimatum Game

Bargaining games are difficult. The equilibrium selection problems they engender represent a major theoretical challenge. At the same time, it is almost inevitable that everyday fairness norms, unadapted to the bargaining game being studied in the laboratory, will be triggered by hints and cues inadvertently or deliberately built into the framing of the game.

Refining Equilibria

The refinement theories that proliferated in the late 1970s and 1980s were largely created in response to frustration with the equilibrium selection problem in bargaining games. In a refinement of Nash equilibrium, assumptions are made about how players will behave *off* the equilibrium path. With such assumptions it is sometimes possible to weed the set of Nash equilibria down to a single possibility.

Rubinstein's (1982) bargaining model is the leading example. In a bargaining game with perfect information in which impatient players alternate in exchanging demands until agreement is reached, he demonstrated the existence of a *unique* subgame-perfect equilibrium, thereby kicking out the props from under a long-standing dogma that characterized the bargaining problem as intrinsically indeterminate.[1] Now that relatively simple proofs of Rubinstein's theorem are available and the idea of a subgame-perfect equilibrium is no longer held in reverence, it is easy to underestimate Rubinstein's achievement. Perhaps this book will help toward putting things back in their proper perspective.

My own attempt to simplify the Rubinstein's approach will serve to illustrate the idea of backward induction that lies behind the notion of a subgame-perfect equilibrium (Binmore 1987).

The feasible set (sometimes called the cake or pie) $X = X_0$ for a bargaining problem is shown in figure 3.1c. Each time an offer is refused,

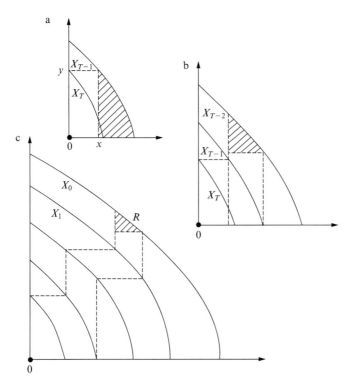

Figure 3.1
Shrinking cakes in Rubinstein's model

the feasible set shrinks. So if no agreement was previously reached, the feasible set when a demand is made at time T will be some smaller set X_T.

Figure 3.1a shows the situation when player I is about to make a demand at time $T - 1$ after all previous demands have been refused. He knows that the cake will shrink from X_{T-1} to X_T if his demand is refused. The final deal therefore can't assign him a payoff of less than x. The reason is that player I would then do better to offer player II a little more than y. A rational player II is sure to accept such an offer, because a payoff of this size will never again be available to her. It follows that if time $T - 1$ is reached without an agreement, the final deal lies in the shaded region of figure 3.1a. A similar argument shows that if time $T - 2$ is reached without an agreement, the final deal lies in the shaded region of figure 3.1b.

Working backward in this way from time T to time 0, we find that the final deal must lie in the shaded set R of figure 3.1c. If we don't get too adventurous when shrinking the cake, and if X_T shrinks away to a single point as $T \to \infty$, then the set R does the same thing. That is to say, only one possible agreement survives the backward induction argument.

It is easy to check that only one pair of strategies can sustain this unique agreement, and so the game has a unique subgame-perfect equilibrium. Although the equilibrium strategies tell the players what to do under all possible contingencies that might arise in the game, what actually happens in equilibrium is that the opening demand is accepted immediately.

Reinhard Selten

The idea of a subgame-perfect equilibrium was invented by Reinhard Selten (1975), who eventually won a Nobel Prize for his contributions to game theory.[2] Before he was widely known outside Germany, I invited him to visit for a week at the London School of Economics, where I was running a workshop in economic theory.

In a long and instructive discussion in the college bar, Selten explained that he had anticipated Rubinstein by exploring the possibility of using subgame-perfect equilibria to analyze some simple bargaining games with his student Ingolf Stahl (1972). He also insisted that his idea of a subgame-perfect equilibrium should be regarded only as an ideal theoretical construct that would be unlikely to predict well in laboratories. In defending this view, he told us of an experiment he had suggested to his student Werner Güth on what became known as the Ultimatum Game.

With colleagues at Köln University, Güth showed that subgame-perfect equilibrium fails to predict even in the simplest version of Rubinstein's model, in which a single demand is followed by a single acceptance or refusal. The subgame-perfect prediction in the Ultimatum Game is that player I will get almost the whole cake, since the alternative to player II accepting such a demand is that she gets nothing. There are wide differences among cultures, but it is now well established that in the Western world, player I commonly offers player II half the cake; it is unwise to offer her less than a third of the cake, since the probability of a refusal is then about a half.

Because a standard response to these results is that they show that people are too nice to pay attention to strategic consideration in bargaining games, it is perhaps worth pointing out immediately that such a naive interpretation is untenable. For example, Mitzkewitz and Nägel (1993) studied the Ultimatum Game in the case where only player I knows how much money is available for division. He mostly then offers half the money when the amount is no more than a third of its maximum possible size. When the amount is larger, he often sneakily makes the offer that would be fair if the amount available for division were equal only to a third of the maximum.

A Two-Stage Game

The Ultimatum Game must now be the single most replicated economic experiment of all time, but it is a reflection on attitudes of the time that nobody took much notice of the paper by Güth et al. (1982) when it was originally published. However, having been much impressed by Selten's arguments, I proposed to my then colleagues, Avner Shaked and John Sutton, that we run an experiment of our own to check things out. At the time we had reservations about the design of the Güth et al. experiment. Was the Ultimatum Game so pathologically simple that the subjects didn't perceive it as a strategic problem? What about the anonymity of subjects in Güth's experiment? And so on.

We had never run an experiment before, but I think we did quite well. I don't know whether we were the first economists to run an experiment with networked computers using animated graphics, but I think it quite likely. I bored a hole with my electric drill through the wall connecting two unused cubicles that the Psychology Department kindly made available. We then passed a wire through the hole to connect two computers, through which our subjects communicated using seat-of-the-pants software. (Commercial networking systems were not then available.)

The general shape of Güth's results survived in our harsher laboratory environment, and so we looked at a two-stage ultimatum game in which player II can follow her refusal of player I's opening demand by making a final demand of her own—but only after the cake has shrunk by a predetermined amount. The subgame-perfect prediction is then that player II will end up with the amount to which the cake shrinks after a refusal, and player I will get the rest.

We found that totally inexperienced subjects in the two-stage game played pretty much as one might expect from observing behavior in the one-shot game. However, subjects who had the experience of playing as player II played quite differently when offered the opportunity to play again, this time in the role of player I. Their initial demands were now close to the subgame-perfect prediction for the particular shrinkage rate of 75 percent that we chose to use.

It was particularly hard to get experimental papers published in those early days. The referees were either theorists who saw no point in theorems being tested in the laboratory, or refugees from psychology who thought they already knew that game theory is irrelevant to human behavior. However, the *American Economic Review* eventually printed the brief note reproduced in this chapter.[3] Unlike the original paper of Güth et al., it attracted a great deal of attention.

This is the only paper that I actively regret publishing, since I think it was instrumental in creating an academic industry in which innumerable variants of the Ultimatum Game continue to be flogged to death in laboratories all over the world to this day. Who cares, for example, how toddlers or victims of Alzheimer's disease play the Ultimatum Game?

Early papers in the genre often began by denouncing the folly of naïve theorists like Binmore, Shaked, and Sutton who were said to believe that subjects in bargaining experiments always behave like selfish optimizers rather than playing fair. Particular criticism was directed at a passage in our experimental instructions which said: "You will be doing us a favor if you simply set out to maximize your winnings."[4] The implication is that we thereby "fixed" our experiment to generate our preferred outcome (Thaler 1988). When our work is mentioned nowadays, it continues to be said that our use of this sentence disqualifies our results from serious attention. But if the sentence persuaded our experienced subjects to behave unfairly, how come it didn't persuade our inexperienced subjects to do the same?

In any case, a glance at the graph of figure 3.2 from Holt and Davies (1993) is enough to show that such critics are simply seizing on an excuse to ignore data they find inconvenient. (Figure 4.1 conveys the same message.) Each point on the graph represents a different two-stage ultimatum game experiment.

When the shrinkage rate is different in different experiments, the subgame-perfect prediction of the opening demand is also different. This prediction is the x coordinate of each point. The y coordinate is the average opening demand actually made in the experiment. If subgame-perfection were a good predictor in these games, *all* the points on the graph would be close to the 45° line—which they evidently aren't. However, the immediate point is that the data point from our experiment isn't an outlier.[5] Since the instructions in these other experiments didn't include our offending phrase, it clearly didn't make much difference to our subjects' behavior.

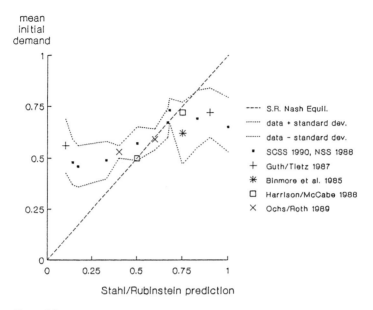

Figure 3.2
Mean initial demands in Alternating-Offer Bargaining Games with two rounds (Source: Spiegel et al. 1994, tab. 6).

Does Backward Induction Work?

We thought that our experiment showed not only that naïve generalizations of the fairness results of Güth et al. in the Ultimatum Game are untenable but that here was at least one case in which subgame-perfection works. However, we were unlucky in having chosen a shrinkage rate that placed our data point near the point of intersection of the graph of subgame-perfect predictions and the graph representing the average opening demands.

When one takes account of the full range of results, it looks as though *both* strategic and fairness considerations somehow combine in determining the subjects' early play.[6] Perhaps different strategic realities trigger different fairness norms. But, whatever the explanation, to use subgame-perfection alone as a predictor is evidently as hopeless as using a fairness norm that ignores the relative bargaining power that the shrinkage rate characterizing a two-stage ultimatum game confers on the players.

Refutations of the idea that experimental subjects commonly reason using backward induction are now legion. My own favorite is the paper by Camerer et al. (1994) in which the *order* in which players click on various screens to examine the payoffs in forthcoming subgames is recorded. But little tendency to work back from the closing subgames to the beginning of the game was observed.

Is the failure of pure subgame-perfection in two-stage ultimatum games a good reason for abandoning Rubinstein's bargaining model as a positive theory? I hope that later chapters will convince skeptics that this would be a bad mistake. There are experimental environments in which the Rubinstein theory works very well indeed.

How can the Rubinstein theory sometimes predict well if subjects don't use backward induction? My guess at the reason isn't very profound. Rubinstein's prediction of the outcome of his bargaining model doesn't change if we replace the subgame-perfect equilibrium of his theorem by what one might call a stationary expectations equilibrium, in which the players always plan to act today as though everybody's plans tomorrow will always be the same as they are today. The point is that it would not be surprising if boundedly rational laboratory subjects were led to such an equilibrium by a simple myopic optimization process that assumes that tomorrow will be much the same as today (chapter 8).[7]

What Does Game Theory Really Predict?

Despite the liberal sentiments expressed above, I guess there is no way I am ever going to escape the lingering odium of being thought so attached to the idea of a subgame-perfect equilibrium that I would fix an experiment to make it seem like it works in the laboratory. Ironically, most of the time that I was being attacked in the behavioral literature for supposedly being an unprincipled supporter of subgame-perfection, I was simultaneously engaged in a debate with Bob Aumann and his followers, in which I was putting the case *against* subgame-perfection as a necessary principle of rationality (Binmore 1996, 1997). Appendix B contains two papers in which I explain why I don't believe that Aumann's (1995, 1996) claim that common knowledge of rationality implies backward induction even has a chance of being true.

Despite Aumann's advocacy, I think some version of my opposing view on this subject is now standard among game theorists. Even Aumann agrees with Selten that subgame-perfection should be regarded as a purely theoretical construct that is unlikely to be decisive in predicting experimental results.

The continuing refrain in papers from the Ultimatum Game industry that "game theory predicts that the subgame-perfect equilibrium will be

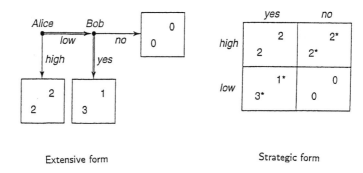

Extensive form   Strategic form

(a) Ultimatum Minigame

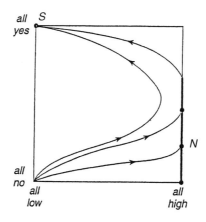

(b) Some trajectories with the replicator dynamics

Figure 3.3
Convergence on weakly dominated equilibria in the Ultimatum Minigame. The Nash equilibria indicated in the right diagram occur in two clusters. The subgame-perfect equilibrium S sits alone in the top left corner of the square. The remaining (weakly dominated) Nash equilibria form a connected set N, indicated by thickening the lower part of the right side of the square. A escape trajectory leads away from the equilibrium at the highest equilibrium in N (where the probability with which player II is planning to say *no* to a low offer makes player I just indifferent between his high and low offers). On arriving in N, the system will presumably drift through N in response to unmodeled noise, until it finally finds it way via the escape trajectory to the subgame-perfect equilibrium S. But the expected waiting time before this eventuality occurs will commonly be so large as to be irrelevant for experimental purposes.

observed" is therefore at best outdated, and at worst dishonest. Refinement theory has been effectively dead for many years now. Current theoretical attempts on the equilibrium selection problem center on trying to model the actual processes of learning or adjustment by means of which actual people find their way to equilibria in the real world. It can't be said that this research program has come up with anything very useful in the way of positive results, but it certainly confirms that we can't afford to throw away unrefined Nash equilibria if we care about the long-run behavior of subjects in laboratories. Simple adjustment processes can be made to converge even on weakly dominated Nash equilibria without any trouble at all.

Consider, for example, the Ultimatum Minigame[8] of figure 3.3a from Binmore et al. (1995). The game has a unique subgame-perfect equilibrium, in which player I makes a high demand and player II acquiesces. It also has many other (weakly dominated) Nash equilibria, in which player I makes the fair demand (which is optimal when player II is planning to say *no* with high probability to the high demand that player I therefore doesn't make).

These equilibria are indicated in figure 3.3b. The trajectories in this figure are those of the replicator dynamics, which evolutionary biologists regard as the simplest model that captures anything significant about evolutionary processes in games. The point is simply that some of these trajectories end up at weakly dominated Nash equilibria.

Appendix C is a theoretical paper that discusses this issue at length in the context of the full Ultimatum Game (Binmore et al. 1995). Among other things, it shows that convergence on weakly dominated equilibria can be robust. Its computer simulations are also in line with those of Roth and Erev (1995) in suggesting that any convergence is likely to be very *slow*.

None of these equilibrium-selection problems exist for the one-shot Prisoners' Dilemma. There are also many other games with only one Nash equilibrium. Any of these games would be a much better test bed for critics of orthodox game theory than the Ultimatum Game, with its many Nash equilibria and slow convergence properties. So why do critics interminably appeal to experiments on the Ultimatum Game? Presumably because they are aware that game theory predicts the behavior of experienced subjects in games like the Prisoners' Dilemma rather well.

Testing Noncooperative Bargaining Theory: A Preliminary Study

Ken Binmore, Avner Shaked, and John Sutton

Bargaining theory has received much attention of late. There has also been a growing interest in experimental work on bargaining, notably by Reinhard Selten (1978) and by Alvin Roth, M. Malouf, and J. Murnighan (1981). This work confirms a view that is common among social psychologists: namely that subjects tend to seek a "fair" outcome to bargaining problems. The thrust of the inquiry is then to determine what the subjects will regard as fair in a given situation.

A tension exists between this work and the theoretical approach revitalized by Ariel Rubinstein (1982). (See also Binmore 1982, 1983; Shaked and Sutton 1984.) This new approach involves modeling the process of offer and counteroffer by means of which agreement can be reached, as a formal noncooperative game, and studying agreements that can be sustained as equilibria of this game.

The tension is sharply illustrated by a recent experimental study of W. Güth, R. Schmittberger, and B. Schwarze (1982). (See also Güth 1983.) Two subjects have to divide a sum of money (the "cake"), using the following primitive procedure: player 1 makes a demand, which player 2 can then accept or refuse. This concludes the game. If the demand is refused, both players receive nothing. A strategic analysis assigns all (or nearly all) of the cake to player 1, but experiments show that a much "fairer" division is usual.

The work of Güth et al. seems to preclude a predictive role for game theory insofar as bargaining behavior is concerned. Our purpose in this

London School of Economics, Houghton St., London WC2A 2AE, UK. We gratefully acknowledge the financial support of the International Centre for Economics and Related Disciplines (Suntory-Toyota Foundation), and the hospitality of the Psychology Department at LSE, where our experimental work was conducted, under the immediate supervision of Yasmin Batliwala, Mimi Bell, and Maria Herrero. We also thank Werner Güth, Alvin Roth, and particularly Reinhard Selten for comments on an early draft.

note is to report briefly on an experiment that shows that this conclusion is unwarranted. (Only the briefest account of the experiment is offered here; for a full account, see our 1984 paper.)

This does not mean that our results are inconsistent with those of Güth et al. Under similar conditions, we obtain similar results.[9] Moreover our full results would seem to refute the more obvious rationalizations of the behavior observed by Güth et al. as "optimising with complex motivations." Instead, our results indicate that this behavior is not stable in the sense that it can be easily displaced by simple optimizing behavior, once small changes are made in the playing conditions.

3.1 The Experiment

In the present work, we went beyond the one-stage "Ultimatum" Game of Güth et al. and examined a two-stage game, as follows:

Stage I: The cake is of size 100 pence. Player 1 makes a proposal (X); player 2 accepts (1 receives X, 2 receives $100 - X$) or rejects (game continues).

Stage II: The cake is of size 25 pence. Player 2 makes a proposal (X'); player 1 accepts (1 receives X', 2 receives $25 - X'$) or rejects (1 receives 0, 2 receives 0).

A game-theoretic analysis requires that player 1 makes an opening demand in the range 74 to 76 pence, and player 2 accepts any opening demand of 74 pence or less (for he cannot do better by refusing, even if he obtains the entire cake in the second stage).

We studied the game, using subjects who were isolated from each other, and who communicated their decisions via linked microcomputers. Following lengthy pilot studies, in which we solicited players' comments after they had played the game, we decided to extend the design, as follows. We invited the subject who had filled the role of player 2 to play the game again, but this time he would fill the role of player 1. We recorded only his opening demand in this second game (game B).

3.2 The Results

We focus here on the main features of interest. The opening demands made in game A and game B, respectively, are shown in the histograms

---

9. See note 10 below.

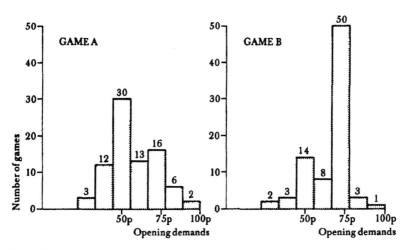

Figure 3.4
Opening demands for main results

in figure 3.4. They exhibit a marked change of behavior between game A and game B. A tendency to "play fair" in game A becomes a strong tendency to play "like a game theorist" in game B.

This marked change in behavior constitutes the first of the two main findings of the present study. The null hypothesis is that the opening demands in each game are drawn from the same population and is rejected at the 0.1 percent level (Kolmogoroff-Smirnoff two-tailed test).

Focusing on those subjects who filled the role of player 2 in game A, we looked at the subsample who faced a "high" demand in that game. A fair player would reject a high demand, and would not himself make a high demand (when offered the chance to act as player 1, in game B). *The results* (shown in table 3.1) *indicate little support for the view that a substantial proportion of the population are "fairmen" as opposed to "gamesmen."* The table shows the relationship between a subject's response to the opening demand made of him in game A, and the opening demand which he later makes when acting as player 1 in game B. Cell *G* denotes gamesmen, cell *F* denotes fairmen. We chose the midpoint between 50 and 75 as our dividing line between low and high demands. The table refers only to the subsample of our population who faced high demands in game A.

What, then, of the players who filled the role of player 1 in game A, and who exhibited a marked tendency to make fair demands? While we have considered various possible explanations, the interpretation that we favor is this: subjects, faced with a new problem, simply choose "equal

Table 3.1

Opening demand in game B	Response to high opening demands $(63 \leq a \leq 77)$ in game A	
	No	Yes
$b \leq 62$	1(F)	2
$b \geq 63$	2	17(G)

division" as an "obvious" and "acceptable" compromise—an idea familiar from the seminal work of Thomas Schelling (1960). We suspect, on
the basis of the present experiments, that such considerations are easily
displaced by calculations of strategic advantage, once players fully appreciate the structure of the game.

Finally, it is important to note that Güth et al. did in fact study subjects playing the one-stage ultimatum game for a second time, without
observing any marked change in behavior.[10] Thus, it is not *only* this feature which distinguishes our results from theirs.

The key feature to note, in this respect, is that *responses to opening
demands in Game A* were strongly biased in favor of "rationality." (Of
22 opening demands in the range $63 \leq a < 77$, only 3 were rejected.) On
the other hand, at the second stage of Game A—following a refusal at
the first stage—subjects showed a strong tendency to reject high demands
(as in the study of Güth et al.).

Our suspicion is that the one-stage ultimatum game is a rather special
case, from which it is dangerous to draw general conclusions. In the ultimatum game, the first player might be dissuaded from making an opening demand at, or close to, the "optimum" level, because his opponent
would then incur a negligible cost in making an "irrational" rejection. In
the two-stage game, these considerations are postponed to the second
stage, and so their impact is attenuated.[11]

---

10. Opening demands were slightly higher, and refusals of these demands *more frequent*.

11. There remains the possibility that the difference between our results and those of Güth et
al. might be traced to differences in the experimental environment rather than to differences
in the game played. Güth et al. operated in an open environment within which subjects
could see each other (although the identity of their current opponent was, of course, a secret). Our assistant, Yasmin Batliwala, has run a controlled experiment to check for this possibility (which will be reported separately). Replicating our experimental conditions, she
compared the behavior of subjects playing our two-stage game with that of a control group
playing the one-stage Ultimatum Game. Broadly, the results confirmed our present interpretation. Behavior in the two-stage game was similar to that reported in this paper. Behavior
in the one-stage Ultimatum Game was consistent with the observations of Güth et al. in that
game theory was a poor predictor of outcomes.

References

Binmore, K. G. 1982. Perfect equilibria in bargaining models. ICERD Discussion paper. London School of Economics.

Binmore, K. G. 1983. Bargaining and coalitions I. ICERD Discussion paper. London School of Economics.

Binmore, K. G., A. Shaked, and J. Sutton. 1984. Fairness or gamesmanship in bargaining: An experimental study. ICERD Discussion paper. London School of Economics.

Güth, W. 1983. Payoff distributions in games and the behavioral theory of distributive justice. Mimeo. Koln.

Güth, W., R. Schmittberger, and B. Schwarze. 1982. An Experimental Analysis of Ultimatum Bargaining. *Journal of Economic Behavior and Organization* 3: 367–88.

Roth, A., M. Malouf, and J. Murnighan. 1981. Sociological versus strategic factors in bargaining. *Journal of Economic Behavior and Organization* 2: 153–77.

Rubinstein, A. 1982. Perfect equilibrium in a bargaining model. *Econometrica* 50: 97–109.

Shaked, A., and J. Sutton. 1984. Involuntary unemployment as a perfect equilibrium in a bargaining model. *Econometrica* 52: 1351–64.

Selten, R. 1978. The equity principle in economic behavior. In H. Gottinger and W. Leinfellner, eds., *Decision Theory and Social Ethics, Issues in Social Choice*. Dordrecht: Reifel Publishing, pp. 289–301.

4 Inequity Aversion?

Camerer (2003, p. 24) explains the behavior of subjects in bargaining experiments who refuse low offers of money in favor of nothing by saying: "According to behavioral game theory, responders reject low offers because they like to earn money but dislike unfair treatment (or like being treated equally)."

I don't see why this should be thought to be a *behavioral* explanation. We aren't even able to predict what people will count as fair in different contexts, so how can we test whether the claim holds true? But this isn't to say that I don't think that the explanation is right at some level. Indeed there are at least two levels at which it surely must be right.

In debriefing sessions, experimental subjects certainly very frequently do say that they like fair outcomes. I might say the same thing myself in similar circumstances. So if we are looking for the way that subjects explain their behavior to themselves, we need look no further. But how well do such subjective explanations predict a person's future behavior?

For example, why do I drive on the left in London? At one level, I do so because I like it. If you ask me in London whether I prefer driving on the left to driving on the right, I will say that I prefer the former. But next week you might find me driving on the right in New York.

The point here is that it isn't an adequate explanation of my behavior in London to say that I choose to drive on the left because I like it. The real question in such instrumental matters is *why* I like it.[1] A major reason is that I want to avoid accidents. This is a more satisfactory explanation for why I drive on the left in London, since it also explains why I drive on the right in New York.

This brings us to the second level at which it can't be wrong to say that people do things because they like doing them. If one includes enough parameters it becomes a tautology that anyone can always be modeled as maximizing a utility function. For example, after observing my driving in appropriate cities, we could summarize our data by saying that I like driving on the left in London, on the right in New York, and at random in Istanbul. But it is surely important not to fall into the Ptolemaic trap of confusing a description of the data with an explanation.

To be useful for predictive purposes, a putative explanation must be reasonably parsimonious. In game theory, people sometimes say that it needs to be *portable*. This means that the predictions should work for some wider class of environments than those from which the data incorporated in the prediction was gathered. For example, if I was seen always driving on the left in London, New York, and Istanbul, then the explanation that I like driving on the left would be portable if I was later observed driving on the left in Paris, Rome, and Tokyo.

The big problem I see with explanations that reduce the behavior of subjects to the maximizing of a suitable utility function is that such explanations commonly fail to be portable over *time*, but this criticism loses much of its force in the context of ultimatum games with only one or two stages, since both theory and experiment suggest that trial-and-error adjustment over a realistic number of trials is then likely to be small.[2] However, other portability problems have to be confronted.

A reasonably satisfactory explanation should be robust to at least some changes in the rules of the game under study, but it turns out that even apparently inessential changes in the *framing* of an experiment can have significant effects on the subjects' behavior.[3] My favorite example is Ball and Eckel's (1996) striking experiment on the Ultimatum Game, in which subjects awarded an otherwise meaningless gold star were the beneficiaries of favored treatment from their bargaining partners.

Is our explanation of this phenomenon to be that subjects like being more-than-fair to people wearing gold stars? Is it the same for white coats or dog collars? What about jackboots or dreadlocks? What of people selling a house or buying a used car?

Rescuing Backward Induction?

In seeking a parsimonious utility function to characterize the behavior of experimental subjects in ultimatum games, Bolton (1991) looked at a case where players care not only about their own money payoff but that of their opponent as well. Fehr and Schmidt (1999) are among others who have similarly found it possible to fit other such functions to Ultimatum Game data—although their claim to have used utility functions "calibrated" in this way to predict the data from other games turn out to be wildly exaggerated.[4] I don't think anyone is especially attached to any particular functional form. Whatever functional form is adopted, there will anyway need to be at least one loose parameter hanging around (to take care of gold-star effects if nothing else).

A question posed by this work is whether subgame-perfection in two-stage ultimatum games can be "rescued" by postulating that the players optimize such other-regarding utility functions rather than the money payoffs provided by the experimenter. The experiment of this chapter answers this question in the negative.

No matter what parameters are chosen in whatever functional form, backward induction isn't portable across different variants of simple ultimatum games, unless the utility functions take account of more than the money payoffs of both players. Because the work of Camerer et al. (1994) and others, we were expecting this negative result, and so we did everything we could to give subgame-perfection its best chance of working, but it failed anyway.

On the positive side, we now have figure 4.1, which provides a less eclectic bunch of data points for the average initial demands in two-stage ultimatum games than the summary of diverse experiments from Holt and Davies (figure 3.2).

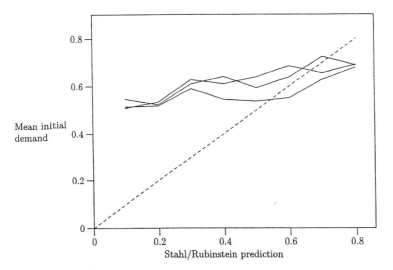

Figure 4.1
Average initial demands in two-stage ultimatum games. The graphs are to be read as in figure 3.2. The groups of subjects corresponding to each graph differed only in having previously played variants of a one-stage Ultimatum Game in which their fractional payoffs after a refusal were respectively $(0.1, 0.1)$, $(0.1, 0.6)$, and $(0.7, 0.1)$.

I want to draw particular attention to the fact that the three graphs of figure 4.1 are systematically different, although all three were compiled from experiments on exactly the same set of games. The only difference between the three groups of subjects corresponding to the three different graphs is that different groups had experienced versions of a one-stage Ultimatum Game that differed in the amounts that each player would receive after a rejection.

So we have another gold-star effect, but this time what matters is the shared history of experience of the subjects in playing a different game. I take this as another confirmation that one comes up with less fragile explanations of experimental data if one thinks of fairness norms as being lodged in the common understandings of a society rather than in the preferences of individuals.

Why do I drive on the left. Because I like it. Why do I like it? Because it helps avoid accidents while I am in London. Why does it avoid accidents in London? Because it is commonly understood in London that everybody drives on the left. Why is it focal to drive on the left in London? Because this is the Nash equilibrium in the Driving Game at which cultural evolution has stranded the British.

In my *Natural Justice* (Binmore 2005), I try to tell the similar but much more complicated story that I think needs to be told for fairness norms. Aside from other issues, behavioral economists might find my treatment of interpersonal comparison relevant to the kind of gold-star effects that have been central in this discussion.

A Backward Induction Experiment

Ken Binmore, John McCarthy, Giovanni Ponti, Larry Samuelson, and Avner Shaked

4.1 Introduction

Experimental subjects frequently fail to play subgame-perfect equilibria in one-stage and two-stage alternating-offers bargaining games. A common response is to question the implicit assumption that players' monetary payoffs and utilities are synonymous. A variety of alternative utility functions have been suggested, typically allowing for "interdependence," or the possibility that a player's utility depends on his opponent's as well as his own monetary payoff.

These alternative utility functions allow some reconciliation of the theory and experimental results but leave open the original question: Does play respect backward induction? And if not, how can the departures from backward induction be characterized? This paper reports an experiment that investigates these questions.[5]

Once we abandon the equivalence of monetary payoffs and utility, we are left without a precise idea of what determines utility. Then how can we examine backward induction? Section 4.2 makes this question more precise and sets the stage for our analysis by splitting backward induction into two components, subgame consistency and truncation consistency. Section 4.3 describes the experimental procedure used to examine subgame and truncation consistency. Section 4.4 presents and discusses the

We thank Menesh Patel and John Straub for research assistance and thank Vince Crawford for helpful comments. The instructions and data for the experiments reported in this paper are posted at http://www.nyu.edu/jet/supplementary.html. Financial support from the ESRC Centre for Economic Learning and Social Evolution at University College London, the National Science Foundation, and the Deutsche Forschungsgemeinschaft, SFB 303 at the University of Bonn, is gratefully acknowledged.

5. The instructions used in the experiment and the data are posted at http://www.nyu.edu/jet/supplementary.html.

results. We find systematic violations of backward induction that cannot be explained by payoff-interdependent preferences. For example, proposers are less aggressive in the second stage of a two-stage bargaining game than in an equivalent one-stage game (violating subgame consistency). Players are less responsive to variations in the expected value of playing a subgame than to equivalent variations in terminal payoffs (violating truncation consistency). Section 4.5 concludes.

4.2 Background

4.2.1 Bargaining Games
Figure 4.2 presents one-stage and two-stage Alternating-Offers Bargaining Games. We take the total surplus to be 100 and measure divisions of the surplus in terms of the percentage allocated to player 1, speaking of 1's actions as "demands" and 2's actions as "offers." The one-stage game is commonly called the Ultimatum Game.

The subgame-perfect equilibrium prediction is that player 1 receives all of the surplus in the Ultimatum Game (or at least all but a penny, if divisions must be made in multiples of pennies), and receives $100(1 - D)$ of the surplus (with $100D$ going to player 2) in the two-stage game, where D is the common discount factor. However, in the original study of the Ultimatum Game, Güth et al. (1982) found that player 1's modal de-

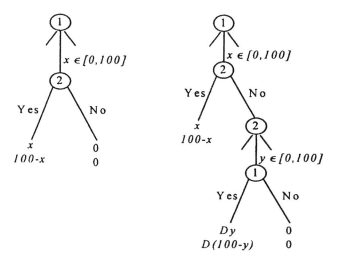

Figure 4.2
One-stage and two-stage alternating-offers bargaining games

mand claimed only half of the surplus, and significantly more aggressive demands were often rejected. Binmore et al. (1985) found similar results, as have a multitude of subsequent studies, surveyed in Bolton and Zwick (1995), Davis and Holt (1993), Güth and Tietz (1990), Roth (1995), and Thaler (1985). Experimental outcomes in the two-stage game similarly tend to be less extreme than the subgame perfect equilibrium.[6]

4.2.2 Payoff-Interdependent Preferences

The experimental results are commonly interpreted as indicating that players have *interdependent preferences*, meaning that preferences depend upon more than simply one's own monetary payoff.[7] Bolton (1991), for example, suggests that utility is increasing in one's own payoff and decreasing in the ratio of one's opponent's to one's own payoff, as do Ochs and Roth (1989).

We concentrate on *payoff-interdependent* preference theories, in which preferences depend *only* upon the payoffs received by the players. For example, applying Bolton and Ockenfels's (2000) ERC (equity, reciprocity, and competition) theory to two-player bargaining games, we can write player i's utility function as

$$u_i(\pi_i, \pi_j) = v_i\left(\pi_i, \frac{\pi_i}{\pi_i + \pi_j}\right), \tag{1}$$

where v_i is assumed to be increasing and concave in its first argument, and to be strictly concave in its second argument, with a zero derivative in the second argument when the latter equals $\frac{1}{2}$.[8] Player i thus prefers higher payoffs but dislikes inequality, and hence may prefer to reject quite asymmetric payoff allocations.

Alternatively, Fehr and Schmidt (1999) work with a utility function (in two-player games)

---

6. Figure 5.6 of Davis and Holt (1993, p. 272) provides a convenient summary of experiments with two-stage games. The results of Camerer et al. (1993) and Johnson et al. (2002), who examine the information-gathering patterns of experimental subjects, raise further questions concerning backward induction.

7. A variety of experiments have investigated the fairness considerations that are often invoked to motivate interdependent preferences. Examples include Abbink et al. (1996), Andreoni et al. (2002), Andreoni and Miller (2002), Bolton et al. (1998), Bolton and Zwick (1995), Dufwenberg and Gneezy (1996), Kagel et al. (1996), Ruffle (1998), Slembeck (1998), Straub and Murnighan (1995), Winter and Zamir (1997), Zwick and Chen (1997), and Zwick and Weg (1996).

8. The function v is continuous and the utility, when $\pi_i = \pi_j = 0$, is defined to equal $v_i(0, 1/2)$ (so $u_i(\pi_i, \pi_j)$ is not continuous).

$$u_i(\pi_i, \pi_j) = \pi_i - \alpha_i \max\{\pi_j - \pi_i, 0\} - \beta_i \max\{\pi_i - \pi_j, 0\}, \tag{2}$$

where $0 < \beta_i < \alpha_i$, so that player i dislikes inequality, and especially dislikes inequality in which i has the smaller payoff. Costa-Gomes and Zauner (2001) examine a utility function whose deterministic part (supplemented by an error designed to facilitate empirical application) is given by

$$u_i(\pi_i, \pi_j) = \pi_i + \alpha_i \pi_j, \tag{3}$$

where α_i may be positive or negative, reflecting a positive or negative concern for the opponent's payoff.

We use (1)–(3) as illustrations, but our results apply to any *payoff-interdependent* utility function $u_i(\pi_i, \pi_j)$ that is strictly quasi-concave on sets of the form $\{(\pi_i, \pi_j) : \pi_i + \pi_j = C\}$ (for some constant C).[9]

A more general interdependent utility specification would allow preferences to be based not only on realized payoffs but also on other characteristics of one's opponent or the structure of the game, including the alternative payoffs offered by unreached outcomes. In Levine (1998), player i's utility may be increasing in j's payoff if j himself is relatively altruistic, while i's utility may be decreasing in j's payoff if j is similarly spiteful. Building on the theory of psychological games, Dufwenberg and Kirchsteiger (1998), Falk and Firshbacher (1999), and Rabin (1993) offer alternatives in which the structure of the game, coupled with beliefs about opponents' intentions, plays an important role. This allows player i to prefer to be kind to kind opponents, but allows i's assessment of whether j has been kind to depend on i's beliefs about what j believed about the consequences of j's actions.

We can be assured of the ability to construct interdependent preferences capable of reconciling experimental data and backward induction, as long as we allow sufficiently flexible preferences and examine a sufficiently narrow class of games.[10] For the interdependent-preferences approach to backward induction to be useful, we require a relatively parsimonious specification of preferences that is readily applicable across a relatively broad class of games. We say that such preferences are relatively "portable." Payoff-interdependent preferences are attractive be-

---

9. Strict quasiconcavity ensures that backward induction solutions are unambiguous.

10. For example, Dufwenberg and Kirchsteiger (1998) argue that their theory creates sufficiently flexible self-referential links across the stages of the game as to render the concept of backward induction vacuous.

cause their simplicity makes them eminently portable. Coupled with the observation that such preferences are consistent with many experimental results, including violations of backward induction (Bolton and Ockenfels 2000; Costa-Gomes and Zauner 2001; Fehr and Schmidt 1999), this makes payoff-interdependent preferences particularly interesting.

4.2.3 Backward Induction

In the Ultimatum Game backward induction requires player 1 to choose 1's most preferred allocation, from the set of allocations that player 2 at least weakly prefers to disagreement. But when preferences exhibit payoff-interdependence, we do not have a precise idea of the latter set. Then how can we examine backward induction?

One experimental approach begins by separating backward induction into its three components:[11]

• *Rationality* Given a choice between two (vectors of) payoffs, a player chooses the most preferred.

• *Subgame consistency* Play in a subgame is independent of the subgame's position in a larger game.

• *Truncation consistency* Replacing a subgame with its equilibrium payoffs does not affect play elsewhere in the game.

In generic, finite games of perfect information, these three requirements are equivalent to backward induction, as captured by the equilibrium notion of subgame perfection.[12] In the case of the Ultimatum Game with ordinary preferences, rationality ensures that a player will always choose a positive amount of money rather than zero. Subgame consistency ensures that a player will accept when this same decision appears as the result of an opponent's offer. Next, truncation consistency allows us to replace this accept/reject decision with its equilibrium payoffs, and then rationality is once again invoked to examine the proposal that opens the game.

---

11. The concepts of subgame consistency and truncation consistency are taken from Harsanyi and Selten (1988). An alternative approach, used by Holt (1999) to examine coordination games, would estimate subjects' utility functions, use these estimates to calculate the backward-induction solution, and then compare the calculated solution with the outcomes of further experiments.

12. In nongeneric, finite games of perfect information, subgame perfection may also require appropriate tie-breaking rules (Harsanyi and Selten 1988, pp. 106–109). Strict quasi-concavity ensures that the relevant genericity condition is satisfied in our games. In games of imperfect information, the possibility of subgames with multiple Nash equilibria obviously allows subgame-perfect equilibria to violate subgame consistency.

Interdependent-preference theories are designed to preserve the maintained assumption of rationality. In order to assess backward induction, our analysis accordingly presumes rationality and examines issues of subgame consistency and truncation consistency.

4.3 The Experiments

4.3.1 The Games

Figure 4.3 presents the games involved in the experiments. Game III is the two-stage game of figure 4.2. We refer to game I as the Ultimatum Game, though the presence of the rejection payoffs (V_1, V_2) causes the

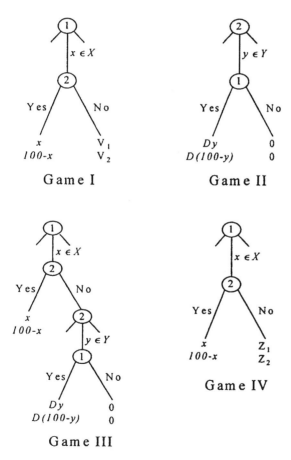

Figure 4.3
Experimental games

game to differ from a standard Ultimatum Game. The rejection payoffs (Z_1, Z_2) in game IV are subject-specific, and are calculated on the basis of the subjects' realized payoffs in game II (details below).

Twenty-four treatments were run, with all four of games I–IV played in each treatment, and with one treatment for each of the twenty-four elements of the set

$$\{(10, 10), (70, 10), (10, 60)\} \times \{0.2, 0.3, 0.4, 0.5, 0.6, 0.7, 0.8, 0.9\},$$

where the first element identifies a rejection-payoff pair (V_1, V_2) that appeared in game I (only) and was common to all of the subjects in the treatment, and the second element identifies the discount factor (again common to all subjects within a treatment) that appeared in games II and III of the treatment.

4.3.2 The Ultimatum Game

The first of our four games, the Ultimatum Game, serves three purposes.

First, the Ultimatum Game with rejection payoffs $(10, 10)$ provides a control. We regard results similar to those obtained in other Ultimatum Game experiments as an essential indication that there is nothing in our procedures that prevents replication of standard experimental results, and would re-examine our procedures in the absence of such results. We choose the Ultimatum Game with the rejection payoffs $(10, 10)$ as a control, rather than the standard Ultimatum Game, to check that the mere introduction of (relatively small) rejection payoffs does not significantly change subjects' behavior.

Second, the Ultimatum Game provides a check on our intuition as to how players respond to varying rejection payoffs. We expect play in the $(10, 60)$, $(10, 10)$, and $(70, 10)$ rejection-payoff games to differ, with player 1 becoming increasing aggressive across these three games, and would again reexamine our procedures if this were not the case.

Finally, the $(10, 60)$ rejection-payoff game provides a setting in which a common form of payoff-interdependence makes a particularly sharp prediction. Payoff-interdependent models typically assume that utility is increasing in one's own payoff and (possibly weakly) decreasing in inequality, as do Bolton and Ockenfels (2000), Fehr and Schmidt (1991), and as does the model of Costa-Gomes and Zauner (2001) when $-1 < \alpha_i < 0$ (in which case it is illuminating to let $u_i(\pi_i, \pi_j) = (1 + \alpha)\pi_i + \alpha(\pi_j - \pi_i)$). Hence player 2 should prefer to accept any allocation in which 2 receives at least 60 percent of the surplus. Player 1 will then demand at least 40, and player 2 will accept 1's demand.

4.3.3 Subgame Consistency

The second stage of the two-stage bargaining game is itself an Ultimatum Game, with player 2 making the initial proposal and with the total surplus given by $100D$ rather than 100. Game II duplicates this second stage as a separate game. We will refer to game II as the *continuation game*. We investigate subgame consistency by comparing play in the continuation game with play in the second stage of the two-stage game:[13]

• Subgame consistency indicates that play in the second stage of the two-stage game, for those cases in which it is reached, should duplicate play in the continuation game.

Isn't the mere fact that the second stage is reached evidence that backward induction fails? If players' preferences are commonly known, the answer is yes. However, different subjects may have different (interdependent) preferences. Player 1 may then be uncertain about the interdependent preferences of the (anonymous) opposing player 2, and hence may optimally make a first-stage demand that some player $2s$ reject, leading to the second stage.

In the presence of such heterogeneity, differing player-2 offers in the second stage of the two-stage game and in the continuation game may reflect not a failure of backward induction, but rather that player 2 has inferred something about player 1, and hence about 2's optimal second-stage offer, from the demand that 2 rejected to reach the second stage of the two-stage game.[14] Depending upon how prior beliefs are specified and how beliefs are updated in response to zero-probability demands, we can construct subgame-perfect equilibria that will account for virtually any outcome. But can this be done with beliefs that are sufficiently straightforward as to yield a useful theoretical model?[15] The evidence

---

13. Violations of subgame consistency are readily found in games with imperfect information and hence multiple backward-induction equilibria, in which the case for subgame consistency is less obvious. See, for example, the Cooper et al. (1994) coordination-game experiments. Much less is known about games with unique backward induction outcomes. In an experiment involving centipede games of varying length, McKelvey and Palfrey (1992) find encouraging results concerning subgame consistency.

14. In the presence of incomplete information, we must now work with perfect Bayesian or sequential rather than subgame-perfect equilibrium, as well as appropriate generalizations of subgame consistency and truncation consistency in terms of Markov perfection. Because we find that incomplete information does not play an important explanatory role, we forgo a formal development, following the common practice of retaining the terms subgame perfection, subgame consistency, and truncation consistency.

15. This consideration is reminiscent of the observation that *some* preferences must exist which support backward induction, while our interest centers on preferences that are sufficiently portable, such as payoff-interdependent preferences.

suggests that the updating of beliefs helps very little in explaining player 2's observed play in the second stage of the two-stage game. Player 2s reject a wide variety of demands in the first stage of game III. If player 2 can draw inferences about player 1 from the latter's period-1 demand, then we would expect player 2's period-2 offer to vary significantly with the identity of the demand rejected by player 2 to reach the second stage. We find no evidence of such a relationship.

Heterogeneous preferences also raise the possibility that the player 2s who reach the second stage of the two-stage game are a biased sample of the complete set of player 2s who participate in the continuation game. We can eliminate this potential selection bias by restricting attention to the continuation-game play of those player 2s who reach the second stage when playing the two-stage game. Doing so only exacerbates (slightly) the observed behavioral differences between the two games.

4.3.4   Truncation Consistency

We next turn to truncation consistency. A rejected demand in game IV leads to the rejection payoffs (Z_1, Z_2). A pair of values (Z_1, Z_2) is assigned to each experimental subject (according to a method that will be important in the next subsection but is not relevant here). When two subjects are matched to play game IV, the value of Z_1 for that interaction is the corresponding value assigned to the subject who plays as player 1, while Z_2 is the corresponding value assigned to the subject who plays as player 2 in game IV. The values Z_1 and Z_2 thus vary across instances of game IV, with subjects always completely informed as to the relevant values.

We can estimate a function describing the relationship between player-1 demands in game IV and the rejection payoffs (Z_1, Z_2). Similarly we can examine a function describing the relationship between player-1 demands in game III and the anticipated values (Z_1^{III}, Z_2^{III}) of play in the second stage of game III, where we estimate the latter values on the basis of the observed second-stage play in game III. If truncation consistency holds, then a change in a game-IV rejection payoff should have the same effect on player-1 demands as an equivalent change in the anticipated value of the game-III second stage:

• Truncation consistency indicates that play in game IV should bear the same relationship to the rejection values (Z_1, Z_2) as does play in the first stage of game III to the anticipated payoffs (Z_1^{III}, Z_2^{III}) of the second stage of the two-stage game.

The primary difficulty here involves identifying and estimating the appropriate anticipated value (Z_1^{III}, Z_2^{III}) of playing the second stage of game III. We find that our results are insensitive to a variety of alternative measures of (Z_1^{III}, Z_2^{III}).

4.3.5 Subgame and Truncation Consistency

Games III and IV differ in that a rejection of a first-period demand in game III leads to a copy of the continuation game, while a rejection in game IV leads to the fixed rejection payoffs (Z_1, Z_2). The latter payoffs are calculated on the basis of observed play in the *continuation* game. A pair of values (Z_1, Z_2) is calculated for each experimental subject, one describing the experience of that subject as player 1 in the continuation game, and one describing the subject's experience as player 2 in the continuation game. When two subjects are matched to play game IV, Z_1 is the estimated continuation-game value for the subject who plays as player 1 in game IV, and Z_2 the estimated continuation-game value for the subject who plays as player 2 in game IV.

If subgame consistency holds, then the continuation-game payoffs (Z_1, Z_2) provide an estimate of the value of entering the second stage of the two-stage game. If truncation consistency holds, then it should not matter whether a first-stage rejection leads to the second-stage game or to the payoff pair (Z_1, Z_2). Hence:

• Subgame and truncation consistency indicate that experimental play in game IV should duplicate that of the first stage of game III.

The primary difficulty here involves ensuring that Z_1 and Z_2 are good estimates of the value of playing the continuation game. Notice that the problem now involves not (Z_1^{III}, Z_2^{III}), which are estimates that appear only in our *analysis* of truncation consistency and whose properties we can examine and adjust in the course of our empirical investigation, but values (Z_1, Z_2), which appear in the specification of game IV and hence whose calculation must be fixed as part of the experimental design.[16]

4.3.6 Procedures

The experiments were conducted at University College London in the fall of 1998 with undergraduate subjects. Each of the twenty-four—one

---

16. Fortunately, this problem does not arise in the test of truncation consistency described in the preceding subsection, where (Z_1, Z_2) need not bear any relationship to the value of the continuation game or second stage of game III.

for each possible combination of three rejection payoff pairs ((10, 10), (70, 10), and (10, 60)) and eight discount factors (0.2, 0.3, 0.4, 0.5, 0.6, 0.7, 0.8, and 0.9)—treatments involved ten subjects, for a total of 240 subjects. Each treatment consisted of eighty rounds, with the ten subjects matched into five pairs for each round, with each pair playing one game. Game I was played in the first twenty rounds, game II in the next twenty, game III in the penultimate twenty rounds, and game IV in the final twenty rounds. We thus have a total of 400 games in each treatment of the experiment and an overall total of 9,600 games, 2,400 each of games I, II, III, and IV. In each of the four games, each subject played about half of the time as player 1 and half of the time as player 2, with the "about" reflecting the fact that roles were assigned randomly. Each of the ten subjects in a treatment could be matched with each of the nine opponents.

All subjects play the four games in the same order. A more complete experimental design would add another dimension to the definition of a treatment, corresponding to different orders in which the four games are played and allowing us to test for the possibility that the results are sensitive to the order of play. Our theoretical design places some constraints on this order, in that game II must be played before game IV so that game-II outcomes can be used in defining the game-IV rejection payoffs (Z_1, Z_2). Even after incorporating this constraint, investigating all possible orderings would require twelve times as many treatments. We discuss possible evidence of order effects as we proceed.

Instructions were provided via a self-paced, interactive computer program that introduced and described the experiment, and provided practice in how to make choices in each of the four games. The surplus was pictured as a wedge-shaped slice of "cake," as shown in figure 4.4. In games I and IV, the left wedge of figure 4.4 appeared, along with two smaller wedges with areas corresponding to the appropriate rejection payoffs of players 1 and 2.

In game II, the right wedge of figure 4.4 appeared, capturing the fact that payoffs in the event of an agreement were discounted. In game III, both wedges appeared, one corresponding to each stage of the game, with the second stage being somewhat fainter while the first stage was being played. Discounting was captured by coloring only an inner segment of the second wedge whose area corresponded to the discounted value of the cake.

Demands and offers were made by using the arrow keys to move a line that rotated about the point of the wedge, with player 1's share lying above the line and player 2's below. To avoid suggesting focal points,

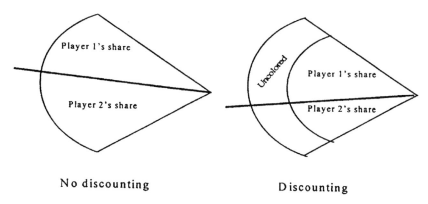

No discounting   **Discounting**

Figure 4.4
Representation of the bargaining games. The wedges were outlined in white against a black
background. The interior of the entire wedge was colored light brown in the no-discounting
case, while only the area within the inner boundary was colored in the discounting case.

there were initially no numbers on the screen. Once a tentative division
was proposed, the percentage of the cake going to each player was indicated, as was the equivalent number of "tickets" going to each player.
The percentages always added to 100. The number of tickets added to
100 in the absence of discounting, and in a discounted stage (game II or
the second stage of game III) was given by $100D$, where D was the discount factor. Players then had a chance to confirm or revise their choice.

After each twenty rounds, and hence after each of games I, II, III, and
IV, an electronic roulette wheel was spun whose surface was divided into
"win" and "lose" areas, with the former being proportional to the number of tickets won in the previous twenty rounds of play.[17] A win paid six
pounds, which was then worth slightly less than ten dollars. Together
with a six-pound initial fee, subjects' earnings were then drawn from the
set $\{6, 12, 18, 24, 30\}$ pounds, with these amounts being won by 4, 28, 79, 106,
and 23 subjects, respectively, for an experiment that took about two hours.

4.4 Results

4.4.1 Game I: The Ultimatum Game

We begin with game I. Figure 4.5 reports player-1 demands and provides
information on player 2's response to those demands.

---

17. Our purpose was not so much to control for risk aversion, as expected-utility maximizers are likely to be risk neutral over the relatively small amounts of money involved in
the experiment but to provide an interlude when switching from one game to the next.

Rounds	(V_1, V_2)	Observations	Mean demand	Median	5th %tile	95th %tile
1–10	(10, 10)	400	64.9	65	50	80
10–20	(10, 10)	400	66.8	68	55.5	76.5
1–10	(70, 10)	400	82.8	85	64	90
10–20	(70, 10)	400	83.4	84	79	88
1–10	(10, 60)	400	39.8	38.5	28	56.5
10–20	(10, 60)	400	36.0	36	26	49

		All demands		Demands in [30, 40]		Demands in [70, 80]	
		Obs.	R %	Obs.	R %	Obs.	R %
1–10	(10, 10)	400	24			111	48
10–20	(10, 10)	400	19			146	34
1–10	(70, 10)	400	30			72	1
10–20	(70, 10)	400	22			61	0
1–10	(10, 60)	400	36	266	23		
10–20	(10, 60)	400	30	313	24		

Figure 4.5
Player-1 demands (measured in terms of the percentage of the surplus demanded by player 1) and player-2 rejection rates (R percent) in the Ultimatum Game. There were five games per round in each of eight treatments for each (V_1, V_2) specification, for a total of 800 observations (or "Obs.") over twenty rounds. No demands from [30, 40] were rejected in the (10, 10) and (70, 10) cases, and none from [70, 80] were accepted in the (10, 60) case.

First, the results for rejection payoff (10, 10) are much like those of conventional Ultimatum Game experiments. The mean and median demands are both near two-thirds of the surplus. A significant number of demands are rejected, with higher rejection rates for higher demands. Demands are slightly higher in the final ten rounds than in the first ten rounds of play, and the distribution of demands is somewhat tighter in the final ten rounds (cf. the 5th and 95th percentiles, and notice that this tightening contributes to the reduction in rejection rates), but the changes are small relative to the variation in Ultimatum Game results reported in the literature.[18] Our experiment replicates familiar Ultimatum Game results.

Second, player-1 demands increase, as expected, as the rejection payoffs change from (10, 60) to (10, 10) to (70, 10). These differences are significant: over the final ten rounds of play, the 90-percentile intervals for the observed demands made under the three specifications, given by

---

18. We frequently compare results for the first and last ten rounds, and often focus on the last ten rounds, in order to isolate any initial subject confusion. The differences are quite small compared to those involved in the hypotheses of interest.

$[26, 49]$, $[55, 77]$, $[79, 88]$,

are disjoint.

When rejection payoffs are $(70, 10)$, player 1 is ensured a payoff (70) larger than player 1 conventionally receives in the ordinary Ultimatum Game. Player 1's mean demand in this case is approximately 83, with a 90-percentile interval (over the last ten rounds) of $[79, 88]$, leaving player 2 with little more than the rejection payoff of 10. This willingness of player 1s to make such aggressive demands reflects the sensitivity of rejection rates to rejection payoffs. Figure 4.5 reports that when rejection payoffs are $(10, 10)$, 40 percent (103 of 257, over all 20 rounds) of demands in the interval $[70, 80]$ are rejected. Only 0.75 percent (1 of 133) are rejected when the rejection payoffs are $(70, 10)$. Figure 4.6 provides an additional

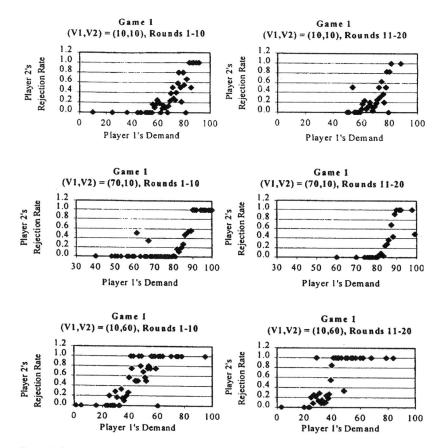

Figure 4.6
Rejection rates in the Ultimatum Game.

summary of the behavior of player 2s. Many player 2s are thus willing to settle for 20 or 25 percent of the surplus if 1 has a rejection payoff of 70 but not if 1's rejection payoff is a mere 10, revealing interdependent preferences for these player 2s of the form:[19]

$$(10, 10) \succ (75, 25) \succ (70, 10). \tag{4}$$

The $(70, 10)$ outcome is consistent with the behavior that would appear if players mentally "assigned" the rejection payoffs 70 to player 1 and 10 to player 2, and then bargained over the remaining surplus as if they were in an ordinary Ultimatum Game with a total surplus of size twenty. For example, player 1's mean demand allocates slightly less than two-thirds of this remaining surplus to player 1. This reaction to rejection payoffs contrasts with the findings of Binmore et al. (1989, 1991, 1998), where players appear to ignore outside options that pose no constraint on the agreement that would be reached in the absence of such an option and make demands close to constraining outside options. In the $(70, 10)$ case, such behavior would produce the agreement that comes closest to that of the ordinary Ultimatum Game while still respecting player 1's rejection payoff, giving player 1 a payoff of (perhaps just over) 70. More important, approaching the surplus remaining after rejection payoffs have been covered as an ordinary Ultimatum Game yields results that contrast sharply with those of the $(10, 60)$ rejection-payoff case, described below.

Finally, the rejection payoffs $(10, 60)$ allow an examination of the most common form of payoff-interdependent theories. If subjects value their own monetary payoff but dislike inequality, as in the models of Bolton and Ockenfels (2000) and Fehr and Schmidt (1999), then subgame perfection calls for player 1 to demand at least forty percent of the surplus, and for such a demand to be accepted.

Figure 4.5 shows that player 1s initially demand about 40 percent of the surplus (the mean player-1 demand over the first ten rounds is 39.8 and the median 38.5), coming very close to the subgame-perfect equilibrium,

19. Would player 2 exhibit the preferences $(10, 10) \succ (75, 25)$ if the choice were given exogenously, rather than arising as a result of player 1's choice? If not, we must question the portability of payoff-interdependent preferences. The generalized dictator games of Andreoni and Miller (2002), in which some dictators give away all of the surplus when faced with exogenously imposed trade-offs that make it efficient to do so, suggest a negative answer. The experiments of Slembeck (1998), in which rejection rates were higher when subjects were presented with exogenously determined choices, and of Blount (1995), in which subjects did not have significantly smaller rejection thresholds when facing a "disinterested" proposer (who did not receive part of the surplus) as when facing an ordinary proposer, are less clear.

and with their demands drifting downward (a mean demand of 36 over the last ten rounds). However, rejection rates are the highest in this treatment, with almost a quarter of the cases in which player 1 demands between 30 and 40 percent of the surplus ending in rejection.[20] A payoff of sixty or slightly higher is not enough to ensure acceptance from player 2.

In summary, we find that (1) our game-I results include replications of standard results for the Ultimatum Game; (2) subjects respond to rejection payoffs, with proposers increasing their demand in response to a high rejection payoff and decreasing their demand when the opponent's rejection payoff is high; and (3) findings for the $(10, 60)$ rejection-payoff specification suggest that something in addition to payoff-interdependent preferences, at least in inequality-aversion forms such as (1)–(2) and (3) (with $\alpha_i \in (-1, 0)$) lies behind the results.

4.4.2 Game II: The Continuation Game

Figure 4.7 provides information on offers and rejection rates in game II. The results in figure 4.7 are reported in terms of the share of the surplus *offered* to player 1, noting that player 1 was the responder in this game.

Game II is an Ultimatum Game, with rejection payoffs of zero. Once we make allowance for the reversal of roles, we again obtain results consistent with previous Ultimatum Game experiments. On average, the proposer demands between 60 and 70 percent of the surplus. Higher demands on the part of the proposer are likely to be rejected, with about 20 percent of plays ending in rejection. Figure 4.8 shows the mean and median percentage of the surplus offered to player 1 by round, showing some initial adjustment followed by relatively unchanging behavior.

Subjects who faced different rejection payoffs in game I face precisely the same game II. However, figures 4.7 and 4.8 suggest that offers in game II vary systematically with the rejection payoffs that prevailed in game I. Subjects who faced rejection payoffs $(10, 60)$ in game I offer more of the surplus to the responder than subjects who experienced rejection payoffs $(10, 10)$, who in turn offer slightly more than those who experienced rejection payoffs $(70, 10)$. Hence rejection payoffs that induced

---

20. Behind the reduction in mean player-1 demand is a more pronounced tightening of the distribution of demands. Over the course of the twenty rounds, there are 146 cases (out of 800) in which player 1 demands more than 40 percent, and hence offers player 2 less than her rejection payoff. However, half (72 of 146) of these demands come in the first four rounds of play. As figure 4.6 shows, some demands that leave player 2 with less than the rejection payoff of 60 are accepted in the early rounds of play, but this behavior has virtually disappeared in the final ten rounds.

Rounds	(V_1, V_2)	Observations	Mean offer	Median	5th %tile	95th %tile
1-10	All	1200	33.4	33	15	50
11-20	All	1200	32.2	31	20	48.5
1-10	(10, 10)	400	32.8	33	19	48
11-20	(10, 10)	400	30.5	30	20	41.5
1-10	(70, 10)	400	28.3	27.5	12	45
11-20	(70, 10)	400	28.0	28	18.5	40
1-10	(10, 60)	400	39.2	41	16.5	55
11-20	(10, 60)	400	38.0	38	24	50

Discount factor	Rejection rates (%)		
	(10, 60)	(70, 10)	(10, 10)
0.2	27	15	22
0.3	22	23	23
0.4	22	23	18
0.5	27	18	16
0.6	25	18	19
0.7	17	22	18
0.8	20	27	12
0.9	17	23	6

Figure 4.7
Player-2 offers (the percentage of the surplus offered to player 1) and player-1 rejection rates in game II. There were five games per round in each of eight treatments per rejection payoffs, for a total of 800 offers in each specification. Rejection rates are given for each combination of rejection payoff and discount factor, over all twenty rounds of play.

more asymmetric divisions of the surplus in game I correspond to game II outcomes with more asymmetric divisions of the surplus. We report tests indicating that these differences are statistically significant in the next section, in the course of comparing games II and III.

It thus appears as if the different game-I specifications condition players to coordinate on different outcomes in game II.[21] On the one hand, this finding provides evidence that subgame consistency fails. At the same time, these results suggest that there are spillovers between games, and hence that the order in which the games are played can matter. The next section shows that play in game III does not vary significantly with the game-I rejection payoff, perhaps because games I and III are less similar than I and II. Could it be that subgame consistency appears to fail, in the form of differing behavior in game II and the second stage of game III,

21. This is reminiscent of the experimental findings of Roth et al. (1991), who find different conventions in Ultimatum Game experiments in different countries.

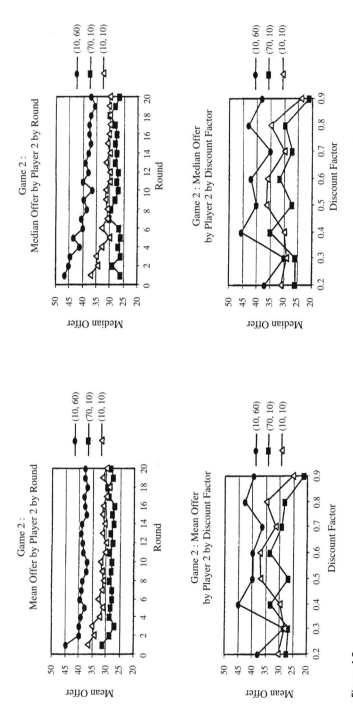

Figure 4.8
Mean and median offers made by player 2 to player 1 in game II, by round and by discount factor, measured as a percentage of the surplus.

simply because game II (and not game III) was affected by previous experience in game I? The differences in game II and the second stage of game III persist even when each of the game-I rejection-payoff cases is examined separately. In addition, these differences take the same direction in each case, even though the three game-I rejection payoffs involve quite different allocations between the two agents and hence would be expected to push game-II behavior in quite different directions. Finally, the effect of game-I rejection payoffs on game-II outcomes are small in comparison to the differences between game II and game III, suggesting that order effects do not lie behind the results.

In contrast to rejection payoffs, differing discount factors, which determine the size of the surplus to be divided, have little effect on the outcome. Figure 4.8 shows mean and median offers by discount factor, revealing no systematic relationship.

In summary, our game-II results are again consistent with standard Ultimatum Game findings.

4.4.3 Games II and III: Subgame Consistency

We now investigate subgame consistency by comparing behavior in the continuation game with that of the second stage of the two-stage game. Of the 2400 initial demands made in the two-stage game, 501 (20.875 percent) were rejected. Figure 4.9 summarizes behavior in the second stage of the two-stage game. As in game II, game-I rejection payoffs are irrelevant in game III, but we will typically report the results for different game-I rejection payoff cases separately.

The mean and median offers for the three rejection-payoff specifications are much closer to one another than they were in game II. Their ranking has also shifted, with the most generous offer now attached to rejection payoff $(10, 10)$ rather than $(10, 60)$. Finally, there is also little pattern to the relationship between discount factors and offers, and there is relatively little difference between the first and last ten rounds of play.

Figures 4.7 and 4.9 show that play in the continuation game and the second stage of game III differs. Proposers are more generous in the second stage of game III, offering a mean percentage of 43.5 (median 44) of the surplus to player 1, as opposed to only 32.8 (median of 32) in the continuation game. This pattern of more generous offers in the second stage of game III holds for every rejection payoff and every discount rate.

Are these differences statistically significant? To address this question, we require an analysis that respects the panel nature of the data. Figure 4.10 reports the results of a random effects regression, with a

Specification	Rounds	Observations	Mean offer	Median	5th %tile	95th %tile
All	1-10	276	43.3	44	23	60
All	11-20	225	43.8	45	25	60
All	1-20	501	43.5	44	25	60
(10, 60)	1-20	136	43.3	44	24	52
(70, 10)	1-20	197	42.0	44	20	59
(10, 10)	1-20	168	45.4	45	32	62
.2	1-20	37	48.6	45	40	62
.3	1-20	47	46.0	47	26	60
.4	1-20	39	43.7	48	15	52
.5	1-20	56	40.3	44	10	75
.6	1-20	44	38.9	37.5	16	53
.7	1-20	70	44.6	45	26	59
.8	1-20	90	41.7	40.5	25	52
.9	1-20	118	44.7	45	33	55

Figure 4.9
Player-2 offers in the second stage of game III, the two-stage game, measured as the percentage of the surplus offered to player 1. "Observations" reports the number of games in which player 2 caused the second stage to be reached by rejecting player 1's first-stage demand. The first three lines report all cases, with a total of 2,400 possible observations over the course of twenty rounds. There are 800 possible observations for each game-I rejection-payoff specification reported in the next three lines, and 300 possible observations for each discount-factor specification.

Independent variable	Estimated coefficient	Standard error	p-value
Intercept (Game II, (10,10))	-.80	.038	.000
Game II, (70,10)	-.19	.054	.001
Game II, (10,60)	.30	.054	.000
Game III, (10,10)	.59	.033	.000
Game III, (70,10)	.56	.059	.000
Game III, (10,60)	.49	.062	.000

Figure 4.10
Random-effects regression results. The dependent variable is $\log y/(100 - y)$, where y is player 2's offer in either the continuation game or the second stage of game III. There are 2,901 observations, 2,400 from the continuation game and 501 from the second stage of game III. Independent variables include an intercept capturing the base case of game II and rejection payoff $(10, 10)$, and dummies capturing departures from the base case for the five remaining combinations of games (II or III) and game-I rejection payoff $((10, 10), (70, 10),$ or $(10, 60))$. "p-Value" is the probability that, given a parameter value of zero, a test statistic appears with absolute value (i.e., a two-tailed test) at least that of the calculated statistic.

transformation of player 2's offer as the dependent variable and with the independent variables including an intercept capturing the base case of game II and rejection payoff $(10, 10)$, and five dummy variables that identify the five remaining combinations of a game (II or III) and one of the three possible rejection payoffs.[22]

The "game II, $(70, 10)$" and "game II, $(10, 60)$" coefficients reported in figure 4.10 identify departures of the game II, $(70, 10)$ and game II, $(10, 60)$ rejection payoff cases from the game II, $(10, 10)$ base case captured by the intercept (shown in bold). These coefficients show that game-II offers are significantly related to game-I rejection payoffs, being highest in the $(10, 60)$ case and lowest in the $(70, 10)$ case. In contrast, a test of the game-III coefficients reveals that offers in game III do not vary significantly in the game-I rejection payoff.

More important, the estimated "game III, $(10, 10)$" coefficient indicates that for the case in which game-I rejection payoffs were $(10, 10)$, game-III offers are higher than game-II offers at any conventional significance level (i.e., a two-tailed test p-value of 0.000), in contrast to the prediction of subgame consistency. It is straightforward to calculate that game-III offers are also higher, at similar significance levels, for the $(70, 10)$ and $(10, 60)$ rejection-payoff cases.

Why are proposers more generous in the second stage of the two-stage game? Figure 4.11 compares rejection rates in the continuation game and the second stage of the two-stage game.

The rates are not too dissimilar, being 29 percent in the second stage of the two-stage game and 20 percent in the continuation game. However, these aggregate rates hide the fact that offers are significantly higher in the second stage of the two-stage game. There are much larger differences in rejection rates conditional on offers. The range of offers [30–40] lies below a typical offer in the second stage of the two-stage game (a mean of 43.5 and median 44), while containing near its bottom end a typical offer in the continuation game (mean of 32.8 and median of 32). Figure 4.11 shows that the rejection rate in the second stage of game III is just

---

22. The transformation of player 2's offer y to $\log y/(100 - y)$, taking $[0, 100]$ into $[-\infty, \infty]$, allows us to capture the restriction that offers must lie in the interval $[0, 100]$. The random effects estimator allows us to capture the fact that the multiple offers of a single player are likely to be correlated. Offers may depend on the history of opponents' actions observed by the offerer. It is appropriate to omit this history from the regression as long as it is not correlated with the offerer-specific error term. Such a correlation could appear, as player i's play could affect the subsequent behavior of opponent j and hence the subsequent history of opponent actions observed by player i, and our implicit assumption is that the resulting correlation is not too large.

		Offers		
Game	Observations	All	30–40	35–45
II	2400	20%		
III	501	29%		
II	1064		15%	
III	131		47%	
II	733			9%
III	190			36%

Figure 4.11
Rejection rates for the continuation game (game II) and the second stage of the two-stage game (game III), in percentages. There were 2,400 plays of each game. In the two-stage game, 501 of these plays reached the second stage.

over three times that of the continuation game, over this range of offers. The range [35–45] lies above a typical offer in the continuation game, and contains near its upper end a typical offer in the second stage of the two-stage game. Here we find rejection rates four times higher in the second stage of the two-stage game. Proposers have good reason to be more generous in the second stage of the two-stage game because responders are much more likely to reject less generous offers.

Are the differences in behavior between the second stage of the two-stage game and the continuation game economically important? Let y_m^{II} be the median offer made in the continuation game, and let y_m^{III} be the median offer in the second stage of the two-stage game. How much would a proposer sacrifice by making offer y_m^{III} in game II? How much by making offer y_m^{II} in game III? Figure 4.12 reports the results. The first eight lines report, for each discount factor, the expected payoff that one would achieve in game II by making the game-II median offer y_m^{II}, and by making the game-III second-stage median offer y_m^{III}. The second eight lines report the payoffs that these offers would receive in the second stage of game III.[23]

In game II, for every discount factor, one is better off making the game-II median offer than the (higher) game-III median, with the latter

---

23. To calculate the expected payoff of an offer y, we must estimate the expected acceptance rate attached to the offer. We first calculated the observed acceptance rate of each offer that appears in the data, given by the proportion of the times the offer was accepted. The "expected" acceptance rate of offer y is then chosen to minimize the sum of the number of higher offers with lower observed acceptance rates and the number of lower offers with higher observed acceptance rates. The minimizer was unique in 24 cases and was an interval in the remaining 8, in which case we chose the midpoint of the interval.

Game	D	II-median, y_m^{II}	Payoff	III-median, y_m^{III}	Payoff
II	.2	31	13	45	11
II	.3	28	19	47	16
II	.4	35	23	48	21
II	.5	33.5	33	44	28
II	.6	35	34	37.5	33
II	.7	31	41	45	39
II	.8	35	52	40.5	48
II	.9	25	68	45	50
III	.2	31	0	45	7
III	.3	28	0	47	13
III	.4	35	0	48	9
III	.5	33.5	0	44	18
III	.6	35	32	37.5	38
III	.7	31	0	45	39
III	.8	35	15	40.5	27
III	.9	25	0	45	41

Figure 4.12
Comparison of expected monetary payoffs in the continuation game (game II) and the second stage of the two-stage game (game III), by discount factor. The y_m^{II} and y_m^{III} columns report the median offers made in games II and III for the relevant discount factor. In the first eight lines, each offer is followed by the expected payoff the offer would receive if made in game II. In the second eight lines, each offer is followed by the expected it would receive if made in the second stage of game III.

sacrificing between 3 ($D = 0.6$) and 27 ($D = 0.9$) percent of the former's expected payoff. These relatively small differences reflect the fact that higher offers reduce the surplus from each agreement but sacrifice no agreements, eliciting a somewhat higher acceptance probability. Results are more dramatic in the second stage of game III. The game-II median offer is sufficiently low as to garner no acceptances in six of the eight cases, hence sacrificing 100 percent of the expected payoff. This reflects the rejection dangers associated with more aggressive offers. The implication is that the differences in game-II and game-III behavior have important payoff consequences, with it being disastrous to treat the second stage of game III as if it were game II.

The differing outcomes of the continuation game and the second stage of game III would be convincing evidence of a failure of subgame consistency if preferences were known and identical across players. However, if preferences are payoff-interdependent, then players may be incompletely informed about their opponents' possibly heterogeneous preferences. This raises two considerations.

First, could proposers in the second stage of the two-stage game be simply reacting to information gleaned about their opponents' preferences

	Accepted demands			Rejected demands		
D	5th %tile	median	95th %tile	5th %tile	median	95th %tile
.2	55	68	77	63	75	81
.3	52	66	77	61	68	80
.4	50	64	70	58	65	80
.5	46	58	66	53	65	78
.6	50	58	66	55	62	70
.7	50	60	65	60	63	79
.8	40	52	60	50	57.5	73
.9	45	51	56	50	55	76

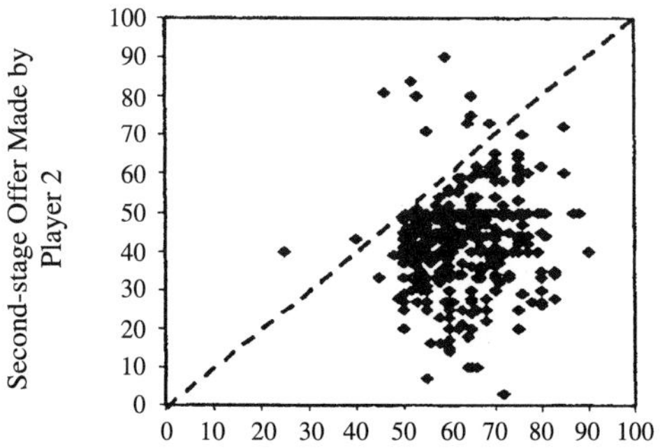

Figure 4.13
The tables show ranges of accepted and rejected demands in the first stage of game III. The figure shows player 2's offer to player 1 in the second stage of the two-stage game, as a function of player 1's demand in the first stage, for those demands that were rejected. Both axes measure the percentage of the surplus accruing to player 1.

from the offer made by their opponents in the first stage? It is not a priori clear which direction this information updating should take. A relatively aggressive demand on the part of player 1 may reveal that 1 is intent on a large share, and hence that player 2 should make a relatively generous offer to player 1 in the next round. Alternatively, an aggressive demand may indicate that 1 is relatively unconcerned with relative-payoff considerations, and hence that 2 can safely make a quite niggardly offer.

In the experiment a wide variety of player-1 demands are rejected. Figure 4.13 shows that there is considerable overlap between the set of accepted and rejected demands. If the value of player 1's demand reveals significant information about player 1, then player-2 offers in the second stage of game III should be systematically related to the value of the player-1 demand that was rejected in order to reach the second stage.

Variable	Estimated coefficient	Standard error	p-value
Intercept, $D = .2$	-.29	1.2	.82
Intercept, $D = .3$	-1.2	.72	.098
Intercept, $D = .4$	-2.4	1.2	.045
Intercept, $D = .5$	-.17	.54	.75
Intercept, $D = .6$	.084	.98	.93
Intercept, $D = .7$	-1.8	.74	.015
Intercept, $D = .8$	.34	.65	.96
Intercept, $D = .9$	-.31	.61	.61
Player-1 demand, $D = .2$	.0073	.017	.67
Player-1 demand, $D = .3$	.015	.010	.152
Player-1 demand, $D = .4$	.036	.018	.044
Player-1 demand, $D = .5$	-.0019	.0082	.82
Player-1 demand, $D = .6$	-.00078	.015	.96
Player-1 demand, $D = .7$	.030	.011	.008
Player-1 demand, $D = .8$	.0016	.010	.88
Player-1 demand, $D = .9$	.0084	.0095	.37
$(V_1, V_2) = (70, 10)$	-.16	.10	.11
$(V_1, V_2) = (10, 60)$	-.064	.10	.54

Figure 4.14
Random effects regression results. The dependent variable is $\log y/(100 - y)$, where y is player 2's offer in the second stage of game III. "Player-1 demand" is the demand rejected by player 2 to reach the second stage. Dummy variables are used to estimate the deviation of the intercept and slope term (on player-1 demand), for each discount factor, from the base-case relationship (shown in bold) of $D = 0.5$.

Figure 4.13 plots player 2's offer to player 1 in the second stage of the two-stage game, as a function of player 1's demand in the first stage, for those 501 demands that were rejected.[24] As expected, the observations cluster below the diagonal: player 2 is generally less generous to player 1 than is player 1. More important, there appears to be little relationship between the rejected demand and the subsequent offer. However, figure 4.13 aggregates over all the discount factor specifications. We expect first-stage demands to vary systematically with the discount factor (as figure 4.17 below confirms), rendering such aggregation suspect. Figure 4.14 reports the results of a random-effects regression of (a transformation of) player 2's second-stage offer on player 1's first-stage demand, once again finding little relationship. In the base case of $D = 0.5$, player 2's second-stage offer does not vary significantly in player 1's first-stage demand.

24. In 217 of the 501 cases in which player 2 rejected, the subsequent offer was "disadvantageous," in the sense that it provided player 2 (if accepted) with a discounted *monetary* payoff lower than the monetary payoff 2 would have secured by accepting player 1's first-stage demand. Ochs and Roth (1989) draw attention to disadvantageous counteroffers in two-stage bargaining experiments, citing them as evidence that subjects must be concerned with more than simply their own monetary payoffs.

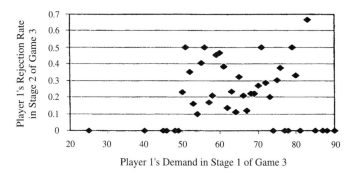

Figure 4.15
Player 1's rejection rate in the second stage of game III, as a function of the first-period demand that player 1 had rejected in order to reach the second stage.

Only the cases $D = 0.7$ and $D = 0.4$ show significant departures from this
base case, with the latter somewhat weaker than the former. Player 2s do
not appear to be drawing useful inferences from the magnitude of player
1's rejected demand.

An examination of player 1's behavior in the second stage of game III
suggests that there is little for player 2 to learn from observing player 1's
first-period demand. Figure 4.15 shows player 1's rejection rate of player
2's offers in the second stage of game III, as a function of the first-period
demand that player 1 had rejected in order to reach the second stage.
There is scant evidence of a systematic relationship. Decomposing these
data by discount factor and controlling for player 2's second-stage offer,
though hampered by very small sample sizes, yields similar results. An
appeal to incomplete information cannot readily reconcile the observed
behavior with payoff-interdependent preferences.

Second, the second stage of game III can only be reached if player 2
rejects player 1's initial demand. Could play in the continuation game differ from that of the second stage of game III because the latter game is
not played by a random sample of player 2s? Notice that one's initial intuition here works the wrong way. We would expect player 2s who reject
to be more aggressive than those who do not, leading to lower rather than
higher offers in the second stage of game III. Figure 4.16 reports results
for game II, analogous to those reported in figure 4.7, but restricts attention to experimental subjects who rejected at least one demand when
playing as player 2 in game III. A comparison with figure 4.7 shows that
the differences are slight and the directions are mixed. The game-II average offer of those with $(10, 60)$ rejection-payoffs who rejected at least one
offer in game III is larger than the overall average, with the opposite rela-

Rounds	(V_1, V_2)	Observations	Mean offer	Median	5th %tile	95th %tile
1-10	All	777	33.5	33	16	50
11-20	All	780	32.4	31	20	49
1-10	(10, 10)	248	32.9	32	20	48
11-20	(10, 10)	242	30.3	30	21	41
1-10	(70, 10)	285	27.6	26	10	45
11-20	(70, 10)	283	27.5	27	17	40
1-10	(10, 60)	244	40.8	43	24	52
11-20	(10, 60)	255	39.9	40	28	50

Figure 4.16
Player-2 offers in game II, measuring the percentage of the surplus offered to player 1, as in figure 4.7, but for those subjects who reject a demand in game III.

tion holding for $(70, 10)$ rejection payoffs. There is little evidence that the second stage of game III is played by a sufficiently atypical group of player 2s as to reconcile game-II and game-III second-stage behavior.[25]

In summary, we find that subgame consistency fails, and does so systematically. Players make less aggressive offers in the second stage of a two-stage game than in an equivalent, stand-alone game. There is evidence that information is incomplete, in the form of rejected first-stage offers in the two-stage game, but the failure of second-stage behavior to depend on the magnitude of the rejected first-stage demand suggests that this does not provide a useful explanation for the differences between game II and the second stage of game III. Similarly the evidence is that self-selection bias in determining which player 2's participate in the second stage of the two-stage game does not provide a useful explanation.

4.4.4 Games III and IV: Truncation Consistency
We next consider truncation consistency, which we examine by comparing the initial demands in games III and IV. Figure 4.17 shows the mean and median demands made by player 1 in the first stage of the two-stage game, as a function of the discount factor and the game-I rejection payoffs. (Again, the game-I rejection payoffs are relevant only in game I.) As

---

25. We can pursue this possibility further by examining "chronic rejecters," namely subjects who frequently rejected demands while playing as player 2 in game III. Consider subjects who rejected five or more demands in the first stage of game III. The average game-II offers made by these subjects (all rounds) were 27.5 (all rejection payoffs), 30.2 (the 10, 10 case), 22.1 (the 70, 10 case), and 35.7 (the 10, 60 case). Hence chronic rejecters made even smaller offers when playing game II, rendering it all the less likely that the relatively large offers encountered in the second stage of game III can be attributed to nonrandomness in the selection of player 2s.

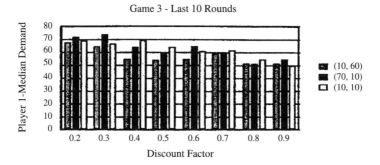

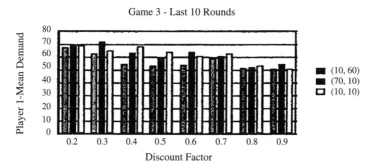

Figure 4.17
Mean and median demands made by player 1 in the first stage of the two-stage game, measured as a percentage of the surplus.

the discount factor increases from 0.2 to 0.9, player 1's mean demand falls from about 70 to about 50 percent of the surplus. Subgame perfection predicts that player 1's demand should decrease in the discount factor, but at a more precipitous rate, falling from 80 percent to 10 percent as D increases from 0.2 to 0.9. The data shown in figure 4.17 are similar to data displayed in figure 5.6 of Davis and Holt (1993, p. 272), which summarizes a variety of experiments with two-stage games.

Each subject i in game IV was characterized by a pair $(Z_1(i), Z_2(i))$, which varied across subjects. Each time two subjects i and j were matched to play the game (in roles 1 and 2), the rejection payoffs were given by $Z_1(i)$ (for player i in role 1) and $Z_2(j)$ (player j in role 2). The following section discusses how the values $(Z_1(i), Z_2(i))$ were determined. For the purposes of this section, it matters only that these values varied across subjects and were commonly known in each game, so the first-stage demands can be expected to vary systematically as do the values (Z_1, Z_2).

We can similarly think of first-stage demands in game III as depending on the player-1 and player-2 values of proceeding to the second stage, which we denote by (Z_1^{III}, Z_2^{III}). If truncation consistency holds, and if play reflects rational behavior given payoff-interdependent preferences, then initial demands in game IV should bear the same relationship to $(Z_1(i), Z_2(j))$ as initial demands in game III to (Z_1^{III}, Z_2^{III}). Our investigation of truncation consistency thus estimates (Z_1^{III}, Z_2^{III}), and then examines the relationship between initial demands in games III and IV and the values (Z_1^{III}, Z_2^{III}) and (Z_1, Z_2), respectively.

Because we are interested in the explanatory power of rational behavior, given payoff-interdependency, we use observed play in the second stage of game III to estimate the expected payoffs (Z_1^{III}, Z_2^{III}). However, some difficulties are raised by the potential heterogeneity in preferences among anonymously matched opponents. In the presence of such heterogeneity, first-stage demands in principle depend on player 1's expectation of (Z_1^{III}, Z_2^{III}), as well as 1's expectation of 2's expectation of (Z_1^{III}, Z_2^{III}), and 1's expectation of 2's expectation of 1's expectation of (Z_1^{III}, Z_2^{III}), and so on. We cannot estimate this entire infinite hierarchy, and must focus on what we expect to be the most salient variables. The greater is the amount of variation in second-stage payoffs explained by variations in the discount factor, and the less important are player idiosyncrasies, the more likely is this hierarchy to be captured by a single pair of values. This observation motivates the wide range of discount factors incorporated in our experimental design.

Since we are interested in the determinants of player 1's initial demand, we first consider player 1's expectation of (Z_1^{III}, Z_2^{III}), which we denote by $(Z_1^{III1}(i), Z_2^{III1}(i))$, where i is the subject acting as player 1 in game III. We take $Z_1^{III1}(i)$ to be the average of the player-1 payoffs in those second-stage games in which player i participated, and take $Z_2^{III1}(i)$ to be the average of the player-2 payoffs in those games.[26]

Figure 4.18 presents the results of random-effects regression with data drawn from games III and IV.[27] The dependent variable is a transforma-

---

26. The more dispersed are realized payoffs, the greater is the extent to which an approach based on such averages requires utility functions that are not too nonlinear, as in (2) or (3).

27. In game III, the sample is restricted to subjects who participated in the second stage of game III at least once, and hence for whom we can estimate $(Z_1^{III1}(i), Z_2^{III1}(i))$. These subjects played game III as player 1 a total of 2,229 times which, together with 2,400 instances of game IV, gives us 4,629 observations.

Independent variable	Estimated coefficient	Standard error	p-value
Intercept	.63	.027	.000
Player-1 payoff	.030	.0011	.000
Player-2 payoff	-.027	.00058	.000
Player-1 payoff, Game III	-.035	.0017	.000
Player-2 payoff, Game III	.025	.0012	.000
(70,10)	.024	.031	.44
(10,60)	-.21	.032	.000

Figure 4.18
Random effects estimates of player 1's first-stage demand in games III and IV. The dependent variable is $\log x/(100 - x)$, where x is player 1's demand in the first stage of game III or game IV. The player-1 and player-2 payoffs are (Z_1, Z_2) for game-IV observations and (Z_1^{III1}, Z_2^{III1}) for game-III observations. "Player-1 payoff, game III" and "player-2 payoff, game III" are dummy variables, indicating how the coefficients on player-1 and player-2 payoffs for game III differ from the game-IV base case. The game-I rejection payoff $(10, 10)$ is the intercept base case, with dummy variables for the $(70, 10)$ and $(10, 60)$ cases.

tion of the demand made by player 1 in the first period of the game, where this is a demand in game III for some observations and a demand in game IV for others. The independent variables include an intercept term and two intercept dummy variables to identify the $(70, 10)$ and $(10, 60)$ game-I rejection payoff cases (the base case is $(10, 10)$). The variables "player-1 payoff" and "player-2 payoff" identify the expected payoffs following a rejection in game III or IV. These variables are given by $(Z_1^{III1}(i), Z_2^{III1}(i))$ for observations taken from game III and by $(Z_1(i), Z_2(j))$ for observations taken from game IV. In addition, we include two slope dummy variables, ("player-1 payoff, game III" and "player-2 payoff, game III"), to capture differences, across games III and IV, in the relationship between initial demands and the payoffs that follow a rejection. If truncation consistency holds, these latter dummy variables should be zero.

The coefficient on "player-2 payoff" in figure 4.18 is negative. Hence the larger is the rejection payoff for player 2, the more moderate is 1's initial demand. The coefficient on the "player-2 payoff, game III" dummy identifies how the dependence of game-III initial demands on player-2 rejection payoffs differs from that of game IV. This coefficient is (significantly) positive, and smaller in absolute value than the "player-2 payoff" coefficient. Hence initial demands in game III are again decreasing in player 2's rejection payoff, but are much less sensitive to the latter.[28] The coefficient on "player-1 payoff" is positive, indicating that player 1

---

28. That is, the sum of the "player-2 payoff" and "player-2 payoff, game III" coefficients is negative, but smaller in absolute value than the "player-2 payoff" coefficient.

tends to be more aggressive in game IV when 1 has a larger rejection payoff. But the "Player-1, game III" dummy is negative, again indicating that this sensitivity is attenuated in game III.[29]

Our basic result is then that player-1 initial demands are significantly less sensitive to rejection payoffs in game III, which appear as the result of play in a continuation game, than to rejection payoffs in game IV, which are part of the specification of the game. In contrast to the prediction of truncation consistency, players react more sharply to variations in fixed terminal payoffs than they do to equivalent variations in the expected value of a continuation game.

Are the differences shown in figure 4.18 economically relevant? From figure 4.18, which gives $\log x/(100 - \log x)$ as a function of V_2, we can calculate that, in game IV, $dx/dV_2 \approx -0.8$, so that 80 percent of an increase in player 2's rejection payoff V_2 is translated into a decrease in player 1's initial demand x. This is a smaller response than the derivative of -1 that would characterize subgame perfection given monetary payoff maximization, but a much larger response than that described by the corresponding derivative for game III, where $dx/dV_2 \approx -0.2$. The latter calculation, which is consistent with the results shown in figure 4.17, shows that players react quite sluggishly to changes in rejection payoffs generated by continuation games.

Are these results robust to our estimation of game III second-stage payoff expectations? We can explore alternatives. First, the average $Z_1^{III1}(i)$ may involve second-stage player-1 payoffs from cases in which subject i occupied the role of player 2. These in turn may involve accept/reject decisions that subject i would have made differently, and which hence may present a misleading estimate of subject i's expected payoff from playing the second stage as player 1. To examine this possibility, we restrict the calculation of $Z_1^{III1}(i)$ to those cases in which i plays the second stage as player 1, calling the estimate $\hat{Z}_1^{III1}$. In addition player 1's expectation of Z_2^{III} may be less important than 1's estimate of 2's estimate of Z_2^{III}, since the latter is likely to play the major role in shaping 2's accept/reject decision in stage 1. We accordingly replace Z_2^{III1} with $\hat{Z}_2^{III21}$, 1's expectation of 2's expectation of 2's payoff in the second stage, calculated as the average payoff realized by player 2 in those second-stage games in which agent i fills the role of player 1.

---

29. In this case, adding the dummy to the base coefficient gives a negative value, indicating that 1's demands in game III are *inversely* related to 1's rejection payoffs. This reflects the fact that Z_1^{III1} and Z_2^{III1} tend to be positively correlated, as both vary positively in the discount factor, with the dominant effect on player-1 demands being the inverse relationship with Z_2^{III1}.

Independent variable	Estimated coefficient	Standard error	p-value
Intercept	.64	.026	.000
Player-1 payoff	.029	.0011	.000
Player-2 payoff	-.027	.00058	.000
Player-1 payoff, Game III	-.030	.0015	.000
Player-2 payoff, Game III	.022	.0010	.000
(70,10)	.028	.032	.38
(10,60)	-.19	.033	.000

Figure 4.19
Random effects estimates of player 1's first-stage demand in games III and IV, as in figure 4.17, but with $(Z_1^{III1}(i), Z_2^{III1}(i))$ replaced by $(\hat{Z}_1^{III1}(i), \hat{Z}_2^{III21}(i))$.

Figure 4.19 duplicates the analysis of figure 4.18, using the alternative measures $(\hat{Z}_1^{III1}(i), \hat{Z}_2^{III21}(i))$. The results are familiar. The coefficient on "Player-2 payoff" is (significantly) negative, so that player 1's game-IV initial demand is more moderate for larger player-2 rejection payoffs. The "Player-2 payoff, game III" dummy is (significantly) positive, and smaller in absolute value. Hence initial demands in game III are again decreasing in player 2's rejection payoff but are much less sensitive to the latter. In this case the calculated derivatives are $dx/dV_2 \approx -0.7$ in game IV, and $dx/dV_2 \approx -0.1$ in game III. Once again, players are much more sensitive to changes in terminal payoffs than to equivalent changes in the expected value of a continuation game.

Next, we would like to investigate the effect of simply using 2's expectation of 2's payoff, rather than 1's expectation of 2's expectation, which suggests replacing $\hat{Z}_2^{III21}(i)$ with $\hat{Z}_2^{III2}(j)$ (when subject i plays j), where the latter measures the average payoff earned in those second-stage games in which subject j acted as player 2.[30] In addition we note that when calculating $\hat{Z}_1^{III1}$, those cases in which subject i, in the role of player 1, rejects a second-stage offer add a zero payoff to $Z_1^{III1}(i)$ while having no effect on $\hat{Z}_2^{III21}(i)$ (or $\hat{Z}_2^{III2}(j)$). This is likely to underestimate i's payoff, since i has revealed that i's realized utility, from payoffs $(0,0)$, is higher than the utility of accepting 2's offer, which in turn is likely to exceed the utility of the effectively recorded outcome $(0, Z_2^{III2}(j))$. The best available correction is to calculate 1's payoff as the average of the *offers* made to subject i when playing the second stage as player 1 (though this still potentially underestimates i's utility in those cases in which i rejects), de-

---

30. If this change makes little difference, then we have evidence that our results are not sensitive to which expectation involving player 2's payoff we choose from the infinite hierarchy of possibilities. More generally, there are numerous alternatives for examining the robustness of the results. We found none that made a significant difference.

Independent variable	Estimated coefficient	Standard error	p-value
Intercept	1.1	.030	.000
Player-1 payoff	.018	.0013	.000
Player-2 payoff	-.032	.00066	.000
Player-1 payoff, Game III	-.027	.0015	.000
Player-2 payoff, Game III	-.022	.00098	.000
(70,10)	.015	.026	.57
(10,60)	-.16	.027	.000

Figure 4.20
Random effects estimates of player 1's first-stage demand in games III and IV, as in figure 4.17, but with $(Z_1^{III1}(i), Z_2^{III1}(i))$ replaced by $(\tilde{Z}_1^{III1}(i), \tilde{Z}_2^{III2}(i))$.

noted by $\tilde{Z}_1^{III1}(i)$. Similarly we are likely to underestimate 2's utility in those cases in which 2 makes a second-stage offer that is rejected. In this case we do not have any attractive alternative estimates of 2's utility available, since (unlike the situation of player 1) we cannot conclude that 2 preferred that the offer be rejected. We accordingly restrict our calculation of 2's payoff to those cases in which 2's offer is accepted, denoted by $\tilde{Z}_1^{III2}(j)$.

Figure 4.20 reports the corresponding estimates, again with familiar results. The coefficient on "player-2 payoff" is (significantly) negative, while the "player-2 payoff, game III" dummy is (significantly) negative but smaller in absolute value. Hence initial demands in games III and IV are both decreasing in player 2's rejection payoff, but are much less sensitive to the latter in game III. In this case the estimated derivatives are $dx/dV_2 \approx -0.8$ in game IV and $dx/dV_2 \approx -0.2$ in game III.

In summary, truncation consistency does not hold. It makes a difference whether a rejected offer is followed by a pair of fixed payoffs, or by a continuation game whose expected outcome matches those fixed payoffs. Initial demands are much more sensitive to changes in terminal payoffs than to equivalent changes in the expected value of a continuation game.[31] These results are consistent across a variety of methods for estimating the expected payoffs following a game-III first-stage rejection.

---

31. Beard and Beil (1994) suggest a similar conclusion. They examine a game in which player 1 can either choose L, ending the game with a known pair of monetary payoffs, or choose R, in which case player 2 chooses between l or r, each ending the game with known payoffs. The payoffs are chosen so that R, r is the unique subgame-perfect equilibrium (if utility depends only upon one's own earnings), but so that R, l is worse for player 1 than L. Their experimental finding is that player 1s quite often choose the "safe" outcome of L rather than risk a suboptimal choice of l on the part of player 2, with the incidence of such choices depending in expected ways upon payoff magnitudes. They suggest that player 1s appear to be more responsive to the payoff following L than to the expected payoff of the subgame following R, attributing this to a preference for certain payoffs that players can ensure over uncertain ones, which players cannot ensure.

4.4.5   Games II, III and IV: Subgame and Truncation Consistency

This section provides a joint test of subgame and truncation consistency, based on comparing first-period demands in game III with demands in game IV.

Each experimental subject i in game IV was characterized by an idiosyncratic pair of rejection payoffs $(Z_1(i), Z_2(i))$, one when playing as player 1 and one when playing as player 2. In each play of game IV, rejection payoffs were commonly known, and given by $(Z_1(i), Z_2(j))$, where player 1 was subject i and player 2 was j. Our intention was that the rejection payoffs (Z_1, Z_2) would equal the subjects' expected payoffs from playing game II, the continuation game. If subgame consistency holds, then these payoffs would also equal the expected payoffs of the second stage of the two-stage game. If truncation consistency also holds, play in the first stage of game III should be identical to play in game IV.

The previous subsection described a variety of alternatives estimating the expected payoff of playing the second stage of game III or, equivalently, playing the continuation game. Our experimental design required one of these estimates to be built into the experiment in the calculation of Z_1 and Z_2. In making this choice, we were anxious to provide the most favorable environment for payoff-interdependent preferences, and hence were anxious not to underestimate *utility* when offers are rejected. We accordingly employed the final alternative investigated in the previous subsection, taking $Z_1(i)$ to be the average offer received by subject i when playing as player 1 in the continuation game, and taking $Z_2(j)$ to be the average payoff realized by subject j player in those periods in which j played as player 2 in the continuation game and made an offer that was accepted.

Figure 4.21 reports the resulting mean rejection payoffs for game IV. As expected, rejection payoffs are larger for larger discount factors. The rejection payoffs allocate about two-thirds of the surplus to player 2 and one-third to player 1. The latter percentage varies with the discount factor, but again in no systematic way. The mean rejection payoffs virtually exhaust the surplus in each case, consistent with a rejection-payoff calculation designed to capture expected utilities, where player 1 prefers disagreement to the offers 1 rejects.

Figure 4.22 compares player-1 demands in games III and IV. We concentrate on the final ten rounds of play in this section, though expanding to all twenty rounds makes virtually no difference. (Once again, the rejection payoffs (V_1, V_2), being $(10, 10)$, $(10, 60)$, or $(70, 10)$, are irrelevant for games III and IV.) If subgame and truncation consistency hold, then

Discount	Obs.	Z_1	Z_2	$Z_1 + Z_2$	Surplus	$Z_1\%$	$Z_2\%$
.2	30	6.3	13.4	19.7	20	32	67
.3	30	8.4	21.5	29.9	30	28	72
.4	30	14.4	25.2	39.6	40	36	63
.5	30	17.2	32.4	49.6	50	34	65
.6	30	22.0	37.4	59.4	60	37	62
.7	30	22.6	46.7	69.3	70	32	67
.8	30	28.1	51.1	79.2	80	35	64
.9	30	25.8	63.7	89.5	90	28	71

Figure 4.21
Mean rejection payoffs for game IV by discount factor. There were three treatments for each discount factor (one for each game-I rejection payoff (V_1, V_2)), with ten subjects in each treatment, for a total of 30 rejection payoffs for each discount factor and player role. The mean of these 30 payoffs is reported in each case. Z_1 and Z_2 percentages are player 1 and 2's average rejection payoff as a percentage of the total surplus.

player-1 demands in games III and IV should be identical. Figure 4.22 indicates that for low discount factors, mean and median demands are similar. However, as the discount factor increases, the mean and median demands fall much more rapidly in game IV than in game III. As a result of this sluggish game-III response, proposers are more aggressive in game III than in game IV, for high discount factors.

Figure 4.23 provides evidence that the differing behavior in games III and IV is important, comparing the mean amount of surplus offered to player 2 in the first stage of games III and IV with player 2's mean rejection payoff in game IV, for large discount factors. In every case the game-IV mean player-1 demand yields a higher payoff to player 2 than does the mean rejection payoff. If the subgame and truncation consistency holds, we can expect the same of the game-III mean demand. However, in every case the game-III mean player-1 demand is sufficiently aggressive as to leave player 2 with a lower payoff than the game-IV mean rejection payoff.

It is intuitive that there should be little difference between games III and IV when discount factors are small. In this case, the rejection payoffs in game IV are small, and the second stage in game III is relatively unimportant. As the discount factor grows, rejection payoffs become larger in game IV and the second stage becomes more important in game III, magnifying behavioral differences.

We can illustrate the difference between games III and IV. For each of the 240 subjects, we can calculate the subject's mean demand as player 1 in games III and IV. Figure 4.24 shows the demands. (Analogous results obtain for median demands.) Low discount factors give rise to relatively

Discount	Obs.	III mean	III median	IV mean	IV median
			Rejection payoffs (10, 10)		
.2	50	69.3	69	70.9	71.5
.3	50	65.5	66.5	65.1	65
.4	50	68.6	69	61.5	61
.5	50	63.9	64	61.1	61
.6	50	61.0	61	55.0	55
.7	50	62.8	62	47.0	47
.8	50	53.4	55	42.3	41
.9	50	50.9	50	29.6	30
			Rejection payoffs (10, 60)		
.2	50	68.0	68	70.5	70
.3	50	62.8	65	67.6	68
.4	50	55.1	55	54.8	55.5
.5	50	53.7	54	54.4	54
.6	50	54.5	55	56.5	55
.7	50	59.0	59	52.4	53
.8	50	51.8	52	50.4	50
.9	50	51.4	51.5	44.5	46
			Rejection payoffs (70, 10)		
.2	50	69.0	72	70.1	70
.3	50	72.5	74	66.4	66
.4	50	63.8	64	57.2	58
.5	50	59.3	59	53.1	53.5
.6	50	64.1	65	51.6	50
.7	50	61.0	60	43.0	43.5
.8	50	52.3	52	36.4	36
.9	50	54.7	55	26.7	26

Figure 4.22
Player-1 demands in the first stage of game III and game IV. Data are taken from the last ten rounds in each case. For each discount-factor and rejection-payoff combination, there were ten rounds of five games each, for 50 observations.

large demands, in which case game-III and game-IV demands are similar. However, higher discount factors give rise to lower demands, in which case player 1s demand significantly more in game III than in game IV, reflecting the relatively sluggish response of game-III demands to discount factors.

To examine the significance of these differences, figure 4.25 reports estimations of subjects' mean and median initial demands in game III as a function of their initial median demands in game IV. Subgame and truncation consistency combine to predict a zero intercept and unitary slope, indicating that there is no systematic difference between the two games.

Discount	(V_1, V_2)	Obs.	100-(III mean)	mean Z_2	100-(IV mean)
.7	(10, 10)	50	37.2	47.3	53.0
.8	(10, 10)	50	46.6	52.0	57.7
.9	(10, 10)	50	49.1	67.2	70.4
.7	(10, 60)	50	41.0	44.2	47.6
.8	(10, 60)	50	48.2	44.5	49.6
.9	(10, 60)	50	48.6	53.7	55.5
.7	(70, 10)	50	39.0	48.3	57.0
.8	(70, 10)	50	47.7	56.7	63.6
.9	(70, 10)	50	45.3	70.1	73.3

Figure 4.23
Amount of the surplus that mean player-1 demands allocate to player 2, in the first stage of game III (100 − (III mean)) and in game IV (100 − (IV mean)).

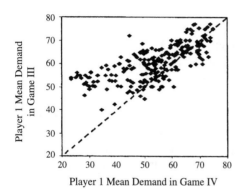

Player 1 Mean Demand in Game IV

Figure 4.24
Plot of player-1 mean demand in game IV (horizontal axis) and the first stage of game III (vertical axis), taken from the last ten rounds of play. There are 240 observations, one for each of the 240 experimental subjects.

Dependent variable	Observations	Intercept	Game-IV demand
Game-III mean demand	240	.37 (.015, (.34, .40))	.43 (0.028, (.37,.48))
Game-III median demand	240	.37 (.016, (.34, .40))	.42 (0.029, (.37,.48))

Figure 4.25
Linear regressions of transformations of player 1's mean and median demand in the first stage of game III on player 1's median and mean demand in game IV confidence intervals.

Instead, the intercept is greater than zero and the slope is less than one (both at a p-value of 0.000), as we would expect if player 1 consistently demands more in game III than in game IV when the discount factor is high.

In summary, our comparison of games III and IV suggests a failure of at least one of subgame and truncation consistency, leading to systematic differences in play in the first stage of game III and play in game IV. The differences appear primarily for high discount factors, when rejection payoffs in game IV are high and the second stage of game III is relatively important. In such cases opening demands are more aggressive in game III than in game IV.

These results are consistent with our separate tests of subgame and truncation consistency. When the discount factor is small, games III and IV are both quite similar to an Ultimatum Game, and yield similar play. As the discount factor rises, so does player 2s payoff in the continuation game, and hence 2's rejection payoff in game IV, leading to lower player-1 demands. A similar force appears in game III as the second stage becomes more valuable. As section 4.4.3 shows, however, player 2s value in the second stage of game III is less than that of the continuation game, reflecting 2's less aggressive play (and 1's more aggressive play) in game III's second stage. In addition section 4.4.4 shows that initial play is less responsive to changes in the expected value of a second stage than to changes in a corresponding terminal payoff. These failures of subgame and truncation consistency reinforce one another. A rising discount factor causes a smaller increase in player 2s rejection value in game III than in game IV, and player 1 is less sensitive to changes in the rejection value in game III than in game IV. Together, the result is that player 1s demands show less variation in game III than in game IV, leading to the result shown in figure 4.24.

4.5 Conclusion

Our experimental results provide several indications that payoff-interdependent preferences and backward induction, in the form of subgame and truncation consistency, are inconsistent. The second stage of the two-stage game features more generous player-2 offers than does the (identical) continuation game. This is a failure of subgame consistency: players regard the second stage of the two-stage game and a seemingly stand-alone equivalent as different strategic situations. Making an offer to someone whose demand you have just rejected, in the second stage of the two-stage game, is not viewed as equivalent to opening the seemingly identical continuation game, with no history of interaction. Truncation consistency also fails. Players are more responsive to variations in future prospects when a rejection leads to a fixed pair of rejection payoffs, as opposed to the case in which a rejection leads to a game involving another offer and response.

Attention now turns either to alternative formulations of preferences or to models of behavior that do not depend on backward induction. Because the self-references or additional arguments built into more complicated preference formulations can deprive backward induction of its content, it is not clear that these are distinct alternatives.

Our findings reinforce those of Andreoni et al. (2002), who show that payoff interdependence alone cannot account for behavior in public-good provision experiments.[32] Instead, changes in the extensive form of the game prompt changes in behavior that are inconsistent with preferences that depend on only payoffs. Our results are similar in spirit, suggesting that preferences in seemingly identical games depend upon the larger context in which the games are played. Andreoni et al. (2002) suggest incorporating the specification of the game into the utility function, allowing players to have different preferences over identical monetary payoff vectors in different games. Given the mounting experimental evidence, such an approach seems inevitable if the results are to be explained in terms of more elaborate utility functions. However, the results will be useful only if some portability of the preferences can be recovered, in the form of some systematic view of the relationship between the specification of the game and preferences.

We suspect the key to such portability lies in a more systematic investigation of how people think about games. Psychologists direct attention to the use of analogy when reasoning about novel problems (e.g., Holyoak and Thagard 1996). We envision players as analyzing unfamiliar games or subgames by drawing analogies to more familiar contexts. Subgame consistency will then obtain if the considerations that shape these analogies are precisely those captured by the extensive-form specification of a game. As a result subgame consistency and backward induction would be compelling in the classical view of game theory, in which games are complete literal representations of strategic interactions. But game theory is typically used not as a literal description but as a *model* of a more

---

32. Prasnikar and Roth (1992) explore similar games and issues.

complicated strategic interaction, and there is no reason to believe that the extensive form constructed by an analyst exactly captures the considerations used by players to analyze the interaction. If not, subgame and truncation consistency can be expected to fail. Anticipating this failure, however, makes many seemingly anomalous experimental findings less puzzling. Framing effects are now expected, for example, as differing details of the experimental environment trigger varying analogies. Nor is it a surprise that rejecting an offer might bring a new analogy into play, or that fixed rejection payoffs and continuation games trigger different analogies. Our hope is that a theory of reasoning by analogy will lead to a more useful model of behavior in games. Samuelson (2001) begins the construction of such a theory.

References

K. Abbink, G. E. Bolton, A. Sadrieh, and F.-F. Tang. 1996. Adaptive learning versus punishment in ultimatum bargaining. Mimeo. University of Bonn and Pennsylvania State University.

J. Andreoni, P. M. Brown, and L. Vesterlund. 2002. What produces fairness? Some experimental results. *Games Econ. Behav.*, 40: 1–24.

J. Andreoni and J. H. Miller. 2002. Giving according to GARP: An experimental test of the rationality of altruism. *Econometrica* 70: 737–54.

T. R. Beard and R. Beil. 1994. Do people rely on the self-interested maximization of others? An experimental test. *Manage. Sci.* 40: 252–62.

K. Binmore, P. Morgan, A. Shaked, and J. Sutton. 1991. Do people exploit their bargaining power? An experimental study. *Games Econ. Behav.* 3: 295–322.

K. Binmore, C. Proulx, L. Samuelson, and J. Swierzbinski. 1998. Hard bargains and lost opportunities. *Econ. J.* 108: 1279–98.

K. Binmore, A. Shaked, and J. Sutton. 1985. Testing noncooperative bargaining theory: A preliminary study. *Amer. Econ. Rev.* 75: 1178–80.

K. Binmore, A. Shaked, and J. Sutton. 1989. An outside option experiment. *Quart. J. Econ.* 104: 753–70.

S. Blount. 1995. When social outcomes aren't fair: The effect of causal attributions on preferences. *Organ. Behav. Human Decision Processes* 63: 131–44.

G. E. Bolton. 1991. A comparative model of bargaining: Theory and evidence. *Amer. Econ. Rev.* 81: 1096–1136.

G. E. Bolton, J. Brandts, and A. Ockenfels. 1998. Measuring motivations for the reciprocal responses observed in a simple dilemma game. *Exper. Econ.* 1: 207–19.

G. E. Bolton and A. Ockenfels. 2000. ERC: A theory of equity, reciprocity and competition. *Amer. Econ. Rev.* 90: 166–93.

G. E. Bolton and R. Zwick. 1995. Anonymity versus punishment in ultimatum bargaining. *Games Econ. Behav.* 10: 95–121.

C. F. Camerer, E. J. Johnson, T. Rymon, and S. Sen. 1993. Cognition and framing in sequential bargaining for gains and losses. In K. Binmore, A. Kirman, and P. Tani, eds., *Frontiers of Game Theory*. Cambridge: MIT Press, pp. 27–48.

R. Cooper, D. V. DeJong, R. Forsythe, and T. W. Ross. 1994. Alternative institutions for resolving coordination problems: Experimental evidence on forward induction and preplay communication. In J. W. Friedman, ed., *Problems of Coordination in Economic Activity.* Boston: Kluwer Academic, pp. 129–46.

M. Costa-Gomez and K. G. Zauner. 2001. Ultimatum bargaining behavior in Israel, Japan, Slovenia, and the United States: A social utility analysis. *Games Econ. Behav.* 34: 238–70.

D. D. Davis and C. A. Holt. 1993. Experimental Economics. Princeton: Princeton University Press.

M. Dufwenberg and U. Gneezy. 1996. Efficiency, reciprocity, and expectations in an experimental game. Discussion paper 9679. CentER for Economic Research, Tilburg University.

M. Dufwenberg and G. Kirchsteiger. 1998. A theory of sequential reciprocity. Discussion paper 9837. CentER for Economic Research, Tilburg University.

A. Falk and U. Fishbacher. 1999. A theory of reciprocity. Mimeo. University of Zurich.

E. Fehr and K. M. Schmidt. 1999. A theory of fairness, competition and cooperation. *Quart. J. Econ.* 114: 817–68.

W. Güth, R. Schmittberger, and B. Schwarze. 1982. An experimental analysis of ultimatum bargaining. *J. Econ. Behav. Organ.* 3: 367–88.

W. Güth and R. Tietz. 1990. Ultimatum bargaining behavior: A survey and comparison of experimental results. *J. Econ. Psych.* 11: 417–49.

J. C. Harsanyi and R. Selten. 1988. *A General Theory of Equilibrium Selection in Games.* Cambridge: MIT Press.

D. J. Holt. 1999. An empirical model of strategic choice with an application to coordination games. *Games Econ. Behav.* 27: 86–105.

K. J. Holyoak and P. Thagard. 1996. *Mental Leaps.* Cambridge: MIT Press.

E. J. Johnson, C. Camerer, S. Sen, and T. Rymon. 2002. Detecting failures of backward induction: Monitoring information search in sequential bargaining. *J. Econ. Theory* 104: 16–47.

J. H. Kagel, C. Kim, and D. Moser. 1996. Fairness in ultimatum games with asymmetric information and asymmetric payoffs. *Games Econ. Behav.* 13: 100–10.

D. K. Levine. 1998. Modeling altruism and spitefulness in experiments. *Rev. Econ. Dynam.* 1: 593–622.

R. D. McKelvey and T. R. Palfrey. 1992. An experimental study of the centipede game. *Econometrica* 60: 803–36.

J. Ochs and A. E. Roth. 1989. An experimental study of sequential bargaining. *Amer. Econ. Rev.* 79: 355–84.

V. Prasnikar and A. E. Roth. 1992. Considerations of fairness and strategy: Experimental data from sequential games. *Quart. J. Econ.* 106: 865–88.

M. Rabin. 1993. Incorporating fairness into game theory and economics. *Amer. Econ. Rev.* 83: 1281–1302.

A. E. Roth. 1995. Bargaining experiments. In J. Kagel and A. E. Roth, eds., *Handbook of Experimental Economics.* Princeton: Princeton University Press, pp. 253–348.

A. E. Roth, V. Prasnikar, M. Okuno-Fujiwara, and S. Zamir. 1991. Bargaining and market power in Jerusalem, Ljubljana, Pittsburgh, and Tokyo: An experimental study. *Amer. Econ. Rev.* 81: 1068–95.

B. J. Ruffle. 1998. More is better, but fair is fair: Tipping in dictator and ultimatum games. *Games Econ. Behav.* 23: 247–65.

L. Samuelson. 1998. Analogies, adaptation, and anomalies. *J. Econ. Theory* 97: 320–67.

T. Slembeck. 1998. As if playing fair—Experimental evidence on the role of information in ultimatum bargaining. Mimeo. University College London.

P. G. Straub and J. Keith Murnighan. 1995. An experimental investigation of ultimatum games: Information, fairness, expectations, and lowest acceptable offers. *J. Econ. Behav. Organ.* 27: 345–64.

R. H. Thaler. 1988. Anomalies: The ultimatum game. *J. Econ. Perspect.* 2: 195–206.

E. Winter and S. Zamir. 1997. An experiment with ultimatum bargaining in a changing environment. Discussion Paper 159. Hebrew University of Jerusalem Center for Rationality and Interactive Decision Making.

R. Zwick and X. P. Chen. 1997. What price for fairness? A bargaining study. Mimeo. Hong Kong University of Science and Technology.

R. Zwick and E. Weg. 1996. An experimental study of buyer-seller negotiation: Self-interest versus other-regarding behavior. Mimeo. Hong Kong University of Science and Technology and Purdue University.

5   Outside Options

Laboratory subjects don't reason by backward induction as Rubinstein (1982) assumed when offering a unique solution to the bargaining problem, but this chapter shows that his solution nevertheless turns out to work a lot better at predicting deals reached in the laboratory than the naïve split-the-difference criterion that was once universal among labor economists.

How can Rubinstein's theory sometimes work if backward induction doesn't? I think the answer is that we don't really need subgame-perfection in his theorem. The idea of a stationary expectations equilibrium will do equally well (chapter 3). For the special case of the theorem considered in this chapter, we could get by with even milder strategic assumptions. All that is necessary for subjects to find their way to the Rubinstein outcome is that they eventually learn to behave in conformity with whatever these mild strategic principles may be.

Nash Bargaining Solution

The story behind the experiment of this chapter begins in 1950, when John Nash (1950) broke with the prevailing orthodoxy by introducing the idea of the Nash bargaining solution. Previously it was held that the bargaining problem is economically indeterminate, in the sense that one has to take account of psychological factors to predict the precise outcome of a negotiation.[1]

Figure 5.1 illustrates three different geometric characterizations of the Nash bargaining solution to a bargaining problem in which rational players must agree on a pair x of payoffs in a given feasible set X, or else remain at a status quo pair ξ.

More notice is usually taken of Nash's axiomatic defense of his bargaining solution than of the bargaining-model defense discussed in

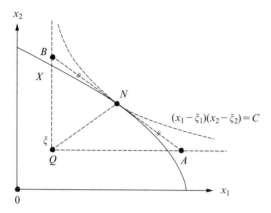

Figure 5.1
Characterizing the Nash bargaining solution. Any rational solution of the bargaining problem must be an efficient point of X that assigns both players at least their status quo payoffs. The Nash bargaining solution can be located within this set of candidates by using any one of the following criteria: (1) maximize the Nash product $(x_1 - \xi_1)(x_2 - \xi_2)$, (2) make $AN = NB$, or (3) make $\angle NQA = \angle NAQ$.

chapter 2. Nash meant the two approaches to be regarded as complimentary, but some residual friction still lingers between theorists who focus on one approach to the exclusion of the other.

Economists were largely ummoved by Nash's work. When I took up his ideas as a newcomer to economics in the 1970s, I was taken aback to be told several times in seminars that "bargaining isn't part of economics." (I was left even more at a loss when I was told some years later that "economics isn't an experimental science.") But I guess the hecklers were right if economics is defined as what economists did at the time.

The world of economics only started paying serious attention in the 1980s to what had been going on in bargaining theory after Rubinstein (1982) had replaced Nash's Demand Game by his much more realistic Alternating-Offers Game.

Rubinstein's discovery opportunely predated a visit to the London School of Economics, where he modestly explained that his efforts to solve the bargaining problem had proved a failure because he could only solve the case with perfect information. To crack the general case of bargaining under incomplete information would indeed have been a triumph, but the theorem he had already was more than good enough for me.

I was sufficiently excited that my next few evenings were spent exploring the implications of the theorem, one of which turned out to be that when the time interval between successive proposals in the Alternating-Offers Game is allowed to become vanishingly small, the predicted deal converges on the Nash bargaining solution (Binmore 1987).[2] I still feel this result to be a striking vindication of the quality of Nash's intuition.

Breakdown and Deadlock

I later applied Rubinstein's bargaining model to the problem of coalition formation in multiplayer games (Binmore 1985). In puzzling over the reason why the outcomes to which I was led are sometimes inconsistent with the Shapley value, I realized that we had all been naïve in accepting Nash's assumption that a disagreement can always be modeled simply as a pair ξ of payoffs.

Nowadays I advocate normally including at least two disagreement points when modeling a negotiation: a deadlock point d, and a breakdown point b. The payoffs at the deadlock point represent the player's incomes while the dispute continues. The payoffs at the breakdown point represent the incomes they will receive if a player abandons the negotiation irrevocably in favor of his or her best *outside option*. Normally the players' breakdown payoffs will exceed their deadlock payoffs.

It was standard practice in labor economics at one time to predict a bargaining outcome using the ordinary Nash bargaining solution with the status quo located at the breakdown point. For example, a worker's payoff at the status quo might be determined by the current level of social benefit. In the case when what is at issue is how an income stream is divided, the outcome then seems very natural. The *extra* surplus created by the players' agreement to cooperate rather than take up their outside options is split fifty:fifty—a practice known as splitting-the-difference.

However, applying the Rubinstein theory doesn't normally lead to the Nash bargaining solution of a bargaining problem with its status quo at the breakdown point b. It leads to the Nash bargaining solution of a bargaining problem with its status quo at the deadlock point d. The breakdown payoffs are relevant only if one of the players would get more than his or her outside option than at the Nash bargaining solution computed as though outside options were absent. The Rubinstein theory predicts that a player with such a large outside option will receive only marginally more than that outside option.[3]

Once we understood this outside option principle, Shaked, Sutton, and I were keen to run an experiment to compare the rival predictions.

A referee made us invent the term deal-me-out for the alternative prediction to split-the-difference generated by Rubinstein's theory when outside options are present. With this terminology, we found that deal-me-out predicts reasonably well, and split-the-difference not at all.

I naïvely thought that our paper would herald the end of split-the-difference in labor economics. Perhaps it would have done so if deal-me-out weren't a bit harder to manage when juggling with equations.

Listening to the Subjects

In addition to the experiment reported in this chapter, we also ran unstructured bargaining sessions with the same bargaining games, taping what the subjects said to each other during the negotiations. The data were broadly consistent with that of our structured experiment but too noisy to be worth reporting without moving to a larger sample size than we could afford. However, I found listening to the tapes very instructive.

There were a number of exchanges in which subjects with low outside options would explain the strategic reality of their positions to a bargaining partner with a larger outside option. In the case where the unequal outside options are both less than a fifty:fifty split of the available money, one of the exchanges might typically go as follows:

Adam argues that his larger outside option entitles him to a larger share of the available money, perhaps because he claims that split-the-difference is fair. Eve demures on the grounds that they should simply split the money fifty:fifty without reference to their outside options. Adam then threatens to take up his outside option. Eve responds that his threat is incredible, since he would lose the difference between what she is offering and his outside option. Adam eventually caves in.

Of course, Eve's debating position is strengthened by the fact that deal-me-out in this situation coincides with the "fair" outcome in which the available money is split fifty:fifty. Our decision to use equal discount rates in the experiment therefore harnesses any bias that may exist in favor of such a fifty:fifty split in favor of deal-me-out. On the other hand, split-the-difference also has some claim to be the "fair" outcome, as we will see in the next chapter. Indeed some of our bargaining games reduced to what seemed like a battle between these two rival "fairness" norms. The subject with the higher outside option would hold out for split-the-difference and the subject with lower outside option for deal-me-out.[4]

Aside from emphasizing that our design by no means buries the fairness issues that bedevil all attempts to get a handle on bargaining behavior, the preceding story of Adam and Eve also puts a finger on the essential strategic insight that players need to recognize in order for deal-me-out to displace split-the-difference. This strategic insight is wrapped up with lots of other baggage in the concept of a subgame-perfect equilibrium, but subjects who wisely don't buy into all the extra baggage will still end up at deal-me-out.

An Outside Option Experiment

Ken Binmore, Avner Shaked, and John Sutton

5.1 Introduction

The Nash bargaining solution has been widely used as a modeling tool for wage negotiations in applied economics. Recent progress in noncooperative, game-theoretic models of bargaining (Binmore 1985; Binmore and Dasgupta 1987; Binmore, Rubinstein, and Wolinsky 1986; Rubinstein 1982; Shaked and Sutton 1984; Sutton 1986) suggests that some of the modeling problems are not quite so simple as is often assumed. The difficulty considered here is the manner in which the bargainers' outside options are incorporated into the Nash solution.

The Nash bargaining solution (Nash 1950) is formulated in terms of a set[5] X of utility pairs that represent possible deals on which two bargainers may agree, and a disagreement pair (d_1, d_2) that represents the utilities the bargainers will receive if there is no agreement. The Nash bargaining solution (s_1, s_2) is then the point in X at which the Nash product $(s_1 - d_1)(s_2 - d_2)$ is maximized subject to the constraints $s_1 \geq d_1$ and $s_2 \geq d_2$. In this paper, and in most applications, the agreements amount to sharing a sum M of money (which will not be available without an agreement) between bargainers whose utilities are linear in money. In this case X is a set of the form $\{(x_1, x_2) : x_1 \geq 0, x_2 \geq 0, x_1 + x_2 \leq M\}$, and $s_i = d_i + (M - d_1 - d_2)/2 \ (i = 1, 2)$. The Nash bargaining solution then assigns each player his disagreement payoff plus half what remains from M after the disagreement payoffs have been made.

However, in applications there is often more than one candidate for the disagreement point. One possible candidate is the *impasse point*, by which

The financial support of STICERD at LSE and of the ESRC; and the excellent research assistance of Yasmin Batliwala, Ami Klin, Nikki Boyce, Maria Herrero, and Carol Van Der Ploeg are acknowledged. Al Roth provided much useful criticism.

5. Which is usually assumed to be convex, closed, bounded above, and comprehensive.

we mean the utility pair that will result if the bargaining continues forever without agreement being reached or the negotiations being abandoned. We always normalize the impasse point at $(0,0)$. But such an impasse is not the only route that may lead to a failure to agree. One or other of the bargainers could unilaterally abandon the negotiations to take up an opportunity elsewhere. Alternatively, if agreement is delayed, the opportunity the bargainers are planning to exploit jointly could be lost through the intervention of some random factor outside the bargainers' control. The utility pairs that arise as a consequence of such breakdowns in the negotiation process provide further candidates for the disagreement point in Nash's solution. In what follows, we assume that only one such *breakdown point* (b_1, b_2) is possible and that $b_1 \geq 0$, $b_2 \geq 0$, and $b_1 + b_2 \leq M$. Breakdown will be assumed to be precipitated by one or other of the players leaving the negotiation table for good in order to take up his outside option b_i. The other bargainer is then assumed to follow suit.

In wage negotiations it is appropriate to think of the points in X as wage-profit flows, the impasse utilities as income flows during a strike and the outside options as the best income flows available to each side if they cease their partnership altogether.

In such a context it is conventional to place the disagreement point for the Nash solution at the *breakdown point* (b_1, b_2) as indicated in figure 5.2. A useful mnemonic for the prediction (p_1, p_2) of the bargaining outcome so generated is *split-the-difference*. The paper contrasts this predic-

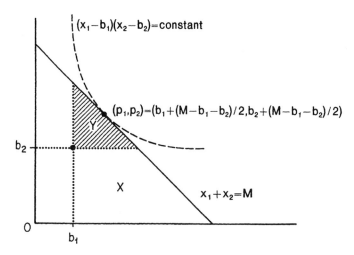

Figure 5.2

tor with a special case of an "outside option principle" derived from an analysis of optimal behavior in a natural game-theoretic model of the bargaining process. The mnemonic used for this special case is *deal-me-out* for reasons to be explained shortly. It selects the bargaining outcome (q_1, q_2) indicated in figures 5.3(a) and (b). This is the Nash bargaining solution for the set $Y = \{(x_1, x_2) : b_1 \leq x_1, b_2 \leq x_2, x_1 + x_2 \leq M\}$ with the disagreement point at $(0, 0)$. Thus outside options are only used as *constraints* on the range of validity of the Nash bargaining solution. The disagreement point is placed at the impasse point $(0, 0)$. With deal-me-out the predicted bargaining outcome is

$$
(q_1, q_2) = \begin{cases}
(b_1, M - b_1) & \text{if } \dfrac{M}{2} < b_1, \\[2mm]
(M - b_2, b_2) & \text{if } \dfrac{M}{2} < b_2, \\[2mm]
\left(\dfrac{M}{2}, \dfrac{M}{2}\right), & \text{otherwise.}
\end{cases}
$$

So each bargainer gets a half-share of the whole sum of money unless this would assign one bargainer less than his outside option. In the latter case that bargainer receives his outside option, and the other bargainer gets the rest.

The appropriate form of the "outside option principle" is justified formally in appendix A by identifying the unique subgame-perfect equilibrium of a Rubinstein-type bargaining game with alternating offers from

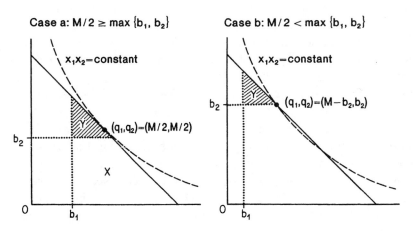

Case a: $M/2 \geq \max \{b_1, b_2\}$ Case b: $M/2 < \max \{b_1, b_2\}$

$x_1 x_2 = \text{constant}$ $x_1 x_2 = \text{constant}$

$(q_1, q_2) = (M/2, M/2)$ $(q_1, q_2) = (M - b_2, b_2)$

Figure 5.3

which either player can secede after refusing an offer to take up his outside option. Deal-me-out arises when the discount factor of δ in this analysis is approximately 1.

Strategically what is involved is very simple. The attraction of split-the-difference lies in the fact that a larger outside option seems to confer greater bargaining power. But how can a bargainer use his outside option to gain leverage? By threatening to play the deal-me-out card. When is such a threat credible? Only when dealing himself out gives the bargainer a bigger payoff than dealing himself in. It follows that the agreement that would be reached *without* outside options is *immune* to deal-me-out threats, unless the deal assigns one of the bargainers less than he can get elsewhere. The opponent need then only offer him epsilon on top of his outside option to keep him at the table. The theory idealizes epsilon to be zero. In real life, epsilon would need to be chosen sufficiently large not to be dismissed as negligible.

This paper reports the result of an experiment in which anonymous subjects played a Rubinstein-type game with outside options. Deal-me-out predicted the outcomes overwhelmingly better than split-the-difference. If one is willing to believe that the stylized negotiations procedure which constrained our subjects bears a sufficient resemblance to that used in relevant real-life situations, and if one is also willing to believe that the laboratory behavior of our subjects is similarly significant, then our results would seem to *refute* the conventional use of split-the-difference in this context.

Is there any point in such an experimental refutation? Is it not enough to show that the conventional predictor attributes suboptimal behavior to the bargainer? Such naïve questions neglect the accumulated evidence that, in laboratory bargaining experiments, subjects seldom take proper account of strategic factors and prefer to settle on deals that are "fair" in some sense (e.g., Güth et al. 1982; Hoffman-Spitzer 1985). Do the current results not contradict this evidence? In brief, one is not entitled to argue that deal-me-out predicts better *because* it represents optimal behavior. We do not, in fact, believe that our subjects know all about subgame-perfect equilibria and are gifted with the capacity for effortless mental arithmetic. Without extensive opportunities for trial-and-error learning, they can only be anticipated to have a *dim* awareness of the strategic realities. Since our game is very simple, being nearly symmetric when both outside options are zero, it may be that such a dim awareness is enough to generate behavior close to the optimum in strategic terms. But the very symmetry that makes such a scenario plausible simultaneously makes it difficult to distinguish such an explanation of the observed behavior from one that postulates that the subjects are partly motivated by "fairness" considerations. The issue of the extent to which "fairness" genuinely motivates subjects in bargaining situations is taken up elsewhere (Binmore, Shaked, and Sutton 1989). The current paper is content to establish that deal-me-out predicts better than split-the-difference without committing itself to *why* this should be so.

5.2   The Bargaining Game

This section briefly describes the rules of the game played by our subjects. The manner in which these rules were operationalized is left to the next section.

A "cake" originally worth £7 (approximately $10 at the time) is to be divided between two players if they can agree on how it is to be divided. The bargainers are constrained to employ the following very specific bargaining procedure. Player 1 begins by proposing a division of the cake to player 2. Player 2 then accepts or refuses this proposal. If he refuses, player 2 may then decide not to continue bargaining but to take up an outside option. In the experiment, games were divided into three groups: in group 1, player 2's outside option was zero; in group 2 it was £2; and in group 3 it was £4. For simplicity, player 1's outside option was *always* zero.[6] If player 2 refuses player 1's offer but does not opt out, then all the sums of money mentioned above are reduced by a factor of $\delta < 1$, and a second round of negotiations takes place, just like the first, but with player 2 making an offer to player 1. This procedure continues with the players alternating in being the proposer until (a) agreement is reached, or (b) a player opts out, or (c) a cutoff point is reached at which the available payoffs have become negligible.[7]

All this information was known to both players,[8] but much care was taken to ensure that neither player became aware of the real-life identity of his bargaining partner.

Figure 5.4 compares the predictions of split-the-difference and deal-me-out. These are appropriate when δ is approximately one. In the experiment, δ was actually taken to be 0.9 so that all sums of money shrank by

---

6. Players with a zero outside option were not explicitly reminded of their opportunity to opt out.

7. In practice this cutoff point was never reached.

8. The game is one of perfect information.

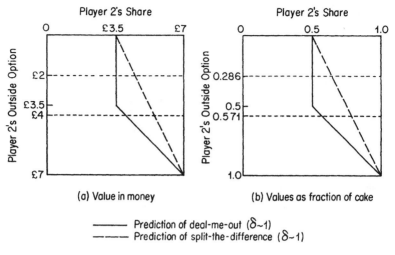

Figure 5.4

10 percent before each new round of negotiation. This explains the slightly different predictions indicated in figures 5.5, 5.6, and 5.7.

Enough information has been provided to appreciate the results of section 5.4, but a detailed analysis requires some further comments on the design of the game.

1. The game is based on a bargaining model of Rubinstein (1982) in the belief that this model, with its explicit pattern of offer and counteroffer, captures an essential aspect of real-world bargaining institutions.

2. The game admits an explicit game-theoretic analysis. It has a unique subgame-perfect equilibrium outcome (as proved in appendix A). In the zero option case this requires the first player to offer $\delta/(1+\delta)$ of the cake to the second player and for the second player to accept. Here δ is the players' common discount factor. With $\delta = 0.9$, as in the experiment, the fraction of the cake to be offered is therefore 0.473. Since this is nearly 0.5, the game-theoretic analysis therefore leads to an approximately fifty:fifty split as would, for example, an analysis based on attributing motives of fairness to the players. With a positive outside option for player 2, all remains precisely the same unless $\delta/(1+\delta)$ of the cake is less than player 2's outside option. If so, then the equilibrium outcome is for player 1 to offer player 2 his or her outside option instead. Since $2 < 0.473 \times 7 = 3.311 < 4$, an equilibrium outcome in groups 1 and 2 of our experiment requires that player 2 gets 0.473 of the cake while, in

group 3, player 2 gets just his outside option (which is worth 0.571 of the value of the cake).

3. The analysis above treats money as infinitely divisible. There is also the fact that equilibrium behavior requires specific selections to be made from actions among which a player is indifferent. In particular, players are always indifferent between accepting or refusing an equilibrium offer, but in equilibrium they accept. With a discrete currency the indifference issue can be resolved in theory, since players can always "play safe" by making their offer better than the alternative by an amount equal to the smallest coin available.[9] Of course, this smallest coin will be regarded as "negligible" by most subjects. One must therefore expect to see larger "token" amounts in practice. Rather than commit ourselves to a view on how large such a "token" amount should be taken to be, we increased the size of the experimental cake from £3 in our pilot study of £7 in the main study so that relevant numbers to be compared were always substantially different.

4. The game-theoretic analysis predicts that agreement will always be reached at the very first opportunity. But implicit in a noncooperative game theory analysis is the hypothesis that it is common knowledge that the players are rational. In real life even a player who is rational himself might reasonably entertain doubts about the rationality of an anonymous opponent. Delaying agreement might then be worthwhile to provide an opportunity of learning whether the opponent is exploitable. However, even when agreement is not immediate, game theory still provides a prediction of future play *conditional* on no agreement having been reached so far. In odd-numbered periods when player 1 makes the offer, the prediction is just as in comment 2 above. In even-numbered periods, player 2 makes the offer. In groups 1 and 2 the equilibrium outcome then gives $1/(1+\delta) = 0.526$ of the available cake to player 2. In group 3 the equilibrium outcome gives player 2 somewhat more than the current value of his outside option (i.e., 0.614 of the value of the currently available cake). It will be noted that a game-theoretic analysis attributes a slight advantage to the player who has the opportunity of making the first proposal.

5. The shrinkage factor $\delta = 0.9$ was chosen with two considerations in mind. The aim was to make the rate of shrinkage fast enough to

---

9. However, this will be only one of many equilibria in the discrete case. These all approximate the unique equilibrium of the continuous case provided that the smallest unit of currency is sufficiently small.

"blanket" any difference in the "natural" rates of time preference of the subjects but slow enough that the first-mover advantage mentioned in item 4 above was relatively small. The situation discussed in the introduction is, strictly speaking, the limiting case as $\delta \to 1-$. In what follows it should be noted that the deal-me-out prediction is the unique subgame-perfect equilibrium outcome calculated for the *actual* shrinkage factor of $\delta = 0.9$ with the first-mover advantage taken into account.

6. A split-the-difference analysis gives 0.5 of the available cake to player 2 in group 1 games, $0.643 = 4.5/7$ in group 2 games, and $0.786 = 5.5/7$ in group 3 games. Split-the-difference can also be used to predict the bargaining outcome *conditional* on no agreement having been reached so far. Because it is favorable to the split-the-difference predictor, we adopt an interpretation in even-numbered periods that takes account of the fact that player 2 must wait one period before his or her outside option is available again. In groups 1, 2, and 3, respectively, the prediction then is that player 2 gets 0.5, 0.629, and 0.757 of the available cake when making an offer.

7. Deal-me-out is only one of various alternatives to split-the-difference that might be considered. Methodologically it has a considerable advantage over the other alternatives in that it yields precise and unambiguous predictions, and hence we cannot be accused of altering our rival predictor to suit the data. Given that our rival predictor does better than split-the-difference, we therefore have a sound case for rejecting the latter. But it is not claimed that we necessarily have a good case for rejecting anything else.

5.3 Experimental Setup

Following the pilot studies, 120 subjects were recruited from a wide cross section of LSE students in the social sciences.[10] Students who had been exposed to game theory or bargaining models were excluded. Recruitment was carried out from teaching classes and not from a pool of subjects accustomed to psychological experiments. Each student was assigned a time slot. To preserve anonymity, two subjects assigned to the same time slot were always drawn from different classes. Much care was taken to ensure that subjects had no knowledge of the identity of their op-

---

10. Including economics, law, demography, social anthropology, politics, management science, sociology, geography, psychology, and computing.

ponent either before or after the game.[11] The 60 pairs were partitioned into the three groups itemized in section 5.2. Group 1 (the "control" group) contained 10 pairs. Groups 2 and 3 each contained 25 pairs.

Subjects were placed in separate rooms before microcomputers linked by a cable. After reading a set of written instructions (appendix B), the subjects were "talked through" the instructions again by a research assistant to ensure that they were clearly understood. Reinforcement of the instructions, together with practice in the use of the necessary computer controls, was provided with the help of a video display unit (VDU). The subjects did *not* play a practice game with the computer, since we were anxious not to offer cues about what type of play was expected. For the same reason we were not present in the room ourselves.

The VDU displayed a picture of a rectangular "cake". The player making an offer could divide the cake into two shares by pressing designated keys that moved the dividing line between the share claimed and the share offered up or down. The monetary value of the cake and the value of the share claimed were also displayed. The responding player registered acceptance or rejection of the offer by pressing the Y or N keys accordingly. Players were paid in cash immediately after the game finished.

5.4 Results

We report the results using diagrams. The raw data appear in our working paper (Sutton et al. 1985). The three histograms, figures 5.5, 5.6, and 5.7, group data in bands equal to a 1 percent share of the cake. Offers and agreements are *always* expressed in terms of the amount of the share proposed for, or received by, *player 2*.

Consider figure 5.6 by way of example. Observe that in group 2 games (with player 2's outside option at £2) 11 of the 25 games concluded with player 2 receiving a share of between 0.50 and 0.51 of the cake available when the bargaining finished. In 6 of these 11 games agreement was reached immediately. Observe that in group 3 games (with player 2's outside option at £4) 7 of the 25 games concluded with player 2 receiving a share of between 0.57 and 0.58 of the cake available when the bargaining finished. In three of these seven games agreement was reached immediately. In the remaining four games agreement was never reached, since

---

11. Thus subjects could not verify that they had a human opponent. But this is unavoidable if anonymity is to be fully preserved.

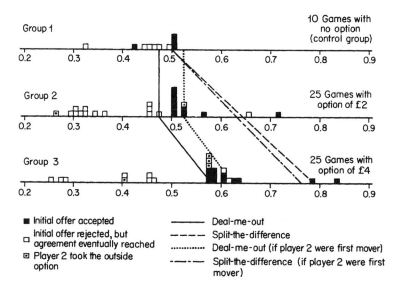

Figure 5.5
Amount received by player 2 as a fraction of the original (£7) cake

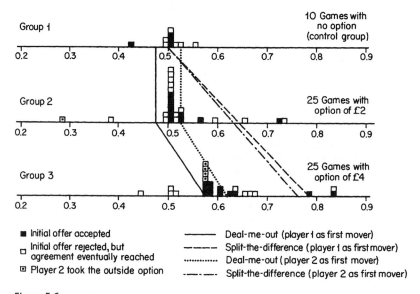

Figure 5.6
Player 2's final payment as a fraction of the cake available when bargaining concluded

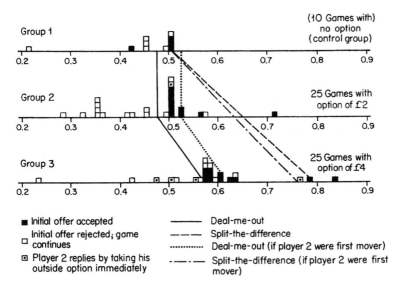

■ Initial offer accepted

□ Initial offer rejected; game continues

⊡ Player 2 replies by taking his outside option immediately

———— Deal-me-out

– – – Split-the-difference

·············· Deal-me-out (if player 2 were first mover)

–·—·– Split-the-difference (if player 2 were first mover)

Figure 5.7
Fraction of the cake originally proposed by player 1 as player 2's share

player 2 chose to take his or her outside option rather than continue bargaining.

5.5 Commentary

The inadequacy of split-the-difference as a predictor, as compared with deal-me-out, is clearly exhibited in figures 5.5, 5.6, and 5.7. A feature of the results is the substantial number of failures to agree at the first opportunity. Figures 5.8 and 5.9 give the full details of the histories of games that lasted at least three rounds. Presumably there would have been more of these games, and with longer histories, if the shrinkage factor $\delta = 0.9$ had been chosen closer to one.[12] None of the currently popular bargaining theories assuming perfect information predict disagreement at all, and to this extent, the data are not supportive of any of them. Further research is clearly necessary on this point.

However, results that may be thought to be surprisingly sharp are obtained by examining what player 2 gets once agreement has been

---

12. On the other hand, the first-mover advantage would have been diminished. However, the final agreements reached do not support the hypothesis that the first player was able to exploit his first-mover advantage even if he perceived that he had one.

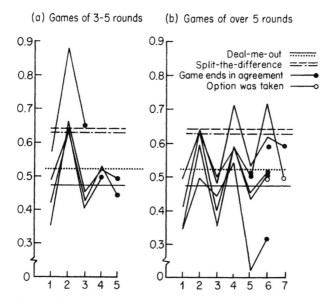

Figure 5.8
Group II (small option) games involving disagreement. The diagram shows the share pro-posed for player 2 in the successive rounds as a fraction of the cake then available.

reached as a fraction of the *cake available at the time of agreement* (see items 4, 5, and 6 of section 5.2). These amounts are shown in figure 5.6. We test the extent to which this impression of sharpness is accurate by asking the following questions:

a. Does the fraction of the available cake obtained by player 2 in a group 2 game (£2 option) exceed the fraction he obtains in a group 1 game (no option)?

b. Is the fraction of the available cake obtained by player 2 in a group 3 game (£4 option) nearer the split-the-difference fraction than the current value of the outside option?

For question a we tested the null hypothesis that the proportion of agreements in which player 2 gets a fraction strictly exceeding 0.5 is equal in both groups 1 and groups 2. (In view of the clustering at 0.5, this seems a more appropriate criterion than does a test for the equality of the me-dian outcome, which is in fact 0.5 in both groups.) In accordance with our rejection of split-the-difference as a predictor, we observe that the null hypothesis is *not* rejected by a χ^2 test at the 5 percent level.

For question b we observe that the fractions of the available cake obtained by player 2 in group 3 games fall into three classes. Four points

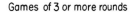

Games of 3 or more rounds

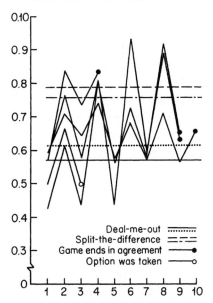

Figure 5.9
Group 3 (large option) games involving disagreement. The diagram shows the share proposed for player 2 in the successive rounds as a fraction of the cake then available.

lie well below 0.571 (which is the value of the outside option to player 2 as a fraction of the available cake when player 1 is proposing). These outcomes are incompatible with either deal-me-out or split-the-difference, however loosely defined. Of the remaining 21 points, 18 are closer to deal-me-out (0.571 for agreement in odd-numbered periods). The null hypothesis—that the fraction of the relevant population generating outcomes closer to deal-me-out is less than one half—is rejected at the 5 percent level by the present data.

Finally, it should be noted that the intuition for split-the-difference is not without some support from the data. The counterproposals made by player 2s who had refused the opening proposal in figure 5.8 (showing group 2 games) cluster around the split-the-difference level. However, most of these counterproposals were refused.

5.6 Conclusion

Split-the-difference has been widely used to predict the outcome of wage negotiations in applied economics. The theoretical foundations for this predictor have been questioned in Binmore (1985) and Shaked and Sutton (1984). The current paper provides experimental support for these doubts.

Some care is necessary in evaluating the implications of the results. They are not immediately relevant if incomplete information or reputation effects are important. Nor are they relevant if breakdown may occur through random events outside the control of the bargainer (see appendix A). Even where they are relevant, it must be remembered that social benefit, for example, may not only be a factor in determining a worker's outside option: it may also be a factor in determining the size of the available "cake."

Finally, it cannot properly be argued that the results demonstrate that our subjects were motivated largely by enlightened self-interest. They were clearly unwilling to settle for less than their outside option, but within this constraint a "fairness" explanation of their behavior is consistent with the data. Our latest experimental study (Binmore, Shaked, and Sutton 1989) bears on these issues. We only observe here that the results of the new study support the rejection of split-the-difference under conditions comparable to those of the current paper.

Appendix A: The Unique Subgame-Perfect Equilibrium Outcome

In this appendix we begin by offering a formal demonstration that the infinite horizon version of the bargaining game of Section II has a unique subgame-perfect equilibrium outcome. We also compute the equilibrium payoffs. (The necessary argument is only sketched in Binmore [1985], while Shaked and Sutton [1984] is unpublished.) We assume a common discount factor δ $(0 < \delta < 1)$ and let player 2's outside option be s $(0 \leq s \leq 1)$. Without loss of generality the original size of the cake is taken to be 1.

Let m_1 and M_1 be the infimum and supremum of equilibrium payoffs to player 1 in the game. Let m_2 and M_2 be the infimum and supremum of equilibrium payoffs to player 2 in the companion game in which it is player 2 who moves first. We claim that the following inequalities hold:

$$m_1 \geq 1 - \max\{\delta M_2, s\}, \tag{1}$$

$$1 - M_1 \geq \max\{m_2, s\}, \tag{2}$$

$$m_2 \geq 1 - \delta M_1, \tag{3}$$

$$1 - M_2 \geq \delta m_1. \tag{4}$$

Inequality (1) follows from the fact that in equilibrium player 2 *must* accept any opening offer y with $y > \max\{\delta M_2, s\}$ because the right-hand side is the *most* that player 2 can get from refusing. Thus in equilibrium player 1 cannot get less than x, where $x < 1 - \max\{\delta M_2, s\}$, because he can always guarantee x by making x his opening demand. Inequality (2) follows from the fact that in equilibrium player 2 must get at least z for each $z < \max\{\delta m_2, s\}$, since z can be guaranteed by refusing player 1's opening offer. Hence player 1 can get at most $1 - a$ in equilibrium. Inequalities (3) and (4) are just the same, but with the roles of players 1 and 2 reversed, and $s = 0$.

We distinguish three cases: (a) $s \leq \delta m_2$, (b) $\delta m_2 < s < \delta M_2$, and (c) $\delta M_2 \leq s$. Case a leads immediately to the conclusion that $1/(1+\delta) \leq m_1 \leq M_1 \leq 1/(1+\delta)$ and $1/(1+\delta) \leq m_2 \leq M_2 \leq 1/(1+\delta)$. Thus in case a, $m_1 = M_1 = m_2 = M_2 = 1/(1+\delta)$. The same argument applied in case b yields the contradiction $1/(1+\delta) < m_2 \leq M_2 \leq 1/(1+\delta)$. In case c the conclusion is that $1 - s \leq m_1 \leq M_1 \leq 1 - s$ and $1 - \delta(1 - s) \leq m_2 \leq M_2 \leq 1 - \delta(1 - s)$. Thus $m_1 = M_1 = 1 - s$ and $m_2 = M_2 = 1 - \delta(1 - s)$. From the computed values of m_2 and M_2, it only remains to observe that case (a) occurs when $s \leq \delta/(1+\delta)$ and case (c) occurs when $s \geq \delta/(1+\delta)$.

This shows that if subgame-perfect equilibria exist, then they generate a unique outcome. Existence, however, is trivial. Each player always demands his equilibrium payoff when proposing and accepts his equilibrium payoff (or more) when responding. Section 5.1 of the paper describes the limiting case as $\delta \to 1-$.

Split-the-difference can also emerge from a noncooperative analysis under suitable conditions. To see this, suppose that the game we have just studied is modified so that outside options are no longer available but that, after each refusal of a proposal, a breakdown in communications occurs with probability π, resulting in the payoff pair $(0, s)$ regardless of any desire the players have to continue negotiating. For simplicity, we take $\delta = 1$. The inequalities of the preceding analysis are replaced by

$$m_1 \geq 1 - \{(1 - \pi)M_2 + \pi s\}, \tag{5}$$

$$1 - M_1 \geq (1 - \pi)m_2 + \pi s, \tag{6}$$

$$m_2 \geq 1 - (1 - \pi)M_1, \tag{7}$$

$$1 - M_2 \geq (1 - \pi)m_1, \tag{8}$$

from which it follows that $m_1 = M_1 = (1 - s)/(2 - \pi)$ and $m_2 = M_2 = \{1 + (1 - \pi)s\}/(2 - \pi)$. The limiting case $\pi \to 0+$ is split-the-difference.

In the finite horizon cases uniqueness is immediate, but the computation of the equilibrium payoffs is tedious. These converge to the infinite horizon payoffs as the horizon is allowed to recede to infinity.

Appendix B: Instructions to Subjects

The following instruction sheet was given to subjects filling the role of player 1 in those games where player 2 had an outside option that was initially worth £4. The instruction sheets given to players in other conditions were similar to this. Having read these instructions, subjects were talked through them by an assistant, and then the rules were explained again by means of a display on the VDU.

Instructions to Player 1

The aim of this exercise is to examine how people behave in bargaining situations.

You will be asked to divide a cake (worth a certain sum of money) between yourself and an opponent.

The initial value of the cake is £7.00.

At certain times, your opponent can, if he/she wishes, "opt out," and be paid a certain sum (initially £4.00); if he/she does this, you will receive nothing.

You do not have any such "outside option."

As bargaining continues over time, these values will be reduced, in a manner to be explained below.

Incidentally, it was decided at random before you came in, who would have the "outside option."

The way bargaining will proceed is as follows:

You will make your opponent an offer of some share of the cake. Your opponent can do one of 3 things:

1. Accept your offer, in which case the game ends. And you and your opponent each receive the agreed amount.

2. Your opponent can decide to "opt out" of the game, in which case he/she will be paid £4.00 and you will receive nothing.

3. Reject the offer—in which case the cake shrinks by 10 percent *and so does the outside option.* Now it becomes your opponent's turn to make you an offer.

The cake is now worth £6.30. Your opponent makes you an offer. You can do one of two things:

1. Accept your opponent's offer, in which case the game ends, and you and your opponent receive the agreed amount.

2. Reject your opponent's offer, in which case the cake, *and the option*, shrink by a further 10 percent, and it becomes your turn once again to make your opponent an offer.

The game continues in this way, with the sums of money shrinking by 10 percent following each rejection, until an agreement is reached.

All this information is known to your opponent.

A computer demonstration now follows.

References

Binmore, K. 1985. Bargaining and coalitions. In A. Roth, ed., *Game Theoretic Models of Bargaining*. Cambridge: Cambridge University Press.

Binmore, K., and P. Dasgupta, eds. 1987. *Economics of Bargaining*. Oxford: Blackwell.

Binmore, K., A. Rubinstein, and A. Wolinsky. 1986. The Nash bargaining solution in economic modeling. *Rand Journal of Economics* 17: 176–88.

Binmore, K., A. Shaked, and J. Sutton. 1985. Testing noncooperative bargaining theory: A preliminary study. *American Economic Review* 75: 1178–80.

Binmore, K., A. Shaked, and J. Sutton. 1989. Testing noncooperative bargaining theory: A reply. *American Economic Review*, forthcoming.

Binmore, K., A. Shaked, and J. Sutton. 1984. Do people exploit their bargaining power? CREST discussion paper. University of Michigan.

Guth, W., R. Schmittberger, and B. Schwarze. 1982. An experimental analysis of ultimatum bargaining. *Journal of Economic Behavior and Organization* 3: 367–88.

Hoffman, E., and M. Spitzer. 1985. Entitlements, rights and fairness: An experimental examination of subjects' concepts of distributive justice. *Journal of Legal Studies* 14: 259–97.

Nash, J. 1950. The bargaining problem. *Econometrica* 18: 155–62.

Rubinstein, A. 1982. Perfect equilibrium in a bargaining model. *Econometrica* 50: 97–110.

Shaked, A., and J. Sutton. 1984. The semi-Walrasian economy. ICERD discussion paper 84/98. London School of Economics.

Sutton, J. 1986. Noncooperative bargaining theory—An introduction. *Review of Economic Studies* 53: 709–24.

Sutton, J., A. Shaked, and K. Binmore. 1989. An outside option experiment. *Quarterly Journal of Economics* 104: 735–70.

6   Forced Breakdown

One of the problems in discussing fairness in bargaining games is that there isn't always a firm consensus among either theorists or subjects about what counts as fair in any particular game. I think that the hints and cues built into the way the game is presented to the subjects matter even more to this question than is generally recognized. If merely pinning a gold star on some people can make a difference, the scope for obtaining variation in this way seems endless (chapter 4).

Controling Frames

I think that we therefore need to *control* the framing of bargaining experiments very carefully, for the same reason that chemists clean their test tubes. If we don't understand what is significant in our input to the subjects, how can we hope to understand their output? It seems to me that a systematic approach to understanding how the framing of a game influences the nature of the fairness norms to which subjects appeal should begin by *minimizing* the cues offered to the subjects by the way the game is framed.

In my experiments I therefore take the opposite tack from authors who evoke the atmosphere of the workplace or some other venue in which the subjects are habituated to operating a norm adapted to whatever game they commonly play in that venue. I seek instead to *avoid* offering any cues that might trigger a focal point adapted to some game other than that being studied in my laboratory. However, Schelling's (1960) essay on the type of information that we unthinkingly make use of in guessing what equilibrium other subjects will regard as focal makes it clear that scrubbing a frame free of inadvertent cues is likely to be difficult. One can easily trigger a focal point simply by representing the feasible set as a familiar geometrical figure, or by labeling some deals with enticingly round numbers.

I think my attempts at controling my experimental frames combine with the comparative richness of the feedback with which I provide my subjects to explain why I see more evidence of learning among my subjects than some other experimenters. The case is particularly clear in the experiment reported in chapter 2 on Nash's Demand Game.

The Demand Game is already abstract in character, and we were careful not to offer any cues in our instructions that might encourage the subjects to identify the game with some more familiar bargaining situation. We then conditioned subjects to accept focal points that we had chosen ourselves. But when they were left to play against each other, we found that only our attempts to condition them on exact equilibria had any success. The most striking fact is that different groups of subjects who ended up at different exact equilibria were ready to say that the focal point that had evolved in their group is the fair outcome of the game.

I think this experiment captures in minature what goes on in the real world when cultural evolution establishes a new norm for a new situation. However, it is the easiest thing in the world to interfere with this process in the laboratory. All one needs to do is to somehow invoke a focal point on which the subjects are very strongly conditioned in the real world. We could have done this in the Demand Game, for example, by taking the set of available payoffs to be a triangle, in which case the central point of the hypotenuse would have been irresistible as a correlate of the fifty:fifty deal that is commonly focal in simple bargaining situations.

Varying the Breakdown Rules

In the Rubinstein bargaining model or in multistage ultimatum games it isn't possible to avoid offering focalizing cues in the framing of the experiment, since the subjects seem to use the strategic structure of the game itself as such a cue (see figures 3.2 and 4.1). However, one can interfere with the rules of the game in a way that is strategically significant but is unlikely to be seen as relevant by inexperienced subjects. We can then see how groups of subjects playing two apparently similar but strategically different bargaining games end up playing. After the experiment is over, we can also ask them what they think is fair in the game they just played.

Rubinstein's Alternating-Offers Game with outside options is a happy playground for someone with such aims, since we can create two strategically different versions of the game simply by making the act of opting out voluntary or not. In the previous chapter we found that the Rubinstein outcome we called deal-me-out works rather well when players who have just refused an offer have the choice of staying around to make a counter-offer or walking off to take up their best outside option. In this case, any breakdowns are voluntary. However, matters change dramatically in the case when we force the players to opt out with some small probability after each refusal. In the case of forced breakdown the Rubinstein outcome is now split-the-difference.

Shaked, Sutton, and I joined forces with Peter Morgan to compare behavior in the Alternating-Offers Game with forced or voluntary breakdown. Behavior differed dramatically in the two cases, with split-the-difference predicting unexpectedly well in the case of forced breakdown. I think it particularly significant that subjects tended to say that what is fair in the game they had just played is the same as the behavior that had evolved in their own particular group. An explanation of fairness in terms of other-regarding preferences therefore has to cope not only with the fact that the subjects' perception of what counts as fair can be altered by an hour's experience in the laboratory, but also that it can be determined by apparently irrelevant alterations to the strategic structure of a game.

It is especially interesting that these conclusions don't hold for the whole subject pool. A minority of around 10 percent insist that fifty:fifty is the fair split of the available money, no matter what the strategic realities may be. Could these be the same kind of people who make up the 10 percent of the subject pool who never learn to switch to defection in the one-shot Prisoners' Dilemma? If such an inflexible minority really exists, they would often make a substantial difference to the convergence properties of simple adjustment processes (chapter 8).

Do People Exploit Their Bargaining Power? An Experimental Study

Ken Binmore, Peter Morgan, Avner Shaked, and John Sutton

6.1 Introduction

Human behavior, even in simple bargaining situations, is not well understood. Numerous rival theories compete for attention, but the data are seldom adequate to justify a rejection of one in favor of another. It is often not even clear what the significant control variables are.

This paper examines only one small aspect of the problem. It describes an experimental attempt to compare the predictions of two qualitatively distinct types of theory. First, there are the fairness/focal theories of bargaining behavior as propounded by Güth (1990), Kahneman et al. (1986), Roth (1985), Selten (1978), and others. Second, there are the strategic theories of bargaining behavior, notably that of Rubinstein (1982). Game-theoretic or strategic models treat the bargainers as rational optimizers and hence predict that the players will exploit whatever bargaining power they possess. Fairness/focal theories view the agreement on which subjects settle as being determined by social norms or conventional understandings that render the agreement focal, given the circumstances in which the bargainers are working. In a bargaining context the social norms often involve "fairness" considerations, but other features of the situation may also be important. For example, deals involving whole numbers of dollars may be salient in some circumstances.

It is not easy to distinguish fairness/focal behavior from strategic behavior. Indeed part of the message of this paper is that what people

We are grateful to the Economics and Social Research Council of the United Kingdom for generously funding this research project. We also thank P. Knox and S. Chew for efficiently programming the experiments, and A. Hoolighan, A. Klin, C. Mirrlees, C. Purkhardt, and B. Thakker for their invaluable help in supervising the experiment and recruiting the subjects. We are also grateful to the Psychology Department at the London School of Economics for the use of their laboratory.

perceive as "fair" or focal can sometimes be explained in terms of the strategic realities of the situation. However, we found it possible to design two simple laboratory games that, superficially at least, seem very similar from a fairness/focal viewpoint but differ significantly in their strategic characteristics.

To summarize the results of the experiments very briefly, the subjects' behavior was biased in the direction of strategically optimal play. Under one of the two conditions the differences in behavior between the two types of game were very marked indeed. The same turned out to be true of what the subjects asserted to be fair when questioned on this issue *after* playing the game.[1] That is to say, what they judged to be fair after experiencing actual play was biased in the direction of the outcome that would result from strategically optimal behavior in the game they had actually played.

Peter Cramton (1988) has run the same experiment using our computer programs with Yale undergraduates as his subjects. His conclusions will be reported elsewhere. We note only that they are broadly consistent with ours. However, his subject population was half the size of ours.

Commentary on the results is left to a concluding section. At this point we observe only that the fairness/focal and strategic bargaining literatures by no means exhaust all possible viewpoints. See, for example, Leventhal (1980), Thibaut (1968), or Walster et al. (1973).

6.2 Bargaining Models

The basic problem for the subjects in all the models considered is that of dividing a sum of money[2] that we call a "cake." If the negotiations break down, player I will receive a payment which is equivalent to a share α of the cake and player II will receive a share β of the cake, where $\alpha + \beta \leq 1$. What is fair in such a situation? Three possible answers to this question merit special attention:

---

1. Individuals in the same pool from which the subjects were drawn but who did *not* play the game were also surveyed on the "fairness" question. There was no significant difference on what was reported as "fair" in the two types of game. This fact could be used for rhetorical purposes in support of the conclusions of the paper, but we do not feel the very dispersed data are good enough for this purpose. In asking inexperienced people for an opinion about a complicated matter, one must expect noisy answers: and it may well be that the data from the poll contain essentially nothing but noise with little or no relevance to the experiment. The best that one would seem entitled to conclude is that the description of the two types of game offered to the subjects for an opinion did not trigger any firmly held preconceptions about what is or is not fair in bargaining situations.

2. We proceed throughout on the questionable assumption that utility can be identified with money.

a. *Split-the-difference* (S-T-D).   With this outcome, player I is assigned α, player II is assigned β, and then they split the remainder of the cake equally. This outcome is the Nash bargaining solution with the *status quo* located at (α, β). Player I's final share is then $(1 + \alpha - \beta)/2$ and player II's share is $(1 + \beta - \alpha)/2$.

b. *Fifty:fifty* (50:50).   With this outcome, the breakdown payments α and β are ignored and each player simply gets half the cake.

c. *Deal-me-out* (D-M-O).   With this outcome, the breakdown payments are ignored and the result is 50:50, *unless* this would assign player i less than i's breakdown payoff of γ. If so, player i gets γ and the other player gets the remaining $1 - \gamma$ of the cake.

The term deal-me-out derives from a previous paper (Binmore et al. 1989c) and is intended to suggest player i's response to the proposed implementation of 50:50 when $\gamma > \frac{1}{2}$. Its possible role as a "fairness" criterion was suggested by critics of the previous paper.

In all the games considered, α was taken to be very small ($\alpha = 0.04$). Two values of β were considered: a high value ($\beta = 0.64$) and a low value ($\beta = 0.36$). Figure 6.1 provides a convenient means of comparing the three different notions for different values of β (but with α fixed at 0.04).

To discuss *strategically optimal* play, it is necessary to be specific about the bargaining procedure to be used. We employ a procedure studied by Rubinstein (1982). Accessible accounts of variants of his model, including those considered here, are to be found, for example, in Binmore et al. (1989b) or Sutton (1986).

In the Rubinstein procedure the players alternate in making proposals indefinitely until a proposal is accepted or the negotiations break down. Some incentive is necessary to encourage the players to reach an early agreement. The two classes of games considered differ in how this incentive is provided and in how breakdowns may occur.

A. *Games with optional breakdown.*   In these games, a player may *opt out* after refusing a proposal[3] made by the opponent (and only then). If a player opts out, the negotiations are deemed to have broken down, and the players receive their breakdown shares, α and β, of the current cake. The incentive for an early agreement is provided by the fact that the cake and the outside options shrink by a factor of δ immediately before each proposal after the first.

---

3. It matters *when* a player may opt out (Shaked 1987).

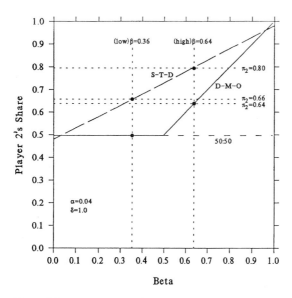

Figure 6.1
The "fairness" criteria.

The game has a unique subgame-perfect equilibrium in which player I offers a share equal to $\max\{\beta, \delta/(1+\delta)\}$ to player II at time 0, and player II accepts (Binmore et al. 1989c). Note that the equilibrium outcome converges to D-M-O as $\delta \to 1-$.

B. *Games with forced breakdown.* In these games, players may not choose to opt out and the cake does not shrink. Instead, after each refusal, a random move decides whether the negotiations will be broken off or allowed to continue. The probability of a continuation is taken to be the same value of δ as in optional breakdown games. The incentive for early agreement is therefore that the cake may disappear altogether if the negotiations are prolonged, leaving each player with only their breakdown payment.

The game has a unique subgame-perfect equilibrium in which player I offers a share equal to $\{\delta(1-\alpha)+\beta\}/(1+\delta)$ to player II at time 0, and player II accepts (Binmore et al. 1989c). Note that the equilibrium outcome converges to S-T-D at $\delta \to 1-$.

Each of these two classes of games was run under two conditions: low β and high β. This yields four different games that are referred to as regimes 0, 1, 2, and 3 as indicated in table 6.1. Thus the labels 0 and 1 refer to optional breakdown games with low and high β, respectively,

Table 6.1

	$\beta = 0.36$	$\beta = 0.64$
Optional breakdown	*Regime 0* Low optional	*Regime 1* High optional
Forced breakdown	*Regime 2* Low forced	*Regime 3* High forced

and the labels 2 and 3 refer to forced breakdown games with low and high β, respectively.

Two points should be noted. The first is that a subgame-perfect analysis predicts future behavior even if past behavior has not been as predicted. Our earlier work (Binmore et al. 1989c) on optional breakdown games indicates that one should not expect instant agreement at time zero from subjects in the laboratory, but that there is reason to believe that the game-theoretic prediction of the final outcome, in terms of the cake then available, may not fare too badly. Results are therefore always reported in terms of player II's share of the cake available *at the time the game ended*. When $\delta \to 1-$, the game-theoretic prediction will always be D-M-O in optional breakdown games, and S-T-D in forced breakdown games. The second point is the more important. For a given value of β, optional breakdown games and forced breakdown games are intended to present a similar payoff profile to the subject, who may therefore be inclined to treat them in the same way in deciding what is or is not fair or focal. Indeed, since a subgame-perfect analysis of an optional breakdown game is *identical* to that of a forced breakdown game when $\alpha = \beta = 0$, one might expect even a strategically minded but inexperienced subject to fail to recognize the rather subtle distinction between the two classes of game. If subjects behave differently in optional breakdown games from the way they behave in forced breakdown games, one would therefore seem to have evidence in favor of the players' bargaining power being a significant factor in determining the final outcome. It is this consideration that provides the major motivation for the experimental design described in this section.

6.3   The Experiment

Subjects were recruited directly from undergraduate classes in economics at the London School of Economics. The students had not studied game theory or bargaining, nor were these topics part of the curriculum for the courses they were attending. The recruiters were graduate students in Psychology who also supervised the fully automated experimental runs in the Psychology Laboratory. Subjects were informed that the experiment was "in economics" rather than "in psychology," but were not informed of the identities of the authors of this paper. As to the details of the game itself, our intention was that the subjects be perfectly informed about the rules of the game and the monetary payoffs to be distributed.

The main experiment ran for 6 days. Each day had four sessions, with each session devoted to a different regime from table 6.1. Each session involved four subjects, who each played 10 games in all. After each game a subject's opponent was changed. On arrival, subjects were seated in isolated booths with a minimum of interaction between them. They communicated via networked microcomputers. They were first asked to read written instructions (appendix A), and then to operate a demonstration program that provided them with hands-on experience on how to make and respond to offers and so on. The cake was represented on the screen by a rectangular slab. The subject made an offer by moving a "knife" up or down the cake until satisfied with the division it indicated. The monetary amounts being proposed were also displayed. The demonstration program did *not* involve any examples of partitions of the cake since we were anxious not to interfere with the natural focal point structure of the game.

After running the demonstration program and asking any questions they might have,[4] the subjects played six "practice games" for which no payments were made. They then played four "real games" in each of which the cake was initially worth £5.00. At the time of the experiment (December 1987) this was worth about $8.00. We felt this sum provided an adequate incentive for the subject to devote some care and attention to the experiment, given that we were asking for only 30 to 45 minutes of their time. Since each group of four subjects in a particular session played a total of 20 games altogether (12 for practice and 8 for real) and since each regime was in force on each of 6 days, we observed a total of 120 games for each of the four regimes (72 for practice and 48 for real).

To minimize on reputation effects, the subjects' bargaining partners were changed after each game. Their role in the game also varied. Half the time they occupied the role of player I (who moves first and has a breakdown payment of α) and half the time they occupied the role of player II (who moves second and has a breakdown payoff of β). We at-

---

4. A supervisor could be summoned by pressing an appropriate key.

tach importance to this alternation of roles in game-theoretic experiments. A rational player bases his strategic analysis of a game on the way he would play if he were in the shoes of the opponent. Alternating roles provides subjects with an opportunity to see things from the other player's viewpoint and hence to understand the game better. In a previous experiment (Binmore et al. 1985, 1988) such role switching influenced the outcome very markedly.

At the end of each session subjects were asked to remain seated until they had completed a questionnaire (appendix B) and had been paid the total amount of money they had successfully bargained for in the four real games that each had played. They were then invited to leave one by one with a view to minimizing interaction.

Under all the four regimes of table 6.1 the cake was worth £5.00 in the main experiment and the parameter δ was taken to be 0.9. In all four regimes player I's breakdown share of $\alpha = 0.04$ was therefore initially worth £0.20 in money.

For optional breakdown games (regimes 0 and 1) the cake shrinks over time according to the discount factor δ, and it is left to the players' discretion whether to force a breakdown by opting out. Under regime 0, player II's breakdown share of $\beta = 0.36$ was initially worth £1.80. Under regime 1, player II's breakdown share of $\beta = 0.64$ was initially worth £3.20.

For forced breakdown games (regimes 2 and 3) the cake does not shrink, but there is a risk of an imposed breakdown every time that an offer is refused. Our intention was that the players should believe that the game continues after a refusal with probability $\delta = 0.9$, but here we met with a difficulty in our pilot experiments. The manner in which we sought to resolve this difficulty requires some explanation.

In our initial pilot the written instructions described the probabilistic mechanism by means of which breakdown occurred, and after each refusal subjects saw a simulated roulette wheel turn on their screens. Nevertheless, they tended to behave as though the possibility of a breakdown ever occurring was negligible.[5] That is to say, they neglected to note that, although 0.9 is nearly 1, $(0.9)^n$ is small when n is sufficiently large. Such misconceptions about probabilistic matters are, of course, commonplace as laboratory phenomena.

After various attempts we sought to evade the difficulty by telling the subjects, in their written instructions, that the maximum length for each

---

5. And, in many cases, confirmed this interpretation of their behavior by their comments on the questionnaire.

game had already been chosen in advance, but that they were not to be told what this length was. However, they were invited to proceed on the assumption that, after each refusal, the probability of the game continuing was 0.9. The precise wording was as follows:

In each of the ten sessions, the number of proposals allowed before a breakdown is announced has been fixed in advance. But we are going to keep you guessing by not telling you what these ten numbers are. All you will know for sure is that a breakdown will occur eventually if agreement is delayed long enough. The maximum number of proposals allowed in each session may be large or it may be small, and knowing what the number turns out to be in one session will not help much in guessing what it will be in another. The numbers have been fixed so that, however many proposals there may already have been in a session, you should still reckon that there is a 90 percent chance of being allowed at least one more proposal. This means for example, that it is more likely that 12 or more proposals will be allowed than 3 or less.

No subject expressed any confusion about the issue on their questionnaire. We chose the maximum lengths for 10 games that each subject played to be:

$$9, 2, 11, 2, 10, 7, 7, 16, 12, 8.$$

The two short games were intended to convince the subjects that breakdown could indeed occur. Otherwise, our intention was that the data available to the subjects should not be such as to allow them rationally to reject the hypothesis that breakdowns occur independently with probability 0.1, even if they participated in games that always ended in breakdown.[6]

6.4   Results

The raw results are available as an appendix to a discussion paper Binmore et al. (1989a). We will be pleased to supply a copy of this discussion paper on request. In this section, the results we believe to be relevant are summarized in six histograms (figures 6.2, 6.3, and 6.4). We always report percentages of the cake obtained by player II. (In optional breakdown games, the cake shrinks over time. The percentage of the cake is then computed in terms of the cake available at the time the game ended.) Games that do not end in agreement are indicated by an empty box.

---

6. We do not, of course, believe that the subjects did carry out any elaborate probabilistic calculations. It is enough for our purposes if the subjects are convinced that the game will end eventually but that it is unlikely to do so immediately.

Player II then gets his or her breakdown share β (36 percent under regimes 0 and 2; 64 percent under regimes 1 and 3).

The immediate issue is whether, in view of the similarity of their payoff profiles and the subtlety of their strategic differences, optional breakdown and forced breakdown games generate the same behavior, although a subgame-perfect analysis predicts D-M-O in the former and S-T-D in the latter. Before considering this question, some preliminary comments are useful:

How Big Is Epsilon?

Game theory treats players as rational optimizers, who are assumed to squeeze the last penny from a situation on the assumption that their opponent will do the same. But in practice one must accept that subjects will treat small enough amounts as negligible. As a rule-of-thumb we proceed as though anything less than the price of a cup of coffee (£0.2 = 4 percent of £5.00 at the time of the experiment) is negligible. In particular, we neglect the fact that the strategically optimal outcomes with the actual discount factor used ($\delta = 0.9$) differ slightly[7] from those in the limiting case when $\delta \to 1-$.

Round Number Focal Points

A further source of possible distortion is the tendency of subjects to settle on deals in round numbers. Under the high β regimes 1 and 3, this tendency makes S-T-D attractive (since 80 percent of the cake is £4.00 at time 0) and creates a possible focal point at 70 percent (which corresponds to £3.50 at time 0). Under the low β regimes 0 and 2, a round number focal point may exist at 60 percent (which corresponds to £3.00 at time 0).

Disagreements

It is sometimes argued that the fact that subjects often fail to agree immediately in bargaining games of perfect information is a serious obstacle to a game-theoretic interpretation of their behavior. It is true that, in the models of this paper, all equilibrium offers will be accepted in equilibrium and hence any refusal is an out-of-equilibrium phenomenon. However, although he accepts in equilibrium, the responder in these models is always

---

7. For example, under regime 0, a subgame-perfect analysis predicts 47.42 percent for player II when player I makes the first offer, and 52.67 percent when player II makes the first offer. These are both approximated by the 50 percent predicted by D-M-O.

indifferent between accepting and refusing. Thus a refusal by a responder does not necessarily represent a large deviation from the game-theoretic prediction if deviations are measured in terms of the responder's anticipated payoffs.[8]

This discussion is particularly relevant to disagreements in the "high optional" games of regime 1. A subgame-perfect equilibrium analysis of such games predicts that player I will offer player II approximately $\beta = 64$ percent at time 0, and that this will be accepted. But such an offer is approximately equal to player II's outside option in such games. If he refuses the offer made to him and instead takes his outside option, it is true that he deviates from what the analysis predicts, but the deviation is negligible in terms of the payoff he receives. For this reason we count disagreements under the high optional regime 1 as being supportive of the game-theoretic prediction (i.e., D-M-O) rather than dismiss them as "noise."

We do not do the same for "forced breakdown" games. The bargaining in the games of this type that the subjects played for money was *unilaterally* terminated by the computer after a minimum of seven offers had been rejected. Disagreements in forced breakdown games therefore convey little information relevant to this study, beyond the fact that disagreements do indeed occur even though they are not predicted.[9] The same goes for the "low optional" games of regime 0.

The Data

A statistical analysis appears in section 6.7. Figure 6.2 summarizes the data for the high β regimes 1 and 3. The difference of behavior between optional breakdown and forced breakdown games is very marked. At this point we note only that game theory predicts the observed behavior much better than the fairness/focal alternatives listed in Section 2 that take no account of strategic issues. It is not surprising that 50:50 does not do well when player II can get 64 percent without the consent of his

---

8. Moreover a prediction based on a subgame-perfect equilibrium analysis presupposes that it is common knowledge that the players are "perfectly rational." If subjects entertain doubts on this score, one might also see deviations from equilibrium by proposers who are "testing the rationality" of their opponent. One might then also observe deviations by responders who anticipate such behavior from their opponent in the future. This latter point is relevant to what follows in the text on opting out.

9. Note in particular that breakdown in the "high forced" regime 3 is *not* compatible with D-M-O when the latter is regarded as a "fairness" criterion because, although player II gets β, player I only gets α instead of his "fair" share of $1 - \beta$.

Regime 1: High–Optional

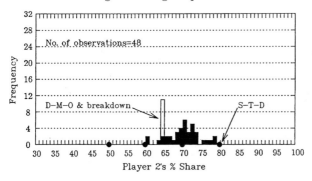

Regime 3: High–Forced

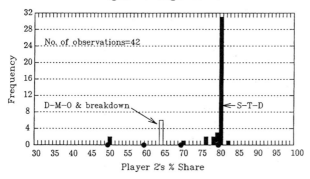

Figure 6.2
A comparison of the paid "high optional" games with the paid "high forced" games for the £5 cake. An open square (□) refers to the games that ended in a breakdown, and a solid square (■) to those that did not. The solid circles (●) on the horizontal axis at 50, 60, 70, and 80 percent indicate possible round number focal points. These percentages of £5 are £2.50, £3.00, £3.50, and £4.00 respectively.

partner,[10] but it is instructive that S-T-D predicts very much better than D-M-O in forced breakdown games, while D-M-O predicts better than S-T-D in optional breakdown games.

The results for the low β regimes 0 and 2 are summarized in figure 6.3. Here the differences between optional breakdown and forced breakdown are slight. The round number focal point at 60 percent (£3.00 at time 0) is perhaps responsible for producing this result, since it lies roughly midway between D-M-O (50 percent) and S-T-D (66 percent).

10. Although a number of researchers have observed systematic violations of individual rationality in related contexts.

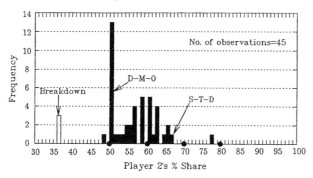

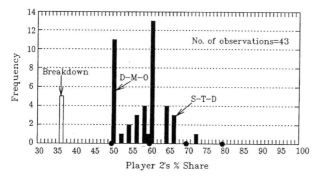

Figure 6.3
A comparison of the paid "low optional" games with the paid "low forced" games for the £5 cake. An open square (□) refers to the games that ended in a breakdown, and a solid square (■) to those that did not. The solid circles (●) on the horizontal axis at 50, 60, 70, and 80 percent indicate possible round number focal points. These percentages of £5 are £2.50, £3.00, £3.50, and £4.00 respectively.

To examine this possibility, we ran the low β regimes 0 and 2 again, but with the £5.00 cake replaced by an $11.00 cake. Subjects were told that their dollar winnings would be paid to them in pounds sterling at the then current exchange rate. Otherwise, the circumstances of the experiment were identical. The point of doing this was to create *two* round number focal points (at $6.00 and $7.00) between the D-M-O prediction of 50 percent and the S-T-D prediction of 66 percent. Figure 6.4 shows the sharper date obtained. The differences between optional breakdown and forced breakdown games are statistically significant (section 6.7). Game theory cannot be said to predict these data well, but it does better than the fairness/focal alternatives being considered.

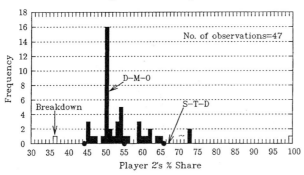

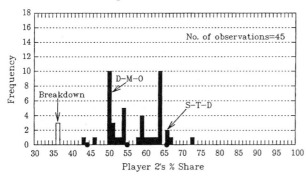

Figure 6.4
A comparison of the paid "low optional" games with the paid "high optional" games for the $11 cake. An open square (□) refers to the games that ended in a breakdown, and a solid square (■) to those that did not. The solid circles (●) on the horizontal axis at 45, 55, and 64 percent indicate possible round number focal points. These percentages of $11 are $5.00, $6,00, and $7.00 respectively.

6.5 Questionnaire

Interesting results were obtained from the subjects' answers to the questionnaire (appendix B). We discuss only[11] the answers to questions 5, 6, and 7. In these questions, the subjects were asked to indicate what they felt to be a fair way to split the cake in three situations. In each situation,

11. It is not clear to us how much weight can be given to the answers to question 8. For the record, we observe that 50 percent of the subjects were unambiguously of the view that it is socially acceptable to use one's bargaining power, and 17 percent were unambiguously of the opinion that one ought to "play fair."

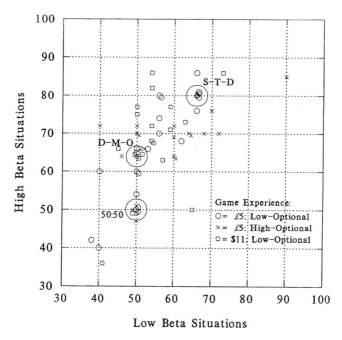

Figure 6.5
The share of the cake for player II proposed as "fair" for low and high β situations by subjects who had experienced optional breakdown games.

player I's breakdown share of the cake was $\alpha = 0.04$ but player II's was
successively $\beta = 0.04$, $\beta = 0.36$, and $\beta = 0.64$. The unanimous response to
question 5 ($\alpha = \beta = 0.04$) was that 50:50 is fair in this symmetric situation.

The answers to question 6 ($\beta = 0.36$) and question 7 ($\beta = 0.64$) are
summarized in figures 6.5 and 6.6. Figure 6.5 shows the views about fairness expressed by all those who had experienced optional breakdown
games (in which D-M-O is strategically optimal). The x-coordinate of
a point[12] in the figure shows what was asserted to be fair in a low-
breakdown payoff situation ($\beta = 36$ percent) and the y-coordinate shows
what was asserted to be fair in a high-breakdown payoff situation ($\beta = 64$
percent). Figure 6.6 similarly shows the views of all those who had experienced forced breakdown games (in which S-T-D is strategically optimal).

12. Too much significance should not be attached to the *precise* location of points in figures
6.5 and 6.6. For example, in figure 6.6, most subjects simply proposed the S-T-D point.
These choices have been indicated by clustering them as close to the S-T-D point as possible
without overlaps. Also subjects were not always very neat in marking their choice of a "fair
division" on their questionnaires.

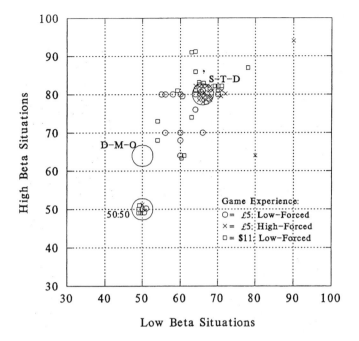

Figure 6.6
Share of the cake for player II proposed as "fair" for low and high β situations by subjects who had experienced forced breakdown games.

The difference between figures 6.5 and 6.6 is striking. (See section 6.7 for a statistical analysis.) Note, in particular, the following features:

1. In both figures a small group (around 10 percent) insists that 50:50 is "fair" despite the asymmetries they are invited to contemplate.

2. Those who had experienced forced breakdown games (S-T-D strategically optimal) were very much more in agreement about what is fair than those who had experienced optional breakdown games (D-M-O) strategically optimal). Results for optional breakdown games were very much more dispersed.

3. In forced breakdown games, S-T-D predicts what was asserted to be fair quite well, and D-M-O predicts very badly.

4. In optional breakdown games, the situation is more confused. However, D-M-O is no longer irrelevant to the data.

We do not feel that these results are conclusive, but they do suggest that people's views about what is fair may be heavily influenced by their strategic experiences in situations about which they do not have established preconceptions.

6.6 Unlearning

We were disappointed not to have sharper results under the optional breakdown regimes 0 and 1, since we had obtained sharp results in a previous study[13] of optional breakdown games (Binmore et al. 1989c), without apparent interference from round number focal points. However, in this previous study, subjects did not play repeatedly and hence had little opportunity to learn. It is therefore of interest to compare the results of our previous study with those shown in figure 6.7 for the first four practice games under the optional breakdown regimes 0 and 1 in the case of the £5.00 cake.[14]

The results from these practice games and those from our previous study are similar, in that D-M-O predicts the data quite well in absolute terms, and overwhelmingly better than S-T-D. The drift away from this distribution is evident from figure 6.3. One can tell a story for the high β regime 1 about subjects learning that player II needs an epsilon on top of what is available from opting out if he or she is to be kept at the negotiating table. However, this would not seem to explain why player II's payoffs should improve over time under the low β regime 0. Presumably round number focal points are somehow relevant. Evidence in support of this would seem to be provided by the differing results obtained for the low β regime 0 with an $11 cake (figure 6.4). More research will perhaps provide an explanation for what is going on here. For the moment, the only safe conclusion would seem to be that if people are indeed "natural gamesmen,"[15] then experience in this context would appear to lead to some "unlearning" of their game-playing skills.

6.7 Statistical Analysis

Here we present the results of nonparametric tests of the null hypothesis that the data sets presented in figures 6.2, 6.3, 6.4, and 6.7 are generated,

13. The size of the cake and the values of α and β were *not* the same.

14. We did not run regime 1 with an $11 cake. The results from practice games under regime 0 for the $11 cake are very similar to those for the £5 case. Only the first four practice games are reported, so the number of observations in each of the histograms of figures 6.2, 6.3, 6.4, and 6.7 is the same.

15. A view that has been wrongly attributed to us in the past.

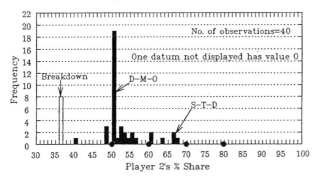

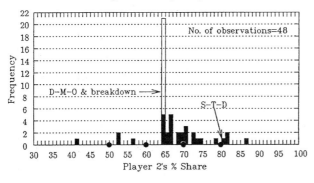

Figure 6.7
The first four *practice* games with optional breakdown for both low and high β in the case of the £5 cake. A open square (□) refers to the games that ended in a breakdown, and a solid square (■) to those that did not. The solid circles (●) on the horizontal axis at 50, 60, 70, and 80 percent indicate possible round number focal points. These percentages of £5 are £2.50, £3.00, £3.50, and £4.00 respectively.

pair by pair, by the same stochastic process. A variety of tests suitable for testing this hypothesis exists. The most commonly used in this context seem to be the Kolomogorov-Smirnov (KS), Cramèr-von Mises (CM), and Anderson-Darling (AD) tests. Each compares empirical cumulative density functions (cdf's). A recent new test of Epps and Singleton (ES) (1986) compares empirical moment-generating functions.

The tests above are "nonparametric" in the sense that their significance levels are not affected by the actual stochastic process generating the observed data. However, the *powers* of the tests do depend on the specifics of the two stochastic processes generating the data. Little is known about the finite sample size ranking of these tests by their powers for various types of stochastic processes. Consequently we conducted a Monte

Table 6.2

Nonpara-metric test results	Test employed											
	KS			CM			AD			ES		
	Value	10%	5%	Value	10%	5%	Value	10%	5%	Value	10%	5%
Figure 6.2	0·845	Yes	Yes	5·84	Yes	Yes	25·9	Yes	Yes	413	Yes	Yes
Figure 6.3	0·180	No	No	0·228	No	No	1·05	No	No	9·58	No	No
Figure 6.4	0·256	Yes	No	0·736	Yes	Yes	3·77	Yes	Yes	14·2	No	No
Figure 6.7	0·842	Yes	Yes	4·48	Yes	Yes	22·2	Yes	Yes	155	Yes	Yes

Carlo study in an effort to deduce if one test or another might "dominate" the others by offering largest power in the context of our study. The results of this study are presented in appendix C. The alternative distributions examined were selected so as approximately to mimic the empirical cdf's observed. We concluded that none of the four tests dominated the others, although the CM and AD tests generally performed at least as well as the KS and ES tests. These findings contrast with the results of the Monte Carlo study of Forsythe et al. (1988), who found that as a pair, the AD and ES tests dominated the others. A number of reasons explain the differing conclusions. In particular, different sample sizes were used (25 in Forsythe et al. 1988 and 40 here) and different alternative hypotheses were examined.

The test results are presented in table 6.2. The "value" columns report the observed values of the statistics. The 10 percent and 5 percent columns report if the tests retain the null hypothesis of no difference in distribution or reject it, at the 10 percent and 5 percent significance levels, respectively. The tests all reject the null hypothesis of no difference in the cases of figures 6.2 and 6.7, and all retain the null hypothesis for figure 6.3. The data for figure 6.4 lead to a strong rejection of the null hypothesis by the CM and AD tests, a rejection by the KS test at the 10 percent significance level, and a retention by the ES test (the prob-value of the ES test is 16.5 percent).

The two histograms of figure 6.4 suggest that the differences in the two data sets are, first, a shift in central location and, second, a difference in the size of a mass point. The Monte Carlo cases 2, 3, and 4 described in appendix C investigate the relative powers of the four tests in the presence of shifts of central location and/or variance. Cases 8 and 9 were intended to reveal the tests's relative powers when a substantial mass point was introduced. In all these cases the ES test is dominated (sometimes sharply) at either significance level by the CM or AD test. For these reasons we attribute more weight to the strong rejections of the null hypothesis of no difference by the CM an AD tests than to the somewhat weaker retention of the null hypothesis by the ES test.

We also tested the null hypothesis that the data presented in figures 6.5 and 6.6 were generated by the same bivariate process. There is a dearth of two-dimensional nonparametric tests available for this task. Extensions of the KS and Wald-Wolfowitz tests from one dimension to two have been developed by Friedman and Rafsky (1979), but as yet they are poorly tabulated. Accordingly we adopted the following approach, which mimics techniques used by spatial statisticians. We categorized the data points into six regions by dividing the rectangle $[30, 100] \times [30, 100]$ vertically at 57.5 and horizontally at 57.5 and 71.5. The regions are labeled 1 to 6 from top left to bottom right. 57.5 is the horizontal coordinate halfway between the D-M-O (and 50:50) and S-T-D points. 71.5 is the vertical coordinate halfway between the D-M-O and S-T-D points. 57 is the vertical coordinate halfway between the D-M-O and 50:50 points. Any data points occurring on a boundary were assigned to the lower region. Doing so weakens the case for rejection of the null hypothesis. The respective numbers of data points in the regions are 10, 14, 20, 9, 12, and 1 for figure 6.5, a total of 66 data points, and 3, 48, 2, 6, 8, and 0 for figure 6.6, a total of 67 data points. The null hypothesis under test is that the two data sets are generated by the same stochastic process. Accordingly we estimate the probability of a data point being generated for a particular region by combining the two samples and then computing the relative frequencies for the region from the combined sample of 133 data points. The respective probabilities so assigned to the six regions are 13/133, 62/133, 22/133, 15/133, 20/133, and 1/133. These probabilities imply that the marginal and conditional probabilities for a data point (x_1, x_2) generated by the estimated stochastic process are

$$\Pr(30 \leq x_1 \leq 57.5) = \frac{55}{133},$$

$$\Pr(57.5 < x_1 \leq 100) = \frac{78}{133},$$

$$\Pr(30 \leq x_2 \leq 57 \mid 30 \leq x_1 \leq 57.5) = \frac{20}{55},$$

$$\Pr(30 \leq x_2 \leq 57 \mid 57.5 < x_1 \leq 100) = \frac{1}{78},$$

$$\Pr(57 < x_2 \le 71.5 \,|\, 30 \le x_1 \le 57.5) = \frac{22}{55},$$

$$\Pr(57 < x_2 \le 71.5 \,|\, 57.5 < x_1 \le 100) = \frac{15}{78},$$

$$\Pr(71 < x_2 \le 100 \,|\, 30 \le x_1 \le 58) = \frac{13}{55},$$

$$\Pr(71.5 < x_2 \le 100 \,|\, 57.5 < x_1 \le 100) = \frac{62}{78}.$$

We used this bivariate stochastic process to generate two independent samples, the first of size 66 and the second of size 67. The "distance" between the two samples was then computed as the sum, over the six regions, of the absolute values of the differences in the relative frequencies. We generated 1,500 pairs of samples and computed the empirical distribution of the resulting 1,500 values of the distance statistic. The range of the statistic is $[0, 2]$, but the observed empirical distribution was concentrated almost entirely between 0.1 and 0.5; the largest observed value was 0.713. The value of the statistic for the data displayed in figures 6.5 and 6.6 is 1.009. We conclude that the null hypothesis that the data presented in figures 6.5 and 6.6 were generated by the same process can be rejected with very high confidence. This conclusion would be unaffected by moderate changes to the positions of the boundaries of regions 1 to 6.

6.8 Concluding Remarks

The results of this experiment are consistent with the view that if the preconceived rules-of-thumb with which players may originally approach a game are not too firmly established, then they can be displaced by more sophisticated rules that take better account of the strategic realities of the situation. Moreover there is evidence that subjects are willing to justify their new behavior by asserting that it is fair. It is *not* argued that these conclusions support the view that fairness/focal theories are mistaken. Nor is it claimed that subjects are natural gamesmen. Our belief is that a more sophisticated type of theory than either of these alternatives is necessary.

We do not believe that people are natural gamesmen, if the term "natural gamesman" is taken to mean an individual who is familiar with all

the results of game theory, who is capable of lightning mental calculations of great complexity, and who takes for granted that other individuals selected at random from the population at large have the same
characteristics as themselves. In so far as people behave like gamesmen,
it is presumably because they are capable, to some extent, of adapting
their behavior to new situations. We do not believe that the manner in
which people learn in game-like situations is optimal or even close to optimal. It is clearly often a hit-and-miss affair that operates below the level
of consciousness to a considerable degree. Nevertheless, we believe that
game theory can be useful in predicting the outcome of such learning
processes.

One may speculate that people are equipped with rules-of-thumb that
they use to settle conflicts of interest that arise in real-life bargaining situations and elsewhere, and that these rules-of-thumb embody fairness
criteria or depend in other ways on salient or focal features of the environment in which they are used. We will follow Dawkins (1976) in referring to such rules-of-thumb as memes. It seems unlikely that people think
very hard about these memes when using them in the real-life situations
to which they are adapted. One tends to question ingrained habits or cus-
toms only when their use generates unsatisfactory results.

What triggers a switch from one meme to another? We have no general
theory to propose. Certainly this experiment was not designed to answer
such a question. Its design specifically excludes the rich variety of conver-
sational or contextual cues that presumably prompt the substitution of
one meme for another under the conditions of everyday life. At best the
experiment only serves to demonstrate that such switches from one meme
to another can occur, and that game theory can be relevant in predicting
the nature of the switch. There are evolutionary reasons why this may be
thought plausible. One may ask: Given a meme that is established in a
human population, how does it manage to survive? Why does it not get
displaced by an alternative meme? The game theorist's answer is that it
survives because it is adapted to the environment in which it is commonly
used. That is to say, it prescribes behavior that is in equilibrium.[16] People
will not usually be conscious of this fact and may be quite truthful in

---

16. It goes without saying that this is a gross simplification. One must take into account the
complexity of the meme's environment. The more complex the environment, the more difficult it will be for better adapted memes to surface, and the longer it will take for them to
become established. One must also consider the cost to individuals of implementing complicated strategies. And so on.

reporting that they are unmotivated by strategic considerations. But it is not necessary for individuals to know why a particular meme survives in order for it to survive.

If this view is correct, a least in some circumstances, then one should expect to observe memes in operation that are triggered by hints or cues in the environment that match the strategic realities of the situation. We hope that the current paper will be seen as a confirmation of the viability of such a standpoint rather than as just a refutation of a naïve version of the fairness/focal explanation of human behavior. Subjects were put in situations for which life did not seem to have equipped them in advance with a strongly established rule-of-thumb. Behavior then evolved that correlated with the strategic situation, and many subjects seemingly developed attitudes toward fairness that allowed them to rationalize this behavior in terms that were familiar to them.

This behavior of our subjects is clearly not supportive of those who might wish to argue that "fairness memes" are altogether irrelevant in describing the behavior of subjects in such laboratory experiments as ours. Moreover we do not doubt that it is possible to construct experiments in which adaptation to the environment of the kind we observed does *not* occur, even with large incentives and long time spans for learning. One might frame the experiment in such a way as to trigger a form of the fairness meme that is very firmly established for use in a particular real-world context but which bears only a surface resemblance to the problem faced in the laboratory.[17] Alternatively, it would not be hard to interfere with the learning process by confusing the issues facing the subjects. Indeed we seem to have done so inadvertently under regimes 0 and 2 with the £5 cake by introducing a round number focal point at £3.00. Such experiments, confirming that fairness is relevant to the way people resolve bargaining problems, would not and do not refute the view that we are defending here.

In summary, in defending the relevance of game theory to actual bargaining behavior, we are not denying that fairness/focal theories are also relevant. We deny only that a theory of this type that ignores strategic considerations is likely to get to what lies at the heart of human bargaining behavior. Most of all we want to emphasize the importance of learning and adaptation in this context.

---

17. Invoking the meme in such pathological circumstances is, of course, precisely what one would wish to do if one's aim were to study the mechanics of a particular established meme.

Appendix A: The Instructions

Different written instructions were offered to subjects depending on the regime of the game they were to play, and whether they would be player I or player II in their first bargaining session. The instructions below are for a subject about to begin as player I under regime 1. The instructions for a subject about to begin as player I under regime 3 were identical with the exception of the fourth paragraph. This was replaced, under regime 3, by the paragraph quoted in section 6.3. Instructions for regimes 0 and 2 were the same except that the figure of £3.20 was replaced by £1.80. The necessary modifications for a subject about to begin as player II will be evident.

Bargaining Experiment: Regime 1, Subject 0

This is an experiment in which you will bargain via the computing equipment in front of you with the persons in the other booths. There will be *ten* separate and distinct bargaining sessions after each of which the person with whom you are paired may change. The initial six sessions are for practice. The remaining four sessions are "for real". The other four persons were recruited in the same way as you and the order in which you and they will be paired has been chosen at random.

In each of the ten sessions a "cake" which is always *nominally* worth £5 will be available for the two bargainers to share, provided they can come to an agreement on how it should be split. You and the other person will alternate in making proposals until *either* a proposal is accepted or the negotiations break down. You will make the first proposal in the *first* session but in five of the ten sessions it will be the other person who makes the first proposal.

Once a proposal is accepted, each of the two parties to the agreement will have his or her agreed share credited to their accounts. *BUT*, if the negotiations get broken off, the opportunity to split the cake will disappear. Instead, each player will receive a *BREAKDOWN* payment. In the *first* session, your breakdown payment is 20p and the other person's is £3.20. But in five of the ten sessions, it will be your breakdown payment which is £3.20 and the other person's which is 20p.

Breakdowns can only occur immediately after a proposal has been refused. It is the person who just refused a proposal who decides whether or not to break off the negotiations. If the decision is to continue bargaining, the cake *SHRINKS TO 90% OF ITS PREVIOUS SIZE* and so, of course, do the breakdown payments.

The final four sessions are for "real" and we will pay you all the money you make in these sessions immediately after the last bargaining session in which you are involved. The preceding six sessions are for practice only. In these sessions you will have to pretend that you are bargaining over real money.

In summary, you have to remember that each proposal which is made may be the last. But even if the negotiations get broken off, the session will not be a complete wash-out for you since you will still get your breakdown payment.

This is not an experiment to find out what sort of person you are. When we see the results, we shall neither know nor care who did what. We are only interested in what happens on average. So please do not feel that some particular kind of behavior is expected of you.

Before the first bargaining session, there will be a demonstration of the computing equipment. The demonstration program is started by pressing the SPACE BAR. But there is no need to hurry. You may have to wait for the other persons to be ready anyway. Read the instructions again if you think this may be helpful, or call the assistant if you need a question answered.

Appendix B: The Questionnaire

It would help us if you would give brief answers to the following questions:

1. Where were you recruited?

2. Were the instructions and the demonstration program clear?

3. Were there any hitches during the experiment?

4. Why did you bargain the way you did?

5. On the scale below, indicate what you feel would be a fair way to split the cake if person 1's and person 2's breakdown payments are both £0.20.

Figure 6.8

6. On the scale below, indicate what you feel would be a fair way to split the cake if person 1's breakdown payment is £0.20 and person 2's breakdown payment is £1.80.

Figure 6.9

7. On the scale below, indicate what you feel would be a fair way to split the cake if person 1's breakdown payment is £0.20 and person 2's breakdown payment is £3.20.

Figure 6.10

8. Is this the sort of situation in which people ought to "play fair" or is it socially acceptable for them to make what use they can of whatever bargaining power they have?

9. Would you bargain in the same way if you were put in the same situation tomorrow?

Appendix C: The Monte Carlo Study

The nonparametric test statistics used were the Kolmogorov-Smirnov (KS), Cramèr-von Mises (CM), Anderson-Darling (AD), and Epps-Singleton (ES) statistics. Let $F_1(x)$ and $F_2(x)$ denote two cumulative density functions (cdf's) defined on an observation space $X \in \mathbb{R}$. The null hypothesis is $H_0 : F_1 \equiv F_2$. The alternative, H_A, is that H_0 is false. Let $\hat{F}_1$ and $\hat{F}_2$ denote the empirical cdf's generated by two independent random samples, of sizes n_1 and n_2, respectively, from X. Let $\hat{F}_{12}$ denote the empirical cdf generated by the combined sample, of size $n_1 + n_2$. The KS, CM, and AD test statistics compare the empirical cdfs $\hat{F}_1$, $\hat{F}_2$, and $\hat{F}_{12}$. They are defined as follows:

$$KS \equiv \sup_{x \in X} |\hat{F}_1(x) - \hat{F}_2(x)|,$$

$$CM \equiv \left(\frac{1}{n_1} + \frac{1}{n_2}\right) \int_X [\hat{F}_1(x) - \hat{F}_2(x)]^2 \, dF_{12}(x),$$

and

$$AD \equiv \left(\frac{1}{n_1} + \frac{1}{n_2}\right) \int_X \frac{(\hat{F}_1(x) - \hat{F}_2(x))^2}{\hat{F}_{12}(x)[1 - \hat{F}_{12}(x)]}.$$

The ES statistic measures the distance between the empirical characteristic functions generated by the two samples. For an arbitrary but fixed integer $J \geq 1$, let $\{t_1, \ldots, t_J\}$ be real and positive numbers. Let X_{ij} denote observation i from sample j. The empirical characteristic function for sample j is

$$\phi_j(t_k) \equiv \frac{1}{n_j} \sum_{i=1}^{n_j} (\cos t_k X_{ij} + i \sin t_k X_{ij})$$

for $k = 1, \ldots, J$ and for $j = 1, 2$.

Denote the $2J \times n_j$ matrix of the real and imaginary parts of ϕ_j by

$$G_j = \begin{pmatrix} \cos t_1 X_{1j} & \cos t_1 X_{2j} & \cdots & \cos t_1 X_{n_j j} \\ \sin t_1 X_{1j} & \sin t_1 X_{2j} & \cdots & \sin t_1 X_{n_j j} \\ \vdots & \vdots & & \vdots \\ \cos t_J X_{1j} & \cos t_J X_{2j} & \cdots & \cos t_j X_{n_j j} \\ \sin t_J X_{1j} & \sin t_J X_{2j} & \cdots & \sin t_J X_{n_j j} \end{pmatrix} \quad \text{for } j = 1, 2.$$

The average row sums of G_j are denoted by the $2J \times 1$ vector

$$g_j = \frac{1}{n_j} \left(\sum_{i=1}^{n_j} \cos t_1 X_{ij}, \sum_{i=1}^{n_j} \sin t_1 X_{ij}, \ldots, \sum_{i=1}^{n_j} \cos t_J X_{ij}, \sum_{i=1}^{n_j} \sin t_J X_{ij} \right)^T$$

for $j = 1, 2$.

The Epps-Singleton statistic is

$$\text{ES} \equiv c \cdot \frac{2n_1 n_2}{n_1 + n_2} (g_1 - g_2)^T (\hat{S}_1 + \hat{S}_2)^{-1} (g_1 - g_2),$$

where $\hat{S}_1$ and $\hat{S}_2$ are the variance-covariance matrices of G_1 and G_2, respectively, and c is a small sample correction factor. The ES statistic is asymptotically distributed as a χ^2 variable with $2J$ degrees of freedom. We chose sample sizes of $n_1 = n_2 = 40$ for our study since the sizes of our data sets are close to these values. Following the recommendations given in Epps and Singleton (1986) for such sample sizes, we chose $J = 5$, $(t_1, t_2, t_3, t_4, t_5) = (0.4, 0.8, 1.2, 1.6, 2.0)$ and $c = 0.849$.

The alternative hypotheses used in our study are listed in table 6.3. The table also presents the estimated powers of each test, for significance levels of 10 and 5 percent. 10,000 independent pairs of samples of 40 data were generated for each case and the power estimates for the 10 and 5 percent significance levels were computed as the fraction of the

Table 6.3

Case number	Distributions		Estimated powers of the test statistics							
			KS		CM		AD		ES	
	F_1	F_2	10%	5%	10%	5%	10%	5%	10%	5%
1	$U[40, 85]$	$U[60, 80]$	0.997	0.975	0.993	0.970	0.999	0.995	0.999	0.996
2	$N(50, 100)$	$N(65, 100)$	1.000	0.999	1.000	1.000	1.000	1.000	1.000	0.999
3	$N(50, 400)$	$N(65, 400)$	0.880	0.723	0.936	0.883	0.939	0.892	0.582	0.452
4	$N(50, 100)$	$N(65, 400)$	0.998	0.983	0.998	0.994	0.999	0.997	0.982	0.963
5	$U(30, 70)$	$N(50, 100)$	0.208	0.060	0.211	0.097	0.249	0.121	0.353	0.240
6	50 with prob. 0.2; $N(50, 100)$ with prob. 0.8	$N(50, 100)$	0.238	0.088	0.212	0.104	0.196	0.098	0.219	0.140
7	50 with prob. 0.2; $N(50, 400)$ with prob. 0.8	$N(50, 400)$	0.232	0.088	0.207	0.098	0.192	0.093	0.221	0.137
8	50 with prob. 0.4; $N(50, 100)$ with prob. 0.6	$N(50, 100)$	0.662	0.355	0.778	0.571	0.720	0.513	0.671	0.558
9	50 with prob. 0.4; $N(50, 400)$ with prob. 0.6	$N(50, 400)$	0.657	0.351	0.774	0.569	0.716	0.515	0.669	0.558

10,000 replications for which the null hypothesis that $F_1 \equiv F_2$ was rejected at these significance levels.

The table suggests that no test dominates the others at the 10 percent level. The KS test never wins at the 5 percent significance level. The CM and AD tests generally do better than the KS and ES tests at either significance level for cases 2, 3, and 4, which present cases of shifts of central location and/or variance. The CM test does best at recognizing differences in distribution due to the existence of a substantial mass point. (The ES test is nonparametric even for discontinuous cdfs. However, the KS, CM, and AD tests assume continuous cdf's and so are not truly nonparametric for cases 6 through 9.) The results above contrast with those obtained by Forsythe et al. who selected the AD and ES tests over the others on the basis of a study using samples of size 25. Our study's results left us unable to discard any of the four tests.

References

Binmore, K., P. Morgan, A. Shaked, and J. Sutton. 1989a. Do people exploit their bargaining power? An experimental study. CREST Working Paper 89-15. University of Michigan.

Binmore, K., M. Osborne, and A. Rubinstein. 1989b. Noncooperative models of bargaining. CREST Working Paper 89-26. University of Michigan; in *The Handbook of Game Theory*, in press.

Binmore, K., A. Shaked, and J. Sutton. 1989c. An outside option experiment. *Quart. J. Econ.* 104: 753–70.

Binmore, K., A. Shaked, and J. Sutton. 1985. Testing noncooperative bargaining theory: A preliminary study. *Amer. Econ. Rev.* 75: 1178–80.

Binmore, K., A. Shaked, and J. Sutton. 1988. A further test of noncooperative bargaining theory: Reply. *Amer. Econ. Rev.* 78: 837–39.

Cramton, P. 1988. Dynamic bargaining with outside options. Unpublished manuscript. Yale School of Management.

Dawkins, R. 1976. *The Selfish Gene*. Oxford: Oxford University Press.

Epps, T. W., and K. J. Singleton. 1986. An omnibus test for the two-sample problem using the empirical characteristic function. *J. Statist. Comput. Simul.* 26: 177–203.

Forsythe, R., J. L. Horowitz, N. E. Savin, and M. Sefton. 1988. Replicability fairness and pay in experiments with simple bargaining games. Working Paper 88-03. Department of Economics, University of Iowa.

Friedman, J. H., and L. C. Rafsky. 1979. Multivariate generalizations of the Wald-Wolfowitz and Smirnov two-sample tests. *Ann. Statist.* 7: 679–717.

Güth, W. 1990. Behavioral theory of distributive justice. In S. Maital, ed., *Applied Behavioral Economics*. Sussex: Brighton.

Kahneman, D., J. Knetsch, and J. Thaler. 1986. Fairness and the assumptions of economics. *J. Bus.* 59: 285–300.

Leventhal, G. 1980. What should be done with equity theory? New approaches to the study of fairness in social relationships. In K. Gergen, M. Greenberg, and R. Willis, eds., *Social Exchange: Advances in Theory and Research*. New York: Plenum.

Roth, A. 1985. Towards a focal point theory of bargaining. In A. Roth, ed., *Game-Theoretic Models of Bargaining*. Cambridge: Cambridge University Press.

Rubinstein, A. 1982. Perfect equilibrium in a bargaining model. *Econometrica* 50: 97–109.

Selten, R. 1978. The equity principle in economic behavior. In H. Gottinger and W. Leinfellner, eds., *Decision Theory and Social Ethics, Issues in Social Choice*. Dordrecht: Reidel.

Shaked, A. 1987. Opting out: Bazaars versus "hi tech" markets. STICERD Discussion Paper TE 87/159. London School of Economics.

Sutton, J. 1986. Noncooperative bargaining theory—An introduction. *Rev. Econ. Stud.* 53: 709–24.

Thibaut, J. 1968. The development of contractual norms in bargaining: Replication and variation. *J. Conflict Resolution* 12: 102–12.

Walster, E., E. Berscheid, and G. Walster. 1973. New directions in equity research. *J. Personality Soc. Psychol.* 25: 151–76.

7 Lost Opportunities

The Coase theorem encapsulates a view that has held sway since at least the time of Edgeworth (1881). It says that rational bargainers with negligible transaction costs will agree on an efficient outcome. If we exclude some pathological cases, modern game theory accords with the Coase theorem in the case where information is perfect.[1]

The Rubinstein (1982) outcome remains efficient even when the costs of delay in his model are large. Layfolk are often disappointed that all the action in the Alternating-Offers Game reduces to an immediate acceptance of the first offer made. But why would perfectly rational people fool around when everybody's cards are on the table right from the start?

However, any perfectly rational subjects who find themselves in real laboratories would be stupid to assume that their fellow subjects are also perfectly rational. It therefore isn't perhaps surprising that the Coase theorem doesn't work well in the Alternating-Offers Game. Sometimes there are many refusals before an agreement is reached.

Players commonly shade down their demands during this period until a compromise is reached. In doing so, they must pay the cost of delaying while learning about their opponent. It is only when the shares finally agreed are evaluated as a fraction of the cake available *at the time of agreement* that the Rubinstein prediction fits reasonably well (chapter 5).

A possible interpretation is that it takes time before an implicit consensus emerges between the players that both are sufficiently rational for Rubinstein's theory to work. In any case, at least as much learning is going on within each Rubinstein game as between games.

Opting Out

A more fundamental source of inefficiency arises when the Rubinstein theory predicts that one of the player's outside options will be active.

This happens if Eve has an outside option that exceeds what she would get if the theory were applied without outside options. The Rubinstein theory then says that Adam will offer Eve her outside option, and that she will accept in equilibrium, although she is then actually indifferent between accepting and refusing. Students who question her predicted behavior in such situations are told that Adam can always prevent her opting out by offering her an extra few pennies. But perhaps he will underestimate the number of extra pennies he needs to offer, and so provoke her into irrevocably ending their negotiation by taking up her outside option.

Although the contract literature seems to ignore the problem, such hard bargaining when a deal is just on the edge being worthwhile for one of the players must surely often result in potentially efficient deals falling through. In any case, this is what happens in the laboratory. Indeed, if it were appropriate to count as negative the cases in which Eve actually opts out when she should strictly accept an offer equal to her outside option, then the support the experiment offers for Rubinstein's theory would be markedly diminished.

The Outside Option Game

In tandem with our experimental work on how people learn in laboratory games, my coauthors and I have also sought to make theoretical contributions to the theory of adjustment processes in games. In the paper reported in this chapter, we join these two strands of research.

Because the Rubinstein bargaining model is too complicated for our theoretical capacity, we return to the relatively simple Nash Demand Game of chapter 2 (but without any fuzzing of the boundary). The opportunity for Eve to take an outside option, leaving Adam with nothing is then added to her strategies.

It is no surprise that the Coase theorem should frequently fail in the laboratory when Eve's outside option is high. Nor is it a surprise by now that the subjects show a strong tendency to characterize their own experience in the laboratory as what fairness recommends. But can we make theoretical sense of how and why subjects don't learn to bargain more efficiently as they gain experience?

I think that we are looking at an example of what Samuelson and I call a hanging valley in our papers on evolutionary drift (Binmore and Samuelson 1997). Figure 7.1 shows a hanging valley in what theoretical biologists call a "fitness landscape." We normally think of a stable equilibrium as lying by itself at the bottom of a fitness valley, but the floor of a valley in a fitness landscape derived even from very simple games com-

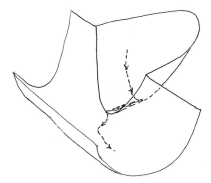

Figure 7.1
A hanging valley in a fitness landscape. A dynamic system can get trapped in such a hanging valley for very long intervals before being flushed out by an unlikely conjunction of random shocks. It can then fall back into the same hanging valley—as in an Escher sketch.

monly consists of a whole connected component of Nash equilibria. For example, the set N in figure 3.3 is the floor of such a valley for the unperturbed replicator dynamics in the Ultimatum Minigame. A similar hanging valley for the three-legged Centipede Game features in the second paper of appendix B.

In the Outside Option Game, a Nash equilibrium in which Eve is left indifferent between taking up her outside option or planning to accept an offer from Adam equal to her outside option is likely to have similar properties to the escape equilibrium in the Ultimatum Minigame. But there is nowhere obvious for the escape trajectory to go in the Outside Option Game but back to the set of equilibria from which it just escaped.[2]

If this speculative story is right, then we shouldn't expect evolution to cure the inefficiencies caused by breakdowns in the Outside Option Game, even if it were given all eternity to accomplish the task. At best we should expect to see the system drift in response to unmodeled noise when the evolutionary pressures fall away in the vicinity of the game's connected component of pure Nash equilibria. For high values of the outside option, the system will then continually be wandering into breakdown territory.

We don't succeed in capturing the complexity of this story with our attempt at a theoretical model in the paper. Current theoretical tools aren't really up to the task. But perhaps the effort that we put into trying to make sense of our data will be compared favorably with the naive stories of those who see no role at all for trial-and-error learning in bargaining experiments.

Hard Bargains and Lost Opportunities

Ken Binmore, Chris Proulx, Larry Samuelson, and Joe Swierzbinski

Orthodox economic theory assumes that the entrepreneurial spirit will call forth individuals or institutions to exploit gains from trade wherever they exist. Implicit in this assumption is the understanding that the parties to any potential deal will agree on a division of the surplus providing each with a share sufficient to ensure their cooperation.

When bargaining over the division of a surplus, each agent has an incentive to extract the largest possible share consistent with the other parties being willing to continue in the relationship. Demands in an alternating-offers negotiation are chosen to drive the responder to indifference between accepting and rejecting (Rubinstein 1982). Demands in a simultaneous-offer negotiation are chosen so that not even the tiniest scrap of surplus remains unclaimed (Nash 1953). In equilibrium, responding players accept in the former case and opposing players make compatible demands in the latter. But only a small misjudgment on either side would be enough to delay agreement or to destroy it altogether. The equilibrium outcome therefore calls for agreement on an efficient deal, but the players' equilibrium strategies leave them precariously perched on the edge of disagreement.

Hard bargaining is entirely consistent with efficiency in a world of perfect information with perfectly rational agents who never make mistakes, but the real world is less accommodating. The leap from models filled

We thank a referee and David Cooper for helpful comments. The support of National Science Foundation grants SES-9122176, SBR-9320678, and especially SES-8821521, for funding the experiments, is gratefully acknowledged. We also thank the University of Michigan for founding the Michigan Economics Laboratory, where the experiments were conducted. The work was completed with the assistance of funding from the UK Economic and Social Research Council grant L122-25-1003. During its progress, Binmore and Samuelson enjoyed the hospitality and support of the Department of Economics at the University of Bonn (Deutsche Forschungsgemeinschaft, Sonderforschungsbereich 303) and the Institute for Advanced Studies at the Hebrew University of Jerusalem. We are grateful to both.

with rational agents to the world of real people is often justified by arguing that learning, imitation, or the discipline of the market will cause low-payoff behavior to be supplanted over time by high-payoff behavior (Alchian 1950; Friedman 1953). If enough money is involved, the school of hard knocks may indeed eventually teach its graduates to approximate the behavior of the idealized agents of orthodox economic theory, but there is no guarantee that they will learn to reproduce all the fine details of perfectly rational bargaining strategies. Instead of reaching a compromise just short of disagreement, one must expect that a bargainer will sometimes overreach himself just enough to push his opponent over the edge. The chance of reaching an efficient deal will then be lost. Even in a world that is only marginally imperfect, a tension therefore arises between the intuition that agents will learn to drive a hard bargain and the claim that economic opportunities will seldom remain unexploited.

Coase (1960) argues that this tension between efficiency and distribution will be resolved in favour of efficiency if transactions costs are negligible. Rubinstein's analysis of alternating-offers bargaining models with perfect information can be regarded as showing that efficient outcomes will also appear even when the transactions costs of refusing an offer are *not* negligible (1982). However, the experiments of Binmore et al. (1989, 1991) with such bargaining models show that substantial fractions of agents inefficiently opt out despite high discount factors (and hence low transactions costs). In contrast to such evidence, the literature on contract theory typically reconciles bargaining and efficiency by assuming that take-it-or-leave-it offers of no more than the responder's outside option will necessarily be accepted, and that responders will opt in to relationships knowing that they will face such offers.[3]

This paper examines an *Outside Option Game* in which one player can sink a cost in order to create a surplus to be divided with another player. The bargaining that follows the decision to opt in by sinking the cost is modeled using a modification of the Nash Demand Game.[4] We report

---

3. See, for example, Chung (1991), Hart and Moore (1988), Hermalin and Katz (1991), and the survey by Hart and Holmstrom (1987). The assumption that an indifferent responder will accept is sometimes defended by observing that she can always be offered an extra $\varepsilon > 0$ to remain in the relationship. But ε itself will be the subject of hard bargaining. If the second player finally accepts ε instead of her outside option of x, it will be because her outside option is not x but $x + \varepsilon$—the *real* amount that just prevents her opting out.

4. A more satisfactory model might employ Rubinstein's alternating-offers game, but its complexity complicates the attempt to offer a theoretical explanation of opting out behaviour, which occurs in experimental alternating-offers games even in the absence of an initial cost-sinking move (Binmore et al. 1989; 1991). The take-it-or-leave-it offers of a Nash Demand Game are also more in line with the standard models of contract theory.

experimental results for the Outside Option Game in which inefficient outcomes are commonplace despite a design intended to facilitate efficient deals. We explain this phenomenon as an equilibrium of an adaptive process in which agents must learn to play the game in an imperfect world. When player 2's outside option is sufficiently high, players do not learn to cooperate and gains from trade remain unexploited.

The following section introduces the Outside Option Game. Section 7.2 discusses the relationship of our work to previous results. Section 7.3 reports the results of an experiment whose instructions appear in the appendix. Section 7.4 analyses the equilibrium behaviour of agents who must play the Outside Option Game in an imperfect world. Section 7.5 concludes.

7.1 The Outside Option Game

The bargaining game we consider involves two players who can keep a ten dollar bill if they can agree on how to divide it. In the classic Nash Demand Game (Nash 1953), players 1 and 2 simultaneously announce take-it-or-leave-it demands, x and y. If $x + y \leq 10$, player 1 receives x and 2 receives y. Otherwise, each gets nothing.

The Outside Option Game modifies the rules of Nash's game in two ways. First, we add an opt-out strategy "O" to player 2's list of strategies. If she opts out instead of making a demand, she receives a payoff of α $(0 < \alpha < 10)$ and player 1 gets nothing, whatever he may have demanded. Second, if player 2 opts in and $x + y \leq 10$, then each player gets half the unclaimed surplus on top of his or her claim. Thus player 1 gets $x + \frac{1}{2}(10 - x - y)$ and player 2 gets $y + \frac{1}{2}(10 - x - y)$. We think of this game as modelling the negotiation over the division of the profits from a partnership worth ten dollars, where only player 2 incurs an opportunity cost of α dollars in joining the partnership.

We sort the pure-strategy Nash equilibria of the Outside Option Game, all of which are also subgame perfect, into two classes:[5]

Efficient equilibria Any pair $(10 - y, y)$ with $y \geq \alpha$ is an efficient Nash equilibrium.

Inefficient equilibria Any pair $(10 - y, O)$ with $y \leq \alpha$ is an inefficient Nash equilibrium.

5. Mixed-strategy Nash equilibria also exist, all of which are inefficient.

Efficiency thus requires player 2 to opt into the game and for the players to make compatible demands that give player 2 a payoff of at least α. There are many such demands, and hence many efficient equilibria. Opting out is always inefficient.

Our basic questions are: *How will the players split the surplus and compensate player 2 for the opportunity cost she incurs in joining the partnership? Will attempts to drive a hard bargain sometimes lead to inefficient outcomes in which player 2 opts out?*

The Outside Option Game focuses attention on the tensions between efficiency and hard bargaining because, when α is large, an efficient outcome can appear only if player 2 aggressively seeks an asymmetrically large share of the total surplus. If she is not convinced that player 1 recognises the need to accommodate such a share, she may simply opt out.[6]

At the same time, the Outside Option Game facilitates efficient outcomes by allowing player 2 to use the fact that any unclaimed surplus is split equally to secure some protection against the risks of hard bargaining. Suppose player 2 is convinced that player 1 will make a demand that leaves 2 a share at least as large as α, but is not certain which of these demands player 1 will make. By opting in and claiming only α, player 2 can ensure that no deals are lost, while still gleaning half of whatever surplus remains when player 1 claims less than $10 - \alpha$, for a payoff exceeding α. Player 2 may even find it profitable to opt in and claim less than α.

How large a share of the surplus should player 2 seek? Among the many efficient equilibria of games like the Outside Option Game, two have attracted attention in the literature:

Split-the-difference. In general, split-the-difference awards each player his outside option plus half of the remaining surplus, and so is the outcome obtained by applying the symmetric Nash bargaining solution after placing the status quo at the pair of outside options. In the Outside Option Game, it assigns $\frac{1}{2}(10 - \alpha)$ to player 1 and $\alpha + \frac{1}{2}(10 - \alpha)$ to player 2.

Deal-me-out. In general, deal-me-out assigns each player half the surplus unless a player would then receive less than his outside option, in which case that player receives his outside option. The deal-me-out outcome is obtained by applying the Nash bargaining solution, with the sta-

---

6. We expect it to be much easier to achieve efficient outcomes when they are consistent with sharing the surplus symmetrically, though the work of van Huyck et al. (1990, 1993) shows that efficiency even then can be elusive.

tus quo at the origin, to the set of outcomes from which alternatives assigning players less than their outside options have been removed (Binmore et al. 1989, 1991). In the Outside Option Game, deal-me-out assigns each player a payoff of 5 unless $\alpha > 5$. If $\alpha > 5$, it assigns $10 - \alpha$ to player 1 and α to player 2.

All bargaining theories agree with split-the-difference and deal-me-out in selecting the fifty-fifty outcome in the Outside Option Game when $\alpha = 0$. When α increases, the appropriate prediction is less clear. Applied workers in labor, trade theory, and elsewhere frequently follow McDonald and Solow (1981) in assuming that a surplus is divided according to split-the-difference. The split-the-difference solution is viewed as capturing the intuition that player 2's share should increase as we strengthen her bargaining position by increasing her outside option. Such models focus their attention on the comparative-static implications of variations in the players' outside options.

However, as long as her outside option falls short of half the surplus, it is not clear that player 2's bargaining position is enhanced by increasing her outside option. Nor is it clear that she can bring pressure to bear on player 1 to secure more than her outside option when the latter exceeds half the surplus. In contrast to models based on split-the-difference, contract theories typically stress Goldberg's (1976) holdup problem (Klein et al. 1978; Williamson 1985), in which one party is forced down precisely to the value of his outside option, giving the deal-me-out outcome. The transactions-cost literature then focuses on the ability of contracts and institutional arrangements to produce efficient outcomes despite holdup problems.

Game theory readily produces models in which deal-me-out is a better description of players' demands than split-the-difference (Binmore et al. 1989, 1991). For example, the Rubinstein (1982) alternating-offers model of bargaining leads to this conclusion when outside options are available. However, we think that such models place too much faith in efficiency. Although the Outside Option Game is designed to make it relatively attractive for player 2 to opt in, it has to be anticipated that player 2 will frequently opt out when α is large.

Why should player 2 opt out? Our view of behavior in the Outside Option Game (and more generally) is that people are ordinarily faced with so many decisions that they cannot possibly conduct a careful analysis in every case. Instead, they equip themselves, not always consciously, with a collection of rules-of-thumb, along with guidelines for the context in which each rule should be applied. When confronted with a novel situation, people then apply what appears to be the best-suited rule-of-thumb. For example, people may propose (and insist on) fifty-fifty as a sharing rule when faced with a bargaining problem. As they accumulate experience, some players will discover better decision rules, and they will then alter their behavior. However, other players will have sufficient demands on their attention from other sources that they may never adapt their behavior to the game in question.[7]

Section 7.4 analyses a very simple model of this phenomenon involving large collections of players who come in two types. All players are repeatedly and randomly matched to play the Outside Option Game. Most players adjust their behavior in the light of their experience with the game until they are playing best responses. We call these agents *maximizers*. However, some agents, referred to as *rule-driven* agents, never bring best-response considerations to bear on the game. Instead, they apply rules-of-thumb that they have become accustomed to using in other games they regard as being analogous to the Outside Option Game. We are interested in the equilibria of this process, taking into account the perturbations caused by the agents who never learn to maximize. We describe conditions under which a maximizing player 2 opts into the game when α is small but opts out when α is large, even if the proportion of rule-driven agents is small.

7.2 Previous Experiments

The point of departure for our analysis is the work of Binmore et al. (1989, 1991) using experimental studies of Rubinstein bargaining models in which players alternate in making offers as often as they please, with the sum of money available for division shrinking fractionally after each refusal. Each player could abandon the negotiations in favor of an outside option whenever he had just refused an offer. The outside options were inefficient in that the sum of opt-out payments was always smaller

---

7. If behavior in the laboratory appears to bear no relationship to optimization theories, the likely reason is then that a rule-or-thumb has been applied that is not well-suited to the game in question. (See Binmore et al. 1985, 1986, 1991 and Roth and Erev 1995*a, b* for discussions of learning in experiments.) Hoffman et al. (1995) similarly suggest that mistakenly applied rules-of-thumb are responsible for much of the behavior that seems anomalous by conventional standards. Camerer and Thaler (1995) indicate that their theory of manners could be viewed as a theory of mistakenly applied rules-of-thumb.

than the current surplus to be divided. In this game, deal-me-out is the unique subgame-perfect equilibrium (Binmore et al. 1986, 1991).[8]

In the experiments of Binmore et al. (1989, 1991), deal-me-out performs well when compared with split-the-difference as a predictor of player 2's share of the money available at the time a deal is struck. However, deal-me-out's prediction that player 2 will never opt out is often wrong. In fact, she frequently opts out when her outside option is sufficiently high. Hard bargaining over how the surplus from an agreement is to be distributed leads to potential gains from trade remaining unexploited.

Rubinstein bargaining games may be reasonably realistic models of many negotiations. However, their complicated structure makes it difficult to explore further the tension between hard bargaining and efficiency revealed by the experimental results. The static structure of the Outside Option Game, along with the absence of an outside option for player 1, yields a simpler game that still captures this tension.

The experimental results of Binmore et al. (1989, 1991) can be compared with the experiments of Hoffman and Spitzer (1982, 1985) and Harrison and McKee (1985), who studied the behavior of subjects in free-form, face-to-face bargaining sessions. One of the subjects in these experiments was designated as the controller. The controller could choose either to receive α dollars (leaving the other subject with nothing) or to split a larger sum of money with the other subject. The two subjects discussed which choice the controller should make and then signed a binding agreement specifying how the total payment should be split between them. In contrast to the results of Binmore et al. (1989, 1991), the deals reached under such circumstances were commonly efficient. In particular, the controller rarely exercised his or her capacity to opt out. More strikingly, the controller in Hoffman and Spitzer's treatments frequently agreed to deals close to a fifty-fifty split, even though he or she could have obtained several dollars more by forgoing an agreement altogether and opting out. Harrison and McKee found fifty-fifty splits to be less prevalent but still observed many cases in which controllers took less than their outside option.

We have doubts about the extent to which the results from such face-to-face bargaining experiments involving relatively small amounts of

---

8. The subgame-perfect equilibrium predicts split-the-difference only if breakdown is *involuntary* (Binmore et al. 1991).

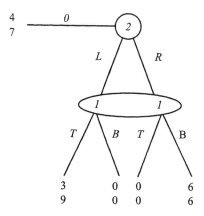

Figure 7.2
The Dalek Game

money are likely to generalize to a wider economic context, because the intimacy generated while the subjects fraternize is likely to inhibit the hard bargaining that we are interested in studying. Our subjects communicate through a computer so that both parties to the negotiation remain anonymous throughout.[9]

Balkenborg (1994) has recently examined a game with an outside option that is simpler than the infinite-horizon games of Binmore et al. and more structured that the experiments of Hoffman et al. Figure 7.2 shows the *Dalek Game*, whose form is taken from Kohlberg and Mertens (1986).

The Dalek Game has two subgame-perfect equilibrium outcomes: one in which players choose (T, L) and so obtain the payoff pair $(3, 9)$, and one in which player 2 takes her outside option (strategy O) because player 1 plays B with probability at least $2/9$. Only the first of these two possibilities is efficient, and only the first satisfies the forward induction criteria that are usually defended in this context by an appeal to the iterated elimination of weakly dominated strategies. However, experimental studies of this game by Balkenborg (1994) show that player 2 virtually always opts out. Cooper et al. (1994) find similar results in related games. The risks associated with the hard bargaining that is required to achieve an efficient outcome are avoided by inefficiently opting out of the game.

9. Hoffman et al. (1992, 1994) have recently argued that the behavior of experimental subjects can be quite sensitive to the details of the experimental setting, including the opportunities to behave anonymously or for behavior to be observed. However, Ochs and Roth (1989) report that their subjects often make disadvantageous offers when anonymously playing alternating-offers bargaining games.

In contrast to the Outside Option Game, there is no counterpart of the deal-me-out solution in the Dalek Game and no flexibility in how player 2 is to be compensated for eschewing her outside option. It is impossible for player 2 to refuse her outside option and receive a payoff in the game just high enough to compensate her for doing so. The Outside Option Game, by presenting more flexibility in this regard, enhances the possibilities for players to forsake outside opportunities and achieve efficient outcomes, thereby providing insights into what it takes to tempt players to enter a game and how players compensate others for doing so.

7.3   Experimental Results

7.3.1   Experimental Design

Section 7.1, in previewing the model of section 7.4, suggests that efficient equilibria will appear when player 2's outside option is small, but equilibria will be inefficient when the outside option is lucrative. Our experiments accordingly call for subjects to play the Outside Option Game with varying values of α. To eliminate the effects of across-subject variations in unobservable characteristics, we arranged for each group of subjects to play a sequence of games with varying values of α. To control for the possibility that behavior in the later games in such a sequence is contaminated by experience in previous games, we conducted two sequences of experimental games, one in which the value of α increased across games and one in which it decreased.

The experiment was conducted at the Michigan Economics Laboratory with undergraduates of the University of Michigan. Each experimental session involved 12 subjects who sat at networked microcomputers that were screened from each other. The subjects were asked to read the written instructions (reproduced in the section 7.6) and given an interactive demonstration of how claims were registered, payoffs determined, and so forth.

Following the demonstration, subjects participated in a series of bargaining sessions. At the beginning of each session, subjects saw on their video displays the outline in white against a black background of a tall, hollow, rectangular "cake." To the left of the cake, in blue print, the number 10 together with brackets reaching from top to bottom reminded subjects that the total height of the cake represented an amount of money that was always nominally worth 10 dollars. Almost as wide and slightly inside the rectangular cake was a second, smaller, hollow rectangle which began at the bottom of the cake and whose height represented the amount of money that player 2 could obtain unilaterally by opting out. The numerical value of the opt-out payment was also indicated. To avoid suggesting focal points, only these two numbers were indicated on the display.

Player 1 indicated his claim by moving a small red cursor that pointed to the right side of his cake up or down using the computer's up and down arrow keys. As the red cursor moved down from its initial position at the top of the cake, the area of the rectangle between the top and the cursor filled with red to represent the amount of player 1's claim. When player 1 was satisfied, he registered his claim by pressing ENTER. At that point the numerical value of his claim was indicated and he had the opportunity to revise the claim by pressing the function key F10 or confirm the claim by pressing SPACE BAR. Claims were made in multiples of dimes.

The procedure by which player 2 indicated a claim was similar except that player 2 moved a small green cursor that was initially positioned at the bottom right hand side of his cake. As the green cursor moved up or down, the area between the bottom of the cake and the cursor filled with green to indicate the amount of player 2's claim. Player 2 could also indicate a decision to opt out by pressing the BACKSPACE key, at which time the area of the rectangle indicating the opt-out payment filled with white to indicate the amount that player 2 could gain by opting out. As with player 1, player 2 was given the opportunity to revise her choice by pressing F10 or confirm it by pressing SPACE BAR.

After both player 1 and player 2 confirmed their choices, the choice of each player's counterpart for the session was displayed by overlying the appropriate red, green, or white region on the player's own display. If the red and green claims of the two players overlapped, then the total claimed by both players was more than 10 dollars, and neither player received anything. The area of overlap was shown in yellow. If the red and green claims did not overlap, then each player received his claim together with half the unclaimed cake. A white line dividing the surplus (i.e., the remaining dark region in the middle of the cake) was displayed together with the numerical value of the player's total payoff. Finally, if player 2 opted out, then she received her opt-out payment while player 1 received nothing. Along with a graphical display of the players' choices and payoffs, a brief written summary of the outcome was displayed.

Subjects did not know with whom they had been paired in each session. After each session, subjects were paired with a new partner who was chosen randomly subject to constraints discussed at the end of this section. Whether a player was player 1 or player 2 in a given session was also determined randomly subject to the constraint that no subject was the same type of player for more than two sessions in a row.[10]

Players participated in twenty "practice" sessions followed by ten "real" sessions. The cake in each session was always nominally worth ten dollars. However, subjects were paid the amounts they succeeded in obtaining in only two of each set of ten sessions. Moreover, for the first ten practice sessions, the subjects were paid at the rate of one *dime* for each dollar they earned. In the second set of practice sessions, subjects were paid at the rate of one *quarter* for each dollar they earned. Only in the final set of ten real sessions were subjects paid at the full rate of one dollar per dollar earned. After each set of ten sessions, a "roulette wheel" appeared on each subject's screen, and the two sessions for which that subject would be paid were randomly selected.

The opt-out payment which a player 2 could receive varied from session to session. There were two types of experiments. In experiments that received the "up" treatment, the opt-out payments for each set of ten practice or real sessions were in the following ascending order: $\{0.90, 0.90, 2.50, 2.50, 4.90, 4.90, 6.40, 6.40, 8.10, 8.10\}$. In experiments that received the "down" treatment, the opt-out payments for each set of ten sessions were in the opposite, descending order.

After the bargaining sessions were over, subjects were asked to complete a computerised questionnaire. For each opt-out payment, subjects answered the question: "What do you feel would be a fair amount for player 2 to get?" by moving a green cursor to indicate a claim on the rectangular cake precisely as in the actual bargaining sessions as player 2. The opt-out payments in the questionnaire were presented in the same (ascending or descending) order that was used in the bargaining sessions.[11]

Our expectation before undertaking the experiment was that player 2 would not take the outside option, with the primary question of interest being how much compensation she would receive for not doing so. However, forgoing a large outside option is potentially risky. When designing the experiment, we attempted to isolate the effect of this risk and attain conditions under which player 2 would not opt out. This motivated our

10. If we had strictly alternated the players' types, then any given subject could have participated in bargaining sessions with only half of the subjects.

11. For each opt-out payment, subjects were also asked to indicate their best guess of the median of the claims that the other subjects in their group designated as fair for a player 2. The subject whose guess was closest to the actual median was awarded $2.

rule calling for unclaimed surplus to be split between the agents. In addition subjects were "filtered" in the practice bargaining sessions.

Our motivation for the filtering was a suspicion that "irrational" behavior by player 1 would be correlated with lower profits and greater risk to player 2 from not taking the outside option. Hence, after the first ten practice sessions, the four subjects with the lowest total profit in these sessions were "filtered out," and, in subsequent practice and real sessions, these subjects were matched only with others in their group. After the second ten practice sessions, the four subjects of the remaining eight who had the lowest cumulative profit in all twenty practice sessions were also grouped. Thus at the start of the real bargaining sessions there were three groups of four subjects who had been selected by their profits in the practice sessions and who bargained in real sessions only with subjects in their own group. Subjects were not informed of this filtering procedure.

Somewhat to our surprise, the differences in the behavior of the average subject in each group during the real sessions and in the average responses to the questionnaire were economically insignificant. For example, pooled over all subjects who experienced the same treatment (either up or down), the frequencies with which subjects in different groups opted out were always within 0.08 of the pooled (across groups) frequency. For each opt-out payment, the median player-1 claims of each group never different from the pooled (across groups) frequency by more than $0.25, and the medians of the claims indicated as fair for player 2 in the questionnaire were identical across all three groups for every value of α and treatment (up or down) except one case, where they differed by only $0.10. As a result tables 7.1 and 7.2 summarize the data pooled across all three groups.

7.3.2 Results

Tables 7.1 and 7.2 summarize the results from the real bargaining sessions of the experiments and the questionnaire. The data are reported separately for each opt-out payment and each treatment.[12] There were a total of 9 experiments where subjects were presented with the opt-out payments in ascending order (the up treatment) and 19 experiments where the opt-out payments were presented in descending order (the down treat-

---

12. The primary difference between the up and down treatment is that, in the down treatment, player 1 was more likely to demand more than α when α was large and player 2 was more likely to opt out. These differences are sufficiently small that our interpretation and conclusions remain unaltered whether working with the up, down, or pooled data, but prompt us to report the up and down treatments separately.

Table 7.1
Summary data for "UP" treatment

	Opt-out payments				
	0.90	2.50	4.90	6.40	8.10
1a. Median claims of player 2 when not opting out	4.95 (4.15–5.20)	5.00 (3.95–5.10)	5.00 (4.90–5.20)	6.40 (5.10–6.80)	8.10 (5.05–8.40)
2a. Median claims of player 1	4.90 (4.20–5.25)	4.90 (4.30–5.00)	4.70 (2.75–5.00)	3.25 (2.20–4.80)	1.60 (0.90–4.00)
3a. Median claims asserted as fair for player 2	5.00 (4.40–5.50)	5.00 (4.05–6.15)	5.00 (4.90–6.80)	6.40 (5.05–7.35)	8.10 (4.90–8.70)
4a. Frequency with which player 2 made claims less than the opt-out value	0.000	0.000	0.019	0.065	0.028
5a. Frequency of player 1 claims greater than 4.50	0.880	0.852	0.574	0.074	0.037
6a. Frequency of player 1 claims providing player 2 a payoff lower than the opt-out value	0.000	0.000	0.009	0.083	0.102
7a. Frequency with which player 2 opted out	0.000	0.019	0.343	0.556	0.750
8a. Mean profit of player 2 when not opting out[a]	4.43 (0.00, 5.00, 5.27)	4.63 (0.00, 5.00, 5.27)	4.72 (0.00, 5.15, 5.65)	5.79 (0.00, 6.60, 7.28)	7.54 (3.35, 8.25, 8.53)
9a. Maximum expected profit of a player 2 who does not opt out[b]	4.77 (4.90)	5.00 (4.90)	5.23 (5.00)	6.13 (6.40)	7.47 (7.80)
10a. Maximum expected profit of a player 1[b]	4.78 (4.80)	4.89 (4.80)	4.70 (4.80)	3.31 (3.10)	1.89 (1.60)

Note: Except where noted, the statistic reported is the median of the observations pooled over all subjects who participated in experiments with the same treatment, and the numbers in parentheses are the 5th and 95th percentile of the observations. Claims and profits are in dollars.
a. Numbers in parentheses are respectively the 5th percentile, median, and 95th percentile of the profits obtained by player twos who did not opt out.
b. See text for details. The number in parenthesis is the optimal claim for such a player.

Table 7.2
Summary data for "DOWN" treatment

	Opt-out payments				
	0.90	2.50	4.90	6.40	8.10
1b. Median claims of player 2 when not opting out	5.00 (3.85–5.20)	4.90 (3.90–5.20)	5.00 (4.90–5.70)	6.40 (4.95–7.00)	8.10 (4.85–8.35)
2b. Median claims of player 1	4.90 (4.10–5.20)	4.90 (4.00–5.10)	4.60 (3.45–5.00)	3.15 (2.05–4.85)	1.70 (1.00–5.00)
3b. Median claims asserted as fair for player 2	5.00 (2.20–5.45)	5.00 (2.50–5.70)	5.00 (4.35–5.70)	6.40 (4.10–6.95)	8.10 (5.00–8.45)
4b. Frequency with which player 2 made claims less than the opt-out value	0.000	0.000	0.013	0.105	0.061
5b. Frequency of player 1 claims greater than 4.50	0.846	0.759	0.535	0.083	0.154
6b. Frequency of player 1 claims providing player 2 a payoff lower than the opt-out value	0.000	0.000	0.009	0.140	0.237
7b. Frequency with which player 2 opted out	0.000	0.000	0.325	0.640	0.868
8b. Mean profit of player 2 when not opting out[a]	4.42 (0.00, 5.00, 5.40)	4.66 (0.00, 5.00, 5.45)	4.88 (0.00, 5.20, 6.00)	5.45 (0.00, 6.57, 7.33)	6.51 (0.00, 8.15, 8.70)
9b. Maximum expected profit of a player 2 who does not opt out[b]	4.85 (4.80)	4.96 (4.80)	5.21 (5.00)	5.82 (5.00)[c]	6.37 (8.00)
10b. Maximum expected profit of a player 1[b]	4.77 (4.80)	4.89 (4.80)	4.56 (4.20)	3.24 (3.00)	2.21 (1.60)

Note: For notes a and b, see table 7.1.
c. The expected profit function was not always a unimodal function of the subject's claim. In this case, for example, there was a second local maximum at 6.40. The expected profit obtained by making a claim of 6.40 was 5.76 dollars.

ment). There were 12 subjects in each experiment and each opt-out payment was presented for two real bargaining sessions. Since half the subjects were player 1 and half were player 2 in each session, for every opt-out payment there were a total of 108 choices by each type of player in real sessions with the up treatment and 228 choices by each type of player for the down treatment.[13]

We summarize the results as follows:

Division of surplus Deal-me-out is in many respects a good predictor of subjects' behavior. As player 1, the median subject made claims that were only slightly less than those predicted by the deal-me-out outcome: for each value of α the median claims depart from the deal-me-out claims of $\min\{5, 10 - \alpha\}$ by less than 50 cents. The median claims player 2 when not opting out were within 10 cents of the deal-me-out claims of $\max\{5, \alpha\}$. With one exception, the expected-profit-maximizing claim for a player 2 who chose not to opt out was within 30 cents of $\max\{5, \alpha\}$. Finally, after the bargaining sessions were over, subjects were asked what would be a fair claim for a player who could opt out. For each opt-out payment, the median claim designated as fair was $\max\{5, \alpha\}$.

Opting Out When α was large, player 2 frequently chose to opt out, yielding an inefficient outcome. The opt-out frequencies for $\alpha = \$4.90$, $\alpha = \$6.40$, and $\alpha = \$8.10$ were 0.33, 0.61, and 0.83, respectively.

Rows 1*a* and 1*b* of tables 7.1 and 7.2 describe the player-2 claims made by players who chose not to opt out, with the median, 5*th* percentile and 95*th* percentile claims indicated (the latter two being the first and second numbers in parentheses, respectively) in each case.[14] Rows 2*a* and 2*b* similarly report player 1 claims, while rows 3*a* and 3*b* report the subjects' estimates of what would be a "fair" claim in each case. The median claims of both player 1 and player 2 reported in rows 1*a*, 1*b*, 2*a*, and 2*b* and the median claims indicated as fair for player 2 in rows 3*a* and 3*b* correspond well to the predictions of the deal-me-out outcome. Moreover

---

13. Since every subject responded once to each questionnaire item, there were also a total of 108 responses to each question for the up treatment and 228 responses for the down treatment.

14. For 108 observations, the 5th percentile is calculated as the mean of the 6th and 7th order statistics, that is, the 6th and 7th elements of a list of the observations sorted from lowest to highest. The 95th percentile is the mean of the 102th and 103th order statistics and the median or 50th percentile is the mean of the 54th and 55th order statistics. For 228 observations, the 5th, 50th, and 95th percentiles are given by the means of the 12th and 13th, the 114th and 115th, and the 216th and 217th order statistics, respectively.

the 95th percentiles reported for player 2's claims indicate that virtually no player 2 expected to receive much more than the deal-me-out claim. In addition, rows 4a and 4b of tables 7.1 and 7.2 show that player 2 rarely opted in and made a claim less than α.

Player 1 behavior is also generally consistent with the deal-me-out outcome, though the 5th percentiles for the player 1 claims for opt-out payments $6.40 and $8.10 show that at least some subjects made claims as player 1 that were close to the split-the-difference outcome.

Rows 5a and 5b report the frequencies with which player 1 made claims greater than 4.50 dollars, that is, claims that were close to the fifty-fifty prediction. Rows 6a and 6b report the frequencies with which player 1 made claims greater that 10 dollars minus the opt-out payment. Such claims give player 2 a smaller payoff than opting out. For both treatments, the frequencies reported in rows 5a, 5b, 6a, and 6b are relatively small for opt-out payments that exceed half the cake, which is consistent with deal-me-out. The most noticeable differences in the data from the up and down treatments are the larger frequencies with which player 1, in sessions with the down treatment, made claims that did not leave player 2 with a payoff larger than α when the opt-out payment was $6.40 or $8.10.[15]

The deal-me-out solution thus matches player 1's behavior reasonably well and matches player 2's behavior reasonably well *when player 2 opts in*. Contrary to the deal-me-out prediction, however, player 2 frequently opts out. Rows 7a and 7b in tables 7.1 and 7.2 report the frequency with which player 2 chose to opt out.[16] The conclusion here is strikingly obvious: player 2 is unlikely to opt out when α is small, but quite likely to do so when α is large.

Why does player 2 opt out? Rows 8a and 8b describe the profit achieved by player 2 when not opting out.[17] The first number is mean profit. In addition to the 5th and 95th percentiles, the middle number reported in parentheses in rows 8a and 8b is the median profit obtained by player 2 when not opting out. In each case the median profit is the same as or slightly larger than the opt-out payment or half the cake,

15. As one might expect, the larger frequencies of such claims for the down treatment coincide with lower mean profits for player 2 as reported in rows 8a and 8b.

16. The overall opt-out frequencies reported in the summary are the weighted average of the frequencies reported in tables 7.1 and 7.2 for the up and the down treatments.

17. For the larger opt-out payments, many player 2s chose to opt out; hence, for these opt-out payments, the numbers of observations summarized in rows 1a, 1b, 8a, and 8b are much smaller than 108 or 228.

whichever is larger. On the other hand, the *mean* profit is always lower than the median profit, often by a substantial margin, and is lower than the opt-out payment for the three largest opt-out payments.

The mean profit reported in rows 8*a* and 8*b* involves only those player 1 claims that were actually matched with a player 2 who did not opt out. In contrast, rows 9*a* and 9*b* report the maximum expected profit that a player 2 could achieve when playing against the entire population of player 1 claims made in bargaining sessions with the designated opt-out payment and treatment. The numbers reported in parentheses are the player 2 claims that achieve this expected profit.[18] The maximum possible expected profit obtained by not opting out is less than the opt-out payment for those opt-out payments which exceed $5.00.[19]

These experimental results reflect the tension between optimization and efficiency. In the quest for a hard bargain, player 1 pushes player 2 toward the fifty-fifty outcome. If the outside option for player 2 is sufficiently small (i.e., outside options $0.90 and $2.50), then the system settles on the fifty-fifty outcome. For higher outside options, hard bargaining on the part of player 1 pushes player 2 to a claim very close to her outside option, with player 1 claiming the rest. This is the deal-me-out outcome, and we expect the system to settle there in a perfect world. However, the experimental world is not perfect. Instead, hard bargaining sometimes leads to disagreements, and this causes the deal-me-out outcome to give player 2 a lower mean payoff than their outside options. As a result player 2 often opts out and the gains from trade go unrealized.

7.4   A Model

This section constructs a simple model of equilibrium play in the Outside Option Game based on ideas outlined in section 7.1. We are interested in the equilibrium of a process that leads most players to choose best responses, but in which some players apply rules-of-thumb borrowed from analogous games. Let θ be the proportion of the agents who, in equilibrium, rely on rules-of-thumb. We refer to such an agent as a *rule-driven* agent. In equilibrium, the remaining $1 - \theta$ of the agents in each

18. In a similar fashion, rows 10*a* and 10*b* report the maximum expected profit and the optimal claim for a player 1 who is matched randomly with one from the designated population of claims made by a player 2 who did not opt out.

19. Because row 9 involves a larger sample of player 1s, it is not contradictory that the maximum profit in row 9*b* (the down treatment) falls short of the mean profit in row 8*b* for outside option 8.10.

population from which players 1 and 2 are randomly drawn play best responses to the opposing population. We refer to these agents as *maximizers*.

Let G_α be a probability distribution on $[0, 10] \cup \{O\}$ describing the claims made by the rule-driven agents in population 2, given the opt-out value α. It will simplify the exposition to let player 1's claims be measured in terms of the share of the ten dollars that they leave as potentially available to player 2. To emphasize this, we will often refer to player 1's actions as *offers*. We let F_α be a probability distribution on $[0, 10]$ describing the offers made by the rule-driven agents in population 1.

We will be primarily interested in the properties of F_α, the key feature of which will be the extent to which F_α concentrates offers around the offer made by maximizers in a pure-strategy equilibrium. We assume that there exists $\psi > 0$ and $\bar{\varepsilon}$ such that in a pure-strategy equilibrium in which maximizing player 2s opt in and demand x, for all $\varepsilon < \bar{\varepsilon}$, we have

$$\frac{F_\alpha([x - \varepsilon, x))}{\varepsilon} \geq \psi. \tag{7.1}$$

Larger values of ψ correspond to a greater concentration of rule-driven offers near x. How large do we expect ψ to be? If F_α is a uniform distribution, so that rule-driven players are completely indiscriminate in their offers, then $\psi = 1$. Our analysis holds for this case, but the results are relatively weak, with large proportions of rule-driven players (large θ) required in order to conclude that player 2 will opt out. However, we expect F_α to be far from uniform and ψ to be much larger than unity. In particular, we expect rule-driven players to appropriate their rules-of-thumb from similar games with similar (though perhaps not precisely the same) equilibria, leading to rules-of-thumb that give offers very close to the equilibrium offer and hence values of ψ that exceed unity.[20]

For a fixed specification of θ, F_α, and G_α, a pure-strategy Nash equilibrium is an offer for player 1, and either a demand or the outside option for player 2, such that it is a best response for each of the maximizing agents in the game to play such a strategy. We have:

---

20. Notice that this allows the distribution F_α to depend not only on the Outside Option Game but also on the *equilibrium* of that game. The factors leading the players to a particular equilibrium of the Outside Option Game, including the strategic structure of the game, the context in which it is played, the characteristics of the players, and the framing of the game, are also the factors that shape the analogies used by rule-driven players in choosing their offers. This leads to rule-driven offers that tend to be near the equilibrium offer but may not precisely equal the equilibrium offer because of imperfect analogies.

Proposition 1 Fix $x \in (0, 10)$, $\alpha < x$, and F_α satisfying (1). Then there exists $\underline{\theta} > 0$ such that if $\theta < \underline{\theta}$, then it is a Nash equilibrium for a maximizing player 2 to demand x and a maximizing player 1 to offer x.

Proposition 2 If $\theta \in (0, 1)$, $\bar{\alpha} \in (5, 10)$, and F_α satisfies (1), then there exists $\bar{\psi}$ such that if $\psi > \bar{\psi}$ and $\alpha > \bar{\alpha}$, then player 2 opts out in every pure-strategy Nash equilibrium. The larger are θ and $\bar{\alpha}$, the smaller can $\bar{\psi}$ be.

Proposition 1 indicates that any pure-strategy Nash equilibrium without rule-driven players remains an equilibrium when there are only a few rule-driven players. This is no surprise. The pure-strategy equilibria in which player 2 enters the game are strict Nash equilibria. As long as the payoff perturbations introduced by rule-driven players are sufficiently small, they cannot disrupt the equilibrium conditions. However, this "sufficiently small" level may be different for different equilibria, which forms the basis for the second statement of the proposition.

Proposition 2 indicates that, for a fixed specification of rule-driven players, there may exist equilibria in which player 2 does not take the outside option as long as α is not too large. But for sufficiently large values of α, such equilibria may fail to exist. For small proportions of rule-driven players and relatively dispersed rule-driven offers (small θ and ψ), efficient equilibria will fail to exist only for a relatively small collection (if any) of high values of α. As either the proportion of rule-driven players increases, or as rule-driven offers become more concentrated, the threshold value of α at which an efficient agreement fails to exist gets smaller. If rule-driven offers are sufficiently concentrated, efficient equilibria may fail to exist for a wide range of large values of α, even though there are few rule-driven agents.

To see why efficient equilibria may not exist for large α, suppose maximizing player 1s offer $x > \alpha$. Player 2 can then demand x, producing an agreement worth x with every maximizing player 1, but yielding disagreements with any rule-driven player 1 who offers less than x. Player 2 could instead reduce her demand slightly, allowing her to conclude agreements with some of the latter players, at the cost of a smaller surplus from existing agreements.[21] If the proportion of rule-driven players is large, this reduction will be advantageous. Even if the proportion of rule-driven

---

21. If player 2 increases her demand, she forces a disagreement with every maximizing player 1, in return for getting a slightly larger share of the surplus from those rule-driven players who are offering more than x. This could be advantageous but only if the proportion of rule-driven players is very high.

players is small, this will be advantageous if their offers are very highly concentrated around x, so that reducing her demand allows player 2 to conclude agreements with a very high proportion of the rule-driven agents. Finally, this reduction is most likely to be advantageous when x is large, and hence the new agreements with rule-driven player 1s are especially valuable. The optimal action for player 2 will then be to reduce her demand, and there is no equilibrium in which player 2 demands x, whenever there are either many rule-driven agents or highly concentrated rule-driven agent offers, and x is large.[22] Rule-driven agents thus preclude equilibria that involve highly asymmetric divisions of the surplus, with more such divisions precluded as there are more rule-driven agents and as their offers are more concentrated. If α is sufficiently large, then every efficient equilibrium must involve a relatively asymmetric division of the surplus with a relative large offer $x \geq \alpha$, and there will be no such equilibria.

Proof of Proposition 1 Proposition 1 follows immediately from the fact that it is a strict Nash equilibrium for player 2 to demand x and player 1 to offer x. We accordingly consider proposition 2. Let $x > \alpha$. Let H_α be a probability distribution on $[0, 10]$ describing the choices of maximizing player ones. In order for maximizers in population 2 to optimally demand x, no demand $x - \varepsilon$ can give a higher payoff, or

$$\int_{y=x}^{10} \frac{x+y}{2} [(1-\theta)\, dH_\alpha(y) + \theta\, dF_\alpha(y)]$$

$$\geq \int_{y=x-\varepsilon}^{10} \frac{x-\varepsilon+y}{2} [(1-\theta)\, dH_\alpha(y) + \theta\, dF_\alpha(y)].$$

A necessary condition for this inequality is

$$\frac{\varepsilon}{2} \int_{y=x}^{10} [(1-\theta)\, dH_\alpha(y) + \theta\, dF_\alpha(y)]$$

$$\geq (x-\varepsilon) \int_{y=x-\varepsilon}^{x} [(1-\theta)\, dH_\alpha(y) + \theta\, dF_\alpha(y)]. \qquad (7.2)$$

---

22. Player 1 faces a similar trade-off when considering whether to increase his offer slightly. However, the fact that $x > \alpha > 5$ ensures that the new agreements achieved by moderating one's demand are more valuable to player 2 than to player 1. This is a variant of the observation by Nash (1953) that players in a noisy environment have an incentive to moderate their demands to achieve more agreements, and that this incentive is greatest for the player receiving the larger share of the surplus, because this is the player for which the additional agreements are particularly valuable.

A necessary condition for inequality (7.2) is (replacing the left and right integrals by upper and lower bounds of 1 and $\theta F_\alpha([x - \varepsilon, x])$ and then using (7.1) for the second inequality):

$$\varepsilon \geq 2(x - \varepsilon)\theta F_\alpha([x - \varepsilon, x]) \geq 2(x - \varepsilon)\theta\psi\varepsilon. \qquad (7.3)$$

The result then follows from noting that (7.3) will be violated whenever the product of α (and hence $x > \alpha$), θ, and ψ is large. ∎

7.5 Conclusion

Experimental subjects in the Outside Option Game inefficiently opt out of the game because efficient equilibria require aggressive bargaining in which small miscalculations can have large costs. We believe that this phenomenon is widespread, and that efficiency will therefore sometimes fail to be achieved even when the agents involved are as close to being rational as real people are ever likely to get.

Contract theorists have recently devoted considerable attention to the holdup problem, in which agents anticipate that promised compensation for incurring sunk costs may be expropriated by others once the costs have been sunk. The traditional line taken by such authors as Coase (1960) or Williamson (1985) is that efficiency is guaranteed if the parties to the deal have a costless opportunity to negotiate a *binding* contract before sinking any costs. More generally, they argue that new property rights and new forms of contracting will emerge to deal with the inefficiencies that can result from a variety of transactions costs and frictions that might impede such contracting.

Our results indicate that if efficiency is to be achieved, attention must also be devoted to providing appropriate compensation *when contracts are negotiated* for opportunity costs that are not yet sunk. This result can be reconciled with the transactions-cost literature by classifying the learning frictions that we study as yet another form of transaction cost whose existence calls for the appearance of new institutions. An obvious possibility is the replacement of primitive bargaining institutions like those built into the Outside Option Game by more sophisticated schemes. However, we first turned our attention to the opting-out phenomenon because of its appearance in the more sophisticated and more forgiving environment provided by Rubinstein bargaining models (Binmore et al. 1989, 1991).

Appendix: Instructions to Subjects

Bargaining Experiment

In this experiment you will bargain via the computing equipment in front of you with people seated at other machines in the room. You will participate in a large number of very short bargaining sessions. Whether you are player 1 or player 2 in these sessions is determined randomly. Sometimes you will be player 1 and sometimes player 2. After each session you will be randomly paired with a new bargaining partner.

In each bargaining session, you and your counterpart for that session will have the opportunity to split a "cake" between you. You will each simultaneously make a claim. If the two claims sum to no more than the value of the cake, then each of you will receive their claim plus half the surplus after the claims have been met. If the two claims sum to more than the value of the cake, each of you will get *nothing* at all.

Only one thing complicates this very simple scenario. Before each bargaining session begins, player 2 *only* is offered the opportunity of opting out. If player 2 opts out, he or she gets a payment that may vary from session to session. But, in each session, both players will know what player 2's opting out payment is for that session. Player 1 gets *nothing* if player 2 opts out.

The cake is always *nominally* worth $10, but you will be paid the amounts you succeed in securing only for *two* of the bargaining sessions. These will be chosen at random from the final ten sessions in which you participate. The preceding two sets of ten sessions are for practice. In each of these two sets of ten practice sessions you will also be paid for two sessions chosen at random, but you will not be paid at the full rate. In the first set of ten practice sessions you will be paid at the rate of one dime for each nominal dollar. In the second set of ten practice sessions, you will be paid at the rate of one quarter for each nominal dollar. Only in the third set of ten sessions will you be bargaining for real and getting paid at the full rate for the two sessions the computer chooses at random.

After the bargaining sessions are over, you will be asked to complete a computerised questionnaire. Money prizes will be awarded during the questionnaire for answers to some questions.

When *all* subjects have completed the questionnaire, the computer will display how much money you have earned during the experiment. This will include the amounts you secured during the bargaining, and any prizes you won while completing the questionnaire. It will not include your $2 attendance fee. Please remain in your seat until the supervisor calls your seat number and then bring your seat tag so that you can be paid.

This is not an experiment to find out what kind of person you are. When we see the results, we will neither know nor care who did what. We are only interested in what happens on average. So please do not feel that some particular sort of behavior is expected of you. However, we do ask that you do not talk to the other subjects or look at their screens. It is important to the experiment that our subjects interact *only* through the computer equipment.

Now press the SPACE BAR on your keyboard. You will see a demonstration that will review the information in these instructions and give you hands-on experience in making claims or opting out. Remember to keep pressing the SPACE BAR to see a new screen. There is no need to hurry. You may have to wait for the other subjects to be ready anyway. If you still have questions after seeing the demonstration, there will be an opportunity to ask the supervisor.

References

Alchian, A. 1950. Uncertainty, evolution, and economic theory. *Journal of Political Economy*, 58: 211–21.

Balkenborg, D. 1994. An experiment on forward versus backward induction. SFB discussion paper B-268. University of Bonn.

Binmore, K., P. Morgan, A. Shaked, and J. Sutton. 1991. Do people exploit their bargaining power? An experimental study. *Games and Economic Behavior* 3: 295–322.

Binmore, K., A. Rubinstein, and A. Wolinsky. 1986. The Nash bargaining solution in economic modelling. *RAND Journal of Economics* 17: 176–88.

Binmore, K., A. Shaked, and J. Sutton. 1985. Testing noncooperative bargaining theory: A preliminary study. *American Economic Review* 75: 1178–80.

Binmore, K., A. Shaked, and J. Sutton. 1989. An outside option experiment. *Quarterly Journal of Economics* 104: 753–70.

Camerer, C., and R. H. Thaler. 1995. Correspondence: Response from Colin Camerer and Richard H. Thaler. *Journal of Economic Perspectives* 9 (4): 239–40.

Chung, T.-Y. 1991. Incomplete contracts, specific investments, and risk sharing. *Review of Economic Studies* 58: 1031–42.

Coase, R. 1960. The problem of social cost. *Journal of Law and Economics* 2: 1–40.

Cooper, R., D. V. DeJong, R. Forsythe, and T. W. Ross. 1994. Alternative institutions for resolving coordination problems: experimental evidence on forward induction and preplay communication. In J. W. Friedman, ed., *Problems of Coordination in Economic Activity*, pp. 129–46. Boston: Kluwer Academic Publishers.

Friedman, M. 1953. *Essays in Positive Economics*. Chicago: University of Chicago Press.

Goldberg, V. P. 1976. Regulation and administered contracts. *Bell Journal of Economics and Management Science* 7: 426–52.

Harrison, G. W., and M. McKee. 1985. Experimental evaluation of the Coase theorem. *Journal of Law and Economics* 28: 653–70.

Hart, O., and B. Holmstrom. 1987. The theory of contracts. In T. Bewley, ed., *Advances in Economic Theory*. Cambridge: Cambridge University Press.

Hart, O., and J. Moore. 1988. Incomplete contracts and renegotiation. *Econometrica* 56: 755–86.

Hermalin, B. E., and M. L. Katz. 1991. Moral hazard and verifiability: The effects of renegotiation in agency. *Econometrica* 59: 1735–54.

Hoffman, E., and M. Spitzer. 1982. The Coase theorem: Some experimental tests. *Journal of Law and Economics* 25: 73–98.

Hoffman, E., and M. Spitzer. 1985. Entitlements, rights and fairness: An experimental examination of subjects' concepts of distributive justice. *Journal of Legal Studies* 14: 259–97.

Hoffman, E., K. McCabe, K. Shachat, and V. Smith. 1992. Preferences, property rights and anonymity in bargaining games. Mimeo. University of Arizona.

Hoffman, E., K. McCabe, and V. Smith. 1994. Social distance and other-regarding behavior in dictator games. Mimeo. University of Arizona Economic Science Laboratory.

Hoffman, E., K. McCabe, and V. Smith. 1995. Correspondence: Ultimatum and dictator games. *Journal of Economic Perspectives* 9 (4): 236–39.

Klein, B., R. G. Crawford, and A. A. Alchian. 1978. Vertical integration, appropriable rents, and the competitive contracting process. *Journal of Law and Economics* 21: 297–326.

Kohlberg, E., and J.-F. Mertens. 1986. On the strategic stability of equilibria. *Econometrica* 54: 1003–38.

McDonald, I. M., and R. M. Solow. 1981. Wage bargaining and employment. *American Economic Review* 71: 896–908.

Nash, J. F. 1953. Two-person cooperative games. *Econometrica* 21: 128–40.

Ochs, J., and A. E. Roth. 1989. An experimental study of sequential bargaining. *American Economic Review* 79: 355–84.

Roth, A. E., and I. Erev. 1995. Learning in extensive-form games: Experimental data and simple dynamic models in the intermediate term. *Games and Economic Behavior* 8: 164–212.

Roth, A. E., and I. Erev. 1995. On the need for low rationality, cognitive game theory: Reinforcement learning in experimental games with unique, mixed strategy equilibria. Mimeo. University of Pittsburgh and The Technion.

Rubinstein, A. 1982. Perfect equilibrium in a bargaining model. *Econometrica* 50: 97–109.

van Huyck, J., R. C. Battalio, and R. O. Beil. 1990. Tacit coordination games, strategic uncertainty, and coordination failure. *American Economic Review* 80: 234–48.

van Huyck, J., R. C. Battalio, and R. O. Beil. 1993. Asset markets as an equilibrium selection mechanism: Coordination failure, game form auctions, and tacit communication. *Games and Economic Behavior* 5: 485–504.

Williamson, O. 1985. *The Economic Institutions of Capitalism*. New York: Free Press.

8 Unequal Bargaining Power

This chapter differs from its predecessors in that it includes neither a published paper nor offers a detailed description of an experiment. Its purpose is to confirm that even small perturbations in the preferences of players, or some disparity in the rate at which they learn, can sometimes have a large impact on game-theoretic predictions. It is therefore unwise to leap to the conclusion that game theory (or neoclassical economics in general) has been refuted by an experiment without first exploring how robust the prediction is to such perturbations.

Although the paper featured in this chapter has this wider aim, it belongs in a book about bargaining because its main example consists of an experiment with a Rubinstein bargaining model in which the players have unequal discount factors (Binmore et al. 2005). The rest of this introductory section explores the background to this experiment, which presents a much greater challenge to Rubinstein's theory than the cases with equal discount rates studied in chapters 5 and 6. The reason is that we can make the Rubinstein prediction differ very markedly from any particular fairness norm when we are allowed to vary the relative sizes of the players' discount rates.

The Asymmetric Nash Bargaining Solution

The axioms with which Nash (1950) originally characterized the Nash bargaining solution include *efficiency* and *symmetry*, although neither is necessary to obtain a result. When the symmetry axiom is abandoned, one is led to an asymmetric bargaining solution obtained by maximizing a generalized Nash product

$$(x_1 - \xi_1)^\alpha (x_2 - \xi_2)^\beta,$$

subject to the requirement that $x \geq \xi$ lies in the set X of feasible alternatives.

I call $\alpha \geq 0$ and $\beta \geq 0$ the *bargaining powers* associated with the particular asymmetric Nash bargaining solution under study. Outside options aren't considered in this chapter, although they fit into the theory exactly as in the symmetric case.

Since we can require that $\alpha + \beta = 1$ without loss of generality, an asymmetric Nash bargaining solution is really determined by the value of only a single parameter. By varying this parameter appropriately, the asymmetric Nash bargaining solution can be made to coincide with any efficient point $x \geq \xi$.

I sometimes get the credit for formulating the asymmetric Nash bargaining solution (Binmore 1987a), but numerous others had done so before, including Kalai (1977), Roth (1979), Roberts (1980), and Myerson (1991). However, it was my linkage of this result with the Rubinstein bargaining model that seems to have put the idea on the map (Binmore 1987b).

Unfortunately, applied workers have relentlessly misapplied the asymmetric Nash bargaining solution in the case where outside options are present. As is traditional in labor economics, they place the status quo at the breakdown point rather than the deadlock point (chapters 5 and 6). They then estimate the bargaining powers that best describe their data as an asymmetric Nash bargaining solution relative to this (wrong) status quo. As when fitting Ptolemaic epicycles to the movements of the planets, this procedure can't fail to fit the data fairly well, but one should normally place the status quo at the deadlock point, and take the bargaining powers to be the reciprocals of the bargainers' discount rates. Because we don't know how to handle the informational problems that are often all-important in real life, the theory would then seldom predict field data well, but at least we would be doing something reasonably scientific.

Rubinstein and the Asymmetric Nash Bargaining Solution

When the bargainers in the Alternating-Offers Game discount time at constant rates, the Rubinstein outcome converges on an asymmetric Nash bargaining solution as the time interval between successive proposals becomes vanishingly small (Binmore 1987b).

The bargaining powers in this asymmetric Nash bargaining solution are given by $\alpha = 1/\rho_1$ and $\beta = 1/\rho_2$, where ρ_1 and ρ_2 are the rates as which players I and II discount time. An impatient player correspondingly has less bargaining power than a patient player. As we saw in chap-

ter 5, equally patient players will end up at the ordinary Nash bargaining
solution with equal bargaining powers.

The following sketch of a proof for the case $\xi = 0$ shows that the result
depends only on the fact that the Rubinstein outcome is a stationary
expectations equilibrium, which is an equilibrium in which players always
plan to optimize on the assumption that, even if a player were to deviate
from the plan he has for today's play, the plans the players have for
tomorrow's play will the same as they are today.

Suppose that the payoff pair a is accepted immediately when proposed
by player I. Let b be the corresponding payoff pair in the companion
game in which it is player II who makes the opening proposal. In equilibrium, an offer will make the responder just indifferent between accepting
and refusing. So in the case of stationary expectations, the equilibrium
values of a and b satisfy $a_2 = b_2 e^{-\rho_2 \tau}$ and $b_1 = a_1 e^{-\rho_1 \tau}$, where $\tau > 0$ is the
time interval between successive proposals. Thus

$$\left(\frac{b_1}{a_1}\right)^\alpha = \left(\frac{a_2}{b_2}\right)^\beta = e^{-\tau}.$$

It follows that a and b are two points on the boundary of the feasible set
X that lie on the same contour $x_1^\alpha x_2^\beta = c$. But x and y converge on the
same point n as $\tau \to 0+$. Their common limit n must therefore be the
asymmetric Nash bargaining solution with bargaining powers $\alpha = 1/\rho_1$
and $\beta = 1/\rho_2$.

It will be evident that much of the fine detail of the bargaining process
in Rubinstein's model is unnecessary for this result to hold true. For example, the subjects don't need to stick to a rigid timetable in which each
makes a demand at a fixed time. It is enough that each has the opportunity to make a demand at least once in any time interval of length τ. In
the experiment on a version of Rubinstein's model that motivates this
chapter, Rubinstein's timetable is retained, but the current proposer is
chosen at random.[1] Subjects then have to look only one move ahead
rather than two when assessing a stationary expectations equilibrium,
but it remains true that we are led to an asymmetric Nash bargaining solution as the time interval between successive proposals becomes vanishingly small.

Myopic Adjustment

As with Reinhard Selten on the subject of subgame-perfect equilibria,
Ariel Rubinstein never thought that his bargaining theorem would predict

behavior in laboratories. He continues to regard his result as an idealization that we shouldn't expect to see realized in the messy world of real life.

I agree to the extent that there seems little chance of the Rubinstein bargaining model with unequal discount rates working at all in the laboratory, unless the subjects use some myopic adjustment process in which they optimize on the assumption that the result of an offer being refused today is that they will have to wait until tomorrow to get the kind of deal other subjects have agreed to already. Joe Swierzbinski (Binmore et al. 2007) has written a simple model of such a myopic adjustment process to confirm that it does indeed eventually converge on the stationary expectations equilibrium of the Rubinstein Alternating-Offers Game.

The model requires that the subjects have a rich source of feedback. They use the deals on which other pairs of subjects have recently agreed to predict the deal that they would reach with their current bargaining partner tomorrow if the proposal on the table today is refused. In an experiment that tests the model, we attempt to provide a surrogate for this feedback by showing a bunch of boxes on a subject's screen that represent six recently agreed payoff pairs discounted to the next period (Binmore et al. 2005).

I don't know of other bargaining experiments in which such a rich source of feedback is provided, although nobody in real life is likely to buy or sell a house or a car without first checking out what similar houses or cars are currently selling for in the market. It is difficult to see how meaningful learning in a population of experimental subjects would be possible without feedback of comparable quality, and so it isn't surprising that other experimenters report little evidence of learning in bargaining games (Camerer 2003).

However, it is impractical for laboratory subjects to play the Rubinstein Game the large number of times that would be necessary to be confident that a myopic adjustment process followed by all subjects would converge. Nor is there much chance that all subjects will follow exactly the same adjustment regime, and the paper that follows confirms that we need only introduce some disparity in how subjects adjust their behavior to divert the system from the Rubinstein track.

Even without further impurities in our test tubes, it would therefore be unreasonable to expect Rubinstein's theory to predict experimental bargaining outcomes without reservation—although it doesn't do too badly in the experiment of Binmore et al. (2005). In fact the myopic optimization hypothesis does sufficiently well that it is hard to see how any future behavioral theory of bargaining can afford not to take it into account. In one treatment, the learning effect is so strong that I even have hope of converting the most intransigent of skeptics to the proposition that learning sometimes matters in bargaining games.

Perturbations

The paper that follows is largely motivated by the fact that we can substantially improve the predictions of our myopic adjustment model in asymmetric versions of Rubinstein's Alternating-Offers Game by introducing perturbations that one may attribute to an initial bias that some subjects are reluctant to abandon.

It is important to note that this model does not deviate from the hypothesis that most subjects will eventually end up as though they are maximizers of expected money, but it nevertheless explains much of the data in our experiment on the Rubinstein bargaining game with unequal discount rates. This finding needs to be contrasted with the claims of those behavioral economists who argue that data from bargaining experiments support the hypothesis that people should be modeled as having a large other-regarding component built into their preferences (chapter 4).

A Little Behavioralism Can Go a Long Way

Ken Binmore and Joe Swierzbinski

8.1 Economic Man Refuted?

There is a school of behavioral economists who have popularized the notion that the neoclassical paradigm of *homo economicus* is refuted by the experimental evidence. We agree that the idea that human behavior can always be modeled as rational optimization in each and every context is off the wall, but who would want to defend such a wild claim? To make their case, behavioral economists need to address the more moderate claim that people often learn to play like income maximizers given sufficient time and adequate incentives.

It isn't adequate to look only at the behavior of inexperienced subjects. Nobody denies that they are unlikely candidates for the role of economic man. Nor is it enough to keep pointing at unusual games like the Ultimatum Game, in which subjects do not seem to adjust their behavior much as they gain experience. Indeed it seems palpably dishonest to harp continually on such games, while simultaneously turning a blind eye to the very much larger literature in which laboratory subjects are reported as converging on the Nash equilibria of games with money payoffs.

Why do we see apparently anomalous behavior in the class of games to which behavioral economists restrict their attention? This paper argues that the explanation lies partly in the fact that behavioral economists are some twenty years behind the times in thinking that economic man must solve games using the principle of backward induction, whereas advances in evolutionary game theory have shown that it is unwise to discard any Nash equilibrium whatever without close attention to the context. The paper then goes on to explore the extent to which the set of Nash equilibria in some games that behavioral economists regard as canonical can be expanded by deviating only slightly from the income-maximizing hypothesis.

The same approach is then applied to an experiment of our own on the Rubinstein bargaining game with unequal discount rates. A full discussion of the experimental details and an analysis of the results is given elsewhere (Binmore et al. 2007).[2] The results are supportive of the pure Rubinstein prediction in some contexts but not in others. For the latter contexts, the Rubinstein bargaining model with unequal discount factors therefore needs to be added to the class of anomalous cases identified by behavioral economists. But we then go on to observe that the anomalies can largely be accommodated by assuming that some fraction of the population of subjects are slow in learning that the fair outcome on which they have been conditioned isn't adapted to the game they are playing in the laboratory.

In brief, we believe that behavioral economists are right to argue that the income-maximizing hypothesis for experienced and adequately incentified subjects needs to be modified to accommodate anomalous cases, but that it is unproved that there is a need for the modifications to be large.

8.2 Ultimatum Game

When subjects first encounter a new game in the laboratory, we do not believe that they commonly recapitulate the principles of game theory in their heads and play accordingly. We therefore do not believe that the subjects are actively optimizing relative to any utility function whatever, whether other-regarding or selfish. We think instead that inexperienced subjects respond to the framing of the experiment by playing according to whatever social norm is triggered by the hints and cues with which they are presented. Game theory is relevant to such social norms, because we believe social norms evolved in the first place as equilibrium selection devices for the *repeated* games of everyday life.

But human beings are not helpless robots, irrevocably programmed by their culture with fixed behaviors. We vary in our flexibility when confronted with new situations, but most of us can and will learn if given the opportunity, and the vast majority of relevant experiments confirm that subjects move toward a Nash equilibrium—calculated with money payoffs—of the laboratory game they are playing, provided that adequate incentives and sufficient time for learning are built into the experimental design.

However, there is a minority of anomalous cases in which subjects do not shift much or at all from their initial behavior. How is such behavior to be explained? Behavioral economists offer the explanation that they are already at or close to a Nash equilibrium of a game in which their payoffs are not measured in money but in units of utility that take into account of the welfare of other players or other social considerations. We agree that one can explain the anomalous cases by arguing that the players are already at or close to a Nash equilibrium, but we see no need to modify the assumption that subjects maximize expected money by very much in order to make this explanation work.

The reason that one does not have to move far (or sometimes at all) from the income-maximizing hypothesis to explain the anomalous cases is that the games involved typically have large numbers of Nash equilibria that behavioral economists neglect to take into account. If the social norm that is triggered by the way an experiment is framed happens to coordinate the behavior of the subjects on or near one of these neglected equilibria, then any learning that follows will have little effect. The subjects will not be led away to a distant Nash equilibrium because they are already in the basin of attraction of a nearby Nash equilibrium.

The leading anomalous case is the Ultimatum Game. In the Ultimatum Game, a sum of money can be divided between Alice and Bob if they can agree on a division. The rules are that Alice proposes a division and that Bob is then restricted to accepting or refusing. If the subgame-perfect equilibrium (in which Bob acquiesces when Alice demands almost all the money) were the only Nash equilibrium of the game, then the fact that Alice's modal offer in the laboratory is a fifty:fifty split would be a serious challenge to the income-maximizing hypothesis for experienced players, since this conclusion seems to be robust when the amount of money is made large or repeated play (against a new opponent each time) is allowed.

However, as with other anomalous cases the Ultimatum Game actually has many Nash equilibria. In fact any split of the money whatsoever is a Nash equilibrium outcome on the income-maximizing hypothesis. Not only does the Ultimatum Game have many Nash equilibria, but computer simulations show that simple models of adaptive learning can easily converge on one of the infinite number of Nash equilibria that are not subgame-perfect (Binmore, Gale and Samuelson 1995).

However, this isn't the point of presenting the computer simulation illustrated in figure 8.1, which was one of a large number of simulations carried out for Binmore et al. (1995). In this simulation the original sum of money is $40, and the simulation begins with Alice offering Bob about $33, leaving $7 for herself. One has to imagine that the operant social norm in the society from which Alice and Bob are drawn selects this

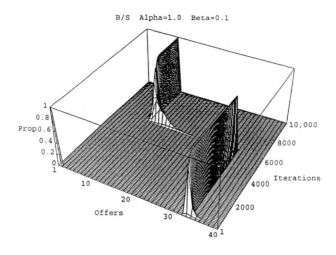

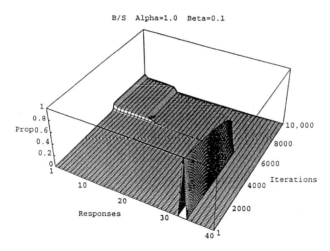

Figure 8.1
Simulated adaptive learning in the Ultimatum Game. The upper diagram shows the evolution over time of the offers a large population of player I's would make to player II if chosen to play. The diagram on the right shows the evolution over time of the acceptance levels of a corresponding population of player II's. A slightly perturbed version of the replicator dynamics is simulated whose parameters have been chosen to make the system converge on a 30:10 split of the $40 available. This takes 5,000 or so iterations when the system is started close to a 7:33 split. (The suddenness of the eventual transition between the Nash equilibria at 7:33 and 30:10 is illusory as the number of iterations during the transition exceeds by far those in any Ultimatum Game experiment.)

Nash equilibrium outcome from all those available when ultimatum situations arise in their repeated game of life. This split (like any other split) is also a Nash equilibrium outcome in the one-shot Ultimatum Game.

The figure shows our slightly perturbed replicator dynamic leading the system away from the vicinity of this $(7, 33)$ equilibrium. The system eventually ends up at a $(30, 10)$ equilibrium. The final equilibrium is not subgame-perfect (where the split would be $(40, 0)$), but this fact is not particularly germane. What is important here is that it takes some 5,000 periods before our simulated adaptive process moves the system any significant distance from the vicinity of the original $(7, 33)$ equilibrium. This enormous number of periods has to be compared with the ten or so commonly considered "ample" for adaptive learning to take place in the laboratory.

One might summarize these remarks by saying that testing the Ultimatum Game isn't an ideal way to go about exploring the extent to which an income-maximizing version of game theory works. Any efficient deal corresponds to a Nash equilibrium that a social norm operating in the society from which the subjects are drawn might render focal. A suitably perturbed adjustment process might eventually lead the subjects elsewhere, but the number of iterations this is likely to take would not be easy to replicate in a laboratory.

8.3 Public Goods Games with Punishment

In games like the Prisoners' Dilemma that can be interpreted as modeling the private provision of public goods, it is uncontroversial that most experienced subjects in laboratory experiments contribute little or nothing. However, Fehr and Gächter's (2000) show that the situation changes when free riders can be punished after the contribution phase is over.

In their modified experiment the subjects can pay a small amount to reduce the payoff of a free rider of their choice by a substantially larger amount. The opportunity to punish free riders in this way is actually used by the subjects, although an income-maximizer can gain nothing from such behavior. Contributions correspondingly rise progressively until most subjects are contributing a substantial amount. The conclusion drawn is that the subjects have a liking for punishing defectors built into their utility functions.

It is doubtless true that most people are disposed to punish antisocial behavior even when there is no money to be made out of this practice. But how firm is this tendency? Will more experience teach people that they gain nothing from punishing malefactors whom they will never meet again? How much of a loss will people endure before giving up the opportunity to punish?

Fehr and Gächter's (2000) experiment is uninformative. They overlook the fact that attributing only the trace of a liking for punishing bad behavior to the subjects is enough to create a Nash equilibrium in their game in which everybody contributes maximally (Steiner 2004). Each player's strategy in this equilibrium calls only for the worst free rider to be punished. Since all players punish the worst free rider, their share of the cost of providing an adequate disincentive becomes tiny. However, the assumption that players are prepared to pay this tiny cost is adequate to support the equilibrium, because nobody wants to be the worst free rider.

8.4   A Gift Exchange Game

An experiment of Fehr et al. (1997, 1999) is based on an idealized competitive labor market in which the workers have the opportunity to reward employers who pay above the competitive rate by putting in more effort. Subjects representing workers turn out to reward generous employers with more effort, although the employers have no way of identifying workers who shirk with a view to punishing them in the future. The result is typical of "gift-exchange" experiments that are offered in support of the hypothesis that people have preferences that incorporate a positive liking for reciprocating.

In a simplified version of the kind of labor market studied in this literature, there are m employers and n workers, where $m < n$. Each of N periods begins with each employer independently publishing either a *high* wage or a *low* wage for all to see. The workers get a negative payoff from being unemployed, and so they compete to get employed. Each worker has an equal chance, and so the probability that any single worker finds employment in any given period is m/n. The matchings are entirely anonymous, so long-term relationships between an employer and a worker are impossible.

A worker on a *low* wage automatically shirks. But a worker on a *high* wage can choose *high* or *low* effort. Both members of a matched pair receive a payoff of s if the wage is *low* (and so the worker shirks). Both receive b if the wage is *high* and the worker puts in *high* effort. The worker receives a payoff of 1 and the employer a payoff of 0 if the wage is *high* and the worker puts in *low* effort. We assume that $0 < s < b < 1$.

All Nash equilibria of this finitely repeated game require that the employer offers a *low* wage along the equilibrium path, but matters change if the game is perturbed slightly. To this end, we assume that each player is independently strategic with probability $1 - \pi$, or a reciprocating robot with probability π. A reciprocating robot makes a *high* offer as an employer and puts in *high* effort when receiving a *high* wage as a worker—until he observes that anyone at all has deviated from this behavior, after which he always plays *low*. The strategic players do not know the value of π but update their subjective probability distribution for this parameter as play proceeds.

For small values of π and large enough values of N, there are Nash equilibria of this finitely repeated game in which everybody plays *high* until near the end of the game. Cooperation is sustained by the contagion mechanism identified by Kandori (1992) for infinitely repeated games. The game is only finitely repeated, but the introduction of a small fraction of reciprocating robots permits a similar cooperating equilibrium to be sustained. As in the gang-of-four paper of Kreps et al. (1982), strategic players find it expedient to mimic the robots until it no longer matters whether a robot is provoked into precipitating a breakdown.

A number of authors, including Reinhard Selten (Selten and Stocker 1986), have shown that the folk theorem often still works in the laboratory when the number of repetitions is finite. The fact that cooperation tends to break down in the final rounds of these experiments adds some support to the relevance of the preceding model, since the same holds true in the experiment of Fehr et al. (1997), with 16 out of 26 workers putting in only the minimum effort in the tenth and final round.

8.5 Bargaining with Unequal Discount Rates

An experiment on Rubinstein's (1982) bargaining model with unequal discount rates reported elsewhere supports the hypothesis that most subjects optimize to a degree that would eventually be sufficient to shift a group of experimental subjects to the Rubinstein solution if all members of the group were to behave in the same way (Binmore et al. 2005). But some subjects presumably do not learn so quickly as others. Perhaps some do not learn at all but remain fixated on operating what they regard as a fair social norm. If we perturb Rubinstein's model by writing such behavioral possibilities into his scenario, what impact will this have on the predicted outcome?

In seeking an answer to this question, we focus on models in which a fraction of the population of possible players are initially conditioned on an outcome f of the bargaining problem, which they regard as fair or focal. However, their behavior is not inflexible. After observing a refused proposal, they sometimes switch to playing strategically with some exogenously determined probability. We find that the existence of such a group can result in significant perturbations of the Rubinstein outcome—even when all the conditioned players will eventually end up playing in the same way as the strategic players.

8.5.1   Experimental Background

This section briefly reviews some relevant experimental evidence.

Subgame Perfection?   The experimental evidence on finite bargaining games with alternating offers is firmly hostile to the idea that laboratory subjects use backward induction in deciding how to play (Camerer 2003). Even when it is assumed that the players care about their opponent's payoffs as well as their own, backward induction performs badly (Binmore et al. 2002).

It is therefore commonly thought that Rubinstein's use of the concept of a subgame-perfect equilibrium in analyzing his infinite-horizon model makes his theorem irrelevant to the behavior of real people. However, in the case of equally patient players, it turns out that the Rubinstein theory does rather well in predicting experimental outcomes when compared with more traditional bargaining approaches (Binmore et al. 1989, 1991). One possible explanation is that the conclusion of Rubinstein's theorem doesn't change if we replace the idea of a subgame-perfect equilibrium by that of a stationary expectations equilibrium—to which subjects can find their way in repeated play using some kind of myopic adjustment procedure, in which tomorrow is always treated as though it will resemble today.

Learning?   Although the experimental evidence that laboratory subjects can adjust their behavior over time to the strategic realities of most simple games is overwhelming, the case of finite bargaining games with alternating offers is more problematic, with nearly all experiments finding little or no evidence of experience changing the subjects' behavior (Camerer 2003).

However, in the bargaining games we have studied experimentally, we have always found evidence of learning—sometimes very rapid learning—

provided that the feedback provided is sufficiently rich. A possible explanation is that simple models of trial-and-error adjustment in the Ultimatum Game (and so presumably in similar games) predict that any learning is likely to be painfully slow (Binmore et al. 1995; Roth and Erev 1995).

Atypical Subjects   A particularly strong body of evidence is presented by Ledyard (1995) in his survey of a very large number of games like the Prisoners' Dilemma that model the private provision of public goods. Novices cooperate somewhat more than half the time, but the frequency of cooperation declines as the subjects gain experience, until about 90 percent of the subjects are defecting. However, the remaining 10 percent of the subject pool is of very considerable interest, especially since we find a similar proportion of subjects in our own bargaining experiments who seem impervious to strategic considerations (Binmore et al. 1991).

A Recent Experiment   In our most recent experiment, subjects played a variant of Rubinstein's (1982) bargaining game in which the next proposer after a disagreement is chosen at random (Binmore et al. 2005). The disagreement point is located at the origin. The feasible set resembles that of figure 8.2. The subjects played a total of 24 games, sometimes as player I and sometimes as player II.

The subjects first knowingly played eight "practice" rounds against a computer programmed to try to condition them either on the approximately utilitarian outcome $(8, 2)$, or on the equal increments or Rawlsian outcome $(4, 4)$. They then knowingly played 16 times against other subjects in their group, chosen unpredictably anew at the start of each game.

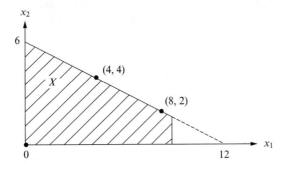

Figure 8.2
A simplified version of the feasible set used in Binmore et al.'s (2005) experiment on Rubinstein's Alternating-Offers Game.

Our intention was to study the extent to which the stability of any focal points established by the conditioning is related to the location of the Rubinstein solution (Binmore et al. 1992).

When player I's discount factor is $\delta_1 = 0.9$ and player II's is $\delta_2 = 0.8$ in the bargaining problem of figure 8.2, the utilitarian outcome $(8, 2)$ is the Rubinstein solution. When the players' discount factors are exchanged, the Rawlsian outcome $(4, 4)$ becomes the Rubinstein solution. Introducing one or other of these pairs of discount factors allows four treatments to be distinguished:

Treatment 1   Subjects conditioned on $(4, 4)$. Rubinstein solution $(4, 4)$.

Treatment 2   Subjects conditioned on $(8, 2)$. Rubinstein solution $(4, 4)$.

Treatment 3   Subjects conditioned on $(4, 4)$. Rubinstein solution $(8, 2)$.

Treatment 4   Subjects conditioned on $(8, 2)$. Rubinstein solution $(8, 2)$.

We succeeded in conditioning the subjects on $(4, 4)$, but we only succeeded in persuading the subjects that player I should get something more than 7 when our target was $(8, 2)$.[3]

Some of our results are shown in figures 8.3 and 8.4. The horizontal axis shows the sixteen games played against a human opponent. The plus signs indicate that player I made the first proposal in a game. The vertical axis shows the mean monetary payoff to player I. The points marked with a cross show the mean payoff to player I in the final agreement, discounted to time zero (in each game). The stars indicate the mean amount assigned to player I by the opening proposal. The circles show the predictions of a myopic best-reply model.[4] The squares show the predictions of a version of the myopic best-reply model, which has been perturbed by introducing a small bias toward the equal-split outcome $(4, 4)$.

The fact that the mean initial proposals always recognize the strategic advantage of the proposer suggests that the Rubinstein approach is basically on track, but the steady movement toward the Rubinstein solution in treatment 2 is absent (or only very slight) in treatments 3 and 4. Why does player I not make more aggressive proposals in treatment 3, and so further shift the trajectory of final agreements toward the Rubinstein solution of $(8, 2)$? Why again does the trajectory in treatment 4 not shift from around $(7, 2.5)$ toward the Rubinstein solution of $(8, 2)$?

We do not see how it is possible to answer such questions in our experiment simply by attributing social preferences to the subjects that lead them to play fair. The data show that the subjects' behavior varies so much over time that any such preferences would sometimes need to be

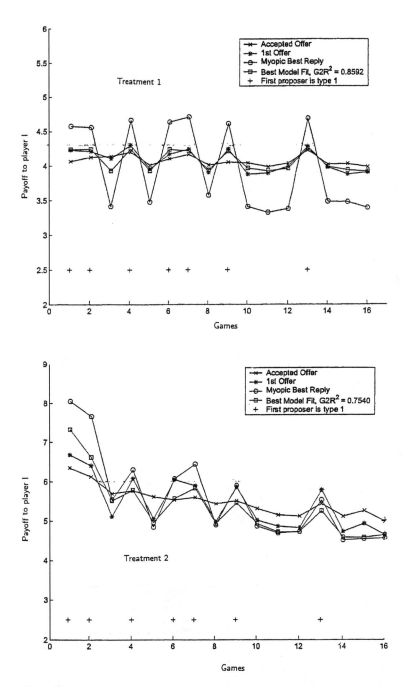

Figure 8.3
Data from treatments 1 and 2 in Binmore et al.'s (2005) experiment on a Rubinstein bargaining game.

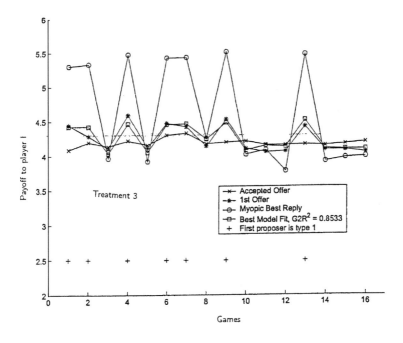

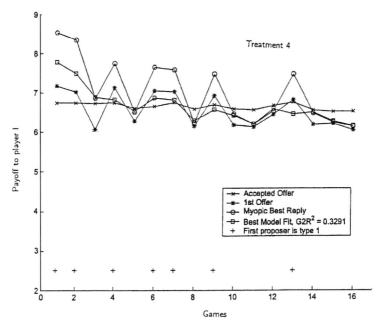

Figure 8.4
Data from Treatments 3 and 4 in Binmore et al.'s (2005) experiment on a Rubinstein bargaining game.

malleable to an extent that would render worthless any attempt to describe the subjects' behavior exclusively in such terms. Their conditioning, their role in the game, and their experience of previous play evidently all matter a great deal. In particular, treatment 2 shows clear evidence of learning—not only within each game—but between games as well.

On the other hand, fairness considerations are clearly relevant to our data—as they are in all bargaining experiments of which we are aware. However, there is an alternative explanation for why people sometimes play fair to the claim that a strong propensity for such behavior is frozen into their preferences. It is that fairness norms evolved as equilibrium selection devices (Binmore 1994, 2005). It is this alternative explanation that motivates the model explored in this paper.

8.6   Perturbing Rubinstein's Model

In Rubinstein's (1982) Alternating Offers Game, two players alternate in proposing how to split a shrinking cake. We model the cake at time 0 as the set

$$X_0 = \{x \in \mathbb{R}^2 : x_2 \le g(x_1)\},$$

Where $g : \mathbb{R} \to \mathbb{R}$ is strictly decreasing and concave. Its inverse function is denoted by $h : \mathbb{R} \to \mathbb{R}$. The set of figure 8.2 will be used as a canonical example. This is really the special case where the boundary of X_0 is $x_1 + 2x_2 = 12$, since the chunk cut away from this set in figure 8.2 is irrelevant to any calculations.[5]

In order that our subjects need only to look one move ahead in computing a stationary expectations equilibrium, our experiment modified the rules of Rubinstein's game so that the new proposer is always decided by the fall of a fair coin. This change does not alter Rubinstein's conclusions in any essential way.

At each time $t = 0, 1, 2, \ldots$ that the modified game is still in progress, an independent chance move chooses player I or II with equal probability to act as proposer or responder at this time. The proposer then makes a demand that the responder can accept or refuse. If the demand is accepted, the proposer receives his demand, and the responder is assigned whatever remains of the cake.

The shrinkage of the cake is modeled by assigning discount factors δ_1 and δ_2 to the two players. After a refusal at time t, the cake shrinks from X_t to

$$X_{t+1} = \{(x_1 \delta_1, x_2 \delta_2) : x \in X_t\}.$$

Since we assume $0 < \delta_i < 1$, the cake shrinks to zero if all proposals are refused.

The game has a unique subgame-perfect equilibrium (Binmore 1987). In equilibrium, the expected payoffs to the two players in our canonical example are[6]

$$r_1 = \frac{12(1 - \delta_2)}{2 - \delta_1 - \delta_2}, \quad r_2 = \frac{6(1 - \delta_1)}{2 - \delta_1 - \delta_2}. \tag{8.1}$$

Such computations are eased by noting that the answer turns out to be a stationary expectations equilibrium. Since a proposer will always make an offer (either $\delta_1 r_1$ or $\delta_2 r_2$) that leaves the responder indifferent between accepting and refusing, we merely need to solve the equations

$$2r_1 = h(\delta_2 r_2) + \delta_1 r_1,$$

$$2r_2 = g(\delta_1 r_1) + \delta_2 r_2.$$

Robots Abreu and Gul (2000) studied the Rubinstein bargaining model in the case where it is common knowledge that there is some probability that an opponent will turn out to be a robot who always plays "fair" regardless of the strategic situation. As in the gang-of-four model (Kreps et al. 1982), they find that a rational player will then sometimes pretend to be such a robot until some randomly determined number of proposals have been refused.

There are two reasons why we do not appeal to the Abreu-Gul model in seeking to make sense of our experimental data. The first is that it seems unlikely that their equilibrium could easily be learned by real people under laboratory conditions. The second is that our experience suggests that even strategically unresponsive subjects are a lot less inflexible than the robots of their model. Our own simpler model seeks to make virtues out of these problems.

Instead of a single chance move that decides whether a player will be a robot or a strategist at the start of the game, we introduce independent chance moves immediately following each refusal that permanently transform a player who has been a robot hitherto into a strategist from now on with probability $1 - \theta < 1$. This way we hope to capture in a crude way the fact that subjects who have been conditioned to play fair have the capability of learning to behave otherwise. If we keep things simple by always assigning the same belief to a newly created strategist as any other strategist would have on reaching the same point in the game, we simultaneously create a game with a stationary structure. Stationary expectations equilibria of this game then have a chance of being learned by subjects who operate some kind of myopic optimization process.

This specification leaves open the initial probability $\phi > 0$ that a player is a robot. In the calculations that follow, we take $\phi = \theta$ to keep things simple (but see section 8.7). It also leaves open the definition of a robot, which we take to be a player who has been conditioned to believe that the correct proposal is some efficient point f of X_0. A robot in the role of player I therefore always demands f_1 when proposing, and accepts f_2 or better when responding. A robot in the role of player II always demands f_2 when proposing, and accepts f_1 or better when responding.

Types of Equilibrium   The plan is to investigate equilibria in which strategists always accept proposals made in equilibrium by strategists. Any refusal therefore signals to a strategist that the opponent is currently a robot, who will remain a robot only with probability θ in the next round. We can therefore employ the same methodology used to characterize stationary expectations equilibria in the unperturbed model. The only difference is that now a proposer sometimes has two possibly optimal demands to compare: a larger demand that makes a strategic responder indifferent between accepting and refusing, and a possibly smaller demand that will also be accepted by a robot responder.

We distinguish three types of equilibrium:

Rubinstein equilibria   A strategist always makes a demand that renders another strategist indifferent between accepting and refusing. In equilibrium, strategists always accept.

Fair equilibria   A strategist always makes the fair demand. In equilibrium, strategists always accept.

Hybrid equilibria   A strategist plays as in a Rubinstein equilibrium or as in a fair equilibrium, depending on whether assigned the role of player I or player II. In equilibrium, strategists always accept.

In designing our experiment, we did not contemplate equilibria other than those of the Rubinstein type, nor did we realize that the existence of a robot fringe could significantly alter the players' behavior in such equilibria. We now think that only the results in treatment 2 look like the subjects are moving toward an equilibrium of the Rubinstein type. In the case of treatment 1, we should have been ready to see a fair equilibrium with $f = (4, 4)$. In treatments 3 and 4, we should have been ready to consider hybrid equilibria.

The point here is not to argue that one or other of these equilibria should be used to predict the data. We think that the modified myopic best-reply model used in Binmore et al. (2007) is to be preferred for this purpose, because it takes better account of the fact that even strategically minded folk need to learn to play equilibria. The point is rather that critics who would like to argue that the Rubinstein theory is altogether refuted by the data need to look harder at possible variants of the theory before they settle on such a draconian conclusion.

Rubinstein Equilibria   Let r be the payoff pair strategic players expect before the game begins. We distinguish three cases.

Case 1. $f_1 > \delta_1 r_1$; $f_2 > \delta_2 r_2$.

Case 2. $f_1 > \delta_1 r_1$; $f_2 < \delta_2 r_2$.

Case 3. $f_1 < \delta_1 r_1$; $f_2 > \delta_2 r_2$.

In case 1, a robot always refuses a strategist's offer of $\delta_2 r_2$ or $\delta_1 r_1$. When a strategic player I proposes, he therefore expects $(1 - \theta)h(\delta_2 r_2) + \theta \delta_1 r_1$. Strategists always accept offers made by strategists, and so expect $\theta f_1 + (1 - \theta)\delta_1 r_1$ when responding as player I. Similar considerations apply to strategic player IIs. The characterizing equations for a Rubinstein equilibrium in case 1 are therefore

$$2r_1 = (1 - \theta)h(\delta_2 r_2) + \theta f_1 + \delta_1 r_1,$$

$$2r_2 = (1 - \theta)g(\delta_1 r_1) + \theta f_2 + \delta_2 r_2,$$

These equations apply if and only if

$$(1 - \theta)h(\delta_2 r_2) + \theta \delta_1 r_1 \geq f_1,$$

$$(1 - \theta)g(\delta_1 r_1) + \theta \delta_2 r_2 \geq f_2,$$

since it would not otherwise be optimal for strategists to tolerate their offers being refused by robots.

In case 2, a robot in the role of player II accepts a a strategist's offer of $\delta_2 r_2$. When a strategic player I proposes, he therefore expects $h(\delta_2 r_2)$. A strategic player II refuses a fair offer, and so expects $\delta_2 r_2$ when responding. The characterizing equations for a Rubinstein equilibrium in case 2 are therefore

$$2r_1 = h(\delta_2 r_2) + \theta f_1 + (1 - \theta)\delta_1 r_1,$$

$$2r_2 = (1 - \theta)g(\delta_1 r_1) + (1 + \theta)\delta_2 r_2.$$

These equations apply if and only if

$$h(\delta_2 r_2) \geq \theta f_1 + (1 - \theta)\delta_1 r_1.$$
$$(1 - \theta)g(\delta_1 r_1) + \theta\delta_2 r_2 \geq f_2,$$

Case 3 is the same as case 2, except that the roles of players I and II are reversed.

Fair Equilibria   Fair equilibria can only exist in case 1, because then $r = f$. The inequalities that need to be satisfied are

$$f_1 \geq (1 - \theta)h(\delta_2 r_2) + \theta\delta_1 r_1,$$
$$f_2 \geq (1 - \theta)g(\delta_1 r_1) + \theta\delta_2 r_2.$$

These inequalities always hold when f coincides with the Rubinstein outcome in the unperturbed game and $\theta \geq 0.5$. (There are no other fair equilibria in our canonical case when $\theta = 0.5$.)

In particular, if $\theta \geq 0.5$ and $f = (4,4)$, it is an equilibrium in our treatments 1 and 2 ($\delta_1 = 0.8$ and $\delta_2 = 0.9$) for everyone always to propose and accept the outcome f. The same holds in our treatments 3 and 4 ($\delta_1 = 0.9$ and $\delta_2 = 0.8$) with $\theta \geq 0.5$ and $f = (8,2)$.

Hybrid Equilibria   We omit the characterization of hybrid equilibria, since it will now be evident how this proceeds.

Existence   In our canonical example, computerized calculations reveal that one of these three types of equilibria exists for all values of θ ($0 \leq \theta \leq 1$) and all values of f ($0 \leq f_1 \leq 12$). There are occasionally multiple equilibria, but mostly only one of the three types of equilibrium exists for each pair (θ, f).

When the two parameters θ and ϕ are not equal, it becomes more complicated to characterize the equilibria. However, computerized calculations again show that one of the three types of equilibrium always exists, except for a few patches in the parameter space. The equilibrium is again typically unique.

8.7   What Do Perturbed Equilibria Look Like?

Figures 8.5 and 8.6 show equilibrium behavior in perturbed versions of Rubinstein's model. They are directly comparable with the experimental

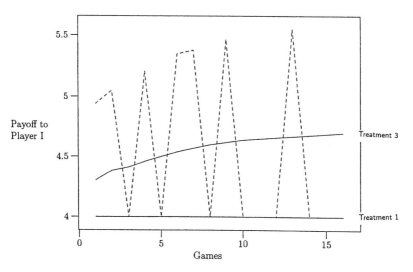

Figure 8.5
Equilibrium behavior in a perturbed Rubinstein model for treatments 1 and 3. The unperturbed Rubinstein outcomes are $(4, 4)$ and $(8, 2)$ respectively. The parameters of the model are $\theta = 0.6$, $\phi = 0.5$, $\psi = 0.1$, and $f = (4, 4)$. Treatment 1 is a fair equilibrium in which nobody ever deviates from proposing or accepting $(4, 4)$. Treatment 3 is a hybrid equilibrium in which only player II proposes $(4, 4)$.

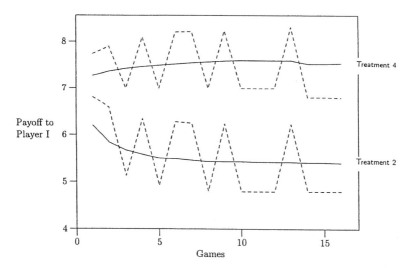

Figure 8.6
Equilibrium behavior in a perturbed Rubinstein model for treatments 2 and 4. The unperturbed Rubinstein outcomes are $(4, 4)$ and $(8, 2)$ respectively. The parameters of the model are $\theta = 0.2$, $\phi = 0.5$, $\psi = 0.1$, with $f = (7.5, 2.25)$ in treatment 2, and $f = (7, 2.5)$ in treatment 4. Treatment 2 is a Rubinstein equilibrium. Treatment 4 begins as a hybrid equilibrium in which only player II proposes $f = (7, 2.5)$ but switches to a Rubinstein equilibrium when the fraction of robots becomes sufficiently small.

data illustrated in figures 8.3 and 8.4. In particular, the choice of who makes the first proposal in each game is exactly the same.

The firm lines in figures 8.5 and 8.6 join points that show the average money payoff to player I in the final agreement, discounted to time zero (in each game). The broken lines join points which show the average money payoff proposed for player I at the outset of each game.

Notice that treatment 1 in figure 8.5 is a fair equilibrium in which both the firm and the broken graph sit on top of each other. Treatment 2 in figure 8.6 is a Rubinstein equilibrium. Treatment 3 in figure 8.5 is a hybrid equilibrium. Treatment 4 in figure 8.6 is begins as a hybrid equilibrium but switches to a Rubinstein equilibrium when the remaining fraction of robots becomes sufficiently small.

The parameter value $\phi = 0.5$ (which gives the fraction of robots at the beginning of the game) was chosen to correspond roughly with the fraction of subjects who begin by cooperating in Prisoners' Dilemma experiments. The parameter value $\psi = 0.1$ (which was taken to be zero in the previous section) is the fraction of robots who are assumed never to alter their conditioned behavior under any circumstances. This was chosen to correspond roughly with the fraction of subjects who persist in cooperating in Prisoners' Dilemma experiments after having enjoyed ample opportunity for learning.[7] The remaining robots behave as described in the preceding section.

In treatments 1 and 3, we took $f = (4, 4)$ to reflect the fact that an attempt was made to condition the subjects on this outcome in the practice rounds. In treatments 2 and 4, we took $f = (7.5, 2.25)$ and $f = (7, 2, 5)$ respectively to reflect the degree of success we enjoyed in seeking to condition the subjects on the outcome $(8, 2)$. However, we would have done better by taking $f = (4, 4)$ in all the treatments—as we do in the modified myopic best-reply model that we fit to the data in Binmore et al. (2007). This observation is reflected in the fact that, although we have made no attempt to fit the current equilibrium model econometrically to the data, we do better by taking $\theta = 0.6$ in treatments 1 and 3, and $\theta = 0.2$ in treatment 2 and 4. Roughly speaking, this means that subjects are assumed to be more reluctant to abandon their conditioning when $f = (4, 4)$ than when $f = (7.5, 2.25)$ or $f = (7, 2.5)$.

8.8   Conclusion

We have argued that anomalous data in bargaining experiments can often be explained without resorting to the extravagant claim that subjects act as optimizers with a large other-regarding component built into their utility function. We believe that a better explanation is that subjects are acting in accordance with a social norm which is adapted to a real-life game that differs from the game they are playing in the laboratory. When subjects fail to adapt their behavior to the laboratory game (with money payoffs) as in a minority of economic experiments, we believe that the explanation is often to be found in the fact that the anomalous games have many Nash equilibria that are commonly overlooked. The field for such an explanation opens wider if one admits the possibility that the subjects may have a *small* other-regarding component built into their utility functions, or if there is some heterogeneity in the speed at which different subjects learn to adjust their behavior away from whatever social norm they brought with them into the laboratory.

In the main part of the paper, we explored the latter possibility using a perturbed version of the Rubinstein bargaining model with unequal discount rates. We find that the crude prediction of the unperturbed Rubinstein model must then be replaced by one of a rich variety of equilibria, some of which share the qualitative features of the available data.

Our general conclusion is that, before critics are entitled to argue that the income-maximizing hypothesis for experienced subjects should be abandoned in bargaining games or elsewhere, they first need to ask whether the behavior they observe is consistent with a neglected Nash equilibrium of the game or with a Nash equilibrium of some perturbed version of the game.

A   More Ultimata

This appendix contains our original unpublished report on the two-stage ultimatum game experiment eventually published as the short note of chapter 3. Both the experimental instructions and the final data are appended.

The authors gratefully acknowledge the financial support provided by the International Centre for Economics and Related Disciplines; the hospitality of the Psychology Department at L.S.E. where the experimental work was carried out and the assistance of Yasmin Batliwala, Mimi Bell, and Maria Jose Herrero who actually ran the experiments. We are particularly indebted to Werner Güth, Alvin Roth, and Reinhard Selten for their detailed and constructive criticism of an earlier draft.

Fairness or Gamesmanship in Bargaining: An Experimental Study

Ken Binmore, John Sutton, and Avner Shaked

A.1 Introduction

A new approach to bargaining theory has led to a major resurgence of interest in the subject over the past few years. The new approach is to study the dynamics of specific bargaining processes using the techniques of noncooperative game theory. This approach presents a marked contrast to the traditional use of axiomatic "bargaining solutions" (e.g., that of Nash) drawn from cooperative game theory. Although useful insights are possible with the traditional methodology, it suffers from the fact that it is seldom clear to what extent the axioms are genuinely appropriate in a given field of application. The new approach, on the other hand, seeks to model explicitly a bargaining process described by a detailed structure of moves; that is, we look for a noncooperative equilibrium where players' strategies describe the offers, and replies they make, at specified stages in the process. One attraction of this approach is that it allows reasoned judgments to be made about the applicability of its conclusions.[1] In some cases, indeed, recent advances have led to conclusions that are sharply testable in the sense that they generate predictions that are directly refutable by experiment (Shaked and Sutton 1983). An investigation of bargaining behavior in a controlled experimental setting is therefore timely.

However, conventional wisdom on experimental bargaining behavior offers little prospect of success for predictions based on game-theoretic

---

1. We think it is important, however, not to regard the two approaches as hostile competitors. We see them instead as providing complementary points of view, each of which provides a different type of insight into bargaining problems. In this we simply follow Nash. According to Nash, intuitions about the appropriate choice of cooperative solution concept should be examined by investigating the extent to which the concept will be implemented by players in a variety of noncooperative negotiation games chosen so as to mimic the manner in which cooperation between individuals may be achieved as a result of their making optimal choices of negotiating posture.

ideas.[2] It is perhaps possible to dismiss some experimental studies on the grounds that the results are too fuzzy to allow an unambiguous interpretation, and because of uncertainties over controls. But a number of recent papers (e.g., Selten et al. 1975; Roth and Malouf 1979; Shaked and Sutton 1983) cannot reasonably be so dismissed. We wish to concentrate particularly on a study of Güth et al. (1982). The reason is that some of the results obtained in that study conflict quite dramatically with the results a game-theoretic analysis would lead one to anticipate.[3] Such results are familiar to social psychologists. However, in most studies subjects bargain in a relatively unstructured environment to which noncooperative game theory cannot be directly applied. In contradistinction, the study by Güth et al. employed an entirely structured environment, so simple that the appropriate game-theoretic analysis would seem completely transparent.

Their most striking experiment used a (one-stage) Ultimatum Game. In this game, two players bargain over the division of a "cake" (which actually consisted of a sum of money between 4 and 10 DM). If the players agree on a division of the cake, then each player receives his agreed share. Otherwise, both players receive nothing. The bargaining procedure is very simple[4] and involves precisely two "moves." The first move is made by player 1 who proposes a division of the cake. The second move is made by player 2 who accepts or rejects the proposal made by player 1.

If the players seek only to maximise the quantity of cake received, a game-theoretic analysis is trivial. Player 1 demands all but the tiniest crumb which player 2 accepts on the grounds that even the tiniest crumb is better than nothing. But the subjects studied by Güth, Schmittberger and Schwarze showed little inclination to act like "gamesmen." Instead they were very much more likely to settle on a *fair* division of the cake.

Güth (1983), along with many social psychologists and others, favours a sociopsychological explanation of this phenomenon in terms of deeply held convictions about "fairness" or "distributive justice." Determined

---

2. Although mention should be made of the work of Fouraker and Siegel (1963) who found evidence of strategic behavior in subjects asked to play bargaining games based on a bilateral monopoly problem.

3. Further similar results are quoted in Güth (1983).

4. Matters would be more complicated if the bargaining game were not a "one-shot" affair but one of a sequence of similar games during the play of which the players would be able to learn the characteristics of their opponents and teach opponents their own characteristics. However, although the study of Güth et al. involved the play of more than one game by some players, care was taken to ensure that a "one-shot" game-theoretic analysis was appropriate in each particular game.

neoclassicists prefer an explanation which assigns a "spite" component[5] to the second player's utility function. This would lead to his rejecting proposals which offer him too little. Knowing this, player 1 would then avoid such proposals.

The two explanations are not necessarily mutually exclusive in that one might attribute a "spite" component in player 2's utility function to righteous indignation at a lack of proper conduct on the part of player 1. At the same time a knowledge that deviations from the path of virtue are likely to be punished might reasonably be expected to reinforce any feelings that player 1 might have about the propriety of "playing fair." Güth (1983) emphasises this latter point.

The chief finding of our experimental study is that these reactions to the observation of "fair play" in certain bargaining situations are unwarranted. Briefly, we feel that our results support the following general conclusions:

Conclusion 1   It is *false* that players *systematically* aim at a "fair" outcome in simple, structured bargaining games.

Conclusion 2   Game theory *can* be useful as a predictor of human behavior in *simple*, structured bargaining games *provided* that the circumstances under which the game is played encourage a little reflection on the part of players. It should be emphasized that we do not make the same claim for *complicated* bargaining games.[6]

Conclusion 3   In so far as subjects hold convictions about "distributive justice," these convictions would seem ephemeral in the sense that they can be quickly displaced by more "rational" considerations once these have been appreciated. Thus the observation that players sometimes divide the cake "half and half" is perhaps better attributed to the subjects finding themselves at a loss as to what play is individually optimal[7] rather than to any firm commitment on their part to some ethical standpoint.

Conclusion 4   Any beliefs that players might entertain about the existence of a "spite" component in their opponent's utility function would seem equally easily displaced.

---

5. This explanation was proposed to us by our colleague Morris Perlman among others. A somewhat less delicate terminology is apparently commonplace.

6. Especially where information is incomplete.

7. Or, perhaps, to their not taking note of the fact that the situation can be seen as a problem in optimisation.

It is not hard to construct plausible "explanations" of these conclusions,[8] but we feel that it would be premature to do so. Much further research is necessary, particularly on the nature of cues that trigger various types of behavior in the laboratory.

Finally it should be noted that many different formulations of a "fairness" or "equity" theory of bargaining behavior are possible. We have chosen to describe particularly simple formulations so that our conclusions are expressible in a reasonably sharp manner. However, we are aware that our results in no way refute more complex formulations of the theory in which both strategic calculations and considerations of fairness play a role in determining the bargaining outcome. Selten and Krischker (1982) offer perhaps the most developed and plausible version of such a theory.

Our stance is a modest one. Game theory provides a simple and testable model, and one that is a natural starting point for explaining observed outcomes in simple bargaining games. Prior to the present work we were much influenced by the current conventional wisdom, which stresses the limitation of game-theoretic predictions. We now feel that this was an overreaction, given the current state of experimental knowledge, and that a more optimistic view is warranted.

A.2 Background

The experimental work described here arose as an offshoot of a more ambitious project that aimed at studying bargaining behavior in multi-stage bargaining games. As a preliminary, we thought it appropriate to seek to reproduce the results of Güth et al. (1982) in a two-stage bargaining game under the laboratory conditions that we thought appropriate to the main project. A two-stage game was chosen to guard against the risk that the

8. Building blocks in such an explanation would presumably include
1. A "limited rationality" model of human behavior such as that proposed by Selten (1978). The essential feature is the possibility that different "problem-solving techniques" might be triggered depending on the "cues" offered by the environment. These "problem-solving techniques" would usually be tailored to real-life bargaining situations rather than those contrived in a laboratory.
2. A recognition that the problems raised by real-life bargaining situations are typically those of coordination and/or reputation-building rather than the competitive issues raised by the game of our study. For "co-ordination"; see Schelling (1960). For "reputations," see Selten (1978) or Wilson (1983).
3. An understanding that the reasons for the survival of a behaviour pattern in a population may have little to do with the explanation that individuals themselves offer for this behavior.

degenerate nature of the one-stage game used by Güth et al. might lead to atypical results in respect of multiple-stage bargaining in general.

A pilot study (pilot I) of such a game led to results that are broadly consistent with those of Güth et al. However, the comments that subjects recorded after the game (about their motivation in playing as they had) led us to doubt that these results in themselves told the whole story. We therefore designed a more complex pilot study (pilot II) with the aim of investigating the doubtful questions. The results of this second pilot study were sufficiently striking that we thought it worth investigating them further by way of an experiment (reported under the heading Main Results) using a much larger sample. It is on this last piece of work that we base the tentative conclusions offered at the end of section A.1.

A.3 The Two-Stage Bargaining Game

As in the (one-stage) Ultimatum Game described in section A.1, two players bargain over the division of a notional cake. If they agree on a division, then each player receives his agreed share. Otherwise, each receives nothing. A rigidly structured bargaining procedure is imposed. Player 1 begins by making a proposal to player 2, which he or she can accept or refuse. If player 2 refuses, then he or she makes a counterproposal, which player 1 can accept or refuse. If player 1 refuses, both players receive nothing.

In the experiment it was common knowledge that the cake was worth a sum of money.[9] When player 1 made his proposal, the cake was worth £1 = 100p. If player 1's proposal was refused, the cake *shrank* to 25p for player 2's proposal. Only proposals involving a whole number of pence were permitted. The amount of 25p for the shrunken cake was chosen so as to be small enough to make a sharp distinction between "fair play" and "gamesmanship" but not so small as to be regarded as negligible.

We leave the experimental conditions under which the game was played until section A.4 and continue this section with a brief game-theoretic analysis. Of course, almost any behavior can be justified along neoclassical lines if one is free to assign sufficiently complicated utility functions to the players. The following analysis, however, assumes that players are interested in maximizing the amount of cake they receive and in nothing else.

---

9. Experimental evidence shows that it can make a substantial difference whether subjects bargain over money or "counters". (See Roth and Malouf 1979.) We are grateful to Professor Selten for advice on the actual amount to make available for bargaining.

An attractive feature of the bargaining games we consider is that further information about the players' preferences (in particular, their attitudes to risk) is irrelevant to the properties of the equilibria with which we are concerned. It is for this reason that we can work directly with monetary payments and do not need to resort to the methods introduced by Roth and Murningham (1982), and others, for the experimental determination of Von Neumann and Morgenstern utilities.

Note first that it cannot be optimal for player 1 to demand 73p or less when he makes the first proposal. The reason is that player 2 can get at most 25p by refusing, and hence he or she will necessarily accept any demand of 74p or less (since this yields a payoff of 26p or more to player 2). Next observe that it cannot be optimal for player 1 to demand 77p or more when he makes the first proposal. The reason is that player 2 will refuse such a demand, and then player 1 will get at most 25p. Player 2 refuses because an acceptance yields a payoff of 23p or less whereas a refusal yields at least 24p. This follows from the fact that any positive offer made by player 2 at the second stage will be accepted by player 1 who otherwise would receive nothing.

A game-theoretic analysis therefore requires that player 1's opening demand lie in the range 74p to 76p inclusive and that player 2 plan to accept any opening demand of 74p or less,[10] but we follow Ståhl (1972) in seeking to minimize rationality assumptions.

If we restrict our attention to opening demands for the moment, then a comparison between "fair play" and "gamesmanship" is easily made. Making some allowance for "noise," the former requires opening demands in the vicinity of 50p while the latter requires opening demands in the vicinity of 75p. This observation is all that is necessary to appreciate the main feature of our results. (See figure A.3 of section A.6.)

We will also make a somewhat more sophisticated comparison that requires our being more specific about the nature of "fair play." Both Güth's (1983) "theory of distributive justice" and the neoclassical "spite" theory require that a substantial proportion of player 2's plan to *refuse* opening demands significantly in excess of 50p. So as to have something precise to say, we offer the following operational labels[11] (it is relevant to their interpretation that $62.5 = (50 + 75)/2$:

---

10. If the players were not constrained by indivisibilities in making demands, then there would be a unique equilibrium involving the acceptance of an opening offer of 75p. In our game there are a multiplicity of (perfect) equilibria due to the fact that players can only make offers in multiples of 1p.

11. Obviously neither definition is either necessary or sufficient for theoretical purposes.

A *gamesman* is a subject who makes an opening demand of 63p or more when filling the role of player 1 and who plans to *accept* opening demands in the range 63p to 77p inclusive[12] when filling the role of player 2.

A *fairman*[13] is a subject who makes an opening demand of 62p or less when filling the role of player 1 and who plans to *refuse* opening demands in the range 63p to 77p inclusive when filling the role of player 2.

The relevant comparison appears in table A.3 of section A.6.

A.4 Experimental Setup

The experiments were conducted in the psychology test-rooms at the London School of Economics under the immediate supervision of Yasmin Batliwala, Mimi Bell, and Maria Jose Herrero.[14] Subjects were placed in separate rooms before two microcomputers linked by a cable. They were then asked to read an account of the rules of the game after which a verbal summary of the instructions was offered.

We felt it was important to offset any reluctance a subject might feel toward maximizing his winnings at the expense of the university, the research fund, or the researchers themselves. We therefore included an instruction as to how subjects should view their objectives, stating that they should set out to maximize their winnings (annex 1).

Reinforcement of the instructions together with practice in the use of the necessary computer controls was then provided via the visual display unit (VDU). The subjects did *not* play a practice game with the computer because we were anxious not to offer any cues about what type of play was expected of them.

After the instructional period, player 1's VDU displayed a picture of a rectangular "cake," which he or she could divide into two "shares" with the aid of a cursor controlled from the keyboard. When satisfied with the proposed division, player 1 pressed a key that transmitted an appropriate display to player 2's VDU. Player 2 responded by pressing key "Y" for acceptance or "N" for refusal. If player 2 refused, his or her VDU then displayed a picture of a new shrunken cake to be divided into two

12. The 77p allows for some noise in the opening demand.

13. Perhaps "strawman" would be a better description, since it is not evident to the authors that a commitment to "fairness" necessarily precludes taking a rational attitude when placed in a "take it or leave it" situation.

14. Maria Jose Herrero is an economist by training; Yasmin Batliwala and Mimi Bell have a background in psychology.

"shares" with the aid of a cursor as before. When ready, player 2's proposal was communicated to player 1 who concluded the game with an acceptance or a refusal.

The players knew throughout the value of the two cakes and were paid the amounts on which they had agreed immediately after the play of the game.

Very considerable care was taken to ensure that the subjects had no knowledge of the identity of their opponent either before or after the game (although this was expensive in so far as the time put in by the research assistants). The fact that strict anonymity was maintained meant that subjects did not have the opportunity to verify whether they were playing against a human opponent, as they had been informed. We thought this a small price to pay in order to eliminate even the slightest possibility of the exchange of hints or cues by the players except via the cable that linked their respective computers.

The players could, of course, make some generalized deductions about their opponents from the manner in which they themselves were recruited. Güth et al. used graduate students in economics at the University of Cologne, but we found it necessary to cast our net more widely. Our subjects included not only graduate and undergraduate students of economics at LSE but also students of related subjects like management science and accounting as well as a sprinkling of students from other disciplines. (Students or former students of the LSE Game Theory course were excluded.) A log-book was kept in which were recorded the particulars of each subject, the course of the game in which he or she took part, and the comments the subject was willing to make afterward about his or her strategy choice. An inspection of these data did not suggest any obvious correlations between the categories of student used and the way they played the game (although this is not to say that such correlations may not exist).

A.5   Pilot Studies

We began by running 38 games (recorded as pilot I) in which the 76 subjects each played one and only one bargaining game each. A histogram of opening demands is given below as figure A.1. These demands are consistent with those observed by Güth et al. (1982) in that there is a clear tendency for player 1 to make a "fair" demand.

It is not so clear that the behavior of player 2 in responding to these demands is consistent with the results obtained by Güth et al. (1982) (see

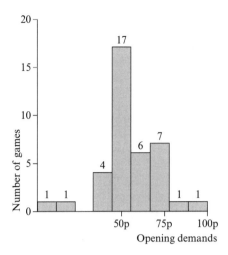

Figure A.1
Opening demands in PILOT I

annex 3). However, our attention was struck, not so much by a disparity of behavior between players 1 and 2 in their play of the game, but by the disparity in their comments about their *motivation* in playing as they had. Those subjects who had occupied the role of player 2 made comments that seemed to us to be very much more to the point. In retrospect, this does not seem very surprising. The role of player 2 is a passive one at the outset, and hence he or she has the opportunity to reflect on the game without the pressure of being in the "hot seat." What is more, player 2 has a much simpler decision problem to contemplate at the first stage. Just two options are available (i.e., accept or refuse) and only the smallest amount of contemplation is necessary to see that a "rational" cake-maximizer should accept demands of 74p or less independently of any beliefs player 2 might have about player 1. In contrast, player 1 has a large number of options to consider, and what is "rational" for him will depend on his beliefs about the manner in which player 2 is likely to respond to his opening demand. In addition player 1 may well feel constrained to act quickly for fear of looking foolish if he procrastinates.

We felt this issue important to explore further. So we ran another 19 games. After each game player 2 was asked to play once more against a *new* opponent,[15] but this time taking the role of player 1 (figure A.2). The

15. Actually the new opponent was a research assistant in the other room instructed to play like a gamesman. However, since we recorded only the opening demand in game B, the identity and manner of play of the new opponent is irrelevant to our results.

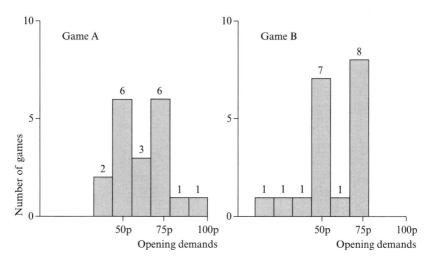

Figure A.2
Opening demands in PILOT II

Table A.1
Response to opening demands

	Response to opening demand of a ($63 \leq a \leq 77$) in game A	
Opening demand in game B	No	Yes
$b \leq 62$	(F) 3	(B?) 0
$b \geq 63$	1	(G) 3

Note: The table refers to the 7 opening demands that fell in the range 63 to 77 in game A of pilot study II. The labels F and G indicate the cells in which a Fairman, and a Gamesman, as defined in section A.3, will lie. A Bayesian with appropriate beliefs about his opponent might lie in the cell labeled B.

results of the ensuing 19 pairs of games are recorded as pilot II. The first of each pair of games is called game A and the second is called game B. We did not seek to study game B beyond the opening demand because of practical difficulties in having suitable subjects available at the necessary times.

The results were sufficiently interesting to induce us to run a further series of 81 game pairs (A and B), which we report under the heading of Main Results. Our immediate aims were as follows:

1. To test for bimodality in the histograms corresponding to those given above.

2. To test the proposition that a substantial proportion of the population are "fairmen" (in the sense of section A.3) by constructing a table corresponding to that given for pilot II in table A.1.

The top left-hand cell in table A.1 is labeled (F) for "fairman" and the bottom right-hand cell is labeled (G) for "gamesman." Note that a "rational cake-maximizer" *must* lie in the right-hand column. A Bayesian player with appropriate beliefs might find himself in cell (B?), but we could think of no rationalization for occupants of the fourth cell.

A.6   Main Results[16]

A complete listing of the course of each game is given as annex 4 and some subsidiary tables are offered in annex 3. In this section we confine our attention to the features of the data that we feel have a direct bearing on the issues raised in section A.1. Recall that we studied 81 pairs of games (game A and game B). Player 1 in game B was the subject who had been player 2 in game A provided with the information that he or she was to play against a *new* opponent in game B. Only the opening demand of game B was recorded. Thus, in game A, the opening demand was made by a totally inexperienced player; in game B, a player had just a little more experience.

The histograms[17] showing opening demands in each game are bimodal but not to a significant degree (figure A.3). Contrary to our expectations, they exhibit a marked change of behavior between game A and game B. A tendency to "play fair" in game A becomes a strong tendency to play "like a game theorist" in game B.

This marked changes in behavior constitutes the central finding of the present study.

To investigate the change in behavior between games A and B, we had planned to test the null hypothesis—that the opening demands in each game are drawn from the same population. The null hypothesis was in-

16. It is necessary to say something about the manner in which we dealt with "mistakes." Several subjects reported, after playing the game, that they had not meant to do what they actually did, chiefly as a consequence of confusing left and right. A pair of games involving a player who reported making such a mistake in understanding the rules of the game was simply discarded. It should be noted, however, that the instructions given to subjects differed slightly as between pilot II and Main Results, the aim being to minimize such mistakes (both reported and unreported). The new instructions emphasized that a subject's share of the cake *always* lay to the left of the cursor both in game A and in game B.

17. Before running the games we decided to split the range of opening demands into nine equal cells so that the cell containing the "fair" demand of 50p would be clearly separated by a third cell from the cell containing the "gamesman" demand of approximately 75p.

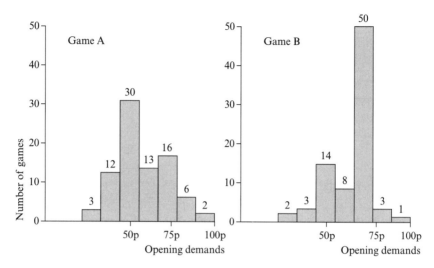

Figure A.3
Opening demands for MAIN RESULTS

deed rejected at the 0.1 percent level (Kolmogoroff-Smirnoff two-tailed test; Siegel 1956, pp. 131, 279).

But, while the pilot results had led us to expect a change in behavior because of a sharpening bimodality, they had not led us to expect a marked shift toward high demands. Given these results, we applied the one-tailed test to observe the more precise question: Are the demands in game B larger? Interestingly, again, the null hypothesis—that the demands in game B are not stochastically larger than those in game A— was rejected at the 0.1 percent level (Kolmogoroff-Smirnoff one tailed test; Siegel 1956, pp. 131, 245).

Our main conclusion is that the results for game B show that game theory *can* be useful as a predictor of human behavior *provided* that the circumstances encourage a little reflection on the part of the players. While this is the interpretation we find most natural, we remark here on a number of qualifications, and on a number of alternative explanations that might appear plausible:

1. *Aping behavior*   It is of course reasonable to ask whether a player in game B might simply by copying the strategy he saw his opponent use in game A. Such aping behavior would lead to a correlation between the opening demand in game A and the opening demand in game B.

A second possibility that would lead to the same correlation is when the opening demands in game B are high because the player in question is reacting to the fact that he was offered very little in game A.

Table A.2
Relationship between the opening demand made to a subject in game A and the opening demand he later made as player 1 in game B.

	Opening demand a in game A	
Opening demand in game B	$a \leq 62$	$a \geq 63$
$b \leq 62$	18 (7)	5 (4)
$b \geq 63$	34 (2)	24 (5)

Note: The figures are those for the Main Results. Those in brackets are for pilot II.

Table A.3
Relationship between a subject's response to the opening demand made of him in game A, and the opening demand that he later makes when acting as player 1 in game B.

	Response to opening demand of a ($63 \leq a \leq 77$) in game A	
Opening demand b in game B	No	Yes
$b \leq 62$	(F) 1	(B?) 2
$b \geq 63$	2	(G) 17

In table A.2 below, we show the relationship between opening demands in game A, and opening demands in game B (Main Results). A Fisher exact test indicates that there is no significant association (at the 5 percent level).

2. *Bayesian decision theory* We were surprised to find little evidence of player 1 choosing an opening demand according to Bayesian criteria— that is, forming a subjective probability distribution for the response behavior of player 2 and then maximizing utility relative to this distribution. Only a small number of subjects explained their behavior in these terms. Instead most subjects who offered a coherent explanation seemed to take it for granted that if they analyzed the game in a particular way, then so would their opponent.

Still it may be interesting to learn what demand a (risk neutral) Bayesian player would make if he correctly forecast the probability of acceptance of demands in each interval (table A.3). However, the data reported here are not adequate to permit any sharp conclusion. The optimal demand for such a player might lie anywhere in the range 50 to 75, within the limits of experimental error.

3. *Fairmen v. Gamesmen* Our study is not at all supportive of the hypothesis that a substantial proportion of the population systematically

play as "fairmen". This is illustrated in table A.2, whose interpretation is noted above.

4. *Comparison with Güth et al.*   Responses to opening demands were strongly biased in favor of "rationality." (Of 22 opening demands in the range $63 \leq a \geq 77$, only 3 were rejected; see annex 3.) On the other hand, at the second stage—following a refusal at the first stage—subjects showed a strong tendency to reject high demands as in the study of Güth et al. (1982). Our suspicion is that the one-stage Ultimatum Game is *pathological* in this respect.

The pathology may be due to the following fact: in the Ultimatum Game, the first player might be dissuaded from making an opening demand at, or close to, the "optimum" level, since his opponent would then incur a negligible cost in making an "irrational" rejection. In the two-stage game, these considerations are postponed to the second stage, and so their impact is attenuated.

There remains the possibility that the difference between our results and those of Güth et al. might be traced to differences in the experimental environment rather than to differences in the game played. Güth et al. operated in an open environment within which subjects could see each other (although the identity of their current opponent was, of course, secret). Our assistant, Yasmin Batliwala, has run a controlled experiment to check for this possibility (which will be reported separately). Replicating our experimental conditions, she compared the behavior of subjects playing our two-stage game with that of a control group playing the one-stage Ultimatum Game. Generally, the results confirmed our present interpretation. Behavior in the two-stage game was similar to that reported in this paper. Behavior in the one-stage Ultimatum Game was consistent with the observations of Güth et al. in that game theory is a poor predictor of outcomes.

A.7   Summary and Conclusions

We have been concerned here to analyze the behavior of experimental subjects in playing a two-stage noncooperative bargaining game. The game we chose was designed to probe more deeply the widely held view that game-theoretic solutions are a poor predictor of bargaining outcomes.

In the game we investigated, the game-theoretic solution turned out to be a fairly successful predictor of outcomes. However, there was a marked difference in behavior between players who were confronted with the game for the first time and those playing it a second time. Many subjects playing for the first time proposed an equal division, even though they enjoyed a strong strategic advantage.

While we have considered various possible explanations, the interpretation we favor is this: when faced with a new problem, subjects simply choose "equal division" as an "obvious" and "acceptable" compromise—an idea familiar from the seminal work of Schelling (1960). We suspect, on the basis of the present experiments, that such considerations are easily displaced by calculation of strategic advantage once players fully appreciate the structure of the game.

Annex 1:   Instructions Given to Player 1

The "Divide a Cake" Game

The aim of this exercise is to examine how people behave in bargaining situations. You will play a game in which you bargain with an opponent, as to how to divide a sum of money between you.

The game has two steps.

In the first step the amount of money involved is £1. You will be given a chance to *make an offer* of a certain share (sum of money) to your opponent.

If your opponent *accepts*, then he or she will be paid the amount that was offered by the organizer.

You will be paid the remaining part of the £1.

And that will end the game.

Suppose your offer is *rejected*, however. Then your opponent will be given a turn to make an offer.

WHAT IS DIFFERENT "SECOND TIME ROUND" IS THAT THE AMOUNT OF MONEY TO BE SPLIT IS LESS.

You will be told at the start of the game, what the size of the cake in this second stage will be. (It may be 75p, 50p, or less.)

But apart from this, the second round is like the first. Your opponent makes you an offer, and you accept: the organizer pays out accordingly.

BUT IF YOU REJECT IT, NO ONE GETS ANYTHING.

And that's all there is to the game!

How Do We Want You to Play?

YOU WILL BE DOING US A FAVOR IF YOU SIMPLY SET OUT TO MAXIMIZE YOUR WINNINGS.

(And since all this will have taken only 5 or 10 minutes, you can make a very respectable "hourly rate of pay" by so doing.)

Before you start the game, there will be a short demonstration routine on the computer, which shows you how to make an offer and how to accept or reject one.

Thank you and over to you!

Annex 2:   The Program

The program presents a series of visual displays accompanied by text. We here show the text of each display in turn (omitting the initial "demonstration" round), together with selected visual displays only. We confine ourselves to player 1. The text displayed to subjects is shown in capitals; our comments on the text are in parentheses.

1. THIS CAKE IS TO BE DIVIDED NOW (figure 2A.1).

2. IT IS NOW YOUR TURN TO MAKE AN OFFER.

3. IF YOUR OFFER IS REJECTED, THE SLICE SHOWN WILL DISAPPEAR (figure 2A.2).

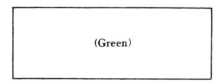

THIS CAKE IS TO BE DIVIDED NOW

Figure 2A.1
The basic color of the display is green. Areas of solid color are indicated in parentheses.

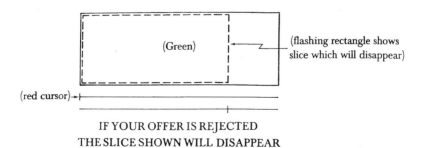

IF YOUR OFFER IS REJECTED
THE SLICE SHOWN WILL DISAPPEAR

Figure 2A.2
Note that the lower (green) cursor records the slice that will disappear and continues to do so.

4. YOU DECIDE YOUR OFFER BY MOVING THE RED CURSOR (figure 2A.3). WAIT!

5. YOUR SHARE WILL BE TO THE LEFT OF THE CURSOR. WAIT!

6. NOW MOVE CURSOR.

PRESS SPACE BAR WHEN YOU HAVE DECIDED.

(The share claimed is now represented by a blue rectangle, shown shaded in figure 2A.3. The lower cursor still shows the 75p slice, which will disappear.)

7. PLEASE WAIT WHILE THE OTHER PLAYER CONSIDERS YOUR OFFER.

(If the player accepts, the game ends. If he rejects, then the game proceeds as follows.)

8. YOUR OFFER WAS REJECTED.

9. THIS CAKE IS TO BE DIVIDED NOW (figure 2A.4).

10. THE OTHER PLAYER WILL NOW MAKE AN OFFER (figure 2A.5).

11. REMEMBER: IF YOU REJECT THIS OFFER, THE *WHOLE* CAKE WILL DISAPPEAR.

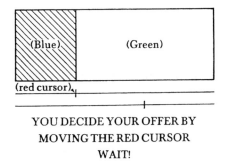

YOU DECIDE YOUR OFFER BY
MOVING THE RED CURSOR
WAIT!

Figure 2A.3

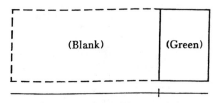

THIS CAKE IS TO BE DIVIDED NOW

Figure 2A.4
Only the lower cursor line is shown in player 1's displays henceforward, since it is player 2 who will make an offer.

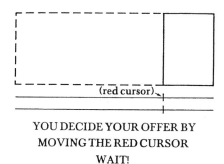

YOU DECIDE YOUR OFFER BY
MOVING THE RED CURSOR
WAIT!

Figure 2A.5
Seen by player 2

12. PLEASE WAIT WHILE THE OTHER PLAYER CONSIDERS WHAT TO OFFER YOU.

13. YOUR OPPONENT OFFERS YOU THE BLUE SHARE.

14. FRACTION OFFERED IS WORTH (VALUE) PENCE.

15. DO YOU AGREE TO THIS OFFER?
PLEASE TYPE Y/N.

16. (IF YES IS TYPED):
YOU ACCEPTED THE OFFER. YOU GET (VALUE) PENCE.
(IF NO IS TYPED):
THE GAME ENDS.

17. THIS IS THE END OF THE GAME. YOUR SCORE: (VALUE) PENCE.
THANK YOU.

Annex 3: Opening Demands and Responses

Opening demand in pence (d)	Number of games				
	Pilot I (game A)	Pilot II		Main Results	
		(game A)	(game B)	(game A)	(game B)
$0 \leq d \leq 11$	1 (1)	0 (0)	0	0 (0)	0
$0 \leq d \leq 22$	1 (1)	0 (0)	1	0 (0)	0
$23 \leq d \leq 33$	0 (0)	0 (0)	1	3 (3)	2
$34 \leq d \leq 44$	4 (4)	2 (1)	1	12 (11)	3
$45 \leq d \leq 55$	17 (12)	6 (6)	7	30 (25)	14
$56 \leq d \leq 66$	6 (4)	3 (2)	1	13 (12)	8
$67 \leq d \leq 77$	7 (4)	6 (2)	8	16 (13)	50
$78 \leq d \leq 88$	1 (0)	1 (0)	0	6 (2)	3
$89 \leq d \leq 99$	1 (0)	1 (0)	0	1 (0)	1

Note: Numbers in parentheses indicate the number of acceptances.

Annex 4:   Listing of Games

Table 4A.1
Pilot 1

Game number	First offer	Second offer	Reply
1	0.99	0.04	R
2	0.54		A
3	0.50		A
4	0.63		A
5	0.39		A
6	0.64		A
7	0.37		A
8	0.85	0.20	A
9	0.50		A
10	0.61		A
11	0.45		A
12	0.75		A
13	0.48		A
14	0.34		A
15	0.44		A
16	0.68		A
17	0.65		A
18	0.71		A
19	0.75	0.16	R
20	0.51	0.12	A
21	0.50		A
22	0.76	0.00	R
23	0.61	0.52	A
24	0.54		A
25	0.18		A
26	0.57	0.48	A
27	0.53		A
28	0.48		A
29	0.50	0.56	A
30	0.55		A
31	0.55	0.52	A
32	0.49		A
33	0.75		A
34	0.75	0.40	R
35	0.48	0.36	R
36	0.02		A
37	0.51	0.32	R
38	0.47		A

Table 4A.2
Pilot 2

First game				Second game	
Game number	First offer	Second offer	Reply	Game number	First offer
1	0.74		A	1	0.74
2	0.74	0.48	A	2	0.51
3	0.37	0.68	A	3	0.32
4	0.48		A	4	0.52
5	0.74		A	5	0.72
6	0.65		A	6	0.74
7	0.58		A	7	0.54
8	1.00	0.04	A	8	0.76
9	0.47		A	9	0.48
10	0.51		A	10	0.75
11	0.67	0.04	R	11	0.72
12	0.44		A	12	0.48
13	0.74	0.36	A	13	0.52
14	0.56	0.40	A	14	0.22
15	0.53		A	15	0.74
16	0.50		A	16	0.75
17	0.74	0.52	R	17	0.51
18	0.87	0.08	A	18	0.36
19	0.48		A	19	0.62

Table 4A.3
Main results

First game				Second game	
Game number	First offer	Second offer	Reply	Game number	First offer
1	0.55		A	1	0.70
2	0.68		A	2	0.31
3	0.43		A	3	0.51
4	0.47		A	4	0.54
5	0.75		A	5	0.74
6	0.47		A	6	0.75
7	0.64		A	7	0.70
8	0.42	0.48	A	8	0.51
9	0.56		A	9	0.65
10	0.68		A	10	0.54
11	0.75		A	11	0.75
12	0.70		A	12	0.75
13	0.71		A	13	0.75
14	0.48		A	14	0.74
15	0.41		A	15	0.48
16	0.88	0.12	R	16	0.75
17	0.74		A	17	0.72
18	0.66		A	18	0.75
19	0.83	0.12	A	19	0.71
20	0.38		A	20	0.74
21	0.81		A	21	0.70
22	0.47		A	22	0.75
23	0.41		A	23	0.70
24	0.50		A	24	0.55
25	0.38		A	25	0.92
26	0.64		A	26	0.75
27	0.49	0.44	A	27	0.52
28	0.38		A	28	0.75
29	0.74	0.40	A	29	0.67
30	0.66		A	30	0.78
31	0.52	0.52	A	31	0.37
32	0.98	0.52	A	32	0.59
33	0.44		A	33	0.77
34	0.54		A	34	0.48
35	0.53		A	35	0.62
36	0.54		A	36	0.74
37	0.52		A	37	0.72
38	0.73		A	38	0.75
39	0.53		A	39	0.75
40	0.86		A	40	0.83
41	0.74	0.48	A	41	0.54
42	0.56		A	42	0.75
43	0.48		A	43	0.74
44	0.54		A	44	0.68
45	0.51		A	45	0.65

Table 4A.3
(continued)

First game				Second game	
Game number	First offer	Second offer	Reply	Game number	First offer
48	0.50		A	48	0.75
49	0.52		A	49	0.77
50	0.38		A	50	0.54
51	0.57	0.44	A	51	0.44
52	0.80		A	52	0.58
53	0.31		A	53	0.74
54	0.81		A	54	0.77
55	0.39		A	55	0.63
56	0.73		A	56	0.76
57	0.31		A	57	0.51
58	0.50		A	58	0.77
59	0.65		A	59	0.74
60	0.61		A	60	0.75
61	0.71		A	61	0.72
62	0.50		A	62	0.75
63	0.47		A	63	0.70
64	0.48		A	64	0.75
65	0.74	0.40	A	65	0.67
66	0.23		A	66	0.38
67	0.57		A	67	0.63
68	0.53	0.48	A	68	0.50
69	0.52	0.00	R	69	0.30
70	0.47		A	70	0.62
71	0.71		A	71	0.72
72	0.43		A	72	0.74
73	0.64		A	73	0.74
74	0.52		A	74	0.75
75	0.38		A	75	0.75
76	0.50		A	76	0.55
77	0.45		A	77	0.69
78	0.75		A	78	0.76
79	0.51		A	79	0.54
80	0.50		A	80	0.88
81	0.75		A	81	0.75

References

Binmore, K. G. 1982. Perfect equilibria in bargaining models. ICERD discussion paper, LSE.

Binmore, K. G. 1983. Bargaining and coalitions I. ICERD discussion paper, LSE.

Fouraker, L. E., and S. Siegel. 1963. *Bargaining Behavior*. New York: McGraw-Hill.

Güth, W., R. Schmittberger, and B. Schwarze. 1982. An experiment analysis of ultimatum bargaining. *Journal of Economic Behaviour and Organisation* 3: 367–88.

Güth, W. 1983. Payoff distributions in games and the behavioural theory of distributive justice. Mimeo, Koln.

Roth, A., and M. Malouf. 1979. Game-theoretic models and the role of information in bargaining. *Psychological Review* 86: 574–94.

Roth, A., and M. Malouf. 1982. Scale changes and shared information in bargaining: An experimental study. *Mathematical Social Sciences* 3: 157–77.

Roth, A., M. Malouf, and J. Murnighan. 1981. Sociological versus strategic factors in bargaining. *Journal of Economic Behaviour and Organisation* 2: 153–77.

Roth, A., and K. Murningham. 1982. The role of information in bargaining: An experimental study. *Econometrica* 50: 1123–42.

Roth, A., and F. Schoumaker. 1983. Expectations and reputations in bargaining: An experimental study. *American Economic Review* 73: 362–72.

Rubinstein, A. 1981. Perfect equilibrium in a bargaining model. *Econometrica* 50: 97–110.

Schelling, T. 1960. *Strategy of Conflict*. Cambridge: Harvard University Press.

Selten, R., et al. 1975. Bargaining experiments with incomplete information. Working paper 39, Institut für Mathematische Wirtschaffsforschung.

Selten, R. 1978. The chain store paradox. *Theory and Decision* 9: 127–59.

Selten, R., and W. Krischker. 1982. Comparison of two theories for characteristic function experiments. Working paper 118, Institute for Mathematical Economics, University of Bielefeld.

Selten, R. nd. Equal division payoff bounds for 3-person characteristic function experiments. Working paper 119, Institute for Mathematical Economics, University of Bielefeld.

Shaked, A., and J. Sutton. 1983. Involuntary unemployment as a perfect equilibrium in a bargaining model. ICERD discussion paper, LSE, forthcoming *Econometrica*.

Shaked, A., and J. Sutton. 1984. The Semi-Walrasian Economy. ICERD Discussion paper 98, LSE.

Siegel, S. 1956. *Nonparametric Statistics for the Behavioral Sciences*. New York: McGraw-Hill.

Ståhl, I. 1972. Bargaining theory. Economic Research Institute, Stockholm.

Wilson, R. 1983. Reputations in games and markets. IMSS discussion paper 434, Stanford.

B Backward Induction?

These papers record my differences with Bob Aumann (1995) on the subject of backward induction. What a lot of trouble I had getting this work published anywhere!

I think the entire literature on refinements of Nash equilibrium was a blind alley for economics, although I guess it will always have a place in the philosophy of rational decision theory (Binmore 1987, 1992). Now that this view is more or less orthodox, it is hard to put oneself back into the frame of mind that once made refinement theory seem such a promising line of inquiry.

A Note on Backward Induction

Ken Binmore

It now seems to be generally accepted that rational players would not necessarily use their backward-induction strategies if there were to be a deviation from the backward-induction path (Binmore 1987). But Aumann (1995) has recently offered a formal defense of the proposition that prior common knowledge of rationality implies that play will nevertheless necessarily follow the backward-induction path. This brief note, extracted from a longer philosophical paper (Binmore 1996), questions the definition of rationality that he employs.

What keeps a rational player on the equilibrium path is his evaluation of what would happen if he were to deviate. But, if he were to deviate, he would behave irrationally. Other players would then be foolish if they were not to take this evidence of irrationality into account in planning their responses to the deviation. A formal model that neglects what *would* happen if a rational player *were* to deviate from rational play must therefore be missing something important, no matter how elaborately it is analyzed. However, Aumann (1995, sec. 5f) is insistent that his conclusions say nothing whatever about what players would do if vertices of the game tree off the backward induction path were to be reached.[1] But, if nothing can be said about what would happen *off* the backward-induction path, then it seems obvious that nothing can be said about the rationality of remaining *on* the backward-induction path. How else do we assess the cleverness of taking an action than by considering what would have happened if one of the alternative actions had been taken? But this is precisely what Aumann's (1995) definition of rationality fails to do.

The support of the ESRC Centre for Economic Learning and Social Evolution and the Leverhulme Trust is gratefully acknowledged.

1. Although he avoids the subjunctive mood, I take this to be the meaning of the apparently oxymoronic sentence, "The results of this paper say nothing about the behavior of the players at vertices that are off the backward induction path and are actually reached."

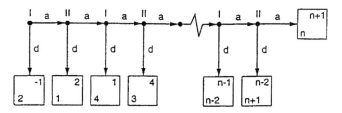

Figure B.1

In Binmore (1987), I used Rosenthal's (1981) Centipede Game of figure B.1 as an example when criticizing the defense of the backward-induction principle that was then current. The same example will also suffice here.

According to Aumann (1995), common knowledge of rationality in the Centipede makes it irrational for player I to choose *across* at his opening move. Aumann supports this conclusion by denying that the rationality of choosing *down* need involve any knowledge at all of what would happen if *across* were played. Instead of saying that it is rational for player I to choose *down* if he knows or believes that choosing *across* would not result in a higher payoff, Aumann says that it is rational for player I to choose *down* if he does not know that choosing *across* would result in a higher payoff. That is to say, Aumann moves the word "not" from one place to another.

But do we really want to deny the standard Bayesian assumption that player I can quantify his ignorance about what would happen if he were to play *across*?[2] If not, then player I must assign a probability p to the event that the result of his playing *across* would be a payoff of at least 4, rather than the payoff of 2 he gets by playing *down*. The latter eventuality would result, for example, if player II were to deduce from player I's choosing *across* at the first node that player I would also choose *across* if the third node were reached.

If *down* is the only Bayesian-rational action at the opening, then $p < \frac{1}{2}$. But why is $p < \frac{1}{2}$?[3] We seem to be stuck with the implication that $p < \frac{1}{2}$ is somehow built into the assumption that there is common knowledge of rationality. But what would be the source of this knowledge? Surely we

---

2. Aumann's (1995, sec. 4c) comments on how his approach can be framed in Bayesian terms are irrelevant to this point, since his formalism does not allow counterfactuals to be expressed.

3. One cannot argue that common knowledge of rationality implies that $p = 0$ because, according to Aumann, the play of *across* at the opening move would refute the hypothesis that player I is rational—and anything whatever follows from a contradiction.

should not be arguing that player I must know or believe something because the action we attribute to him is rational. The causal chain should run from knowledge to action rather than the reverse.

In denying Aumann's (1995) claim that common knowledge of rationality necessarily implies backward induction, I do not want to argue that backward induction is irrelevant to game-theoretic analyses. For example, one may use induction to demonstrate that all Nash equilibria in the Centipede require player I to choose *down* with probability one at the opening move. Personally, I think that the Nash equilibria of interest for the issues that Rosenthal (1981) invented the Centipede to explore are those in which player I is actually indifferent between playing *down* and *across* at the opening move—but this is another story told elsewhere (Binmore 1996).

References

Aumann, R. 1995. Backward induction and common knowledge of rationality. *Games and Economic Behavior* 8: 6–19.

Binmore, K. 1987. Modeling rational players, I. *Economics and Philosophy* 3: 9–55.

Binmore, K. 1996. Rationality and backward induction. Centre for Economic Learning and Social Evolution at University College London. (http://ada.econ.ucl.ac.uk).

Rosenthal, R. 1981. Games of perfect information, predatory pricing, and chain-store paradox. *Journal of Economic Theory* 25: 92–100.

Rationality and Backward Induction

Ken Binmore

I have a text, it always is the same,
And always has been,
Since I learnt the game.
(Chaucer, *The Pardoner's Tale*)

B.1 Introduction

In 1987, I wrote a paper (Binmore 1987a) that questioned the rationality of the backward-induction principle in finite games of perfect information. Since that time, a small literature has grown up in which Antonelli and Bicchieri (1994), Ben-Porath (1992), Bicchieri (1988, 1989), Bonanno (1991, 1994), Pettit and Sugden (1989), Reny (1992), Samet (1994), Stalnaker (1992a, b), and numerous others have attempted with varying success to treat the issues formally.

I believe my claim that rational players would not necessarily use their backward-induction strategies if there were to be a deviation from the backward-induction path is now generally accepted. But Aumann (1995) has recently offered a formal defense of the proposition that prior common knowledge of the players' rationality implies that play will nevertheless necessarily follow the backward-induction path. He argues that the conclusion is counterintuitive in certain games, but attributes our discomfort with the result to a failure to appreciate how strong his assumptions are. However, although Aumann's deep and thought-provoking contributions to the foundations of game theory provide the chief inspiration for this article, my purpose is not to comment specifically on his recent article. Its purpose is to question the *significance* of this and other results of the formalist genre.

Without intending any disrespect to the authors,[1] I believe that there is little of genuine significance to be learned from any of the literature that applies various formal methods to backward-induction problems—even when the authors find their way to conclusions that I believe to be correct. It seems to me that all the *analytical* issues relating to backward induction lie entirely on the surface. Inventing fancy formalisms serves only to confuse matters. The related literature on the Surprise Test Paradox provides a particularly blatant example. The paradox has a trivial resolution (Quine 1996; Binmore 1994), but the various exotic logics that have been brought to bear on the problem never come near exposing the piece of legerdemain by means of which we are deceived when the problem is posed.

Formalists will object, saying that an argument is open to serious evaluation only after it has been properly formalized. But this is a disingenuous response. It is true that if we were in serious doubt about whether an author had succeeded in analyzing his or her model correctly, then it would be foolish not to insist that the argument be given in precise terms. However, the literature on backward induction seldom provokes doubts at this level. The issue is almost never whether a particular model has been analyzed correctly—but whether the correct model has been analyzed.

In brief, I think that the backward-induction problem—like much else in the foundations of game theory—poses only a very small challenge to our powers of formal analysis. The real challenge is not to our powers of analysis but to our ability to find tractable models that successfully incorporate everything that matters. In particular, it seems entirely elementary that whatever model of a player is used, it must be rich enough to encompass *irrational* behavior as well as rational behavior (Binmore 1987a). What keeps a rational player on the equilibrium path is his evaluation of what would happen if he were to deviate. But, if he were to deviate, he would behave irrationally. Other players would then be foolish if they were not to take this evidence of irrationality into account in planning their responses to the deviation. A formal model that neglects what *would* happen if a rational player *were* to deviate from rational play must therefore be missing something important, no matter how elaborately it is analyzed. However, Aumann (1995, sec. 5c), for example, is insistent that his conclusions say nothing whatever about what players would do if vertices

---

1. It is always easy to predict which line of research will be fruitful *after* the event.

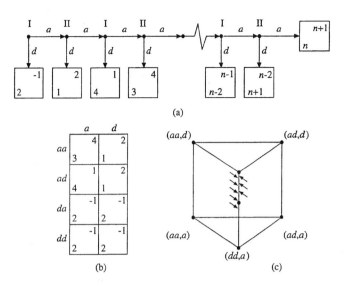

Figure B.2
The Centipede Game

of the game tree off the backward-induction path were to be reached.[2] But, if nothing can be said about what would happen *off* the backward-induction path, then it seems obvious that nothing can be said about the rationality of remaining *on* the backward-induction path. How else do we assess the cleverness of taking an action than by considering what would have happened if one of the alternative actions had been taken? But this is precisely what Aumann's (1995) definition of rationality fails to do. (See justification 6 of section B.4.)

In Binmore (1987a), I used Rosenthal's (1980) Centipede Game of figure B.2(a) as an example when criticizing the defense of the backward induction principle that was then current. Figure B.2(b) shows the strategic form of the special case when $n = 3$ (the three-legged Centipede). In this note, I plan to use the same example to elaborate on the criticism just expressed of the tighter defense of the principle that is possible if one follows Aumann (1995) in abandoning claims about what would happen off the backward-induction path.

It is easy to verify that the backward-induction principle requires that each player always plan to play *down* in the Centipede. In particular, the

---

2. Although he avoids the subjunctive mood, I take this to be the meaning of the apparently oxymoronic sentence, "The results of this paper say nothing about the behavior of the players at vertices that are off the backward induction and are actually reached."

unique subgame-perfect equilibrium S in the three-legged Centipede is (dd, d). However, the three-legged Centipede has other Nash equilibria. Part of the reason for writing this article is to argue that such alternative Nash equilibria have been too readily dismissed in the past—a theme pursued at greater length in Binmore et al. (1995) and Binmore and Samuelson (1995). In particular, the three-legged Centipede has a mixed Nash equilibrium N in which player I uses his backward-induction strategy with probability one, but player II mixes between a and d, using the former with probability $1/2$.[3] If player I knows that player II will play *across* with this probability, it is false that rationality requires that he play *down*. In fact he is indifferent between playing *down* and *across*. Although he plays *down* with probability one in equilibrium, it is nevertheless equally rational for him to play *across*.

Among other things, this article argues that prior common knowledge of rationality should not lead us to reject the equilibrium N. On the contrary, it is argued that N, rather than S, is the equilibrium of interest for the issues that the Centipede was constructed to explore. It is tempting to wave this point aside by conceding that perhaps prior common knowledge of rationality in the Centipede may lead to the play of N and so does not, after all, necessitate that player I open the Centipede by playing *down*. But who cares if player I only plays *across* with probability zero? But there is more riding on this issue than immediately meets the eye, as I hope will be evident by the end of this article. In particular, I hope that it will become apparent that we need not follow Aumann (1992, 1995) in perceiving a sharp discontinuity between what happens when there is perfect common knowledge of rationality and when this condition is relaxed slightly. In particular, there is no need for game theorists to seek to insulate themselves from the criticism of experimentalists by claiming that their theorems have no relevance to how real people behave.

---

3. The three-legged Centipede has other mixed Nash equilibria. Figure B.2(c) shows a prism, the points of which represent all pairs of mixed strategies for the reduced strategic form of the three-legged Centipede (obtained by deleting the row da). A point in the prism corresponds to a Nash equilibrium if and only if it lies on the closed line segment NS. This article discusses possible eductive analyses of the Centipede (Binmore 1987a). In an evolutive analysis it would be of interest to note the trajectories of the replicator dynamics indicated in Figure B.2(c). No Nash equilibrium is an asymptotic attractor in these dynamics. Moreover after an equilibrium E in the relative interior of NS has been perturbed by introducing a small fraction of player I's who use aa, the system returns to an equilibrium that is nearer N than E. Drift induced by a tendency on the part of player I to use aa rather than ad when making an out-of-equilibrium deviation will therefore result in a movement along NS towards N. A tendency to use ad rather than aa will result in a drift in the opposite direction toward S.

Section B.2 comments briefly on the importance of common knowledge assumptions in general. Section B.3 explores one of the reasons for the popularity of the claim that prior common knowledge of rationality implies the backward-induction principle. It describes my version of a folk argument that purports to demonstrate that prior common knowledge of rationality in the Centipede Game implies that its opening move will necessarily be *down*. As with Aumann's (1995) more complicated theorem, the argument is correct, in the sense that the conclusion does indeed follow from the premises. But something must be wrong at the conceptual level, because the conclusion that player I will begin by playing *down* is obtained without any reference to his beliefs about what would happen if he were to play *across*. But if the probability that player I assigns to the event that player II would then also play *across* is sufficiently high, it is obviously not optimal for player I to begin by playing *down*. I believe that this apparent paradox arises partly as a consequence of a failure to appreciate how counterfactual reasoning works. Section B.4 therefore seeks to demystify this question. Section B.5 attempts to resolve the paradox by retelling the story with a less restrictive background model. However, once a paradox-free model has been adopted, the door is no longer closed on the Nash equilibrium N. Finally, Section B.6 tries to say something about what the conclusions mean by taking up a clarion call from one of Aumann's (1985) previous papers, and asking what we are trying to accomplish when we prove theorems in game theory. Personally, I think it is because this question has been so neglected that the foundations of game theory are now in such a mess.

B.2   Common Knowledge

Before Aumann (1976) put the concept of common knowledge on an operational footing, game theorists were very casual about what their players did or did not know. More recently it became fashionable to insist that everything is to be assumed to be common knowledge, regardless of its relevance to the issue at hand. Now the wheel has turned again, with Aumann and Brandenburger (1995) insisting that no common knowledge at all is necessary to justify Nash equilibrium. As they observe, it is obviously true that justifying Nash equilibrium requires no more than that each player knows the game and the strategies used by his opponents. In the hope of averting confusion, this section is devoted to pointing out that this truth, and its elaborations to more complex situations, are largely beside the point.

The purpose of prescriptive game theory is to advise players about the rational course of action in a game. If a prescriptive theory begins with the assumption that the players already know its prescriptions, then it preempts its own reason for existing. To be useful, a prescriptive theory needs to begin with assumptions that not trivialize the problem. It is important to insist that such assumptions often *do* require that various things are common knowledge—notably, the rules of the game, the preferences of the players over the outcomes, and the players' beliefs about chance moves in the game. One may summarize these assumptions as the requirement that the game being played is common knowledge among the players.[4]. Examples that demonstrate how slight relaxations of this requirement can sometimes have big effects are a commonplace of the theory. For example, all Nash equilibria in the N-times repeated Prisoners' Dilemma result in each player defecting at each stage with probability 1. However, this conclusion evaporates if the value of N is not common knowledge (Binmore 1991, ch. 10).

Of course, *after* a game-theoretic analysis has been brought to a successful conclusion and the results published in a book, it may well be reasonable to assume that each player knows that his opponents will play as the book prescribes. But it does not follow that one can then discard the knowledge assumptions that led its author to write what he wrote. The reason that rational players know what their opponents will do after reading the book is because they are able to check that the author's conclusions do indeed follow from his hypotheses. However, within the static formalism that Aumann (1987, 1989; Aumann and Brandenburger 1995) now favors, there is no way to compare the state of things before and after an analysis, or even to ask why a player takes one action rather than another. As Aumann (1987) puts it, players "just do what they do." An analyst can only look on from outside the world in which the game is played and comment that if the players happen to make a Bayesian-rational choice then they will be operating a correlated equilibrium. As Aumann (1987) insists, such a model is neither prescriptive nor descriptive, but what he calls "analytic." Personally, I think that such analytic models have their uses, but they will not suffice as a foundation stone for all of game theory. If it sometimes seems otherwise, it is because, as with George Orwell's *newspeak*, criticism of the defects of analytic models

4. Harsanyi's theory of incomplete information does not provide a counterexample. His theory provides a recipe for adding information to a situation in which information is incomplete until a game has been constructed whose structure is common knowledge (Binmore 1991, ch. 11).

sometimes cannot even be expressed in the language within which they are formalized.

Although I believe it would be a mistake to follow Aumann and Brandenburger (1995) in focusing attention away from the underlying common knowledge assumptions of game theory, this is not because I think one will often be led to wrong conclusions by treating common knowledge considerations in an informal manner. It is at the *interpretive* level that the importance of common knowledge assumptions needs to be acknowledged. In Harsanyi's theory of incomplete information, for example, one really does need to assume that the underlying distribution of types is common knowledge. But the theory is nevertheless widely applied to situations in which this assumption is highly implausible. In any case, although no formal definitions are introduced, it is important to emphasize that this article takes both common knowledge of the game and prior common knowledge of rationality for granted. If they feel the need, those familiar with Aumann (1995) will have no difficulty in formalizing what it means for something to be common knowledge in the simple case covered by proposition 1. My own view is that we run into conceptual difficulties when considering the implications of prior common knowledge of rationality in finite games of perfect information because we are unsure how rationality should be defined—not because we are unable to handle the technicalities of common knowledge.

Finally, while on the subject of rationality, I am anxious to clear the air by stipulating that the general difficulties I have raised elsewhere (Binmore 1987) about the coherence of the notion of "perfect rationality" evaporate in the context of a finite game of perfect information. In such games the issue of whether rational players are so perfect that they can decide the undecidable does not arise.

B.3 "Proving" Backward Induction

Knowledge of a finite game of perfect information can be summarized as a list of conditional sentences of the type: "If both players were always to play *across*, then player I would get a payoff of n and player II would get $n + 1$." A player's knowledge of the characteristics of his opponents (including what the opponents know or do not know about him) is not always accorded a formal role in game-theoretic analyses. Usually the assumptions being made about what players know about each other are implicit in the equilibrium concept that an analyst chooses to consider. However, in what follows, I will assume that part of our enterprise is to

seek to label each node x in the Centipede Game with a pair (S, T) of finite sets. The interpretation is that if node x were to be reached, then it would be common knowledge that player I lies in set S and player II lies in set T. With such a convention, the assumption of prior common knowledge of rationality can be expressed by labeling the first node with a pair (R_1, R_2), where both R_1 and R_2 contain only "rational" players. (When the word "rational" appears in quotes, there will be reason later to ask whether the framework within which it is being used is capable of bearing the load.)

During the course of a game, the actions that a player takes will enrich the information about his characteristics available to his opponent. Suppose that node x is labeled with the pair (S, T). Suppose also that, if player I were to take action a at node x, then the next node would be y. Finally, suppose that there is at least one player in the set S who sometimes would play a if node x were reached. Then it will be assumed[5] that y may be labeled with a pair (S', T), where $S' \subseteq S$. A similar assumption is made if it is player II who moves at node x. The perennial problem of refinement theory arises when *no* player in S would ever take action a if node x were reached. How then should node y be labeled? This problem will not go away, but it will be put to one side for the moment.

If the first node of the n-legged Centipede Game of figure B.2(a) is labeled (S, T), then it will be denoted by $G_n(S, T)$. An elaborate definition of a "rational" player is not needed if the aim is only to show that the "rational" opening move is necessarily *down* in $G_n(R_1, R_2)$, where R_1 and R_2 will always denote sets of "rational" players. A "rational" player need only be taken to be someone who would maximize his payoff when making the first move in all games $G_n(R_1, R_2)$.

Proposition 1   When there is prior common knowledge that everybody is a "rational" player, the Centipede Game necessarily begins with the play of *down*.

Proof   For all R_1 and R_2, it follows immediately from the definition of a "rational" player that *down* is always played in $G_1(R_1, R_2)$. As an induction hypothesis, suppose that the first move of $G_{n-1}(R_1, R_2)$ is *down* for all R_1 and R_2. Now consider the first move of $G_n(R_1, R_2)$. If the play of *across* is a possible opening move of $G_n(R_1, R_2)$, then the second node $G_n(R_1, R_2)$ should be labeled (R_1', R_2), where $R_1' \subseteq R_1$. But we know that

---

5. The assumption implies that actions taken by one player are not informative about the other. I make this assumption only to keep things simple. Binmore (1987) uses Selten's Horse Game as an example when exploring the alternative hypothesis.

down is the opening move of $G_{n-1}(R'_1, R_2)$ if this is reached. Moreover the common knowledge assumption implies that the player making the opening move $G_n(R_1, R_2)$ knows this also. It follows that a "rational" player in the set R_1 makes a suboptimal move by playing *across*, since he knows that his payoff from playing *down* would be greater. From this contradiction, we deduce that no "rational player" in the set R_1 ever opens $G_n(R_1, R_2)$ by playing *across*.   ■

The proposition shows that, with prior common knowledge of "rationality," the opening move of the Centipede Game cannot be *across*. A formalist might be satisfied to stop at this point, but I think it important to continue by asking the seemingly stupid question:

Is it rational to be "rational"?

To address this question, consider the labeling of the second node of $G_3(R_1, R_2)$. Since it has been shown that this node cannot be reached, we have no rule to assist in its labeling. We therefore lack the information we need to predict what would happen if the second node were reached. Nevertheless, to assess the rationality of a "rational" player who plays *down* at the opening move, we need to ask what payoff he *would* get if he *were* to play *across*.

The subjunctives in the preceding sentence have been italicized to emphasize that we have a counterfactual conditional to evaluate. Aumann's (1995) discussion of such counterfactuals, which actually play no role whatsoever in his formal analysis, obscures the important point that the interpretation of a counterfactual depends on the *context* in which it arises. An aside on this issue is therefore necessary.

B.4   Conditionals

Sanford's (1989) book, *If P, then Q*, reviews the many attempts that have been made to provide an adequate account of conditional reasoning. The debate began in ancient times and continues unabated into the present. There seems to be no consensus even on definitions. However, I will adopt the terminology of Flew's widely quoted *Dictionary of Philosophy* (1979). Flew distinguishes material conditionals, subjunctive conditionals[6] and counterfactual conditionals.

---

6. Aumann (1995) invents the term *substantive conditional* for what Flew calls a subjunctive conditional, arguing that the subjunctive is colloquially used only with a false antecedent. If I were ever take up residence in New York, perhaps I would come round to his point of view.

A *material conditional* is usually called a material implication by mathematicians and written as $P \Rightarrow Q$. Such conditionals are all that is needed in pure mathematics and so mathematicians are often reluctant to concede that other types of conditional may sometimes be useful. However, the *subjunctive conditional*, "If my dean were a man, then my salary would be astronomical" is false as used in ordinary conversation—even though my dean is actually a woman and so the conditional has a false antecedent (which would make it true if interpreted in the material sense). A subjunctive conditional with such a false antecedent is said to be a *counterfactual conditional*.

How are subjunctive conditionals to be interpreted? The simplest approach uses the notion of a *possible world*. For example, since my dean is actually a woman, someone interpreting the counterfactual conditional, "If my dean were a man, then my salary would be astronomical" needs to consider what possible world I have in mind when seeking to make sense of the sentence. In these enlightened times, the relevant possible world is clear enough. It is created by replacing my current female dean by a male dean, leaving everything else the same. However, were Isaac Newton to have said "If my dean were a woman, my salary would be astronomical," we would certainly not have thought it appropriate simply to replace his male dean by a female dean, leaving everything else the same. For a female dean to be possible in the seventeenth century, all sorts of other changes in society would need to be postulated. How a subjunctive conditional is to be interpreted therefore depends on the context in which it arises. If the context is uncertain, it is the duty of the analyst to clarify the context that he has in mind by making formal assumptions if necessary.

In section B.3, all three types of conditional appear. Subjunctive conditionals appear in the description of the game. When we are told, "If both players were always to play *across*, then player I would get a payoff of n," we are accepting a constraint on the possible worlds we are allowed to postulate during an analysis of the game. The definition of a "rational" player makes a similar use of subjunctive conditionals. We are told something about what such a player would do if he were to play the game $G_n(R_1, R_2)$. (I find it helpful to think of a "rational" player as a computer program that would produce certain outputs if it were offered certain inputs. However, only some of the many potential inputs it might receive will actually be realized.)

Section B.3 continues with the proof of proposition 1. Wherever the indicative mood has been used in this proof, the conditionals are intended as material conditionals—as in a regular mathematical proof. In such arguments by contradiction, it is of some importance to be clear on this point. As Sanford (1989) documents, it is easy to go astray when attempting to argue by contradiction when the conditionals are subjunctive, because nothing says that all subjunctive conditionals that appear in an argument must be interpeted within the same possible world.

Section B.3 ends by questioning the rationality of a "rational" player who opens $G_n(R_1, R_2)$ with the play of *down*, by asking what such a player would get if he were to play *across*. Here we are definitely faced with a counterfactual conditional. As stressed in Binmore (1987), the standard definition of a game tells us nothing whatever about the nature of the possible world or worlds within which such a counterfactual conditional is to be interpreted. It is true that, when arguing by contradiction in proposition 1, we maintained the hypothesis that common knowledge of "rationality" was still in place when contemplating the possibility that player I might start by playing *across*. But after proposition 1 has been proved, we have to live with the fact that common knowledge of "rationality" would be refuted if player I's opening move were *across*. The meaning of the counterfactual conditional, "If a 'rational' player were to open $G_n(R_1, R_2)$ by playing *across*, he would get a smaller payoff than if he played *down*" therefore remains open for debate unless further information is supplied to establish a context for its interpretation.

One way of specifying a context for our troublesome counterfactual conditional is to name a label (S, R_2) for the second node of $G_3(R_1, R_2)$. To make the traditional backward-induction argument work, we need that $S \subseteq R_1$. However, the assumption that $S \subseteq R_1$ seems strange to the layman, who argues that the play of *across* has refuted the hypothesis that player I lies in the set R_1. This leads him to propose that $S \subseteq CR_1$.

One possibility for the set S is then that its members would always play *across* no matter what. Backward induction would then fail, since player II would play *across* if the second node of $G_3(R_1, R_2)$ were reached, because player II would then believe player I would play *across* if the third node were reached. In this situation it would definitely be irrational to be a "rational" player. If a precondition of being rational is to be "rational," we are therefore led to the odd conclusion that a rational player cannot know that if an opponent ever were to play *across* in the Centipede, then he would always play *across*. But, when we assumed prior common knowledge of the players' rationality, did we really intend to restrict what the players might or might not believe in the counterfactual event that someone were to play irrationally?

But nothing compels us to adopt either $S \subseteq R_1$ or $S \subseteq CR_1$ as properties of the relevant possible world within which to interpret our troublesome counterfactual.[7] If we wish to justify the rationality of a "rational" player, we therefore need to add something to the assumption of prior common knowledge of "rationality"—something that tells us what *would* be known if a "rational" player *were* to play *across*. I can think of a number of ways in which someone defending backward induction might seek to justify or evade the requirement that $S \subseteq R_1$:

Justification 1 One could simply add the assumption $S \subseteq R_1$ to the other assumptions being made. For example, in the spirit of Selten's (1975) agent-normal form of a game, it is not unknown for authors to propose that a player be modeled as a collection of independently acting agents, one for each decision node at which the player might have to make a decision. As Binmore and Samuelson (1993) observe, it then seems relatively innocent to propose that, if prior common knowledge of the rationality of one of the players were to be refuted during the course of the game by some display of irrational behavior on the part of one or more of his agents, then rationality should still be attributed to those of his agents who have yet to play. One might even be forgiven for regarding the assumption as being so natural that it need not be explicitly stated when assigning a meaning to the counterfactual conditionals that arise when irrational play needs to be contemplated. However, since a rational player is clearly not simply a collection of independently acting agents, there seems little point in deducing the backward-induction principle from the assumption that he is.

Justification 2 One could follow Selten (1975) in his defense of perfect equilibrium by attributing any "irrationalities" that may arise during the game to transient random errors that have no significance for a player's future play.

Justification 3 One might follow Zermelo (1913) in his study of chess by proceeding on the assumption that each player needs always to take the least favorable view of his opponent when assessing possible futures. This is certainly the correct procedure when computing a player's security level in a game—and security strategies are what we care about in two-person, zero-sum games like chess. Moreover in such games the least favorable assumption is always that the opponent will behave rationally in the fu-

7. The logic of the layman's argument is flawed because anything follows from a contradiction. But it does not therefore follow that his suggestion that $S \subseteq CR_1$ can be rejected.

ture no matter how irrationally he may have behaved in the past. But the Centipede Game is not zero-sum. Zermelo is therefore irrelevant as an authority in this context.

Justification 4 One might adopt a strict revealed-preference line as in Binmore (1994). If we take the choices that would be made at nodes as fundamental, then the reason, for example, that *down* is assigned a larger payoff at the final node of the Centipede than *across* is because it is part of the data of the problem that if player I were to reach the final node and make whatever deductions about his situation that he then thought fit, he would definitely choose *down* and not *across*.

But the literature on backward induction does not adopt a strict revealed-preference approach because it then becomes a tautology that backward induction holds. Whatever behavior we might observe in a finite game of perfect information is compatible with backward induction if we are allowed to fill in the payoffs after the event. Binmore (1994) makes this point to refute philosophers who argue that prior common knowledge of rationality in games like the Centipede makes backward induction necessarily *irrational*—as opposed to Aumann's (1995) claim to the contrary.

Justification 5 Alternatively, one might argue as follows. Because player I is known to be rational, if he plays *down* at the first node of the Centipede Game, then he must know that he would get a worse payoff from playing *across*. That is to say, his rationality includes his knowing that if he were to play *across*, then player II would not conclude that he is the type of person who always plays *across*. But what would be the source of this knowledge? Surely the causal chain should run from knowledge to action rather than from action to knowledge.[8] However, if rationality implies "rationality," we have already seen that the assumption of prior common knowledge of rationality commits us to precisely this difficulty.

Justification 6 Aumann (1995) seeks to evade the requirement that $S \subseteq R_1$ by denying that the rationality of choosing *down* need involve any knowledge at all of what would happen if *across* were played. Instead of saying that it is rational for a player to choose *down* if he knows or

---

8. More generally, we should not argue that an action is rational because it has been chosen by a rational person. We should argue that a person is rational because he always chooses rational actions given his knowledge or beliefs. If this principle is denied, how does one deal with the fallacy for rational cooperation in the Prisoners' Dilemma that goes, "I am rational. So anything I decide to do will necessarily be rational. Player II is also rational and hence will aways make the same decision as I make when placed in identical circumstances. Therefore, she will do whatever I do in the Prisoners' Dilemma. Hence I should cooperate."

believes that choosing *across* would not result in a higher payoff, the strategem is to say that it is rational for a player to choose *down* if he does not know that choosing *across* would result in a higher payoff.[9] But does this mean that we are to assume that he is so ignorant that the standard Bayesian assumption that he can quantify his ignorance with a probability distribution is to be denied?[10] If not, then he must assign a probability p to the event that the result of his playing *across* would be a payoff of 4 rather than the payoff of 2 he gets by playing *down*. If only *down* is Bayesian-rational, then $p < \frac{1}{2}$. But how come $p < \frac{1}{2}$? We seem to be stuck with the implication that this fact is somehow built into the assumption that there is prior common knowledge of rationality. That is to say, we have essentially the same problem that we faced in justification 5.

Of the preceding attempts to justify or evade the assumption that $S \subseteq R_1$, it is the second that I feel has most to be said for it. It is an upfront attempt to explain how a "rational" player might come to act "irrationally." Often the need for such an explanation is expressed by asserting that each equilibrium concept needs to incorporate a "theory of mistakes." However, nothing says that Selten's (1975) trembling-hand story is the only story of mistakes that can be told. Indeed adopting such a story would seem to close the door on any hopes that game-theoretic results might be relevant to the play of real people. We all know that bad play by actual people is usually the result of a failure to think things through properly—and people who have reasoned badly in the past are likely to reason badly in the future.

Kreps, Milgrom, Roberts, and Wilson's (1982) "gang of four" paper tells a different story in which there are irrational types as well as rational types of players. Within such a story, the observation of an action that would be a mistake for a rational player is explained by attributing it to an irrational player—just as our layman would wish. In Selten's terminology, trembles are then correlated, and so backward induction cannot be justified. Indeed within such a framework Fudenberg, Kreps, and Levine (1988) have shown that no refinements of Nash equilibrium can be justi-

9. Such a movement of the word "not" from one place to another in the sentence may seem innocuous. But do we really want to argue that it is rational never to take any action that would reduce our ignorance? But the very nature of such an action precludes our knowing what its outcome would be.

10. Aumann's (1995, sec. 4c) comments on how his approach can be framed in Bayesian terms are irrelevant to this point, since his formalism does not allow counterfactuals to be expressed.

fied at all. Of course, the analysis of a game with a realistic theory of mistakes is much harder than with Selten's trembling-hand story. But if we want a theory that is at all relevant to what real people do when they play games, it seems to me that this is the route we must follow.

B.5 Paradox of Rationality?

The previous section argues that it may not be rational to be "rational." But, whatever full rationality may be, surely it includes being "rational"?

In my view, the appearance of a paradox arises only because we have been working with an inadequate background model. To explore this viewpoint, let us first consider the case when it is not true that there is prior common knowledge that all the players are rational. Instead there is prior common knowledge that a player is rational with probability $1 - \varepsilon > 0$ and irrational with probability $\varepsilon > 0$. Only the extreme case in which irrational players always play *across* will be considered. This setup was analyzed in Binmore (1987) in much the same way that the gang of four Kreps et al. (1982) analyzed the finitely repeated Prisoners' Dilemma. The analysis shows that equilibrium play in the Centipede requires the rational players to mix between *across* and *down* at each stage of the game. If the Centipede has sufficiently many legs, they play *across* with probability one in the early stages of the game. At the final stage, they necessarily play *across* with probability zero. At intermediate stages, they play *across* with a probability that declines over time from one to zero.

For an equilibrium in the three-legged Centipede, the initial phase in which rational players choose *across* with probability one is absent. Equilibrium play requires that rational players use both *across* and *down* with positive probabilities at nodes 1 and 2. The probabilities with which a rational player mixes at one of these nodes are chosen to make a rational player at the other node indifferent between playing *down* or *across*. As $\varepsilon \to 0$, the probability that a rational opening player chooses *across* declines to zero. However, he remains indifferent between choosing *across* or *down* all the way up to the limit, where the players' behavior is summarized by the Nash equilibrium N introduced in section B.1.

To capture this phenomenon while actually working at the limit, it is necessary to abandon the assumption of section B.3 that the sets of players to be considered are finite, in favor of a model in which a set may be of measure zero without being empty. Knowledge must also be reinterpreted as being "belief with probability one." The existence of irrational players in $G_3(R_1, R_2)$ is then not ruled out altogether. They may exist with probability zero. One can then contemplate a mixed equilibrium in which a null set of rational players open $G_3(R_1, R_2)$ by playing *across*.[11] (A rerun of the backward induction argument of section B.3 shows only that the set of "rational" players who play *across* cannot have positive measure.) It is then not true that a rational player *must* play *down* at the opening move of $G_3(R_1, R_2)$. He will be indifferent between his two choices. This is particularly important when the general question of backward induction in the Centipede is at issue. Although only a null set of rational players would begin $G_n(R_1, R_2)$ by playing *across*, the existence of this set nevertheless has an enormous impact on what would happen if later nodes were to be reached.

The general procedure followed in this section seems usable whenever a puzzling counterfactual arises. Instead of ignoring the difficulty or inventing exotic methods of analysis to deal with the problem of what would happen if impossible events were to occur, one enlarges the model so that the impossible events cease to be impossible (Selten and Leopold 1982; Binmore 1987). One then returns to the idealized world in which the problem first arose by allowing appropriate parameters to approach their extremal values. In this section, for example, we studied a world parametrized by $\varepsilon > 0$, and then considered the limit as $\varepsilon \to 0$. The idealized world obtained in this way then retains the essential properties of the less idealized worlds in which the analysis was conducted—albeit sometimes in vestigial form, as with the null set of rational players who may begin the Centipede by playing *across* according to the analysis of this section.

In my opinion, we neglect such vestiges of realism at our peril, especially if we hope that the theories we propound will have some relevance to applied work. We know from the work of McKelvey and Palfrey (1992) that real people are not inclined to open the Centipede by playing *down*. Such behavior is simply irreconcilable with Aumann's (1995) idealization of a player. But with the approach outlined in this section, one is offered a clue about which idealizing assumptions need to be relaxed to accommodate the data.

---

11. The size of this null set must, of course, be carefully chosen so that the probability that player II at node 2 attaches to the event that his opponent is irrational is just sufficient to make him indifferent between his two choices. Those concerned about conditioning on a null event will find an appropriate formalism in Blume et al. (1991).

B.6 What Are We Trying to Accomplish?

Early game theorists seem to have taken for granted that their role was *prescriptive*—to advise players on how to optimize given their information, on the often tacit assumption that it is common knowledge that the other players are receiving similar advice. On the standard assumption of neoclassical economics that all agents behave as though in receipt of such advice, one would then have a *descriptive* model—one that allows predictions to be made about the world. Confusion at the conceptual level is therefore possible because the same theorem may be useful in both prescriptive and descriptive game theory. Such confusion may be compounded when theorems are proved whose interesting interpretations lie in what Aumann (1987) calls *analytic* game theory.

I have commented on Aumann's (1987) careful distinction between an analytic model and models constructed for other purposes elsewhere (Binmore 1992). The issues are simpler in the case of the Centipede Game. In brief, proposition 1 makes perfectly good sense when interpreted in terms of an analytic model. In Aumann's (1987) expressive catchphrase, players in an analytic model "just do what they do." We do not ask how it comes about that they behave like they do, we simply write down some conditions that are assumed to constrain their behavior and explore their implications. In the case of the Centipede Game, common knowledge of "rationality" turns out to imply that player I begins by playing *down*. But it also turns out to imply that player I acts as though he knows or believes that if he were to play *across*, then the probability that player II would then play *across* is less than $\frac{1}{2}$.

But suppose that we try to use proposition 1 for prescriptive purposes. Imagine that it is common knowledge that players I and II have hired Von Neumann and Morgenstern respectively to give them advice. Von Neumann applies proposition 1 and advises player I to choose *down* at the first node. Morgenstern tells player II that she will not require his services since the second node will not be reached. Player I now asks Von Neumann *why* he should choose *down* at the first node, and the reply is that this conclusion follows from proposition 1. But player I very reasonably finds this answer inadequate and persists by asking what advice Von Neumann predicts that player II will receive from Morgenstern. On receiving the reply that Morgenstern will offer her no advice because he will believe that the second node will not be reached, player I then tells Von Neumann that he is sure that player II would play *across* if node 2 were reached, and she had to act without the benefit of Morgenstern's advice. Von Neumann objects that this is not part of the data of the problem as proposed to him, and player I agrees that Von Neumann was only asked to offer advice on the assumption that player II would act as advised by Morgenstern. However, player I explains that he has private information about player II's past history of play when she acts without advice, that he thought irrelevant when he learned that player II had retained Morgenstern's services.

Can Von Neumann now plausibly reply that it follows from proposition 1 that player I cannot have this information? If he dared, player I would simply respond that Von Neumann should adjust his model to the data rather than trying to adjust the data to his model.

As for possible alternative models, Von Neumann can reason as in section B.5 and so reconcile player I's claim to have private information about player II with a version of proposition 1 in which the players are drawn from an infinite population. He will then be led to the mixed Nash equilibrium N of the Centipede Game introduced in section B.2. When player I now asks what advice Von Neumann predicts that Morgenstern will give player II, Von Neumann answers that Morgenstern will randomize, and sometimes advise her to play *across* and sometimes *down*, with the probabilities chosen so that it doesn't matter to player I whether he takes Von Neumann's advice or not. If player I now asks Von Neumann why he should therefore take Von Neumann's advice, does Von Neumann now reply that he must do so because Morgenstern predicted that it was almost certain that he would? Player I would just respond that he doesn't care whether Morgenstern's prediction is verified or not.

Notice that the problem has now ceased to have backward induction *per se* as its focus. It now pivots around the old chestnut of why a player should mix between strategies that all yield the same payoff. But the standard defenses of mixed Nash equilibria all require introducing trembles of some sort and then taking a limit. However, if Von Neumann appeals to one of these defenses, he must abandon the postulates of proposition 1 and argue instead that the world is such that players do not always follow the advice of their tame game theorists with probability one. Indeed we already had to contemplate this possibility when finding a way for Von Neumann to accommodate player I's private information about player II in the first place.

However hard we struggle, it is therefore necessary to face the fact that the story we are telling is only fully coherent in a world to which the postulates of proposition 1 are only an idealizing approximation. The source of the paradox in the prescriptive case is that the story cannot be told while actually at the limit without fudging one issue or another.

What of the possibility of applying proposition 1 to a neoclassical descriptive model? As a referee comments, in practice N and the subgame-perfect equilibrium S predict the same thing in such a model: namely that player I will play *down* with probability one. If the trembles are sufficiently small, what difference does it then make whether we predict N or S? But, as the difficulties we have encountered in seeking to interpret proposition 1 should have warned us, it turns out that it may matter very much if one is interpreting an equilibrium as the end-product of some equilibrating process. One then needs to worry about the stability of equilibria. The case of the *four*-legged Centipede is particularly striking in this regard, since Cressman and Schlag (1995) have recently shown that, although the subgame-perfect equilibrium S is locally stable with respect to the standard replicator dynamics, the same is not true of the equilibrium N at the other end of the component of Nash equilibria.[12] In fact, trajectories *lead away* from N far into the interior of the phase space, where they wander all over the place before approaching the component of Nash equilibria again. The equilibrium N is therefore unsafe as a prediction of the end-product of an equilibrating process like the replicator dynamics.[13] I know that these remarks on interpretation just seem like waffle to formalists. However, I hope that some readers at least will agree that it is a mistake to invent definitions of rationality that make it look as though theorems that are strictly applicable only in analytic models can be applied without careful appraisal to prescriptive or descriptive purposes.

Acknowledgments

The support of National Science Foundation grant SES 9122176 is gratefully acknowledged, together with the hospitality of the Deutsche Forschungsgemeinschaft, Sonderforschungsbereich 303 at the University of Bonn, where the first draft of the paper was written. The final version of

12. Their work was partly inspired by the very informative simulations of perturbed and unperturbed replicator dynamics carried out by Giovanni Ponti at University College London. Actually his simulations show that it is enough to study a slightly perturbed version of the replicator dynamics in the *three*-legged Centipede to make a sufficiently similar point.

13. For more general comments on when it is unsafe to use an equilibrium of an idealized model as a prediction of behavior in an unidealized model that it approximates, see Binmore and Samuelson (1995).

the paper was prepared as part of the Economic and Social Science "Belief and Behavior" program L 122 251 024. An extended abstract of a predecessor of the paper appears in the proceedings of the fifth TARK conference on Theoretical Aspects of Reasoning about Knowledge. An extract commenting on Aumann's (1995) definition of rationality as *A Note on Backward Induction* in Binmore (1996).

References

Antonelli, G., and C. Biechieri. 1994. Game-theoretic axioms for local rationality and bounded knowledge. Philosophy Working Paper. Carnegie-Mellon University.

Aumann, R. 1976. Agreeing to disagree. *Annals of Statistics* 4: 1236–39.

Aumann, R. 1985. What is game theory trying to accomplish? In K. Arrow and S. Honkapohja, eds., *Frontiers of Economics*. Oxford: Basil Blackwell, pp. 28–88.

Aumann, R. 1987. Correlated equilibrium as an expression of Bayesian rationality. *Econometrica* 55: 1–18.

Aumann, R. 1989. Interactive epistemology. Working paper. Cowles Foundation, Yale University.

Aumann, R. 1992. Irrationality in game theory. In P. Dasgupta, D. Gale, O. Hart, and E. Maskin, eds., *Economic Analysis of Markets and Games: Essays in Honor of Frank Hahn*. Cambridge: MIT Press, pp. 214–17.

Aumann, R. 1995. Backward induction and common knowledge of rationality. *Games and Economic Behavior* 8: 6–19.

Aumann, R., and A. Brandenburger. 1995. Epistemic conditions for Nash equilibrium. *Econometrica* 63: 1161–80.

Ben-Porath, E. 1992. Rationality, Nash equilibrium, and backward induction in perfect information games. Working paper. Tel Aviv University.

Bicchieri, C. 1988. Common knowledge and backwards induction: A solution to the paradox. In M. Vardi, ed., *Theoretical Aspects of Reasoning About Knowledge*. Los Altos: Morgan Kaufmann.

Bicchieri, C. 1987a. Strategic behavior and counterfactuals. *Erkerntnis* 30: 69–85.

Binmore, K. 1987. Modeling rational plays I. *Economics and Philosophy* 3: 9–55.

Binmore, K. 1987b. Modeling rational players II. *Economics and Philosophy* 4: 179–214.

Binmore, K. 1991. *Fun and Games*. Lexington, MA: D.C. Heath.

Binmore, K. 1992. Foundations of game theory. In J.-J. Laffont, ed., *Advances in Economic Theory*. Sixth World Congress of the Econometric Society. Cambridge: Cambridge University Press.

Binmore, K. 1994. *Playing Fair: Game Theory and the Social Contract I*. Cambridge: MIT Press.

Binmore, K. 1996. A Note on backward induction. *Games and Economic Behavior* 17: 135–37.

Binmore, K., J. Gale, and L. Samuelson. 1995. Learning to be imperfect: The ultimatum game. *Games and Economic Behavior* 8: 56–90.

Binmore, K., and L. Samuelson. 1993. Rationalizing backward induction? Forthcoming in the Proceedings of the International Economics Association conference in Turin on "Rationality."

Binmore, K., and L. Samuelson. 1995. Equilibrium selection and drift. University of Wisconsin discussion paper.

Blume, L., A. Brandenburger, and E. Dekel. 1991. Lexicographic probabilities and choice under uncertainty. *Econometrica* 59: 61–80.

Bonanno, G. 1991. The logic of rational play in games with perfect information. *Economics and Philosophy* 7: 37–65.

Bonanno, G. 1994. Knowledge, rationality and equilibrium in extensive games. Mimeo. Harvard University.

Cressman, R., and K. Schlag. 1995. The dynamic (in)stability of backwards induction. Discussion paper B-347. University of Bonn.

Flew, A. 1979. *A Dictionary of Philosophy*. London: Macmillan.

Fudenberg, D., D. Kreps, and D. Levine. 1988. On the robustness of equilibrium refinements. *Journal of Economic Theory* 44: 354–80.

Kreps, D., P. Milgrom, J. Roberts, and R. Wilson. 1982. Rational co-operation in the finitely repeated Prisoners' Dilemma. *Journal of Economic Theory* 27: 245–52.

McKelvey, R., and T. Palfrey. 1992. An experimental study of the Centipede Game. *Econometrica* 60: 803–36.

Pettit, P., and R. Sugden. 1989. The backwards induction paradox. *Journal of Philosophy* 4: 1–14.

Quine, W. 1996. *The Ways of Paradox and Other Essays*. Cambridge: Harvard University Press.

Reny, P. 1992. Rationality in extensive form games. *Journal of Economic Perspectives* 6: 103–18.

Rosenthal, R. 1981. Games of perfect information, predatory pricing, and chain-store paradox. *Journal of Economic Theory* 25: 92–100.

Samet, D. 1994. Hypothetical knowledge in games of perfect information. Working paper. Tel Aviv University.

Sandford, D. 1989. *If P, Then Q*. London: Routledge.

Selten, R. 1975. Reexamination of the perfectness concept for equilibrium points in extensive-games. *International Journal of Game Theory* 4: 25–55.

Selten, R., and Leopold. 1982. Subjunctive conditionals in decision theory and game theory. In W. Stegmüller, W. Balzer, and W. Spohn, eds., *Philosophy of Economics*. Berlin: Springer-Verlag.

Stalnaker, R. 1992a. *Knowledge, Belief and Counterfactual Reasoning in Games*. Cambridge: MIT Press.

Stalnaker, R. 1992b. On the evaluation of solution concepts. Cambridge: MIT Press.

Zermelo, E. 1913. Uber eine anwendung der Mengenlehre auf die Theorie des Schachspiels. In *Proceedings of the Fifth International Congress of Mathematicians*, vol. II. Cambridge: Cambridge University Press.

C Equilibrium Selection in the Ultimatum Game

The paper reproduced here is one of a long sequence of papers with Larry Samuelson on evolutionary dynamics and equilibrium selection. His excellent book sets the paper in a wider context (Samuelson 1997). But no matter how often modern game theorists multiply examples in which evolutionary processes fail to select subgame-perfect equilibria, it will continue to be said that game theory always predicts that a subgame-perfect equilibrium will be played.

Learning to be Imperfect: The Ultimatum Game

Ken Binmore, John Gale, and Larry Samuelson

C.1   The Ultimatum Game

Consider two players with a dollar to divide. The rules of the Ultimatum Game specify that player I begins by making an offer of $x \in [0, 1]$ to player II, who then accepts or refuses. If player II accepts, player I gets $1 - x$ and player II gets x. If player II refuses, both get nothing. Traditional game theory predicts that the play of this game will result in the unique subgame-perfect equilibrium in which player II plans to accept whatever she is offered and player I offers player II nothing.[1]

In the first of many experiments on this and related games by numerous authors, Güth et al. (1982) found that the modal offer was $\frac{1}{2}$ and that player I had roughly half a chance of being rejected if he offered about $\frac{1}{3}$ of the sum of money available. Binmore et al. (1989) reported qualitatively similar results in their replication of the Ultimatum Game experiment. There have been many related studies in the interim, surveyed by Bolton and Zwick (1993), Güth and Tietz (1990), Roth (1994), and Thaler (1988).

Critics of traditional game theory have quoted these results (along with the early results on the finitely repeated Prisoners' Dilemma and games

Financial support from National Science Foundation Grant SES-9122176 and the Deutsche Forschungsgemeinschaft, Sonderforschungsbereich 303 at the University of Bonn, is gratefully acknowledged. We thank Drew Fudenberg and Joseph Harrington for helpful discussions, and thank two referees and an associate editor for helpful comments. We are grateful to the Department of Economics at the University of Bonn and the Institute for Advanced Studies at the Hebrew University of Jerusalem, where part of this work was done, for their hospitality. The authors first encountered the possibility of using the replicator dynamics to obtain unusual results in the Ultimatum Game in a manuscript of James Andreoni and John Miller. This paper was prepared for the Nobel Symposium at Björkborn, Sweden, June 18–20, 1993.

1. If offers must be made in whole numbers of cents, other subgame-perfect equilibria also exist, but player II never gets more than one cent in any of these.

involving the private provision of public goods) as demonstrating that the
optimizing paradigm on which game theory is based is fundamentally
mistaken. Instead, so the story goes, people simply honor whatever social
norm is appropriate to the situation. Frank (1988) is particularly eloquent
on this subject. In bargaining games, for example, it is popular to assert
that people "just play fair."

Many game theorists have responded by dismissing laboratory results
as irrelevant to actual behavior. We agree that the results of poorly
designed experiments are irrelevant. Binmore (1992, p. 51) stresses that
an experimentalist or game theorist should be cautious about making predictions unless the following criteria are satisfied:[2]

- The game is reasonably simple;
- The incentives are adequate;
- Sufficient opportunity for trial-and-error learning is provided.

On the other hand, game theorists cannot ignore experiments that persis-
tently refute their predictions when all three criteria are satisfied. In the
case of the Ultimatum Game, the relevant experiments have been replicated too often for doubts about the data to persist. A theory predicting
that real people will use the subgame-perfect equilibrium in the Ultimatum Game is therefore open to question.

At first glance the case for subgame-perfection in the Ultimatum Game
seems ironclad. This is a two-player game of perfect information in which
each player moves only once.[3] Player I need only believe that player II
will not play a weakly dominated strategy to arrive at the subgame-
perfect offer. But the deletion of weakly dominated strategies is an
eductive principle (see Binmore 1987, 1988), whereas we believe that the
principles to which one must appeal when predicting actual behavior, in
the laboratory or elsewhere, are almost always *evolutive* in character.

---

2. As experimental techniques in economics have become increasingly sophisticated, the importance of these factors has come to the fore. As advocated by Smith (1991), it is now commonplace to offer experimental subjects large incentives instead of the negligible amounts
considered appropriate by many psychologists. At the same time the introduction of computer technology has made it possible to use interactive demonstrations to teach subjects
the rules of the game quickly and efficiently and to give the subjects the experience of large
numbers of repetitions of the game. A survey to Ledyard (1992) of recent experiments concerning the private provision of public goods is revealing. In experiment after experiment,
subjects are reported to approach the game-theoretic equilibrium as the incentives increase
and the subjects' experience with the game becomes extensive.

3. In particular, the criticism that subgame-perfection calls for players to regard their opponents as perfectly rational after having received evidence to the contrary (cf. Binmore 1987/
1988) has no force in the Ultimatum Game.

That is to say, the outcomes we observe are not the product of careful reasoning but of trial-and-error learning.

This paper demonstrates that interactive learning processes readily lead to outcomes in the Ultimatum Game that are Nash equilibria but not subgame-perfect.[4] We argue that game theorists were therefore wrong to put all their eggs in the subgame-perfect basket when predicting laboratory behavior in the Ultimatum Game. A case exists for predicting that interactive learning will result in the selection of one of the other Nash equilibria of the game.

Section C.2 begins by showing that if the initial conditions are not too close to the subgame-perfect equilibrium, then the replicator dynamics can converge to Nash equilibria in the Ultimatum Game that are not subgame-perfect. Given the relation between trembles and subgame-perfect equilibria (Selten 1975), such a result is of interest only if it is robust in the presence of relevant perturbations. We therefore introduce noise into the replicator dynamics. When this noise is small in absolute terms but relatively larger in the population of responders, we find that asymptotic attractors survive which are Nash equilibria but not subgame-perfect. But why do we expect responders to be noisier than proposers? Our reason is to be found in the structure of the Ultimatum Game. When noise levels are allowed to depend on the potential cost of making an error, the system can endogenously produce a situation with more noise in the responding population.

Section C.3 explains how we think these calculations should be interpreted in the light of the experimental data. In the process, we comment on a complementary learning-based analysis of the Ultimatum Game due to Roth and Erev (1993). We also explain why we expect to see initial conditions in laboratory experiments that lead the dynamics to equilibria that are not subgame-perfect. In particular, we suggest that initial play reflects decision rules that have evolved in real-life bargaining situations that are superficially similar to the Ultimatum Game. These bargaining games generally feature more symmetric allocations of bargaining power than the Ultimatum Game, yielding initial play in Ultimatum Game experiments that need not be close to the subgame-perfect equilibrium.

Section C.4 discusses how we think (out-of-equilibrium) behavior can persist in which people "leave money on the table." This section also

---

4. This finding is not without precedent. Binmore (1990), Samuelson (1988, 1993, 1994), and Samuelson and Zhang (1992) give simple examples showing that the deletion of weakly dominated strategies is at best a dubious activity in an evolutionary context.

comments on the use of "fairness" explanations for the outcomes of Ulti-matum Game experiments.

The results of section C.2 are established by numerically computing trajectories for the replicator dynamics. In order to provide some insight into the forces that drive these results, section C.5 studies a variant of Sel-ten's (1978) Chain-Store Game, which we reinterpret as a two-offer sim-plification of the Ultimatum Game. In this simpler setting an analytic study of the evolutionary dynamics is possible. The same analysis also provides a possible resolution of the well-known chain-store paradox that does not require incomplete information assumptions and applies even when only one potential entrant exists.

We employ the replicator dynamics throughout. Why are such bio-logically motivated dynamics relevant? First, section C.6 presents an aspiration-level model of learning that leads to the replicator dynamics. Börgers and Sarin (1993), Binmore and Samuelson (1993), Cabrales (1993), and Schlag (1994) similarly present learning models that lead to the replicator dynamics, suggesting that the replicator dynamics are of more than merely biological interest. Second, the analysis of section C.5 isolates the smoothness properties of the learning model that drive our results, revealing that qualitatively similar results will hold in a wide variety of learning models (including variants of Roth and Erev's 1993 model).

C.2   Numerical Calculations

This section studies a version of the Ultimatum Game. The players must split a "pie" of size 40. The set of offers available to the proposer is $I = \{1, 2, \ldots, 40\}$.[5] (Note that an offer i is the amount that player I pro-poses that player II should get rather than the amount player I demands for himself.) An action for player II is a choice from the set $\{Y, N\}$. Her strategies are therefore functions $f : \{1, 2, \ldots, 40\} \to \{Y, N\}$. How-ever, we assume that player II is restricted to functions of the form $f(i) = Y$ $(i \geq j)$ and $f(i) = N$ $(i < j)$ for some $j \in \{1, 2, \ldots, 40\}$. We can then identify player II's strategy with the minimum acceptable offer j and the set of pure-strategy pairs can be identified with $I \times I$. The forty pure-strategy Nash equilibria are (i, i) $(i = 1, 2, \ldots, 40)$. Since $i = 0$ is excluded, the unique subgame-perfect equilibrium is $(1, 1)$.

---

5. In what seemed crucial cases, we also computed solutions for games with $I = \{1, 2, \ldots, 100\}$ without significantly altering the results.

Table C.1
Fixed noise calculations

δ_I	δ_{II}				
	0.1	0.01	0.001	0.0001	0
0.1	7	2	1	1	1
0.01	9	7	3	1	1
0.001	9	9	7	3	1
0.0001	9	9	9	7	1
0	9	9	9	9	9

For an evolutionary analysis, we assume that player I is drawn from an infinite population of proposers and that player II is drawn from an infinite population of responders. The fraction of proposers who make offer i at time t is denoted by $x_i(t)$. The fitness $\pi_i(t)$ of a proposer using offer i at time t is taken to be the expected payoff to a player I who makes offer i when his opponent is drawn at random from the population of responders at time t. Average fitness in the population of proposers at time t is $\bar{\pi}_I(t) = x_1(t)\pi_1(t) + \cdots + x_{40}\pi_{40}(t)$. The standard replicator equation for the evolution of $x_i(t)$ is given by

$$\dot{x}_i = x_i(\pi_i - \bar{\pi}_I), \qquad i \in \{1, 2, \ldots, 40\}. \tag{1}$$

Similarly we let $y_j(t)$ be the fraction of responders playing strategy j at time t, with $\pi_j(t)$ being the fitness of a responder using strategy j and $\bar{\pi}_{II}(t)$ be the average fitness of responders, so that

$$\dot{y}_j = y_j(\pi_j - \bar{\pi}_{II}), \qquad j \in \{1, 2, \ldots, 40\}. \tag{2}$$

The evolution of the whole system is determined by the 80 equations given by (1) and (2).

In the terminology of Hofbauer and Sigmund (1988), every Nash equilibrium is a rest point of the replicator dynamics.[6] It is easy to show that many of these Nash equilibria are local attractors. In addition, the calculation reported in cell $(0, 0)$ of table C.1 shows that, with uniform initial conditions,[7] the system converges to an equilibrium in which

---

6. A *rest point* r is a fixed point of the dynamics. A *local attractor* l has the property that for each neighborhood V with $l \in V$, there is another neighborhood U with $l \in U \subseteq V$ such that any trajectory that begins in U remains in V. An *asymptotic attractor* a is a local attractor with the property that all trajectories which begin in a small enough neighborhood of a converge to a.

7. That is, each population begins with each strategy being played by $\frac{1}{40}$ of the agents in that population.

player II receives a little more than 20 percent of the pie. We therefore have immediate occasion to cast doubt on the subgame-perfect prediction in an evolutive context.

However, it may appear that Nash equilibria which fail to be subgame-perfect equilibria are attractors only because the long-run operation of the replicator dynamics allows some strategies to approach extinction, and hence artificially excludes the evolutionary pressure against weakly dominated strategies that would otherwise eliminate them. We therefore turn our attention to models in which small fractions of all possible strategies are continually injected into the population—including those that test the "rationality" of responders who refuse positive offers. Only if the survival of Nash equilibria that are not subgame-perfect is robust in the presence of such noise can we realistically argue against the subgame-perfect prediction.

It is natural to see the noisy model as an evolutionary gloss on Selten's (1975) trembling-hand story, which he used to justify subgame-perfect equilibria in games like the Ultimatum Game. However, caution is necessary before pressing the analogy too far. Samuelson and Zhang (1992) show that adding noise to the replicator and other evolutionary dynamics does not necessarily lead to the elimination of weakly dominated strategies. The question of whether only subgame-perfect equilibria can survive in a noisy evolutionary environment therefore remains open.

Noise in an interactive learning system may arise in many ways and cause perturbations of various types. We therefore think it important to be clear on the source of the noise to be studied.[8] This in turn requires that we take a little more care than is usual in modeling the agents.

We envisage an agent as a stimulus–response mechanism with two modes of operation: a playing mode and a learning mode. Its playing mode operates when it is called upon to choose a strategy in one of a large number of games that it repeatedly plays against different opponents. Its behavior in each game is triggered by a stimulus that is determined by the manner in which the game is framed. (By a "game-frame," we mean more than the game itself. We include also the context in which the game is encountered and the manner in which its rules are described.[9]) When it receives such a stimulus s it responds by playing a

8. We depart from that part of the refinement literature which follows Kohlberg and Mertens (1986) in demanding robustness in the face of all conceivable perturbations. There is no reason to suppose that a system will necessarily be adapted to types of noise that it has experienced only rarely if at all.

9. For example, it may be relevant whether the interacting agents are a monopoly seller and a buyer or whether they are the joint winners of a lottery.

strategy $D(s)$. If the learning mode were absent, an agent could therefore be identified with a fixed decision rule D that maps a set of stimuli into a set of strategies. However, sometimes an agent will enter its learning mode between games to adjust its current decision rule. When learning, it takes a stimulus s and some information f about the relative success of strategies in the game labeled by s to modify the value of $D(s)$. The learning rule L that it uses for this purpose is assumed to be fixed. We restrict our attention to learning rules that lead to the replicator dynamics largely because this dynamic has been widely discussed in the literature on evolutionary game theory and hence will be familiar (but see section C.6).

Noise may perturb an agent in its decision mode or in its learning mode. Here and in section C.6, we simplify by considering only the second possibility. We then simplify further by assuming that the only source of error lies in the possibility that an agent may mistakenly learn to play a strategy that is adapted to the wrong game.[10] We do not explicitly model the situations that may be confused with the Ultimatum Game. In the case of a misguided proposer, we simply assume that he makes each offer i in the Ultimatum Game with probability θ_i. If the fraction of proposers at time t who misread the game is always δ_{I}, and the usual arguments leading to the replicator equation apply to the fraction $1 - \delta_{\mathrm{I}}$ of the proposing population who do not misread the game, then we are led to the "noisy replicator equation"

$$\dot{x}_i = (1 - \delta_{\mathrm{I}})x_i(\pi_i - \bar{\pi}_{\mathrm{I}}) + \delta_{\mathrm{I}}(\theta_i - x_i) \tag{3}$$

for the evolution of the fraction $x_i(t)$ of agents in the proposing population who play strategy i. The corresponding equation for the population of responders is

$$\dot{y}_j = (1 - \delta_{\mathrm{II}})y_j(\pi_j - \bar{\pi}_{\mathrm{II}}) + \delta_{\mathrm{II}}(\psi_j - y_j), \tag{4}$$

where δ_{II} is the fraction of the responding population who misread the game and ψ_j describes the choices of such agents.

Section C.6 derives (1)–(2) and (3)–(4) from an explicit choice model in which agents sometimes misread their strategic situation. Other choice

---

10. Although the English language forces us into speaking of players' misreading the game or learning to play better, it should be emphasized that our agents do not monitor what is going on except insofar as this is modeled by the learning rule with which they are endowed. The face that they have a learning rule at all makes them more flexible than the stimulus–response machines that are often considered, since their decision rules for playing games evolve over time, but the learning rule that governs how decision rules evolve is fixed.

models can lead to different versions of the dynamics. For example, if a proportion $\delta_I \tau$ of the agents die (or leave the game, or choose to experiment with new strategies) in each time period of length τ, to be replaced by novices who play each strategy i with probability θ_i, then we are led to the equation $\dot{x}_i = x_i(\pi_i - \bar{\pi}_I) + \delta_I(\theta_i - x_i)$. This corresponds to noise in agents' playing mode rather than their learning mode. Our theoretical analysis in section C.5 includes this case as well as (3) by examining dynamics of the form $\dot{x}_i = \Delta_I x_i(\pi_i - \bar{\pi}_I) + \delta_I(\theta_i - x_i)$. Alternatively, Binmore et al. (1993) examine a choice model that gives rise to the dynamics $\dot{x}_i = x_i(\pi_i - \bar{\pi}_I)/\bar{\pi}_I$. Van Damme (1987) and others work with a discrete version of this dynamic. We have reported numerical calculations using this discrete dynamic in Binmore and Samuelson (1994), and we indicate how the results differ from those reported here as we proceed.

What determines θ_i and ψ_j? These presumably reflect rules of thumb or behavior learned in other games, and as a result we have little to say about their precise form. For most of our calculations we will assume that these represent a uniform distribution over strategies. We discuss how the specification of θ_i and ψ_j affects the results at the end of this section.

Table C.1 reports calculations for various values of δ_I and δ_{II}.[11] The rows in table C.1 correspond to different values of δ_I. The columns correspond to different values of δ_{II}. In each case the system was initialized with each of the 40 possible strategies being played by $\frac{1}{40}$ of each population. The mistake probabilities were also taken to be uniform, so that $\theta_i = \psi_j = \frac{1}{40}$.

The entries in table C.1 are the model offers made by player I after the system has converged to a point where the proportion of each population playing each strategy is unchanging in its first 15 decimal places. In each case the frequency with which the model offer is played at this point is 1.00 to at least two decimal places. The equilibrium behavior of responders is much more diffuse, but is very highly concentrated on strategies less than or equal to the modal offer. Hence offers are rejected with only a very tiny probability. For example, in the cases when the model equilibrium offer made by player I is 9, a significant fraction of responders would accept each of the offers between 1 and 9 in equilibrium (with virtually no responders insisting on more than 9)—but the fraction

---

11. The difference equation $x_i(t + \tau) - x_i(t) = \tau[(1 - \delta_I)x_i(\pi_i - \bar{\pi}) + \delta_I(\theta_i - x_i)]$ is used to approximate Eq. (3) where we set $\tau = 0.01$. The robustness of the approximation was tested by repeating a sample of the calculations with much smaller values of τ.

of responders who will refuse anything lower than 9 is high enough to make it unprofitable for proposers to reduce their offer.

Table C.1 shows that, if the noise level among responders is sufficiently small relative to that of proposers, then the subgame-perfect equilibrium appears. However, if the noise level in the responding population fails to be small enough compared with the noise level in the proposing population, then outcomes appear that are far from the subgame-perfect equilibrium. If responders are noisy enough compared with proposers, then player II gets a little more than 20 percent of the pie.[12]

Section C.5 provides an analytic explanation of these results for a simple special case, but the intuition is straightforward. It is, for example, weakly dominated for player II to refuse an offer of 10 percent. There will therefore always be some evolutionary pressure against this strategy because, in a noisy population, the set of proposers who make such low offers is continually renewed. However, if this fraction of the proposing population becomes sufficiently small, the pressure against refusals of 10 percent will be negligible compared with the drift engendered by the noise in the responding population. Hence, if responders are noisy enough relative to proposers, then sufficiently many responders can reject offers of 10 percent that it is not a best response for proposers to offer less and we can reach outcomes that are not subgame-perfect.

Why should we anticipate that there will be more noise in the population of responders than in the population of proposers? Recall that we envision the noise arising as a result of an agent misreading the game when learning and hence acquiring an inappropriate behavior. The context is that of a boundedly rational agent without sufficient computational power to devote full attention to all of the many games that compete for its attention. However, the frequency with which learning errors are made is unlikely to be independent of the potential costs. Instead we expect the likelihood of a learning error to depend on how much it currently matters in payoff terms what strategy is played in the game.[13] In more familiar

---

12. For the dynamic $x_i(t + 1) = x_i(t) + x_i(t)(\pi_i - \bar{\pi})/\bar{\pi}$, Binmore and Samuelson (1994) find results that are much the same as reported in this paper, though in (1994) we find that player I's noise level need only be at least as high as player II's in order to give subgame-perfection. The outcome for cases in which player II's noise level is higher is again 9. This difference arises because, near the subgame-perfect equilibrium, the divisor π becomes especially small for responders. This accentuates the learning portion of the noisy replicator dynamic, causing the responding population to seem less noisy.

13. This formulation is consistent with the spirit of Myerson's (1991) proper equilibrium, which refines the idea of a trembling-hand equilibrium by making more costly mistakes less likely.

terms, the assumption will be that the players are more diligent in identifying games correctly when their potential gains and losses are large, and more prone to misread games when their potential gains or losses are small.[14]

In the Ultimatum Game the result of making such an assumption is that responders will tend to be noisier when proposers are making low offers, because the responders will then have less at stake. In particular, such endogenously determined noise will lead responders to be noisier than proposers if the system should get close to the subgame-perfect equilibrium.

To explore this question further, we performed calculations in which the noise levels were endogenized along the lines discussed above. We took

$$\delta_k(t) = \frac{\alpha\beta}{\alpha + \lambda_k(t)}, \qquad k = \mathrm{I}, \mathrm{II}, \tag{5}$$

where α and β are constant and $\lambda_k(t)$ is the difference between the maximum and minimum of the expected payoffs attached to player k's strategies, given the current distribution of strategies in the opposing population. When this difference is zero, as is nearly the case for responders at the subgame-perfect equilibrium, the noise level takes its highest value of β. If the difference could increase all the way to infinity, $\delta_k(t)$ would decrease to zero.[15]

Table C.2 summarizes calculations with endogenized noise for various values of the two constants α and β listed in the first and second columns. The third column shows the modal offer made in equilibrium. The frequency with which the modal offer made in equilibrium is again 1.00 to at least two decimal places, and responders' strategies range between the

14. Such an assumption adds more complexity to the stimulus–response mechanism used to model an agent. The mechanism must now incorporate a device that responds to changes in its environment by diverting computational capacity between monitoring and other tasks according to the estimated rewards from the different activities. Like the learning rule, this device is assumed to be fixed.

15. The difference between the maximum and minimum payoff is an arbitrary measure of the payoffs that are at stake in a game. Calculations using alternative measures, such as the variance of the payoffs to player k's strategies, with each strategy taken to be equally likely in the variance calculation, produced analogous results (Binmore and Samuelson 1994). A more realistic measure would perhaps use a sample of past payoffs rather than employing all current payoffs. On the other hand, we suspect that people are indeed often able to make educated guesses about their compatriots' current payoffs without necessarily being at all well informed about the strategies that secure the payoffs. Academic economists, for example, are often able to estimate their colleagues' salaries quite closely. Extreme payoffs are especially likely to attract comment.

Table C.2
Calculations with endogenous noise

α	β	Offer	$\delta_I(\infty)$	$\delta_{II}(\infty)$
10	1	9	0.26	0.52
10	0.1	9	0.024	0.053
10	0.01	9	0.0024	0.0053
10	0.001	9	0.00024	0.00053
1	1	9	0.032	0.1
1	0.1	9	0.0031	0.01
1	0.01	9	0.00031	0.001
1	0.001	9	0.000031	0.0001
0.1	1	9	0.0032	0.011
0.1	0.1	9	0.00032	0.0011
0.1	0.01	9	0.000032	0.00011
0.1	0.001	9	0.0000032	0.000011
0.01	1	9	0.00032	0.0011
0.01	0.1	9	0.000032	0.00011
0.01	0.01	9	0.0000032	0.000011
0.01	0.001	9	0.00000032	0.0000011

modal offer and zero, with virtually no rejections. The fifth and sixth columns show the noise levels in the two populations after equilibrium is achieved.

Endogenizing the noise leads to an equilibrium in which the responder population is noisier than the proposer population. It is therefore not surprising that the equilibrium outcome is not subgame-perfect. In fact the equilibrium offer is again close to 20 percent.

How robust are these results? First, consider the question of initial conditions. The calculations reported in tables C.1 and C.2 are based on a uniform initial distribution of offers over $I \times I$. We also performed $1,600 = 40 \times 40$ other calculations to explore the dependence of the results on the initial conditions. Table C.3 shows the modal equilibrium offers for some of these initial conditions for the case of endogenous noise with $\alpha = 1$ and $\beta = 0.1$. The entry in row i and column j is the modal equilibrium offer when the system is started with all proposers playing i and all responders playing j. The frequency of the modal equilibrium offer remains 1.00 to at least two decimal places.

Space precludes showing the whole table. The table extends downward just as one would anticipate on the basis of its existing pattern. For cases in which proposers initially play at least 10, it extends to the right as one would expect (expect that the cells $(38, 37)$, $(38, 38)$, $(39, 37)$, $(39, 38)$, $(39, 39)$, $(40, 37)$, $(40, 38)$, $(40, 39)$, and $(40, 40)$ yield outcomes of 9 rather than 10). For cases in which the initial offer is less than 10, we

Table C.3
Calculations with varying initial conditions

	1	2	3	4	5	6	7	8	9	10	11	12	13	14	
1	1	2	3	4	5	6	7	8	9	10	10	10	10	10	⋯
2	1	2	3	4	5	6	7	8	9	10	10	10	10	10	⋯
3	1	2	3	4	5	6	7	8	9	10	10	10	10	10	⋯
4	1	2	3	4	5	6	7	8	9	10	10	10	10	10	⋯
5	1	2	3	4	5	6	7	8	9	10	10	10	10	10	⋯
6	1	2	3	4	5	6	7	8	9	10	10	10	10	10	⋯
7	1	2	3	4	5	6	7	8	9	10	10	10	10	10	⋯
8	1	2	3	4	5	6	7	8	9	10	10	10	10	10	⋯
9	1	2	3	4	5	6	7	8	9	10	10	10	10	10	⋯
10	1	2	3	4	5	6	7	8	9	10	10	10	10	10	⋯
11	1	2	3	4	5	6	7	8	9	10	10	10	10	10	⋯
12	1	2	3	4	5	6	7	8	9	10	10	10	10	10	⋯
13	1	2	3	4	5	6	7	8	9	10	10	10	10	10	⋯
14	1	2	3	4	5	6	7	8	9	10	10	10	10	10	⋯
15	1	2	3	4	5	6	7	8	9	10	10	10	10	10	⋯
16	1	2	3	4	5	6	7	8	9	10	10	10	10	10	⋯
17	1	2	3	4	5	6	7	8	9	10	10	10	10	10	⋯
18	1	2	3	4	5	6	7	8	9	10	10	10	10	10	⋯
19	1	2	3	4	5	6	7	8	9	10	10	10	10	10	⋯
20	1	2	3	4	5	6	7	8	9	10	10	10	10	10	⋯
21	1	2	3	4	5	6	7	8	9	10	10	10	10	10	⋯
22	1	2	3	4	5	6	7	8	9	10	10	10	10	10	⋯
23	1	2	3	4	5	6	7	8	9	10	10	10	10	10	⋯
24	1	2	3	4	5	6	7	8	9	10	10	10	10	10	⋯
25	1	2	3	4	5	6	7	8	9	10	10	10	10	10	⋯
⋮	⋮	⋮	⋮	⋮	⋮	⋮	⋮	⋮	⋮	⋮	⋮	⋮	⋮	⋮	⋮

find the outcome to be 10 as long as the initial response is not too high (generally, up to 25, though higher for lower initial proposals). Higher initial responses yield lower final outcomes. We found the outcomes of initial conditions in which the proposer offers at least 10 to be robust to the values of α and β.[16] The outcomes for cases in which proposers initially offered less than 10 were somewhat more sensitive, though the outcome was always at least as large as the minimum of the initial offer and initial proposal.[17]

The most striking feature of table C.3 is the robustness of a modal equilibrium offer above 20 percent. This offer appears for a large collection of initial conditions, including all those in which the initial proposal and response are at least 20 percent. The next section explains why we believe these are most likely to be the relevant initial conditions.

How do our results depend on the specification of noise, that is, on θ_i and ψ_j? By changing these specifications, we can obtain different results. The distribution of noise among the responders is especially important. If we alter ψ_j to put relatively more weight on offers and responses near zero, equilibrium outcomes can be achieved in which the responder gets less that 20 percent of the pie. Causing more weight to be put on somewhat higher offers gives outcomes in which the responders get more than 20 percent of the pie.

It is interesting to note, however, that changing the values of θ_i and ψ_j that are attached to relatively high offers has virtually no effect on the outcome. For example, we changed the mistake probabilities so that θ_{20} and ψ_{20}, the probabilities of the "fair" offer and response, took various values up to 0.95 (with the remaining values of θ_i and ψ_j remaining equal to one another). We might view this as a case in which the rule of thumb to which most noisy players resort when not paying attention to the game is to split the pie evenly, with a minority of such players adopting completely random rules of thumb that attach equal probability to all strategies. This change had almost no impact on the results of the calculations.

---

16. Using the specification of the basic dynamic as $x_i(t+1) = x_i(t) + x_i(t)(\pi_i - \bar{\pi})/\bar{\pi}$ and taking $\lambda_k(t)$ to be the variance of the payoffs accruing to each of agent k's strategies (rather than the difference between the maximum and minimum payoff) gives similar results, though the 10's are replaced by 9's.

17. Whenever proposers initially make smaller offers than responders will accept, the dynamics begin with a race between proposers and responders, with each adjusting to match the other's strategy. The outcome of this race can be sensitive to parameters of the model when all responders initially get very low payoffs, as is the case for low proposer offers.

   Probability attached to the "fair" response of 20 has little effect because this offer lies above the range of potential modal equilibrium offers (given that the remaining noise is uniformly distributed). As a result the response earns a low payoff and the learning dynamics ensure that little probability accumulates on this response. The important considerations involve the distribution of noise over those responses that are lower than potential modal equilibrium offers. These responses earn almost identical payoffs and noise plays a major role in determining the equilibrium proportions of responders choosing each of these strategies. The key here is whether the noise in the responder population can amass a sufficient proportion of responders on a strategy y to make it unprofitable for proposers to make offers $x < y$ and hence sustain an outcome in which the modal offer is y. This depends on the relative noise level of the two populations and on the specification of the noise. With uniform noise and sufficiently noisy responders, offers less than or equal to 10 can be sustained (see table C.3) but higher offers cannot. If the responder's noise concentrates more of its probability near (away from) zero, then lower (higher) modal offers will result (provided in the latter case that the increased weight is not directed to offers such as 20 that are too high to be possible equilibrium modal offers).

   It is clear that we cannot place too much significance on the particular value of the equilibrium offer of a little more than 20 percent that repeatedly emerges in the calculations, and we are anxious that our results not be remembered for this number. Different specifications of the model can give different numbers. The important feature of the results is that the equilibrium offer is frequently far from subgame-perfect, even when the noise levels are made very small indeed. This result requires primarily that the responding population be relatively more noisy than the proposing population. But this is the configuration of noise levels that appears if players tend to be less noisy when making decisions that are more important.

C.3   Relevance to Experimental Data?

How do we think the calculations of the previous section might be relevant to the experimental data? We think it useful to distinguish four time spans:[18]

---

18. Our general views on the evolution of social norms inside and outside laboratories have been reported elsewhere (Binmore and Samuelson (1994)).

1. In the *short run*, one should anticipate that behavior is driven primarily by norms that are triggered by the framing of the problem. The framing may well elicit norms that are ill-adapted to the laboratory situation. If these norms have been strongly reinforced outside the laboratory, they may be hard to shift. We suspect that the "irrational" behavior studied by the school of Kahneman and Tversky (1987) often falls into this category.

2. In the *medium run*, subjects begin to learn—as emphasized by Andreoni and Miller (1993), Crawford (1991, 1992), Miller and Andreoni (1991), Roth and Erev (1993), and numerous other authors.

3. In the *long run*, this interactive learning process may converge on an equilibrium of the game.

4. In the *ultralong run*, there may be jumps between equilibria when random shocks jolt the system from one basin of attraction to another—as emphasized by Young (1993), Kandori et al. (1993), and Samuelson (1994).

In the ultralong run we expect an evolutionary process to select the subgame-perfect equilibrium. However, our guess is that the ultralong run is *too* long a run to be relevant to the available experimental data. We also do not think that the replicator dynamics provide a useful model of the ultralong run.[19]

But, as we have argued, the replicator dynamics do have a role to play as long-run approximations to certain simple learning rules. We therefore believe that the asymptotic properties of the replicator dynamics may be relevant to the long-run outcome of interactive learning in the laboratory. If so, then it is significant that our calculations of the long-run behavior of noisy replicator dynamics in the Ultimatum Game should generate equilibria that are far from subgame-perfect.

We believe that our calculations are relevant to the short run as well as the long run. As section C.6 explains, we think it possible to regard our dynamics as a crude but instructive model of social evolution (as well as of interactive learning in the laboratory).

---

19. In section C.6, an implicit appeal is made to the law of large numbers when studying the long run, so that the underlying stoachastic learning is smoothed into a deterministic process. Binmore and Samuelson (1993) argue that one must refrain from such appeals when studying the ultralong run, and work directly with the stochastic system instead. If one were to work directly with the stochastic system in the current paper, results would emerge concerning the expected waiting time until reaching the subgame-perfect equilibrium in the ultralong run. The noisier the responding population relative to the proposing population, the longer the system lingers near long-run equilibria that are not subgame-perfect—and hence the longer and less relevant the ultralong run.

More important, the social norm (or norms) triggered in the short term by laboratory experiments on the Ultimatum Game have presumably evolved to guide behavior in real-life bargaining situations that are superficially similar to the Ultimatum Game in some respects. We must therefore examine long-run behavior in these external situations for the origin of the norms that guide short-run behavior in laboratory experiments on the Ultimatum Game.

The real-life bargaining situations that have shaped the norms which subjects bring to the laboratory will be complicated by informational, reputational and other effects that are controlled away in the laboratory. The pure Ultimatum Game represents an extremal case in the class of real-life bargaining situations, because all the power is on the side of the proposer. If a social norm adapted to the pure Ultimatum Game leads to the proposer offering about 20 percent to the responder, we should therefore anticipate that bargaining norms adapted to a wider class of bargaining games will assign *more* than 20 percent to the responder. If this guess is correct, we should therefore envisage the initial conditions for learning in the laboratory as allocating more than 20 percent to the responder and hence as lying in the basin of attraction of the 20 percent equilibrium offer of table C.3.

What do our calculations tell us about the medium run? Table C.4 is a medium-run version of table C.1. It differs from table C.1 in that the modal offer is reported on the first occasion at which no change in consecutive iterations was detected in the first five decimal places of the fractions of proposers making each offer. (Table C.1 does the same, but with fifteen decimal places.) The number in parentheses following each model offer is a measure of how much learning was necessary before a temporary stability in the first five decimal places was achieved.[20] In table C.1, the frequency with which modal offers were used was 1.00 to at least two decimal places. The frequency with which the modal offers were used at the time reported in table C.4 is at least 0.98.[21]

---

20. The measure is the number of iterations of the discrete dynamic described in note 11 multiplied by the step size. In the model of section C.6, τ of the population has an opportunity to change strategies in each iteration of the discrete equation. Our measure therefore provides a crude approximation to the aggregate number of times that members of the entire population have assessed their strategies. The measure is intended to serve as a correlate for the number of rounds of an experiment required to reach temporary stability.

21. If we ask for stability in only the first three decimal places, the first line of this table would read 9 (7) 9 (6) 9 (6) 9 (6), with the modal offer being played with frequency at least 0.85 in each case.

Table C.4
Medium-run equivalent of table C.1

δ_I	δ_{II}				
	0.1	0.01	0.001	0.0001	0
0.1	9 (13)	7 (74)	7 (69)	7 (69)	7 (69)
0.01	9 (15)	9 (12)	9 (12)	9 (12)	9 (12)
0.001	9 (15)	9 (12)	9 (12)	9 (12)	9 (12)
0.0001	9 (15)	9 (12)	9 (12)	9 (12)	9 (12)
0	9 (15)	9 (12)	9 (12)	9 (12)	9 (12)

Table C.4 shows that the system *always* (with uniform initial conditions and perturbations) goes quite quickly to a modal offer of about 20 percent. But table C.1 shows this to be a medium-run result. In the long run, the system sometimes moves away to the subgame-perfect equilibrium. Only when $\delta_I < \delta_{II}$ is the medium-run behavior a useful guide to the long-run behavior of the system.

These results complement those of Roth and Erev (1993), who report Ultimatum Game simulations that spend extended periods of time, in the medium run, near equilibria that are Nash but no subgame-perfect. Roth and Erev suggest explaining the experimental data on the Ultimatum Game as a set of medium-run observations of a learning process.

We agree that much experimental data consists of a series of snapshots of medium-run phenomena. This is especially true of Ultimatum Game experiments, where both dispersion in proposals as well as rejected offers often persist into the later rounds of the experiments, both of which can only be medium-run phenomena in our model. However, we do not think it follows that theories of long-run behavior can be neglected. As our analysis of section C.5 suggests, long-run predictions of theoretical models of interactive learning will often depend only on *qualitative* features of the models. By contrast, medium-run predictions must be expected to depend on the fine details of the interactive learning process. We therefore think that current theoretical techniques are more likely to be successful when applied to long-run rather than medium-run phenomena. Rather than seeking to explain experimental data in which medium-run behavior has been elicited, we therefore think there is a strong case for designing experiments with a view to eliciting long-run behavior.[22] The contribution of this paper is to argue that, in such

---

22. Binmore et al. (1992), for example, obtain very close convergence to equilibrium in less than 40 repetitions in a complicated bargaining game by offering high incentives and helping the subjects with sophisticated computer graphics.

experiments, there is no compelling reason why predictions should favor
subgame-perfect equilibria over other Nash equilibria.

C.4 Leaving Money on the Table

The previous sections argue that attention needs to be paid to Nash equilibria in the Ultimatum Game that are not subgame-perfect. Such equilibria require that the responder be prepared to refuse low positive offers.
If offered a choice between something and nothing, such a responder
would therefore sometimes choose nothing. Such behavior is outlawed in
conventional economic modeling. Perhaps for this reason, a common response to our argument is an incredulous "Why would anyone leave
money on the table?"

That positive offers should be refused in the short term is easy to understand. Short-term behavior in the Ultimatum Game is likely to be governed by social norms that are triggered by the framing of the laboratory
experiment. Rather than being adapted to the pure Ultimatum Game,
such social norms will presumably have evolved for use in everyday
cousins of the Ultimatum Game. In everyday life we rarely play pure
take-it-or-leave-it games. In particular, real-life games are seldom played
under conditions of total anonymity. A refusal of something positive may
therefore serve to maintain a reputation for toughness. Even when we do
play anonymously, outside options are often available. For example, in
the take-it-or-leave-it auction used by stores to sell their goods, a refusal
of something positive may simply indicate a willingness to search elsewhere for a better deal. Norms that call for refusals in commonly occurring "take-it-or-leave-it" situations therefore make good evolutionary
sense. Given that such norms exist, it is unsurprising if they are sometimes inappropriately triggered in laboratory experiments. Short-run
refusals of positive offers in the pure Ultimatum Game therefore create
no problem for orthodox game theory.

However, we argue that Nash equilibria that are not subgame-perfect
should be taken seriously even in the long run. Notice first that such equilibria actually require very few offers to be rejected, because proposers
learn not to make such offers. Nevertheless, responders must stand ready
to reject some positive offers.

On this subject, it is useful to observe that people clearly *do* sometimes
leave money on the table. Frank (1988), for example, reminds us about
tipping behavior in restaurants that are never to be visited again. After
the waiter makes your change, you can either pocket the entire amount

or leave the customary percentage on the table. Nearly everyone chooses the latter option—including economists!

A kibitzer may ask *why* we leave money on the table. Most people are satisfied with the explanation that leaving a tip is a custom that it would be uncomfortable to violate. If pressed, they might attribute the discomfort to the unfairness involved in disappointing the server's expectations.

Such considerations have led a number of authors to downplay strategic explanations of experimental behavior in favor of various theories of "fair play." Sophisticated versions of this approach sometimes build a taste for "fairness" into the utility functions attributed to the subjects. Ochs and Roth (1989) discuss such a utility function in explaining the mediumrun results of an alternating offers bargaining experiment. Bolton (1991) explicitly constructs such a utility function for this purpose.

We agree that subjects find their emotions engaged in bargaining situations. They also frequently explain their bargaining behavior in the laboratory in terms of "fairness." But an approach that takes these facts at their face value is in danger of explaining too much and too little. Fairness theories explain too much because, by choosing one's fairness notion with sufficient care, one can justify a very wide range of outcomes. At the same time such theories explain too little because they provide no insight into the origin of the fairness norms to which appeal is made.

We believe that a more fruitful approach is to ask how the custom of leaving money on the table can survive. Our answer is simple. The amounts involved and the frequency with which the situation arises are too small to provide sufficient evolutionary pressure to eliminate the phenomenon in a noisy environment. What then of the folk explanation in terms of the discomfort felt at violating a fairness norm?

In responding to such questions, it is important to appreciate that the evolutionary approach we advocate reverses the standard *explicans* and *explicandum* of the folk explanation and of economic theory. Our players are not members of the species *Homo economicus*. They do not optimize relative to fixed preferences. They simply have decision rules for playing games. When a player switches from a less profitable to a more profitable strategy, he does not do so because he thinks that the switch is optimal— he is just acting as a stimulus–response mechanism.

This model of *Homo sapiens* raises the question of how it *feels* for one's actions to be programmed as a result of past experience. Here the *post hoc, ergo propter hoc* fallacy awaits the unwary. It is easy to say that I preferred to take this foolish action rather than that wise action *because* I got angry. But we feel angry because adrenalin and other chemicals have been released into our bloodstream by a process which is only very partially under our conscious control. Angry feelings are a conditioned reflex to certain learned stimuli. Such conditioned reflexes survive because the behaviors they induce have evolutionary advantages. Rather than seeking to explain a particular behavior in terms of the angry feelings that accompany it, we therefore do better to explain the angry feelings in terms of the evolutionary advantages of the behavior. In brief, being angry or fearful or amorous is how it feels to be a stimulus–response mechanism.

Of course, none of us like to admit that much of our behavior is little more than a set of conditioned reflexes. We prefer to offer more flattering rationalizations of the behavior. For example, the stimulus of receiving an offer of only 10 percent in the Ultimatum Game may be sufficiently irritating that we turn the offer down. If asked *why* we refused, we may then rationalize our behavior by arguing that irritation is an entirely appropriate response to an "unfair" offer of 10 percent. Indeed, such an explanation may become institutionalized and so reinforce the behavior that it "explains." But we see no more reason to believe that "fairness norms" are fixed and immutable than that economic agents always maximize money. We believe that players usually find their way to a long-run equilibrium of trial-and-error learning without having any clear understanding of the strategic realities of the game they are playing. They simply learn that certain stimulus–response behaviors are effective. After the game they may rationalize their behavior in various ways. In bargaining experiments they often say that the long-run equilibrium to which they found their way is "fair." But, from an evolutionary perspective, how they explain their own behavior to themselves and others is an epiphenomenon. If they had found their way to another equilibrium, they would be offering some other explanation.[23] Economists who fit utility functions to observed behavior would similarly find themselves proposing a different utility function.

In summary, we believe that attention should be focused on the evolution of *behavior*. If a type of behavior that prompts people to leave money on the table survives, it will be because there is insufficient evolutionary pressure to remove it. Fairness explanations may be offered as rational-

---

23. One can observe the fairness norms evolving in the laboratory. In Binmore et al. (1992), the median long-run equilibrium claim in a laboratory implementation of the Nash Demand Game turns out to be a very good predictor of the median claim said to be "fair" in a computerized postexperimental debriefing, even though subjects are randomly chosen for an initial conditioning that directs their subsequent play to different long-run equilibrium claims.

izations of the behavior. Such stories may even be incorporated into the workings of the stimulus–response mechanism. But the details of how the mechanism actually works or how we explain its workings to ourselves are secondary. The primary consideration is why some behavior patterns survive in a population while others will necessarily perish. Only after this question has been answered is it worthwhile to ask why some of the stories we tell ourselves are washed away by the evolutionary tide while others remain high and dry.

C.5 An Ultimatum Minigame

To identify the forces that drive our computational results, this section provides an analytical study of the simplified version of the Ultimatum Game shown in figure C.1. In this Ultimatum Minigame, player I can make a high offer (H) or a low offer (L). If he makes a high offer, it is assumed that player II accepts. If he makes a low offer, player II may accept (Y) or refuse (N).

The Ultimatum Minigame has the same structure as Selten's (1978) Chain-Store Game. Although we do not press the point, our conclusions in this section therefore provide a possible resolution of the chain-store paradox that applies even in the case when there is just one potential entrant.

Figure C.1c shows the pairs (x, y) that represent equilibria in the Ultimatum Minigame, where x and y are the probabilities with which H and Y are played. There is a unique subgame-perfect equilibrium S at $(0, 1)$ in figure C.1c, and a component N of Nash equilibria occupying the closed line segment joining $\left(1, \frac{2}{3}\right)$ and $(1, 0)$.

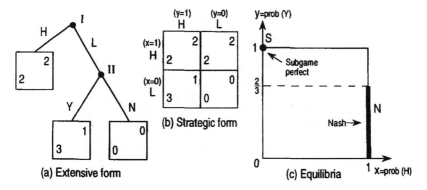

Figure C.1
Ultimatum Minigame.

s

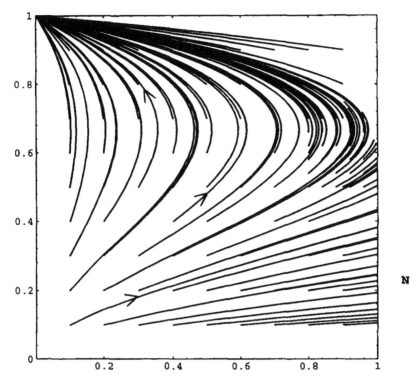

Figure C.2
Phase diagram, no noise.

Figure C.2 shows the trajectories of the standard replicator dynamics in the Ultimatum Minigame:

$$\dot{x} = x(1 - x)(2 - 3y) \tag{6}$$

$$\dot{y} = y(1 - y)(1 - x). \tag{7}$$

We summarize the key properties of these trajectories in proposition 1 (see note 6):

Proposition 1 The subgame-perfect equilibrium S is the unique asymptotic attractor of the unperturbed replicator dynamics. With the exception of $\left(1, \frac{2}{3}\right)$, the Nash equilibria in the set N are local attractors.

The fact that interior points of N are local attractors does not seem to us an adequate reason for regarding them as alternatives to the subgame-perfect equilibrium S. To draw this conclusion, we feel it necessary that the result should survive in the presence of noise that continually replaces strategies that the replicator dynamics drives to extinction. We accordingly require strategies to be at least local attractors in slightly perturbed versions of the dynamics where extinction is not a possibility. We accordingly study the perturbed replicator dynamics, defined by

$$\dot{x} = \Delta_I x (1 - x)(2 - 3y) + \delta_I \left(\frac{1}{2} - x \right), \tag{8}$$

$$\dot{y} = \Delta_{II} y (1 - y)(1 - x) + \delta_{II} \left(\frac{1}{2} - y \right). \tag{9}$$

In the case when $\Delta_k = 1 - \delta_k$ $(k = I, II)$, these equations are analogues to (3)–(4) of section C.3.

Figures C.3 and C.4 show the trajectories for the perturbed replicator dynamics. None of the points in N is a local attractor in figure C.3, where responders and proposers are equally noisy; but there exists an asymptotic attractor in figure C.4, where responders are noisier than proposers.

More formally, we are interested in what happens when the noise in (8)–(9) is small, so that $(\delta_I, \delta_{II}, \Delta_I, \Delta_{II})$ is close to $(0, 0, 1, 1)$. We fix $\phi = \delta_{II} \Delta_I / \delta_I \Delta_{II}$ and consider the limit as $(\delta_I, \delta_{II}, \Delta_I, \Delta_{II}) \to (0, 0, 1, 1)$ in two cases:

Case 1. $0 < \phi < 3 + 2\sqrt{2}$.
Case 2. $3 + 2\sqrt{2} < \phi$.

Since $3 + 2\sqrt{2} \sim 5.8$, responders are appreciably noisier than proposers in the second case.

Lemma 1 Let R be the set of rest points of the system (8)–(9) for values of $(\delta_I, \delta_{II}, \Delta_I, \Delta_{II})$ near $(0, 0, 1, 1)$.

In case 1, the set R has at most one limit point, which is the subgame-perfect equilibrium $S = (0, 1)$.

In case 2, the set R has at most three limit point $S = (0, 1), (1, \underline{y})$ and $(1, \bar{y})$. The points $(1, \underline{y})$ and $(1, \bar{y})$ lie in the set N of Nash equilibria.

Proof Writing $\dot{x} = \dot{y} = 0$ and $(\delta_I, \delta_{II}, \Delta_I, \Delta_{II}) = (0, 0, 1, 1)$ in (8)–(9) yields $(0, 0)$, $(0, 1)$ and $(1, y)$ as candidates for the limit points of R. The first point is a source for the unperturbed dynamics, and is easily excluded as a limit point of R. We now consider the possible values of y. To this end, write $\dot{x} = \dot{y} = 0$ in (8)–(9) and then set $x = 1$. We then obtain the equation

S

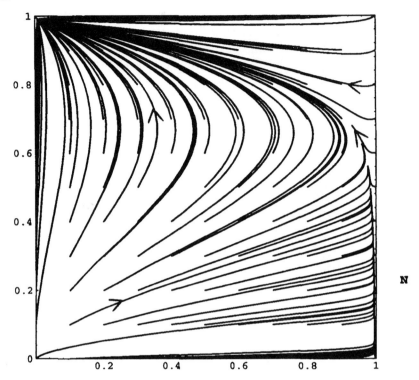

Figure C.3
Phase diagram, comparable noise ($\delta_{\mathrm{I}} = \delta_{\mathrm{II}} = 0.01$).

$$\phi = \frac{y(1-y)}{(2-3y)(2y-1)}.$$

This equation, illustrated in figure C.6, has two solutions, $\underline{y}$ and $\bar{y}$, satisfying $\frac{1}{2} < \underline{y} < 2 - \sqrt{2} < \bar{y} < \frac{2}{3}$ when $\phi > 3 + 2\sqrt{2}$. When $\phi < 3 + \sqrt{2}$, the equation has no solutions y satisfying $0 \le y \le 1$. ∎

Proposition 2 Let $A(\delta_{\mathrm{I}}, \delta_{\mathrm{II}}, \Delta_{\mathrm{I}}, \Delta_{\mathrm{II}})$ be the set of asymptotic attractors of the system (8)–(9) given values $(\delta_{\mathrm{I}}, \delta_{\mathrm{II}}, \Delta_{\mathrm{I}}, \Delta_{\mathrm{II}})$.

In case 1, the set A has a unique limit point as $(\delta_{\mathrm{I}}, \delta_{\mathrm{II}}, \Delta_{\mathrm{I}}, \Delta_{\mathrm{II}}) \to (0, 0, 1, 1)$, which is the subgame-perfect equilibrium $S = (0, 1)$.

In case 2, the set A has two limit points as $(\delta_{\mathrm{I}}, \delta_{\mathrm{II}}, \Delta_{\mathrm{I}}, \Delta_{\mathrm{II}}) \to (0, 0, 1, 1)$, which are $S = (0, 1)$ and $(1, \underline{y})$. (The point $(1, \bar{y})$ is a limit of saddles.)

s

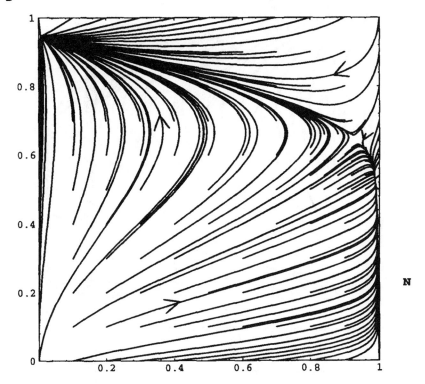

Figure C.4
Phase diagram, more noise in population II ($\delta_{\mathrm{I}} = 0.01, \delta_{\mathrm{II}} = 0.1$).

The first case gives rise to the phase diagram in figure C.3; the second case to the phase diagram in figure C.4.

Proof The proof of the first statement is straightforward, and we consider only the second. The right side of (8)–(9) defines a function $F : \mathbb{R}^2 \to \mathbb{R}^2$ for which

$$DF(x, y) = \begin{pmatrix} \Delta_{\mathrm{I}}(2 - 3y)(1 - 2x) - \delta_{\mathrm{I}} & -3\Delta_{\mathrm{I}}x(1 - x) \\ -\Delta_{\mathrm{II}}y(1 - y) & \Delta_{\mathrm{II}}(1 - 2y)(1 - x) - \delta_{\mathrm{II}} \end{pmatrix}.$$

The trace of this matrix is negative when $\frac{1}{2} < y < \frac{2}{3}$ and $x > \frac{1}{2}$. We therefore consider the limiting value of its determinant.

Multiply the second column of $\det DF(x, y)$ by $2y - 1$ and then make the substitution $\delta_{\mathrm{II}}(2y - 1) = 2\Delta_{\mathrm{II}}y(1 - y)(1 - x)$, which holds at a rest point by virtue of (8)–(9). Factor out the term $\Delta_{\mathrm{I}}\Delta_{\mathrm{II}}(1 - x)$ and write $\delta_{\mathrm{I}} = 0$ and $x = 1$ in what remains. We then have to sign the determinant

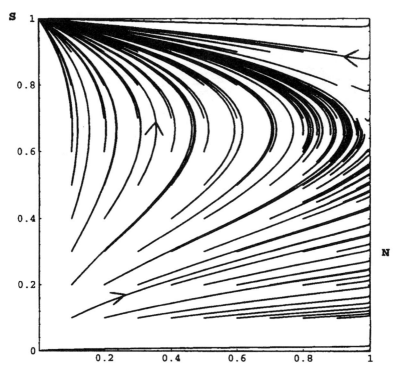

Figure C.5
Phase diagram, endogenous noise ($\alpha - \beta = 0.01$).

$$\begin{vmatrix} 2 - 3y & 3(2y - 1) \\ y(1 - y) & 2y^2 - 2y + 1 \end{vmatrix} = y^2 - 4y + 2.$$

The roots of the quadratic equation $y^2 - 4y + 2 = 0$ are $2 - \sqrt{2}$ and $2 + \sqrt{2}$. It follows that the determinant is positive when $y = \underline{y} \leq 2 - \sqrt{2}$ and negative when $y = \bar{y} < \frac{2}{3} < 2 + \sqrt{2}$. Thus $\underline{y}$ is an asymptotic attractor and $\bar{y}$ is not.   ∎

We next briefly consider the effect of endogenizing the noise in (8)–(9) by writing $\Delta_{\mathrm{I}} = c_{\mathrm{I}}(1 - \delta_{\mathrm{I}}(t))$ and $\Delta_{\mathrm{II}} = c_{\mathrm{II}}(1 - \delta_{\mathrm{II}}(t))$, where c_{I} and c_{II} are constants and $\delta_{\mathrm{I}}(t)$ and $\delta_{\mathrm{II}}(t)$ are given by (5). We study the rest points of this system as β approaches zero, for small values of α. Figure C.5 shows the trajectories for this case.[24] We have:

24. An asymptotic attractor exists, though it is difficult to see, at approximately $(1, 0.505)$.

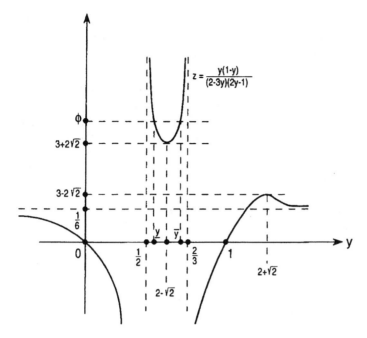

Figure C.6
Determining $\underline{y}$ and $\bar{y}$.

Proposition 3   Let A be the set of asymptotic attractors for (8)–(9) with endogenous noise when $\beta > 0$ is small. For sufficiently small α, A has two limit points $S = (0, 1)$ and $(1, \underline{y})$ as $\beta \to 0$. As $\alpha \to 0$, these limit points converger to $(0, 1)$ and $\left(1, \frac{1}{2}\right)$.

Proof   The first statement follows from an argument analogous to that of the previous proposition, along with the observation that, as $x \to 1$, the difference between the minimum and maximum of player II's payoffs approaches zero, so that $\delta_{II}(t)/\delta_{I}(t)$ gets very large for sufficiently small α. As $\alpha \to 0$, the limiting ratio of $\delta_{II}(t)/\delta_{I}(t)$ approaches infinity, in which case we see from figure C.6 that the limiting values of $\underline{y}$ and $\bar{y}$ approach $\frac{1}{2}$ and $\frac{2}{3}$ respectively.   ∎

We can identify the forces behind these results. When nearly all proposers are playing H, the pressure for a responder to play Y is weak. Adding noise to the strategies of the proposer pushes the population of proposers away from H, and increases the pressure for responders to move towards Y. This pushes the system toward the subgame-perfect equilibrium. However, the responders are also noisy. In the absence of other forces, this noise creates a drift that would eventually result in the responding population being split equally between agents who play Y and agents who play N. But the best reply for a proposer against such a mix in the responding population is to play H. If the drift in the responding population is sufficiently strong, it overpowers the countervailing tendency towards the subgame-perfect equilibrium. As a result the responding population remains close enough to a half–half mix of Y and N that the best reply for proposers continues to be H. The subgame-perfect equilibrium then fails to be selected.

The same intuition can be expressed in a more quantitative form. The dynamic system give by (6)–(7) can be represented as a vector field on the state space $[0,1]^2$, associating with each point (x, y) a vector

$$(x(1-x)(2-3y), y(1-y)(1-x)) \tag{10}$$

indicating the direction and strength of moment at (x, y). Along the component N illustrated in figure C.1c, these vectors are all zero vectors. The perturbed system (8)–(9) is the sum of the vector field given by (10) and a vector field of perturbations given by

$$\left((\Delta_{\mathrm{I}} - 1)x(1-x)(2-3y) + \delta_{\mathrm{I}}\left(\frac{1}{2} - x \right), \right.$$

$$\left. (\Delta_{\mathrm{II}} - 1)y(1-y)(1-x) + \delta_{\mathrm{II}}\left(\frac{1}{2} - y \right) \right). \tag{11}$$

Because the vector (10) is zero on N, the behavior of (8)–(9) on N is driven by the perturbations given in (11). The key question here is whether we can find a subset $\overline{N} \subset N$ such that the perturbations on $\overline{N}$ point into the basin of attraction of $\overline{N}$ in the *unperturbed* dynamics given by (10). If such an $\overline{N}$ exists, then the perturbations have the effect of continually pushing points near $\overline{N}$ back into the basin of attraction of $\overline{N}$. The dynamics (8)–(9) will then have an asymptotic attractor that is close to $\overline{N}$ and that converges to $\overline{N}$ as noise levels become small.

What does this have to do with relative noise levels? Let $\overline{N} = [0, y + \varepsilon)$ for some small $\varepsilon > 0$. Notice that this set includes the half-half mixture between Y and N, and recall that responder perturbations are pushing responders toward the half–half mixture of Y and N. At the same time, proposer perturbations are pushing proposers toward the strategy L, which in turn creates pressure for responders to switch to Y. The larger the ratio δ_{II} to δ_{I}, the stronger the net perturbation pushing responders toward the half–half mixture, and the more likely the resulting perturbations to point into the basin of attraction of $\bar{N}$. Notice that only relative noise levels matter in determining the *direction* of the perturbation vectors, which (combined with the fact that (10) is zero on N) explains why the argument holds for arbitrarily small absolute noise levels.

Two implications of this argument are immediate. First, if the payoff 3 is replaced by 5 in the Ultimatum Minigame, then the best response to a half–half mixture of Y and N is L, so that the preturbed dynamics can never point into the basin of attraction of a subset of N. The dynamics then lead to the subgame-perfect equilibrium regardless of relative noise levels. Second, even after replacing 3 by 5, we could induce the perturbations to point into the basin of attraction of a subset of N if we altered the specification of the responders' behavior (when noisy) to put a large probability on N rather than a probability of $\frac{1}{2}$ on N. We see here the sensitivity of the results to the specification of noisy behavior.

This argument also provides an idea as to how sensitive our results are to the specification of the unperturbed learning dynamic, which we have taken to be the replicator dynamic. The precise form of this dynamic is not particularly important, as long as the points in N are rest points and the set N has a basin of attraction into which perturbations can point. This excludes pure best-reply dynamics, in which even an arbitrarily small payoff difference between Y and N causes all responders to immediately switch to Y. However, virtually any system in which growth rates of strategy proportions are smooth, increasing functions of expected payoff differences (with growth rates being zero when all strategies have the same expected payoff) has the desired property.[25] The existence of an asymptotic attractor close to the component of equilibria that are not subgame perfect therefore holds for a wide class of dynamic processes, although the precise location of this attractor will be sensitive to the specification of the process.

These results address long-run behavior. What about the medium run? Figures C.3 and C.4 reveal medium-run behavior matching that reported in table C.4 for the full Ultimatum Game. The trajectories in figure C.3 reach the subgame-perfect equilibrium S in the long run, but in the medium run they can first approach the set N of Nash equilibria that are not subgame perfect. In figure C.4 (where $\delta_I < \delta_{II}$), some trajectories again approach N in the medium run, but in these case these trajectories never leave the vicinity of N.

---

25. Samuelson (1988) describes such systems as "cardinal" (as opposed to "ordinal").

These results allow us to return to the question of fairness. Experimental results in bargaining games are now seldom explained *purely* in terms of fairness norms. Prasnikar and Roth (1992) and Roth et al. (1991), for example, suggest that some experimental results are best described in terms of a trade-off between strategic and fairness factors. Their most striking example contrasts the Ultimatum Game with the Best Shot Game. The latter is a public-goods-provision game that, like the Ultimatum Game, features a unique subgame-perfect equilibrium in which the first mover's payoff is much higher than the second mover's.

Prasnikar and Roth find experimental outcomes for the Ultimatum Game that are not close to subgame perfection. On the other hand, their Best Shot outcomes are consistent with a subgame-perfect explanation. They suggest that fairness considerations are able to wrestle outcomes away from subgame-perfection in the Ultimatum Game, but are overwhelmed by strategic considerations in the Best Shot Game. In adopting this interpretation, they note that the Best Shot Game has only one pure-strategy Nash equilibrium that is not subgame perfect. The payoff pair resulting from this Nash equilibrium is $(0.4, 3.7)$. The payoff pair at the rival subgame-perfect equilibrium is $(3.7, 0.4)$. Prasnikar and Roth argue that there is then very little scope for learning to reinforce movements of behavior away from the subgame-perfect equilibrium, and hence very little scope for fairness considerations to gain a foothold. This contrasts with the Ultimatum Game, where the presence of Nash equilibria that are close to the unique subgame-perfect outcome provides opportunity for movements away from subgame perfection (perhaps induced by fairness considerations) to be reinforced.

Our methodology offers a potential explanation of such results that, in keeping with our discussion in section C.4, does not require treating "fairness" as a primitive concept. To make this point, we contrast the Best Shot Minigame of figure C.7 with the Ultimatum Minigame of figure C.1. In the Best Shot Minigame, player I has the option of making a high (H) or low (L) contribution to the public good. If player I makes a high contribution, the player II is assumed to make a low contribution. If player I makes a low contribution, then player II has the choice of a high or low contribution. The payoffs are such that there is no gain to both players making a high contribution and each player is better off if the other player makes the high contribution.

As figure C.7 indicates, the Best Shot Minigame has the same qualitative features as the Ultimatum Game, with a subgame-perfect equilibrium

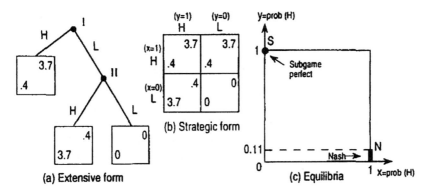

Figure C.7
Best Shot Minigame.

S of (L, H) and a component N of Nash equilibria in which player I plays H. However, the strategic incentives associated with these equilibria differ, with this difference making it very much more likely that our model will select a Nash equilibrium that is not subgame-perfect in the Ultimatum Minigame than in the Best Shot Minigame. In particular, notice that N is much smaller than the corresponding Ultimatum Game component. Nash equilibria that are not subgame perfect in the Best Shot Game require that player II uses H with a probability no higher than approximately 0.11. As a result the basin of attraction of this component relative to the unperturbed replicator dynamics is small. Moreover, if perturbations are introduced in which H and L receive the same probability from players who misread the game, then the perturbed dynamics cannot point into the basin of attraction of N. In contrast to the Ultimatum Minigame, no local attractor can therefore be found close to N and the subgame-perfect equilibrium is necessarily selected in the Best Shot Minigame.[26]

C.6   The Relevance of Replicator Dynamics

Why do we think the replicator dynamics, with their origins in biology, are relevant? Börgers and Sarin (1993) have shown that the replicator dynamics can serve as an approximation to simple learning models related

---

26. A local attractor could be created close to N, but this requires perturbations that are very heavily weighted toward L.

to that used by Roth and Erev (1993). In this section we present a simple model of social evolution that also leads to the replicator dynamic. Our purpose is not to argue that the replicator dynamics represent "the" right model but only to argue that dynamics of their general type are worthy of our attention.[27]

We interpret our model as one of social evolution because it relies on the ability of players to observe others' strategies; information that is generally not available in the laboratory. The reinforcement learning model of Börgers and Sarin (1993) is perhaps better suited as a model of learning in experiments. As explained in section C.3, both types of learning seem relevant to explaining experimental data.

Divide time into discrete periods of length τ. In every period, each agent retains his current strategy with probability $1 - \tau$. With probability τ, the agent compares his payoff with an aspiration level Λ, which is random and uniformly distributed on $[l, L]$. If the agent receives a payoff exceeding Λ, then the agent does not switch strategies. If the agent's payoff falls short of Λ, then the agent randomly chooses a new strategy. The probability that a given strategy is chosen is taken to be the proportion of the population playing that strategy. For example, it may be that the agent chooses a new strategy by randomly selecting another member of the population and imitating his strategy.

Why is Λ random? Our preferred interpretation here is that the aspiration level is actually fixed while the payoffs in the game are random,[28] though we find it analytically convenient to work with the equivalent formulation of a random aspiration level. This is consistent with the view we used to motivate our noisy dynamics, namely that players are constantly involved in a multitude of different games and may misperceive the precise nature of the game.

Let $p_i(t)$ be the probability that the aspiration level Λ exceeds the payoff from a proposer's strategy i in period t. We assume that exactly $p_i(t)$ of the proposers playing strategy i at time t are dealt an aspiration level in excess of their payoffs, and that these proposers switch to new strategies in exactly the same proportions as these strategies are used in the population of proposers. Then

27. See Binmore and Samuelson (1993) and Cabrales (1993) for similar arguments. See Bendor et al. (1991) for another aspiration learning model.

28. We then implicitly assume that the dispersion of the payoff distribution around its mean does not vary over strategies or players. More realistic assumptions would lead to more complex dynamics.

$$x_i(t + \tau) = x_i(t)(1 - \tau p_i(t)) + \sum_{j \in S} \tau p_j(t) x_j(t) x_i(t). \tag{12}$$

Note that $p_i(t) = (L - \pi_i(t))/(L - l)$, where $\pi_i(t)$ is the payoff to strategy i in period t. Hence

$$\frac{x_i(t + \tau) - x_i(t)}{\tau} = x_i(t) \frac{\pi_i(t) - \bar{\pi}_I(t)}{L - l},$$

where $\bar{\pi}_I(t)$ is the average payoff over all proposers' strategies. Taking the limit as $\tau \to 0$ leads to a continuous-time version of the dynamic:

$$\dot{x}_i = x_i \frac{\pi_i - \bar{\pi}_I}{L - l}. \tag{13}$$

A similar equation can be derived for responders. The replicator dynamic given by (1)–(2) is the special case in which time has been rescaled so as to eliminate the constant $L - l$.[29]

Now suppose that each proposer ignores the learning process with probability δ_I in each period. Given that the learning process is ignored, with probability τ such an agent abandons his strategy regardless of aspiration level considerations and randomly chooses a new strategy, giving strategy i probability θ_i.

The dynamic given by (12) now becomes[30]

$$x_i(t + \tau) = (1 - \delta_I) \left\{ x_i(t)(1 - \tau p_i(t)) + \sum_{j \in S} \tau p_j(t) x_j(t) x_i(t) \right\}$$

$$+ \delta_I [x_i(t) + \tau(\theta_i(t) - x_i(t))].$$

But $p_i(t) = (L - \pi_i(t))/(L - l)$. As $\tau \to 0$, we obtain

$$\dot{x}_i = (1 - \delta_I) x_i(t) \frac{\pi_i(t) - \bar{\pi}_I(t)}{L - l} + \delta_I(\theta_i - x_i(t)). \tag{14}$$

The noisy replicator dynamic given by (3)–(4) is the special case in which $L - l = 1$ for both populations.

We have assumed that the two populations are governed by identical learning rules. There are two obvious ways in which they may not be.

29. See Taylor and Jonker (1978) and Hofbauer and Sigmund (1988). This rescaling depends on an assumption that the distribution of the aspiration level is the same for the two players.

30. Samuelson and Zhang (1992) examine an analogous dynamic, with the random choices interpreted as errors in passing strategies (or genes) from one generation to the next.

First, the populations may be characterized by different values of $L - l$. This is equivalent to saying that the unperturbed dynamics presented in (1)–(2) may proceed at different speeds of the two populations.[31] Consider the Ultimatum Minigame. The faster is the relative rate at which population I learns, the larger is the basin of attraction of the component of Nash equilibria N that are not subgame perfect. This makes it more likely that the perturbations on this component will point into its basin of attraction, and hence more likely that the dynamics do not lead to the subgame-perfect equilibria.

Alternatively, the rates of learning in the perturbed dynamics (3)–(4) may be different. This would correspond to a situation in which learn draws come at different rates for the two populations.[32] It is easy to show that changing the rate at which learning proceeds is equivalent to rescaling payoffs (i.e., multiplying by a constant) and noise levels.[33] As the relative rate at which learning procees for population II increases, we are again more likely to observe outcomes that are not subgame-perfect.

C.7   Conclusion

To the question of whether the subgame-perfect equilibrium should be regarded as the one and only game-theoretic prediction for the Ultimatum Game, we hope that we have provided a convincing and firmly negative answer. But what distinguishes our model from other theories of equilibrium selection in the long run, notably fairness theories? Neither our theory nor fairness theories are open to straightforward refutation, since both leave an apologist with ample room for maneuver in explaining the data. In particular, our theory requires tailoring the initial conditions and the noise that perturbes the dynamics to the experimental environment. We hope that our models will not have to be altered radically in moving between environments, as seems to be necessary with fairness models. However, the final word on these questions will have to await further research on a variety of other games. We hope to report such results soon.

---

31. One might, for example, make the speed of learning endogenous by linking it to the payoff magnitudes involved, just as we have done with noise levels.

32. Again, these rates might be linked to payoff differences.

33. For example, increasing the rate at which time proceeds by replacing $\dot{x}$ with $k\dot{x}$ for $k < 1$ is equivalent to multiplying all payoffs by $1/k > 1$ and multiplying the noise level by $1/k$ (or multiplying the parameters α and β by $1/k$ in our endogenous noise cases).

References

Andreoni, J., and J. H. Miller. 1993. Auctions with aritificial adaptive agents. Mimeo. University of Wisconsin, Madison, WI; Carnegie Mellon University, Pittsburgh, PA.

Bendor, J., D. Mookherjee, and D. Ray. 1991. Aspiration-based adaptive learning in two person repeated games. Mimeo. Indian Statistical Institute.

Binmore, K. 1987/1988. Modeling rational players: I and II. *Economics and Philosophy* 3: 179–214; 4: 9–55.

Binmore, K. 1990. *Essays on the Foundations of Game Theory*. Cambridge, MA: Basil Blackwell.

Binmore, K. 1992. *Fun and Games*. Lexington, MA: D.C. Heath.

Binmore, K., and L. Samuelson. 1993. Muddling through: Noisy equilibrium selection. Mimeo. University College London; University of Wisconsin.

Binmore, K., and L. Samuelson. 1994. An economist's perspective on the evolution of norms. *Journal of Institutional Theoretical Economics* 150: 45–63.

Binmore, K., L. Samuelson, and R. Vaughan. 1993. Musical chairs: Modelling noisy evolution. Mimeo. University College London; University of Wisconsin.

Binmore, K., A. Shaked, and J. Sutton. 1989. An outside option experiment. *Quarterly Journal of Economics* 104: 753–70.

Binmore, K., J. Swierzbinski, S. Hsu, and C. Proulx. 1992. Focal points and bargaining. Discussion paper. University of Michigan.

Bolton, G. E. 1991. A comparative model of bargaining: Theory and evidence. *American Economic Review* 81: 1096–1136.

Bolton, G. E., and R. Zwick. 1993. Anonymity versus punishment in ultimatum bargaining. Mimeo. Pennsylvania State University.

Börgers, T., and R. Sarin. 1993. Learning through reinforcement and replicator dynamics. Technical report. University College London.

Cabrales, A. 1993. Stochastic replicator dynamics. Mimeo. University of California, San Diego.

Crawford, V. P. 1991. An "evolutionary" interpretation of Van Huyck, Battalio, and Beil's experimental results on coordination. *Games and Economic Behavior* 3: 25–59.

Crawford, V. R. 1992. Adaptive dynamics in coordination games. Department of Economics working paper 92-02R. University of California, San Diego.

Frank, R. 1988. *Passions within Reason*. New York: Norton.

Güth, W., R. Schmittberger, and B. Schwarze. 1982. An experimental analysis of ultimatum bargaining. *Journal of the Economic Behavior Organization* 3: 367–88.

Güth, W., and R. Tietz. 1990. Ultimatum bargaining behavior: A survey and comparison of experimental results. *Journal of Economic Psychology* 11: 417–49.

Hofbauer, J., and K. Sigmund. 1988. *The Theory of Evolution and Dynamical Systems*. Cambridge: Cambridge University Press.

Kahneman, D., and A. Tversky. 1988. Rational choice and the framing of decisions. In *Decision Making*. Cambridge: Cambridge University Press.

Kandori, M., G. J. Mailath, and R. Rob. 1993. Learning, mutation, and long run equilibria in games. *Econometrica* 61: 29–56.

Kohlberg, E., and J.-F. Mertens. 1986. On the strategic stability of equilibria. *Econometrica* 54: 1003–38.

Ledyard, J. 1992. Public goods: A survey of experimental research. Working paper. California Institute of Technology.

Miller, J. H., and J. Andreoni. 1991. Can evolutionary dynamics explain free riding in experiments? *Economic Letters* 36: 9–15.

Myerson, R. B. 1991. *Game Theory: Analysis of Conflict.* Cambridge: Harvard University Press.

Ochs, J., and A. E. Roth. 1989. An experimental study of sequential bargaining. *American Economic Review* 79: 355–84.

Prasnikar, V., and A. E. Roth. 1992. Considerations of fairness and strategy: Experimental data from sequential games. *Quarterly Journal of Economics* 106: 865–88.

Roth, A. E. 1994. Bargaining experiments. In J. Kagel and A. E. Roth, eds., *Handbook of Experimental Economics.* Princeton: Princeton University Press.

Roth, A. E., and I. Erev. 1993. Learning in extensive-form games: Experimental data and simple dynamic models in the intermediate term. Mimeo. University of Pittsburgh; The Technion.

Roth, A. E., V. Prasnikar, M. Okuno-Fujiwara, and S. Zamir. 1991. Bargaining and market power in Jerusalem, Ljubljana, Pittsburgh, and Tokyo: An experimental study. *American Economic Review* 81: 1068–95.

Samuelson, L. 1988. Evolutionary foundations of solution concepts for finite, two-player, normal-form games. In M. Y. Vardi, ed., *Theoretical Aspects of Reasoning about Knowledge.* San Mateo, CA: Morgan Kaufmann.

Samuelson, L. 1993. Does evolution eliminate dominated strategies? In K. Binmore, A. Kirman, and P. Tani, eds., *Frontiers of Game Theory.* Cambridge: MIT Press.

Samuelson, L., 1994. Stochastic stability in games with alternative best replies. *Journal of Economic Theory* 64: 35–65.

Samuelson, L., and J. Zhang. 1992. Evolutionary stability in asymmetric games. *Journal of Economic Theory* 57: 363–91.

Schlag, K. H. 1994. Why imitate, and if so, how? Mimeo. University of Bonn.

Selten, R. 1975. Reexamination of the perfectness concept for equilibrium points in extensive-form games. *International Journal of Game Theory* 4: 25–55.

Selten, R. 1978. The chain-store paradox. *Theory Decision* 9: 127–59.

Smith, V. 1976. Experimental economics: Induced value theory. *American Economic Review* 66: 274–79.

Taylor, P. D., and L. B. Jonker. 1978. Evolutionarily stable strategies and game dynamics. *Mathematical Biosciences* 40: 145–56.

Thaler, R. H. 1988. Anomalies: The Ultimatum Game. *Journal of Economic Perspective* 2: 185–206.

van Damme, E. 1987. *Stability and Perfection of Nash Equilibria.* Berlin: Springer-Verlag.

Young, P. 1993. The evolution of conventions. *Econometrica* 61: 57–84.

D Generalizing Rubinstein

Various accounts of extensions of Rubinstein's ideas are available, for example, Binmore et al. (1982, 1992), Binmore (1985), Binmore and Dasgupta (1987), Osborne and Rubinstein (1990), and Muthoo (1999). The paper reproduced here is an attempt to offer a mathematically undemanding version of the theory that remains sufficiently general for most applied work.

Bargaining Theory without Tears

Ken Binmore

D.1 Introduction

The purpose of this article is twofold. The primary aim is to provide a simple proof of a version of Rubinstein's (1982) bargaining theorem in a setting that is sufficiently general to cover the situations that typically arise in applications. In particular, the feasible set is not assumed to be convex and a reasonably general view is taken of the manner is which disagreement may arise.

The secondary aim pursues some points made in Binmore et al. (1986). A detailed analysis of subgame-perfect equilibria in a complicated non-cooperative bargaining model is unnecessary for most applications. Much heavy computation can be short-circuited by applying certain simple principles directly rather than deriving them anew each time they are required. The methodology is illustrated in section D.8 for a model of decentralized price formation.

D.2 The Alternating-Offers Model

Rather than setting the story directly in utility space, it will be told in terms of the classic problem of "dividing the dollar." A philanthropist donates a dollar to Adam and Eve on condition that they are able to agree on how to share it. Disagreement may arise in various ways. A player may abandon the negotiations in favor of his or her best outside option leaving the other to do the same. Or the philanthropist may lose patience if agreement is delayed and withdraw his offer. If either of these eventualities occurs, the negotiations will be said to have broken down. Even without a breakdown, agreement may not be reached since it is open to the players to sit at the negotiation table for ever.

The result of bargaining under precisely specified rules will be studied. All action takes place at times $n\tau$ $(n = 0, 1, 2, \ldots)$, where $\tau > 0$. Adam is active when n is even. Eve is active when n is odd. If the game has not already ended at time $n\tau > 0$, the philanthropist begins by withdrawing his dollar with probability $\pi = \lambda\tau < 1$. The game continues with probability $\bar{\pi} = 1 - \pi$. The active player then decides whether to opt out. If the active player opts in, then he or she continues by making a proposal on how to split the dollar. The passive player then accepts or refuses. Only after a refusal does the clock advance by τ. The passive player then becomes active and the above sequence of events is repeated. The game begins at time $n = 0$ but, in this first period, the steps in which the dollar may be withdrawn and in which Adam may opt out are skipped. The very first move therefore consists of Adam's making a proposal. The second move consists of Eve's response. If she refuses, the sequence of events described in the previous paragraph commences with $n = 1$. Figure D.1 illustrates the order of moves.[1]

D.3   Preferences

Adam is taken to be player 1 and Eve to be player 2. The set of possible deals is identified with

$$\Omega - \{\omega : \omega_1 + \omega_2 \leq 1\}.$$

Notice that it is assumed that money can be burned or borrowed and transferred freely between the players. Osborne and Rubinstein (1990), for example, assume that such transactions are impossible.[2] The point $\beta \in \Omega$ represents a pair of breakdown payments. These are the payments that each player will receive if the negotiations break down.[3]

---

1. Most of the sequencing in this specification is unimportant to the results. That chosen is largely for mathematical convenience. However, it is important that the active player's opting out decision does not occur immediately *after* the passive player has refused an offer. Otherwise, further equilibria appear (Shaked 1987). But a model in which a player cannot leave without hearing one final offer from the opponent seems more realistic. The anomalous first period allows a more elegant statement of some results since then Adam will never actually opt out in equilibrium. It is, of course, trivial to extend the analysis using backward induction to the case when the first period is not anomalous.

2. Hence Osborne and Rubinstein (1990) are able to find equilibria in circumstances when they would not otherwise exist. The approach taken here seems more natural.

3. The case when *different* payments are received depending on whether someone opts out or the dollar is withdrawn has been considered elsewhere (e.g., Binmore et al. 1992). The only new difficulties are combinatorial, but the interest of this more general case does not seem sufficient to justify the extra algebra.

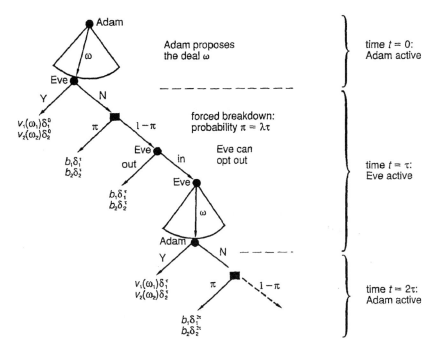

Figure D.1
Rules of the bargaining game

Player i's utility for the outcome $\omega \in \Omega$ at time t is taken to be

$$u_i(\omega, t) = v_i(\omega_i)\delta_i^t, \tag{1}$$

where the discount factor δ_i satisfies $0 < \delta_i \leq 1$. (The corresponding discount rate ρ_i is defined by $\delta_i = e^{-\rho_i}$). To economize on notation, we write $\Delta_i = \delta_i^\tau$. Recall that $\pi = \lambda\tau$. Thus, in what follows, both Δ_i and π are always functions of τ. The function $v_i : \mathbb{R} \to \mathbb{R}$ is assumed to be continuous and strictly increasing. Its range is an open interval R_1. We take $b_i = v_i(\beta_i)$. The breakdown point b then lies in $R_1 \times R_2$.

The Pareto frontier of the set X of utility pairs available at time 0 is the graph of the function f defined by

$$f(x_1) = v_2(1 - v_1^{-1}(x_1)).$$

Both $f : R_1 \to R_2$ and its inverse $f^{-1} : R_2 \to R_1$ are continuous and strictly decreasing. Note that $b \in X$ so that $b_2 \leq f(b_1)$ and $b_1 \leq f^{-1}(b_2)$.

It remains to discuss how the players assess the consequences of the perpetual disagreement outcome D. This is assigned utility $u_i(D) = 0$ so as to be consistent with the result of allowing $t \to \infty$ in (1). In addition it is assumed that $0 \in \bar{R}_1 \times \bar{R}_2$ and $b \geq 0$.

A situation in which the players use strategies that rule out the possibility of agreement being reached but do not result in either player ever opting out will be called a deadlock. A deadlock leads to the outcome D with positive probability only when $\pi = 0$. Otherwise, the expected utility to player i from a deadlock is

$$\pi b_i \Delta_i + \pi b_i \Delta_i (\bar{\pi}\Delta_i) + \pi b_i \Delta_i (\bar{\pi}\Delta_i)^2 + \cdots = \frac{\pi b_i \Delta_i}{1 - \bar{\pi}\Delta_i} \tag{2}$$

If v_1 and v_2 are concave, then so is f. It follows that X is convex. If X is not convex, we specifically do *not* replace it by its convex hull as is normal practice. It is frequently unrealistic to suppose that agreement on a lottery is feasible. A union boss, for example, cannot report to his members that their wage settlement was decided by tossing a coin. Where lotteries are feasible, Ω should be replaced by the set of all lotteries with prizes in Ω. A simpler theory then results.

Notes

1. Fishburn and Rubinstein (1982) show that relatively mild assumptions on preference relations guarantee a utility representation of the form (1). In particular, (1) substitutes in this paper for the conditions (A1) through (A5) of Osborne and Rubinstein (1990). Their condition (A6) is not used here.

2. Expressing the basic problem in terms of "dividing the dollar" clarifies the interpretation but may obscure the generality of the treatment. All that really matters is the shape of the set X of feasible utility pairs and the values of δ_1, δ_2, π, and b. Geometric characterizations of the equilibrium outcomes in such a setting are easily obtained (Binmore 1987). Algebraic characterizations, as studied here, require more labor.

3. If $\pi > 0$, the utility functions must be understood in the sense of Von Neumann and Morgenstern. If $\pi = 0$, expected utility calculations are not necessary and so any utility function representation will suffice. This observation permits the study of various cases not obviously included in the scope of the analysis. In particular, Rubinstein's (1982) case of "fixed costs of disagreement" is accessible. Player i's utility for the deal w at time t is then $U_i(w, t) = w_i - \gamma_i t$, where $\gamma_i > 0$. Rubinstein's version has to be supplemented here by requiring that, if someone opts out at time t,

then player i gets $-\gamma_i t$. One takes $u_i(w,t) = \exp U_i(w,t)$ and $\delta_i = e^{-\gamma_i}$. Then $v_i(x) = e^x$ is far from concave. Notice that $f : (0, \infty) \rightarrow (0, \infty)$ is given by $f(x) = e/x$ and $b = (1,1)$. The example is useful because it exhibits various pathologies.

D.4 Stationary Subgame-Perfect Equilibria

In this section, η and ξ are Pareto-efficient deals in Ω. The utilities assigned to these deals at time 0 by the two players are given by $y_i = v_i(\eta_i)$ and $z_i = v_i(\xi_i)$. Notice that $y_2 = f(y_1)$ and $z_2 = f(z_1)$.

Adam will be assumed to use a pure strategy s that requires him to

1. Propose η whenever called upon for a proposal;

2. Accept ξ or better and to refuse anything worse whenever called upon for a response.

Eve will be assumed to use a pure strategy t that has the same properties except that the roles of η and ξ are reversed.

When do strategies with these properties constitute a subgame-perfect equilibrium? The current section explores this question in a series of lemmas. The simple proofs are relegated to an appendix.

Define: $m_i : R_i \rightarrow \mathbb{R}$ by

$$m_i(x) = \Delta_i(\pi b_i + \bar{\pi} \max\{b_i, x\}),$$

and restrict attention to those η and ξ for which

$$\left. \begin{array}{l} y_2 = m_2(z_2) \\ z_1 = m_1(y_1) \end{array} \right\}. \tag{3}$$

These equations express the fact that the passive player will always be indifferent between accepting and refusing what is proposed.

Lemma 1 If (3) holds, then $y_1 \geq b_1$ or $z_2 \geq b_2$. Also $z_1 \leq y_1$ and $y_2 \leq z_2$.

Proof If $y_1 < b_1$, then $z_1 = \Delta_1 b_1 \leq b_1$. Since z is Pareto-efficient, it therefore cannot be that $z_2 < b_2$. If $y_1 \geq b_1$. Then $z_1 = \Delta_1(\bar{\pi} y_1 + \pi b_1) \leq \Delta_1 y_1 \leq y_1$. Thus $z_2 = f(z_1) \geq f(y_1) = y_2$. A similar argument applies if $z_2 \geq b_2$. ∎

Lemma 2 If y and z satisfy [3], then there exists a corresponding subgame-perfect equilibrium pair (s, t).

The properties given for s and t do not specify whether or not a player should opt out when the opportunity arises. Adam should opt in if $y_1 \geq b_1$ and opt out if $y_1 < b_1$. Eve should opt in if $z_2 \geq b_2$ and opt out if $z_2 < b_2$.

Proof It needs to be confirmed that proposing decisions are optimal. They are optimal because the active player cannot demand more without being refused, and he or she prefers not to be refused. In checking this last point, lemma 1 makes all the cases immediate except for that in which the active player opts out in equilibrium. Suppose, in particular, that $y_1 \geq b_1$ and $z_2 < b_2$. Then $y_2 = \Delta_2 b_2$. Hence

$$z_2 \geq y_2 = \Delta_2 b_2 \geq \Delta_2(\bar{\pi}\Delta_2 b_2 + \pi b_2) = \Delta_2(\bar{\pi} y_2 + \pi b_2).$$

It follows that Eve prefers z to be accepted than to have her proposal refused. A similar argument applies when $y_1 < b_1$ and $z_2 \geq b_2$. ∎

Lemma 3 The pair (y, z) satisfies (3) and hence specifies a stationary subgame-perfect equilibrium if and only if y_1 is a zero of the function $g : R_1 \to \mathbb{R}$ defined by

$$g(x) = f(x) - (m_2 \circ f \circ m_1)(x)$$

and $y_2 = f(y_1)$, $z_1 = m_1(y_1)$, $z_2 = f(z_1)$.

It will be necessary to investigate the properties of the function g in some detail. Note to begin with that

$$g(x) = \begin{cases} f(x) - \Delta_2[\pi b_2 + \bar{\pi} f(\Delta_1 b_1)] & \text{if } x \leq b_1, \\ f(x) - \Delta_2[\pi b_2 + \bar{\pi} f(\Delta_1(\pi b_1 + \bar{\pi} x))] & \text{if } b_1 \leq x \leq c_1, \\ f(x) - \Delta_2 b_2 & \text{if } x \geq c_1, \end{cases}$$

where $\bar{\pi} c_1 = \Delta_1^{-1} f^{-1}(b_2) - \pi b_1$. The dependence of g on r is not made explicit, since it turns out to be more convenient to study $G : R_1 \times (0, \infty) \to \mathbb{R}$, which is defined by

$$G(x, r) = \tau^{-1} g(x) \tag{4}$$

when this dependence matters.

Lemma 4 The function $g : R_1 \to \mathbb{R}$ has the following properties:

i. $x < \Delta_1 b_1 \Rightarrow g(x) > 0.$
ii. $x > f^{-1}(\Delta_2 b_2) \Rightarrow g(x) < 0.$

Proof

i. If $x < \Delta_1 b_1$, then

$$g(x) > f(\Delta_1 b_1) - \Delta_2[\pi b_2 + \bar{\pi} f(\Delta_1 b_1)]$$

$$= (1 - \Delta_2 \bar{\pi}) f(\Delta_1 b_1) - \Delta_2 \pi b_2$$

$$\geq (1 - \Delta_2 \bar{\pi}) b_2 - \Delta_2 \pi b_2$$

$$= b_2 (1 - \Delta_2) \geq 0.$$

ii. If $x > f^{-1}(\Delta_2 b_2)$, then $f(x) < \Delta_2 b_2$. If it is also true that $g(x) \geq 0$, then

$$\Delta_2 b_2 - \Delta_2[\pi b_2 + \bar{\pi} f(\Delta_1(\pi b_1 + \bar{\pi} x))] > 0$$

$$b_2 > f(\Delta_1(\pi b_1 + \bar{\pi} x))$$

$$f^{-1}(b_2) < \Delta_1(\pi b_1 + \bar{\pi} x)$$

$$x > c_1.$$

Now suppose that $f^{-1}(\Delta_2 b_2) \leq c_1$. Then $g(x) < 0$ for $f^{-1}(\Delta_2 b_2) < x \leq c_1$. Hence, $g(x) < 0$ for $x > f^{-1}(\Delta_2 b_2)$, because g is continuous and decreases on (c_1, ∞). On the other hand, if $f^{-1}(\Delta_2 b_2) > c_1$, then $x > f^{-1}(\Delta_2 b_2)$ implies that $g(x) = f(x) - \Delta_2 b_2 < 0$. ∎

Lemma 5 The function $g : R_1 \to \mathbb{R}$ always has a zero in $[\Delta_1 b_1, f^{-1}(\Delta_2 b_2)]$ and hence a stationary subgame-perfect equilibrium exists.

Proof This follows from the previous lemma because g is continuous. ∎

D.5 Nonstationary Equilibria

This section proves a generalized version of a theorem of Rubinstein (1982). The proof follows Binmore (1987), Shaked and Sutton (1984) and Binmore et al. (1989).

Let S be the set of all subgame-perfect equilibrium outcomes. The first result demonstrates that S is necessarily a large set when more than one stationary subgame-perfect equilibrium of the type considered in section D.4 exists. In particular, Pareto-inefficient outcomes lie in S.

Multiple stationary subgame-perfect equilibria exist when $g : R_1 \to \mathbb{R}$ has more than one zero. Let $(\underline{s}, \underline{t})$ be the strategy pair that corresponds to the smallest zero y_1 of g. Let $(\bar{s}, \bar{t})$ be the strategy pair corresponding to the largest zero $\bar{y}_1$.

Let T be the set of all feasible payoff pairs x that satisfy $x \geq (y_1, \bar{y}_2)$.

Lemma 6   If $x \in T$, then there exists a subgame-perfect equilibrium (s, t) in which Adam proposes a deal ξ at time 0 worth x and Eve accepts. Thus $T \subseteq S$.

Proof   Three "states of mind," UP, DOWN, and MIDDLE are distinguished. Players begin in the MIDDLE state. In this state, the subgame-perfect equilibrium (s, t) to be constructed requires Adam to propose ξ when called upon to make a proposal. Eve accepts ξ and anything at least as good as ξ. She refuses anything else.   ∎

In the UP state, (s, t) requires that the players play according to $(\bar{s}, \bar{t})$ in the remainder of the game. In the DOWN state, (s, t) requires playing according to $(\underline{s}, \underline{t})$ in the remainder of the game.

Once in the UP state, players remain there. The same applies to the DOWN state. Transitions from the MIDDLE state are made as follows. If Adam proposes ξ, then a refusal by Eve shifts both players to the UP state. If Eve refuses any other proposal, both players shift to the DOWN state.

Why is the schedule for proposal and response in the MIDDLE state optimal? Eve should accept ξ because $x_2 \geq y_2 = m_2(\bar{z}_2)$. Her response to other proposals is optimal because she gets $y_2 = m_2(z_2)$ from refusing. Adam should propose ξ because he gets at most y_1 from deviating and $x_1 \geq y_1$. (If Adam deviates to a proposal that is refused, either Eve opts out because $z_2 < b_2$ or she opts in because $z_2 \geq b_2$. In the latter case, Adam gets $\bar{\Delta}_1(\pi b_1 + \bar{\pi} z_1) \leq \Delta_1 z_1 \leq z_1 \leq y_1 \leq x_1$. In the former case, he gets $\Delta_1 b_1 \leq b_1 \leq y_2 \leq x_1$ by lemma 1.)

Next it will be shown that $S \subseteq T$. A preliminary lemma is needed.

Lemma 7   The set Y of all subgame-perfect equilibrium payoffs to Adam is $[y_1, \bar{y}_1]$.

Proof   Let $a = \inf Y$ and $A = \sup Y$. Let Z be the set of all subgame-perfect equilibrium payoffs to Eve in the companion game in which it is Eve who makes the first proposal at time 0. Write $e = \inf Z$ and $E = \sup Z$.

1. It is open to Eve to refuse whatever Adam proposes at time 0. If equilibrium strategies are used in the continuation of the game, then Eve will

get an expected payoff of at least $m_2(e)$ because the companion game will be played after a time delay of τ unless the dollar is withdrawn of Eve opts out in the interim. If equilibrium strategies are used, it follows that Eve gets at least $m_2(e)$, and so Adam gets at most $f^{-1}(m_2(e))$. Thus $A \leq f^{-1}(m_2(e))$, and so

$$f(A) \geq m_2(e). \tag{5}$$

On applying a similar argument in the companion game,

$$E \leq f(m_1(a)). \tag{6}$$

2. It is optimal for Eve to accept any proposal from Adam that assigns her a payoff $w_2 > m_2(E)$, provided that equilibrium strategies are used after a refusal. Thus Adam must get at least $f^{-1}(w_2)$. Hence $f^{-1}(w_2)$ is a lower bound for S whenever $w_2 > m_2(E)$. Thus $a \geq f^{-1}(m_2(E))$, and so

$$f(a) \leq m_2(E). \tag{7}$$

On applying a similar argument in the companion game,

$$e \geq f(m_1(A)). \tag{8}$$

3. From (5) and (8),

$$f(A) \geq m_2(e) \geq (m_2 \circ f \circ m_1)(A),$$

and hence $g(A) \geq 0$. But $g(x) < 0$ for $x > \bar{y}_1$. Thus $A \leq \bar{y}_1$. But $\bar{y}_1 \in Y$, and so $A = \bar{y}_1$.

From (6) and (7),

$$f(a) \leq m_2(E) \leq (m_2 \circ f \circ m_1)(a),$$

and hence $g(a) \leq 0$. But $g(x) > 0$ for $x < \underline{y}_1$. Thus $a \geq \underline{y}_1$. But $\underline{y}_1 \in Y$, and so $a = \underline{y}_1$.

4. It remains to confirm that $\underline{y}_1 \leq y_1 \leq \bar{y}_1$ implies $y_1 \in Y$. This follows immediately from lemma 6. ∎

Theorem 1 $S = T$.

Proof By the preceding lemma, Adam's equilibrium payoffs lie in the set $[\underline{y}_1, \bar{y}_1]$. Similarly Eve's equilibrium payoffs in the companion game lie in $[\bar{z}_2, \underline{z}_2]$. It follows that her equilibrium payoffs in the original game lie in $[\bar{y}_2, \underline{y}_2]$, since $\bar{y}_2 = m_2(\bar{z}_2)$ and $\underline{y}_2 = m_2(\underline{z}_2)$. Thus $S \subseteq T$. On the other hand, lemma 6 shows that $T \subseteq S$. ∎

Notes

1. When multiple equilibria exist, there may be subgame-perfect equilibria in which agreement is not reached immediately (Osborne and Rubinstein 1990, sec. 3.10.1).

The second and third notes concern two cases of special interest considered by Rubinstein (1982). The reason that the conclusions quoted differ from his is because the bargaining models considered are not identical.

2. In the notation of section D.3, take $v_1(x) = v_2(x) = x$ and $\pi = 0$. Then $R_1 = R_2 = \mathbb{R}$ and $f(x) = 1 - x$. The zeros of the function g are the stationary subgame-perfect equilibrium outcomes for Adam. In this case g is strictly decreasing. It follows that there is a unique equilibrium outcome. If $u = (1 - \Delta_2)/(1 - \Delta_1\Delta_2)$ satisfies $b_1 \le u \le \Delta_1^{-1}(1 - b_2)$, then Adam gets u. If $u < b_1$, then Adam will be planning to take his outside option should the opportunity arise. He gets $1 - \Delta_2(1 - \Delta_1 b_1)$ when proposing. If $u > \Delta_1^{-1}(1 - b_2)$, Eve is planning to take her outside option. Adam gets $1 - \Delta_2 b_2$.

3. The second case of interest is described in note 3 of section D.3. When $\Delta_1 > \Delta_2$, g has a unique zero at Δ_2^{-1}. In terms of money payoffs, this means that when $\gamma_1 < \gamma_2$, Adam gets $1 + \gamma_2\tau$ in equilibrium. (Eve plans to take her outside option.) When $\Delta_1 < \Delta_2$, g has a unique zero at $\Delta_1\Delta_2^{-1}$. In terms of money payoffs this means that when $\gamma_1 < \gamma_2$, Adam gets $(\gamma_2 - \gamma_1)\tau$ in equilibrium. (Adam plans to take his outside option.) When $\Delta_1 = \Delta_2 = \Delta$, g is zero on $[1, e\Delta^{-1}]$. Thus, with the notation of section D.4, $\underline{y}_1 = 1$ and, $\bar{y}_1 = e\Delta^{-1}$. Hence $\bar{y}_2 = \Delta$. Any feasible pair $x \ge (1, \Delta)$ is therefore an equilibrium outcome. In terms of money payoffs this means that when $\gamma_1 = \gamma_2 = \gamma$, the set of equilibrium outcomes is $\{\omega : \omega_1 + \omega_2 \le 1, \omega_1 \ge 0, \omega_2 \ge -\gamma r\}$.

D.6 Generalized Nash Bargaining Solutions

Much of the interest of the bargaining model described in the previous sections lies in the fact that, in the limit as $\tau \to 0+$, the equilibrium outcomes can be characterized in terms of a suitably generalized version of Nash's bargaining solution. The case $\tau \to 0+$ deserves special emphasis for at least two reasons. The first reason is that there will often be nothing that constrains players to keep to the timetable specified in the model. After refusing a proposal, they will then wish to make a counterproposal at the earliest possible opportunity.[4] The second reason is that Adam's first-mover advantage disappears in the limit as $\tau \to 0+$. In this section a generalized Nash bargaining solution will be described. Axiomatizations of the point-valued version can be found in Kalai (1977), Roth (1979), and elsewhere.

An abstract bargaining problem will be identified with a triple (X, b, d) in which X is interpreted as the set of feasible payoff pairs, b is a breakdown point whose coordinates are the players' outside options, and d is a deadlock point. As in section D.2, R_1 and R_2 are open intervals, $f : R_1 \to R_2$ is a strictly decreasing surjection and $X = \{(x_1, x_2) \in R_1 \times R_2 : x_2 \le f(x_1)\}$. Also $0 \in \bar{R}_1 \times R_2$ and $0 \le d \le b \in X$. For the remainder of the paper it will also be assumed that f is twice differentiable on R_1.

A generalized Nash product with bargaining powers $\alpha > 0$ and $\beta > 0$ is defined to be an expression of the form

$$P(x_1, x_2) = (x_1 - d_1)^\alpha (x_2 - d_2)^\beta. \tag{9}$$

When X is convex and $b = d$, the regular Nash bargaining solution introduced by Nash (1950) identifies the solution of (X, d, d) with the point n at which the Nash product P with $\alpha = \beta$ is maximized subject to the constraints $x \in X$ and $x \ge d$.

When X is not convex, a more elaborate definition is necessary. Let $p : R_1 \to \mathbb{R}$ be given by

$$p(x) = P(x, f(x)). \tag{10}$$

Attention will be restricted to the case in which $p'(x)$ is zero neither at an endpoint of the interval $[b_1, f^{-1}(b_2)]$, nor at an interior point x where $p''(x) = 0$. Only pathological cases are excluded by this restriction. The function $H : R_1 \to \mathbb{R}$ is defined by

$$H(x) = \begin{cases} +\infty & \text{if } x < b_1, \\ f'(x)\left(\dfrac{x - d_1}{\alpha}\right) + \left(\dfrac{f(x) - d_2}{\beta}\right) & \text{if } b_1 \le x \le f^{-1}(b_2), \\ -\infty & \text{if } x > f^{-1}(b_2). \end{cases}$$

This has the same sign as p' on the interval $[b_1, f^{-1}(b_2)]$. A 'zero' of H will be understood to be any $x \in R_1$ which has the property that all of its neighborhoods contain both positive and negative values of H. In view of

---

4. The limiting factors will then be physical or physiological. Modeling these will involve a reinterpretation of δ_1 and δ_2.

the preceding restrictions on p, a 'zero' of H is either an interior point z of the interval $[b_1, f^{-1}(b_2)]$, at which $H(z) = 0$, or an endpoint of the interval.

A Nash bargaining point n can now be defined to be a Pareto-efficient point of X for which n_1 is a 'zero' of H. Of all Nash bargaining points, let $\bar{n}$ be that which assigns Adam the greatest payoff (and Eve the least). Let $\underline{n}$ be that which assigns Eve the greatest payoff (and Adam the least). The generalized Nash bargaining solution corresponding to the bargaining powers $\alpha > 0$ and $\beta > 0$ for the bargaining problem (X, b, d) is the set N of all feasible payoff pairs $x \geq (\underline{n}_1, \bar{n}_2)$. The definition is illustrated in figure D.2.

Proposition 1 The point $\bar{n}$ is the local maximum of the Nash product (9) subject to $x \in X$ and $x \geq b$ that assigns Adam the greatest payoff. The point $\underline{n}$ is the local maximum that assigns Eve the greatest payoff.

Proposition 2 A sufficient condition that N consist of a single point is that $(x - d_1)f'(x)$ be concave on $[b_1, f^{-1}(b_2)]$. In particular, it is sufficient if f is concave and so X is convex.

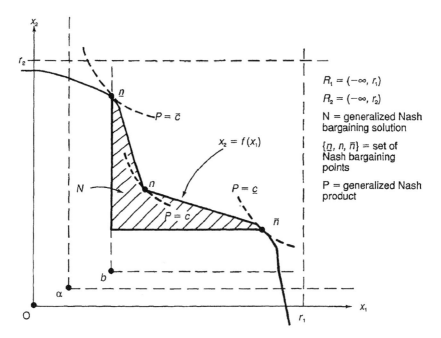

Figure D.2
A generalized Nash bargaining solution

Proof The condition implies that H is strictly decreasing on $[b_1, f^{-1}(b_2)]$.   ∎

D.7   The Nash Program

The aim of the Nash program is to provide noncooperative justifications, where possible, for the solution concepts of cooperative game theory (see, for example, the introduction to Binmore and Dasgupta 1987). The alternating offers model of sections D.2 through D.5 is important in this context since it provides a defense for the Nash bargaining solution.

Theorem 2 As $\tau \to 0$, the set of subgame-perfect equilibrium outcomes in the alternating offers model converges to the generalized Nash bargaining solution N corresponding to the bargaining powers $\alpha = 1/(\lambda + \rho_1)$ and $\beta = 1/(\lambda + \rho_2)$ for the bargaining problem (X, b, d), in which the deadlock payoff $d_i = \lambda b_i/(\lambda + \rho_i)$ is the limiting value of (2) as $\tau \to 0+$.

Proof It will be shown that the set of values of x for which the function G defined by (4) is zero converges to the set of "zeros" of the function H defined in the preceding section. The first step is the observation that for each $x \in R_1$,

$$G(x, \tau) \to H(x) \quad \text{as } \tau \to 0+.$$

On the interval $[b_1, f^{-1}(b_2)]$, this follows from L'Hôpital's rule because $c_1 > f^{-1}(b_2)$. Outside the interval, one may appeal to lemma 4 to determine the sign of G.

1. Every neighborhood of a "zero" of H contains a zero of G, provided τ is sufficiently small. With the restriction introduced in section D.6, each such neighborhood contains a point at which H is positive and a point at which H is negative. The same is therefore true of G if τ is sufficiently small. Since G is continuous, it follows that G has a zero in the neighborhood.

2. Every neighborhood that contains zeros of G for all sufficiently small τ also contains a "zero" of H. The inverval $[b_1, f^{-1}(b_2)]$ is compact, and hence G converges uniformly to H on this interval. This observation takes care of neighborhoods centered at points of $(b_1, f^{-1}(b_2))$. A trivial argument extends the conclusion to neighborhoods centered at the endpoints.   ∎

In summary, where the defense of the use of the Nash bargaining theory is to be based on an alternating offers model,[5] the "status quo" should correspond to the consequences of a deadlock (during which the players remain at the negotiation table but never reach an agreement). The outside options that they may obtain by abandoning the negotiations serve only as constraints on the range of validity of the Nash bargaining solution. Often it is convenient to apply these principles to payoff *flows*. In a wage negotiation, for example, the deadlock flows may be the income per period for the two sides during a strike.

The final result of this section is offered without a proof. In provides a criterion for the uniqueness of an equilibrium in the alternating offers model that does not depend on τ being small.

Proposition 3   A necessary condition that the alternating offers model have a unique subgame-perfect equilibrium is that N consist of a single point.

Some special cases of theorem 2 deserve mention. In each case X is assumed to be convex so that N consists of a single point.

1. $p_1 = p_2 = 0$. In this case the equilibrium outcome converges to the regular Nash bargaining solution for the problem (X, b, b). Here the breakdown and deadlock points are the same, and there is no difficulty in deciding on an appropriate "status quo" in using Nash's theory. This case arises when it is not impatience that motivates an early agreement but fear that the opportunity to reach an agreement may disappear if an agreement is delayed.

2. $p_1 = p_2 = p > 0$. In this case the equilibrium outcome converges to the regular Nash bargaining solution for the problem (X, b, d), where $d = \lambda b / (\lambda + p)$. Note the displacement of the "status quo" from b. In *symmetric* situations, this displacement leaves the location of the Nash bargaining solution unaltered. Models that mistakenly place the "status quo" at b will therefore nevertheless lead to the correct conclusions in symmetric situations.

3. $\lambda = 0$. In this case the equilibrium outcome converges to an *asymmetric*, Nash bargaining solution with bargaining powers $\alpha = 1/p_1$ and $\beta = 1/p_2$ for the problem $(X, b, 0)$. Recall that the payoff pair 0 corresponds to the perpetual disagreement point D which therefore serves as

5. Rather than, for example, Nash's (1950) own model in which players simultaneously make take-it-or-leave-it offers.

the appropriate "status quo" under these circumstances. This case arises when the players are unconcerned about the risk of losing the opportunity to reach an agreement and are motivated simply by their impatience with delays.

D.8 Decentralized Price Formation

To illustrate the principles of the preceding section, a model will now be studied in which the price at which a good is traded is determined by bargaining between buyers and sellers rather than through some centralized auctioneering mechanism. Insofar as there is an innovation as compared with Rubinstein and Wolinsky (1985), Gale (1986), or Binmore and Herrero (1988), it lies in the more realistic modeling of the circumstances of a bargaining breakdown. Wolinsky (1988) and Bester (1988) consider other variants of the model.

Each seller owns a house. If he sells the house at time t for price p, his utility is $p\delta_1^t$. The buyer gets $(1 - p)\delta_2^t$. An agent who opts out of the market or who never succeeds in consummating a deal gets zero utility. After a sale the buyer and seller leave the market but are immediately replaced by a new buyer and a new seller so that things remain in a steady state. The market therefore always contains a pool of unmatched agents looking for a bargaining partner.

The price at which the house is exchanged is determined by bargaining between individual buyers and sellers who have succeeded in finding each other. The bargaining model is based on that of section D.2, but various modifications are necessary. In particular, account needs to be taken of buyers and sellers who have yet to find a bargaining partner. Such unmatched agents are always deemed to be active.

At the beginning of each time period, *all* active agents are matched with a new partner with probability $\lambda_i \tau > 0$ $(i = 1, 2)$. A player who was passive in the preceding period and refused the proposal made by his or her partner may therefore have *two* partners in the current period. Such a player is in a powerful position because this creates an auctioning scenario.[6] The modeling of this scenario is discussed below. The next event is a decision by active players on whether or not to opt out. An unmatched player may opt out of the market altogether. A matched active player may do the same or abandon his or her current partner and

---

6. Usually this possibility is neglected by assuming that the rejection of a proposal or the discovery of a new partner dissolves the partnership.

so become unmatched. If a matched active player opts in, he or she makes a proposal that the passive player may accept or refuse. Before further events, the clock advances by τ. Any remaining passive players become active and the cycle of events is repeated.

This is a more complex problem than that discussed in preceding sections, but a full noncooperative analysis will not be described. Instead, the result of such an analysis will be predicted using the principles outlined in section D.7. These apply only in the limiting case when $\tau \to 0+$ (the case of "no bargaining frictions"). The prediction is framed in terms of an appropriate Nash bargaining solution of an appropriate bargaining problem (X, b, d). Note first that the average probability that bilateral bargaining will break down during a period of length τ is $\lambda\tau = \frac{1}{2}(\lambda_1 + \lambda_2)\tau$. The appropriate bargaining powers are therefore $\alpha = 1/(\lambda + \rho_1)$ and $\beta = 1/(\lambda + \rho_2)$. The feasible set X is the unit simplex. The value of the generalized Nash bargaining solution is therefore a payoff pair of the form $(p, 1 - p)$, where p is the price at which the house is sold. Agreement on this price will be immediate when a buyer and seller get matched.

The seller's outside option b_1 is $\lambda_1 p/(\lambda_1 + \rho_1)$. Similarly $b_2 = \lambda_2(1 - p)/(\lambda_2 + \rho_2)$. Notice that since $b_1 < p$ and $b_2 < 1 - p$, no player opts out in equilibrium. It remains to consider the deadlock point d. Matters and less simple than in section D.7. We take

$$d_1 = \frac{1}{2(\rho_1 + \lambda)}\{\lambda_2 b_1 + \lambda_1(1 - b_2)\},$$

$$d_2 = \frac{1}{2(\rho_2 + \lambda)}\{\lambda_1 b_2 + \lambda_2(1 - b_1)\}.$$

The assumption is that when *two* sellers are matched simultaneously with one buyer, the house is sold at a price equal to a seller's outside option b_1. The buyer then gets $1 - b_1$, and similarly if *two* buyers are matched with one seller.[7] The deadlock payoffs are then calculated by considering the consequences of a matched buyer and seller continuing to negotiate without reaching agreement until one finds a second partner.

The equilibrium price is then found by solving the equation

$$p = \left(\frac{\alpha}{\alpha + \beta}\right)(1 - d_2) + \left(\frac{\beta}{\alpha + \beta}\right)d_1.$$

---

7. The auction envisaged can be modeled as a noncooperative game as in Binmore (1987) or Wilson (1984).

In the case when $\rho_1 = \rho_2 = \rho$, $\rho = (\lambda_1 + \rho)/2(\lambda + \rho)$, and so the unit of surplus gets divided in the ratio $(\lambda_1 + \rho) : (\lambda_2 + \rho)$. This is the conclusion reached in Rubinstein (1982) and Wolinsky (1988).[8]

Opting out plays no role in the preceding discussion. One may, however, follow Gale (1986) and enrich the model by replacing the assumption that agents get zero utility from leaving the market by something more realistic. To this end, continuous, strictly increasing functions $S : [0, 1] \to \mathbb{R}$ and $B : [0, 1] \to \mathbb{R}$ are introduced. In each period it is assumed that $S(1)\tau$ and $B(1)\tau$ are the measures of sellers and buyers who appear in the market in one period.[9] The quantity $S(x_1)\tau$ is interpreted as the measure of these new sellers who can get a utility of at most x_1 outside the market. A similar interpretation applies to $B(x_2)\tau$.

For a steady-state equilibrium, the measures of new buyers and sellers who choose not to opt out by leaving the market must be equal. In the limiting case as $\tau \to 0+$, this reduces to the requirement that $S(b_1) = B(b_2)$. The measures S_τ^* and B_τ^* of sellers and buyers in the market at the beginning of a period will consist of $S(b_1)\tau$ and $B(b_2)\tau$ together with those sellers and buyers who were in the market in the previous period but did not get matched (A matched pair will agree immediately in equilibrium). The values S^* and B^* need to be related to the rates λ_1 and λ_2 at which agents are matched. One of many possible assumptions is that there is a fixed constant $k > 0$ for which

$$\lambda_1 = \frac{kB^*}{S^* + B^*}, \quad \lambda_2 = \frac{kS^*}{S^* + B^*}.$$

The measure of sellers who get matched in a period and hence leave the market after concluding a deal is then $\tau k S^* B^*/(S^* + B^*)$. This is equal to the measure of buyers who get matched in the same period. For a steady state it is therefore necessary that

$$S(b_1) = B(b_2) = \frac{kS^*B^*}{S^* + B^*}. \tag{11}$$

The principle that a bargainer's outside option acts only as a constraint on the range of validity of the bargaining solution is now applied. The conclusion is that the analysis that led to the equilibrium price p in the

8. But note that the same conclusion would not be reached if $\rho_1 \neq \rho_2$ because the breakdown assumptions differ.

9. They appear after the matching move but before the opting out move.

case when outside options were zero remains valid. The players do not even need to be informed of their partner's outside option.

In the case $p_1 = p_2 = p$, the value of the equilibrium price was given in terms of λ_1 and λ_2. This allows b_1 and b_2 to be calculated in terms of λ_1 and λ_2. However, λ_1 and λ_2 are functions of S^* and B^* and so the model can be solved.

When $p \to 0+$ (the case of "no search frictions"), b_1 and b_2 reduce to p and $1 - p$ respectively. The equations $q = S(p)$ and $q = B(1 - p)$ can then be interpreted as defining supply and demand curves. The equilibrium price p is then simply the Walrasian price. Note, however, that the "law of one price" applies even when search frictions are not negligible.

It is interesting to explore the manner in which models like that discussed here relate to classical intuitions about price formation. However, my own view is that the value of such models lies more in their capacity to provide insight into situations which are not amenable to a classical approach because relevant frictions cannot be dismissed as negligible.

D.9   Conclusion

This paper has largely been an attempt to convince the reader that the material it covers is fairly straightforward as a piece of theory. However, one does not need to penetrate very deeply into the theory in order to be able to apply the principles to which it leads. In particular, a wide variety of matching-and-bargaining models is amenable to the analysis outlined in section D.8.

References

Bester, H. 1988. Bargaining, search costs and equilibrium price distributions. *Review of Economic Studies* 55: 201–14.

Binmore, K. G. 1985. Bargaining and coalitions. In A. E. Roth, ed., *Game-Theoretic Models of Bargaining*. Cambridge: Cambridge University Press.

Binmore, K. G. 1987. Perfect equilibria in bargaining models. In K. G. Binmore and P. Dasgupta, eds., *The Economics of Bargaining*. Oxford: Blackwell.

Binmore, K. G., and P. Dasgupta. 1987. *The Economics of Bargaining*. Oxford: Basil Blackwell.

Binmore, K. G., and M. J. Herrero. 1988. Matching and bargaining in dynamics markets. *Review of Economic Studies* 55: 17–31.

Binmore, K. G., M. Osborne, and A. Rubinstein. 1992. Noncooperative models of bargaining. In R. Aumann and S. Hart, eds., *Handbook of Game Theory*, vol. 1. Amsterdam: North Holland.

Binmore, K. G., A. Rubinstein, and A. Wolinsky. 1986. The Nash bargaining solution in economic modeling. *Rand Journal of Economics* 17: 176–88.

Binmore, K. G., A. Shaked, and J. Sutton. 1989. An outside option experiment. *Quarterly Journal of Economics* 753–70.

Fishburn, P. G., and A. Rubinstein. 1982. Time preference. *International Economics Review* 23: 677–94.

Gale, D. 1986. A simple characterization of bargaining equilibrium in a large market without the assumption of dispersed characteristics. Technical report working paper 8605. Center for Analytic Research in Economics and Social Science. University of Pennsylvania.

Kalai, E. 1977. Nonsymmetric Nash solutions and replications of 2-person bargaining. *International Journal of Game Theory* 6: 129–33.

Nash, J. 1950. The bargaining problem. *Econometrica* 18: 155–62.

Osborne, M., and A. Rubinstein. 1990. *Bargaining and Markets*. San Diego: Academic Press.

Roth, A. E. 1979. *Axiomatic Models of Bargaining*. Berlin: Springer-Verlag.

Rubinstein, A. 1982. Perfect equilibrium in a bargaining model. *Econometrica* 50: 97–109.

Shaked, A. 1987. Opting out: Bazaars versus high tech' markets. Technical report discussion paper 87-159. Suntory Toyota International Centre for Economics and Related Disciplines.

Shaked, A., and J. Sutton. 1984. Involuntary unemployment as a perfect equilibrium in a bargaining model. *Econometrica* 52: 1351–64.

Wilson, R. 1984. Notes on market games with complete information. Technical report. Graduate School of Business, Standford University (Unpublished paper).

Wolinsky, A. 1988. Dynamic markets with competitive bidding. *Review of Economic Studies* 55: 71–84.

Notes to Chapter Introductory Remarks and Reprint Acknowledgments

Introduction

1. A game is said to be one-shot when it is worth emphasizing that it is to be played just once, without further interaction between the players.

2. In a "public goods game," the subjects privately choose how much to contribute to a public project that enhances the value of the total contribution. This enhanced value is enjoyed by everyone, including the "free riders" who contributed nothing.

3. Using average behavior as a summary statistic can be seriously misleading in public goods games even for inexperienced subjects, since they tend to split into those who contribute a lot and those who contribute nothing (Camerer 2003, p. 46).

4. For example, Deutsch (1985), Homans (1961), Kayser et al. (1984), Lerner (1981, 1991), Reis (1984), Sampson (1975), Schwartz (1975), Wagstaff (2001), Walster et al. (1973), and Walster and Walster (1975).

5. Healy (2004) reports similar final-round effects, not only in his own instructive gift-exchange experiment, but also in those of Rigdon (2002) and Riedl and Tyran (2005).

6. Tversky, who sadly died before the award of the prize, was Kahneman's long-time collaborator.

7. One might perhaps call the behavioral position *retro*-classical, since it abandons the neo-classical theory of revealed preference in favor of the psychological interpretation of utility functions held by economists in Victorian times.

8. Fehr and Schmidt (2005) actually tell us in their reply to Shaked's critique that they "picked the value $\beta_i = 0.6$" on the grounds that it "seemed more plausible to us." It certainly fits the data they claim to predict better than other values in the range between 0.5 and 1, which is all the accuracy their "calibration" allows.

9. A student recently told me that I figured explicitly in the course in behavioral economics he had just taken as an awful example of how *not* to run experiments.

Chapter 1

The paper was first published in the *Economic Journal* 111 (2001): 445–64. It is reproduced here by kind permission of the editors.

Chapter 2

The paper was first published in the *International Journal of Game Theory* 22 (1993): 381–409. It is reproduced here by kind permission of the editors.

1. Even if the games had multiple equilibria, the equilibrium selection problem wouldn't have arisen. This is because the equilibria of two-person, zero-sum games are both interchangeable and payoff-equivalent, which implies that it doesn't matter which equilibrium the players go for.

Chapter 3

The paper was first published (with A. Shaked and J. Sutton) in *American Economic Review* 75 (1985): 1178–80. It is reproduced here with kind permission of the publisher.

1. Von Neumann and Morgenstern (1944) endorse the dogma in their pathbreaking *Theory of Games and Economic Behavior*. It may seem incredible now, but the bargaining model of Nash (1950) studied in the previous chapter was largely ignored at the time Rubinstein wrote his paper.

2. Selten's formal definition of a subgame-perfect equilibrium is that it is a Nash equilibrium that induces Nash equilibrium play in every subgame, whether or not the subgame is reached in equilibrium. He originally said such equilibria are perfect, but later used the term perfect equilibria for his more general notion of a trembling-hand perfect equilibrium.

3. Our orginal discussion paper of 1984, with the experimental instructions and the data, appears as appendix A.

4. Our inexperience as experimenters at the time is evident not only in this sentence, but in the fact that the dollar rewards we offered were so painfully small.

5. Spiegel et al. inappropriately averaged our results over the two trials to obtain a single data point for our experiment in their figure. If only demands made by the more experienced subjects are recorded, our data point moves even closer to the results reported by later experimenters.

6. Few experiments have as many as ten repetitions. Camerer (2003, p. 469) summarizes the experimental results so far from all multistage Ultimatum Games by saying that they lie somewhere between an equal-split and the subgame-perfect outcome. Is it only another accident that these are precisely the outcomes that are evolutionarily stable in a version of Rubinstein's model when simple strategies are assumed to supplant more complicated strategies if they do the same job? (Binmore et al. 1991).

7. One might perhaps call the behavioral position retro-classical, since it abandons the neoclassical theory of revealed preference in favor of the psychological interpretation of utility functions held by economists in Victorian times.

8. This is also the stage game in Selten's (1988) chain-store paradox. The behavioral literature has taken to referring to it as the Mini-ultimatum Game, although it is the game that is small rather then the ultimata.

Chapter 4

The paper was first published in the *Journal of Economic Theory* 104 (2002): 48–88. It is reproduced here by kind permission of the editors.

1. From what direct utility function has my revealed indirect utility function been derived?

2. Substantial switches in behavior, as in Binmore et al. (1985) are unusual.

3. Plott and Zeiler's (2003) painstaking study of framing sensitivities in the endowment effect is particularly instructive.

4. See Shaked (2005) and Fehr and Schmidt's (2005) reply.

Chapter 5

The paper was first published in the *Quarterly Journal of Economics* 104 (1989): 753–70. It is reproduced here by kind permission of the editors.

1. Von Neumann and Morgenstern (1944) were still saying this in the *Theory of Games and Economic Behavior*.

2. It is assumed that the available cake shrinks at a constant rate as offers are refused. If the players discount the shrinkage at different rates, one is led to an *asymmetric* variant of the Nash bargaining solution, for the reasons explained in chapter 8.

3. People usually reference Binmore et al. (1982) for this result, thereby neglecting the role of Shaked and Sutton (1989, 1991). Appendix D reproduces what is intended to be a user-friendly version of the general theory (Binmore 1994).

4. In reporting on old-time collective bargaining in Sweden, Elster (1992) notes that each side in a wage negotiation would similarly advocate the use of a fairness norm that favored their own side rather than crudely exchanging demands for higher or lower wages.

Chapter 6

The paper was first published in *Games and Economic Behavior* 3 (1991): 295–322. It is reproduced here by kind permission of the editors.

Chapter 7

The paper was first published in the *Economic Journal* 108 (1998): 1279–99. It is reproduced here by kind permission of the editors.

1. Coasians commonly exclude other cases on the grounds that there are then significant informational costs.

2. I doubt that biologists commonly appreciate that fitness landscapes derived from simple games can resemble Escher sketches in which you keep walking downstairs but eventually find yourself above your starting point.

Chapter 8

1. This doesn't affect the players' bargaining powers when their probabilities of being chosen are equal (Binmore 1987).

2. We do not attribute the laboratory successes that the Rubinstein theory has enjoyed to its use of backward induction, but to the fact that the unique subgame-perfect equilibrium in Rubinstein's model happens to be a stationary expectations equilibrium. (See Binmore et al. 1989, 1991.)

3. The computer randomized over a small range centered on $(8, 2)$. The subjects responded by moving close to an optimal response to this behavior.

4. Responders were shown the outcome of six recent final agreements discounted to the next period that they could use in estimating a best reply.

5. Although not to focal point considerations, as the midpoint $(6, 3)$ on the hypotenuse would clearly have strong focal properties if the cutaway chunk were present.

6. Replacing δ_i by $e^{-\rho_i \tau}$ and allowing $\tau \to 0$ (to capture the case where the interval between successive proposals becomes vanishingly small), we are led to an asymmetric Nash bargaining solution of the bargaining problem $(X_0, 0)$ with bargaining powers $1/\rho_1$ and $1/\rho_2$.

7. The results look much the same with $\psi = 0$.

Appendix B

"A Note on Backward Induction": First published in *Games and Economic Behavior* 17 (1996): 135–37. It is reproduced here by kind permission of the editors.

"Rationality and Backward Induction": First published in the *Journal of Economic Methodology* 4 (1997): 23–41. It is reproduced here by kind permission of the editors.

Appendix C

First published in *Games and Economic Behavior* 8 (1995): 56–90 with the alphabetical order of the authors' names somehow scrambled. It is reproduced here by kind permission of the editors.

Appendix D

First published in *Investigaciones Económicas* 17 (1994): 403–19. It is reproduced here by kind permission of the editors.

Bibliography for Chapter Introductory Remarks

Abreu, D., and F. Gul. 2000. Bargaining and reputation. *Econometrica* 68: 85–117.

Aumann, R. 1995. Backward induction and common knowledge of rationality. *Games and Economic Behavior* 8: 6–19.

Aumann, R. 1996. Reply to Binmore. *Games and Economic Behavior* 17: 138–46.

Axelrod, R. 1984. *The Evolution of Cooperation*. New York: Basic Books.

Ball, S., and C. Eckel. 1996. Buying status: Experimental evidence on status in negotiation. *Psychology and Marketing* 105: 381–405.

Binmore, K. Bargaining and coalitions. In A. Roth, ed., *Game-Theoretic Models of Bargaining*. Cambridge: Cambridge University Press.

Binmore, K. 1987. Modeling rational players, I and II. *Economics and Philosophy*, 3 and 4: 179–214 and 9–55.

Binmore, K. 1987a. Nash bargaining theory I. In K. Binmore and P. Dasgupta, eds., *Economics of Bargaining*. Cambridge: Cambridge University Press.

Binmore, K. 1987b. Nash bargaining theory II. In K. Binmore and P. Dasgupta, eds., *Economics of Bargaining*. Cambridge: Cambridge University Press.

Binmore, K. 1987c. Perfect equilibria in bargaining models. In K. Binmore and P. Dasgupta, eds., *Economics of Bargaining*. Cambridge: Cambridge University Press.

Binmore, K. 1992. Foundations of game theory. In J.-J. Laffont, ed., *Advances in Economic Theory*. Cambridge: Cambridge University Press.

Binmore, K. 1994a. Bargaining theory without tears. *Investigaciones Economicas* 18: 403–19.

Binmore, K. 1994b. *Playing Fair: Game Theory and the Social Contract I*. Cambridge: MIT Press.

Binmore, K. 1996. A note on backward induction. *Games and Economic Behavior* 17: 135–37.

Binmore, K. 1997. Rationality and backward induction. *Journal of Economic Methodology* 4: 23–41.

Binmore, K. 1998. *Just Playing: Game Theory and the Social Contract II*. Cambridge: MIT Press.

Binmore, K. 2005. *Natural Justice*. New York: Oxford University Press.

Binmore, K., and P. Dasgupta. 1987. *The Economics of Bargaining*. Oxford: Blackwell.

Binmore, K., J. Gale, and L. Samuelson. 1995. Learning to be imperfect: The Ultimatum Game. *Games and Economic Behavior* 8: 56–90.

Binmore, K., J. McCarthy, G. Ponti, L. Samuelson, and A. Shaked. 2002. A backward induction experiment. *Journal of Economic Theory* 104: 48–88.

Binmore, K., P. Morgan, A. Shaked, and J. Sutton. 1991. Do people exploit their bargaining power? An experimental study. *Games and Economic Behavior* 3: 295–322.

Binmore, K., M. Osborne, and A. Rubinstein. 1992. Noncooperative models of bargaining. In R. Aumann and S. Hart, eds., *Handbook of Game Theory I.* Amsterdam: North Holland.

Binmore, K., M. Piccione, and L. Samuelson. 1998. Evolutionary stability in alternating offers bargaining models. *Journal of Economic Theory* 80: 257–91.

Binmore, K., A. Rubinstein, and A. Wolinsky. 1982. The Nash bargaining solution in economic modelling. *Rand Journal of Economics* 17: 176–88.

Binmore, K., and L. Samuelson. 1997. *Muddling through: Noisy equilibrium selection. Journal of Economic Theory* 74: 235–65.

Binmore, K., A. Shaked, and J. Sutton. 1985. Testing noncooperative game theory: A preliminary study. *American Economic Review* 75: 1178–80.

Binmore, K., A. Shaked, and J. Sutton. 1989. An outside option experiment. *Quarterly Journal of Economics* 104: 753–70.

Binmore, K., J. Swierzbinski, S. Hsu, and C. Proulx. 1992. Focal points and bargaining. Discussion paper. University of Michigan.

Binmore, K., J. Swierzbinski, and C. Tomlinson. 2007. An experimental test of Rubinstein's bargaining model. Else discussion paper. University College London.

Bolton, G. 1991. A comparative model of bargaining: Theory and evidence. *American Economic Review* 81: 1096–1136.

Bowles, G., and H. Gintis. 2002. Behavioural science: Homo reciprocans. *Nature* 415: 125–28.

Brown, J., and R. Rosenthal. 1990. Testing the minimax hypothesis: A re-examination of O'Neill's game experiment. *Econometrica* 58: 1065–81.

Camerer, C. 2003. *Behavioral Game Theory: Experiments in Strategic Interaction.* Princeton: Princeton University Press.

Camerer, C., and D. Harless. 1994. The predictive utility of generalized expected utility theories. *Econometrica* 62: 1251–90.

Camerer, C., E. Johnson, T. Rymon, and S. Sen. 1994. Cognition and framing in sequential bargaining for gains and losses. In A. Kirman K. Binmore, and P. Tani, eds., *Frontiers of Game Theory.* Cambridge: MIT Press.

Cameron, L. 1999. Raising the stakes in the Ultimatum Game: Experimental evidence from Indonesia. *Economic Inquiry* 27: 47–59.

Deutsch, M. 1985. *Distributive Justice: A Social Psychological Perspective.* New Haven: Yale University Press.

Dunbar, R., and H. Plotkin. 2004. A cross-cultural study of altruism. University College London.

Edgeworth, F. 1881. *Mathematical Psychics.* London: Kegan Paul.

Elster, J. 1992. *Local Justice: How Institutions Allocate Scarce Goods and Necessary Burdens.* New York: Russell Sage Foundation.

Estes, W. 1957. Of models and men. *American Psychologist* 12: 609–17.

Fehr, E., and S. Gächter. 2000a. Cooperation and punishment in public goods experiments. *American Economic Review* 90: 980–94.

Fehr, E., and S. Gächter. 2000b. Fairness and retaliation: The economics of reciprocity. *Journal of Economic Perspectives* 14: 159–81.

Fehr, E., and S. Gächter. 2002. Altruistic punishment in humans. *Nature* 415: 137–40.

Fehr, E., S. Gächter, and G. Kirchsteiger. 1997. Reciprocity as a contract enforcement device: Experimental evidence. *Econometrica* 65: 833–60.

Fehr, E., and K. Schmidt. 1999. A theory of fairness, competition and cooperation. *Quarterly Journal of Economics* 114: 817–68.

Fehr, E., and K. Schmidt. 2005. The rhetoric of inequity aversion—A reply. See ⟨http://www.wiwi.uni-bonn.de/shaked/rhetoric/⟩.

Frank, R. 2004. *What Price the Moral High Ground?* Princeton: Princeton University Press.

Frank, R., T. Gilovich, and D. Regan. 1993. Does studying economics inhibit cooperation? *Journal of Economic Perspectives* 7: 159–71.

Gigerenzer, G. 2004. Striking a blow for sanity in theories of rationality. In M. Augier and J. March, eds., *Models of a Man: Essays in Honor of Herbert A. Simon.* Cambridge: MIT Press.

Güth, W., and H. Kliemt. 1998. The indirect evolutionary approach: Bridging the gap between rationality and apaptation. *Rationality and Society* 10: 377–99.

Güth, W., R. Schmittberger, and B. Schwarze. 1982. An experimental analysis of ultimatum bargaining. *Journal of Behavior and Organization* 3: 367–88.

Hamilton, W. 1995. *The Narrow Roads of Geneland.* Oxford: Freeman.

Harsanyi, J. 1977. *Rational Behavior and Bargaining Equilibrium in Games and Social Situations.* Cambridge: Cambridge University Press.

Henrich, J., et al. 2004. *Foundations of Human Sociality: Economic Experiments and Ethnographic Evidence from Fifteen Small-Scale Societies.* New York: Oxford University Press.

Henrich, J., et al. 2005. "Economic man" in cross-cultural perspective. *Behavioral and Brain Sciences* 28: 795–855.

Hey, J., and C. Orme. 1994. Investigating generalizations of expected utility theory using experimental data. *Econometrica* 62: 1251–90.

Hines, W., and J. Maynard Smith. 1979. Games between relatives. *Journal of Theoretical Biology* 79: 19–30.

Holt, C., and D. Davis. 1993. *Experimental Economics.* Princeton: Princeton University Press.

Homans, G. 1961. *Social Behavior: Its Elementary Forms.* New York: Harcourt, Brace and World.

Healy, P. J. 2004. Group reputations and stereotypes as contract enforcement devices. Caltech working paper.

Kahneman, D., and A. Tversky. 1979. Prospect theory: An analysis of decision under risk. *Econometrica* 47: 263–91.

Kahneman, D., and A. Tversky. 1988. Rational choice and the framing of decisions. In *Decision Making.* Cambridge: Cambridge University Press.

Kalai, E. 1977. Nonsymmetric Nash solutions and replications of two-person bargaining. *International Journal of Game Theory* 6: 129–33.

Kandori, M. 1992. Social norms and community enforcement. *Review of Economic Studies* 59: 63–80.

Kayser, E., T. Schwinger, and R. Cohen. 1984. Layperson's conceptions of social relationships: A test of contract theory. *Journal of Social and Personal Relationships* 1: 433–548.

Kreps, D., P. Milgrom, J. Roberts, and R. Wilson. 1982. Rational cooperation in the finitely repeated Prisoners' Dilemma. *Journal of Economic Theory* 27: 245–52.

Ledyard, J. 1995. Public goods: A survey of experimental research. In J. Kagel and A. Roth, eds., *Handbook of Experimental Economics.* Princeton: Princeton University Press.

Lerner, M. 1981. The justice motive in human relations: Some thoughts about what we need to know about justice. In M. Lerner and S. Lerner, eds., *The Justice Motive In Social Behavior.* New York: Plenum.

Lerner, M. 1991. Integrating societal and psychological rules of entitlement: The basic task of each social actor and a fundamental problem for the social sciences. In R. Vermunt and H. Steensa, eds., *Social Justice in Human Relations I: Societal and Psychological Origins of Justice*. New York: Plenum.

Mitzkewitz, M., and R. Nagel. 1993. Experimental results on ultimatum games with incomplete information. *International Journal of Game Theory* 22: 171–98.

Muthoo, A. 1999. *Bargaining Theory with Applications*. Cambridge: Cambridge University Press.

Myerson, R. 1991. *Game Theory: Analysis of Conflict*. Cambridge: Harvard University Press.

Nash, J. 1950. The bargaining problem. *Econometrica* 18: 155–62.

O'Neill, B. 1987. Nonmetric test of the minimax theory of two-person zero-sum games. *Proceedings of the National Academy of Sciences* 84: 2106–2109.

Osborne, M., and A. Rubinstein. 1990. *Bargaining and Markets*. San Diego: Academic Press.

Plott, C., and K. Zeiler. 2005. The willingness to pay/willingness to accept gap, the "endowment effect" and experimental procedures for eliciting valuations. Social Science Working Paper 1132R. California Institute of Technology. To appear in *American Economic Review* 95: 530–45.

Reis, H. 1984. The mutidimensionality of justice. In R. Folger, ed., *The Sense of Injustice: Social Psychological Perspectives*. New York: Plenum.

Riedl, A., and J.-R. Tyran. 2005. Tax liability side equivalence in gift-exchange labor markets. *Journal of Public Economics* 89: 2369–82.

Rigdon, M. 2002. Efficiency wages in an experimental labor market. *Proceedings of the National Academy of Sciences* 99: 13348–351.

Roberts, K. 1980. Interpersonal comparability and social choice theory. *Review of Economic Studies* 47: 421–39.

Roth, A. 1979. *Axiomatic Models of Bargaining*. Berlin: Springer-Verlag.

Roth, A., and I. Erev. 1995. Learning in extensive-form games: Experimental data and simple dynamic models in the medium term. *Games and Economic Behavior* 8: 164–212.

Roth, A., and I. Erev. 1995. Learning in extensive-form games: Experimental data and simple dynamic models in the medium term. *Games and Economic Behavior* 8: 164–212.

Rubinstein, A. 1982. Perfect equilibrium in a bargaining model. *Econometrica* 50: 97–109.

Rubinstein, A. 1998. *Modeling Bounded Rationality*. Cambridge: MIT Press.

Sally, D. 1992. Conversation and cooperation in social dilemmas: A meta-analysis of experiments from 1958 to 1992. *Rationality and Society* 7: 58–92.

Sampson, E. 1975. On justice as equality. *Journal of Social Issues* 31: 54–64.

Samuelson, L. 1997. *Evolutionary Games and Equilibrium Selection*. Cambridge: MIT Press.

Samuelson, L. 2004. Information-based relative consumption effects. *Econometrica* 72: 93–118.

Schelling, T. 1960. *The Strategy of Conflict*. Cambridge: Harvard University Press.

Schwartz, S. 1975. The justice of need and the activation of humanitarian norms. *Journal of Social Issues* 31: 11–136.

Selten, R. 1975. Reexamination of the perfectness concept for equilibrium points in extensive-games. *International Journal of Game Theory* 4: 25–55.

Selten, R. 1988. Anticipatory learning in two-person games. Working paper B-93. Friedrich-Wilhelms-Universität Bonn.

Selten, R., and R. Stocker. 1986. End behavior in finite sequences of prisoners' dilemma supergames: A learning theory approach. *Journal of Economic Behavior and Organization* 7: 47–70.

Shaked, A. 2005. The rhetoric of inequity aversion. See ⟨http://www.wiwi.uni-bonn.de/shaked/rhetoric/⟩.

Smith, V. 1976. Experimental economics: Induced value theory. *American Economic Review* 66: 274–79.

Smith, V. 1991. *Papers in Experimental Economics.* Cambridge: Cambridge University Press.

Spiegel, M., J. Currie, H. Sonnenschein, and A. Sen. 1994. Understanding when agents are fairmen or gamesmen. *Games and Economic Behavior* 7: 104–15.

Stahl, I. 1972. *Bargaining Theory.* Economics Research Institute, Stockholm.

Steiner, J. 2004. A trace of anger is enough: On the enforcement of social norms. CERGE-EI working paper. Prague.

Thaler, R. 1988. Anomalies: The Ultimatum Game. *Journal of Economic Perspectives* 2: 195–206.

Von Neumann, J., and O. Morgenstern. 1944. *The Theory of Games and Economic Behavior.* Princeton: Princeton University Press.

Wagstaff, G. 2001. *An Integrated Psychological and Philosophical Approach to Justice.* Lampeter, Wales: Edwin Mellen Press.

Walster, E., E. Berscheid, and G. Walster. 1973. New directions in equity research. *Journal of Personality and Social Psychology* 25: 151–76.

Walster, E., and G. Walster. 1975. Equity and social justice. *Journal of Social Issues* 31: 21–43.

Weibull, J., and M. Salomonsson. 2005. Natural selection and social preferences. *Journal of Theoretical Biology*, to appear.

Index